The Cinema of Ozu Yasujiro

EDINBURGH STUDIES IN EAST ASIAN FILM
Series Editor: Margaret Hillenbrand

Available and forthcoming titles

Independent Chinese Documentary
Dan Edwards

The Cinema of Ozu Yasujiro
Woojeong Joo

Eclipsed Cinema
Dong Hoon Kim

Memory, Subjectivity and Independent Chinese Cinema
Qi Wang

Hong Kong Neo-Noir
Edited by Esther C. M. Yau and Tony Williams

www.edinburghuniversitypress.com/series/eseaf

The Cinema of Ozu Yasujiro

Histories of the Everyday

Woojeong Joo

EDINBURGH
University Press

Edinburgh University Press is one of the leading university presses in the UK.
We publish academic books and journals in our selected subject areas across the
humanities and social sciences, combining cutting-edge scholarship with high
editorial and production values to produce academic works of lasting importance.
For more information visit our website: edinburghuniversitypress.com

© Woojeong Joo, 2017

Edinburgh University Press Ltd
The Tun – Holyrood Road
12 (2f) Jackson's Entry
Edinburgh EH8 8PJ

Typeset in 10/13 Chaparral Pro by
IDSUK (DataConnection) Ltd

A CIP record for this book is available from the British Library

ISBN 978 0 7486 9632 1 (hardback)
ISBN 978 0 7486 9633 8 (webready PDF)
ISBN 978 1 4744 2454 7 (epub)

The right of Woojeong Joo to be identified as author of this work has been asserted in
accordance with the Copyright, Designs and Patents Act 1988 and the Copyright and
Related Rights Regulations 2003 (SI No. 2498).

Contents

List of Figures	vii
List of Tables	ix
Acknowledgements	xi
Introduction: Ozu, History and the Everyday	1
1 Early Ozu: *Shōshimin* Film and Everyday Realism	21
2 Ozu in Transition: The Coming of Sound and Family Melodrama	59
3 Wartime Ozu: Between Bourgeois Drama and National Policy Film	103
4 Postwar Ozu: Ozu's Occupation-era Film and Tokyo Regained	141
5 Late Ozu: New Generation and New Salaryman Film	186
Conclusion	209
Notes	216
Glossary of Japanese Terms	243
Select Filmography	247
Select Bibliography	251
Index	267

Figures

1.1	A road that connects city and suburb in *I Was Born But...*	42
1.2	Unemployed Okajima is seen alienated from his family	47
1.3	The moment of revelation in *Tokyo Chorus*	48
1.4	Yoshii clowns in his boss's amateur film	49
1.5	A day in the life in an empty field	51
1.6	A day in the life at school	51
1.7	A day in the life at a workplace	52
1.8	A public park, a deviated everyday space for adults as well as children	53
1.9	A breakfast of contemplation	55
2.1	Kihachi drinks imaginary *sake*	79
2.2	A failed *moga* observes a *ryōsai kenbo*	90
2.3 & 2.4	Okajima surveys Date Satoko's modern girl appearance	91
2.5	A moment of revelation for a husband to witness his wife working in a bar	92
2.6	Chikako examines the bruise on her cheek in a mirror	95
2.7	A stove always separates Ryōichi and Harue in *mise en scène*	96
2.8	Chikako violates the stove line and gets punished	97
2.9 & 2.10	Harue watches Chikako in sorrow	98
2.11	The stove at the side conjoins the two women in one space	99
2.12	A kiss by *moga* and *ryōsai kenbo*	100
3.1	Ozu, an imperial soldier, in Jiujiang, China	112
3.2	Bourgeois ladies in close conversation	123
3.3	A picture of his father that Ryōhei observes	133
4.1	Somiya utters the 'Kyoto versus Tokyo' remark when looking at the scenery of Kyoto's Kiyomizudera temple	154
4.2	Kōichi sits alienated from his wife and sister, while a bowl of rice is handed between the two women	161
4.3	Father Munekata reads a magazine article called 'Atomic Bomb'	163
4.4 & 4.5	An ardent energy is dormant in the unidirectional look of the postwar masses	170

4.6	Hirayama's room inside his *pachinko* parlour	172
4.7	Looking at Tokyo from a rooftop	179
4.8	Shūkichi and Tomi look at a photograph of their dead son, Shōji	180
4.9	Coexistence in divergence: Shige eats rice while Shūkichi drinks *sake*	183
5.1	A family spending evening time together in *Good Morning*	203
5.2	Kōichi's commodity fetishism	205
5.3	Children engrossed in watching television	207

Tables

2.1	The number of all-talkie versus part-talkie, and *saundoban* from Kamata studio	62
2.2	Key Shochiku directors' transition to talkie films	63
2.3	Representative *kateishōsetsu* adapted to *shinpa* melodrama	88
4.1	Top grossing Shochiku films in the early 1950s	176

Acknowledgements

A long time has passed since I began thinking about Ozu, during which period I have owed a great deal to so many people. Below is only a partial record of those names that I cannot forget and that will stay longer in my heart, with my gratitude and respect.

From spawning the idea of this study to fulfilling it in printed form, I always received kind help and warm encouragement from Professor Alastair Phillips, without which I would not have been able to finish this work. I admire his love of Ozu as well as cinema in general, and it was a very fortunate chance for me to share my thoughts with him during and after my graduate study at the University of Warwick. I am also grateful to the late Victor Perkins, whose insightful teaching (including on *Late Spring*) still remains a precious memory from the past. Since the day I began to live as well as study in Japan, I have owed so much to Professor Fujiki Hideaki for his kind assistance in my ongoing research and teaching at Nagoya University. His passion for film studies has always been a great impetus for me, and I wish this book can be a little *ongaeshi* for what he has done for me so far. I would also like to thank Professor Mitsuyo Wada-Marciano, Jeong Suwan, Rayna Denison, Kitamura Hiroshi, Tsuboi Hideto, Ma Ran and Ham Chungbeom for their kind interest in my work and their encouragement, and Charlotte Brunsdon and Isolde Standish for their helpful comments and advice as examiners of my doctoral thesis on which the content of this book is based.

My research in Japan was assisted by several funding organisations: the Japan Student Services Organisation, the Japan Korea Cultural Foundation and the Japan Society for the Promotion of Science, for whose generous support I would like to express my deep sense of gratitude. Many thanks also go to the staff in these institutions and at Nagoya University for their administrative support, and to Mika Ko for her great help and advice in the application process. I also appreciate the kind help from the Kamakura Museum of Literature in searching for Ozu's images and contacting the Ozu family on my behalf.

Parts of Chapter 1 and Chapter 4 are based on two previously published journal articles, which are edited and republished here with kind permissions from the publishers: 'I Was Born Middle Class, But . . .: Ozu Yasujiro's *Shōshimin Eiga* in the Early 1930s', in *Journal of Japanese and Korean Cinema* 4: 2 (2012), pp.103–18, http://dx.doi.org/10.1386/jjkc.4.2.103_1 (Routledge, part of Taylor and Francis Group); and 'Rethinking Noriko: Marriage Narrative as Historical Allegory in Ozu Yasujiro's *The Moon Has Risen* and Other Occupation-Era Films', in *Screen* 56: 3 (2015), pp. 335–6, doi: '10.1093/screen/hjv045 (Oxford University Press).

Special thanks go to the people who have been directly involved in the long production process of this book. I would like to thank Professor Margaret Hillenbrand for her great help and support in preparing my proposal, and also for reviewing my manuscript as the Series Editor. I am also very grateful to all the staff at Edinburgh University Press, especially my Commissioning Editors, Gillian Leslie and Richard Strachan, who have supported this work with great kindness and patience from the beginning. I would also like to thank the Project Manager, Rebecca Mackenzie, for managing the cover design work, and the Desk Editor, Edward Clark, for supervising the editing process. Last but not least, I really appreciate the detailed copyediting work by Sarah Burnett.

I also owe deep gratitude to my colleagues and friends at the University of Warwick and Nagoya University. I would especially like to thank Michael Piggot, Paul Cuff and Dogase Masato for not only sharing their love of cinema with me but also reviewing my manuscript at its early stage to give me invaluable ideas and comments. I am also grateful to all the faculties and students at Nagoya University's Japan-in-Asia Cultural Studies Program and Japanese Culture Studies Program, especially the film studies majors, whose knowledge and endeavour in their own fields became a great intellectual stimulus for me.

My last special thanks go to my family. I am so grateful to my parents for their love and support throughout my lifetime. I also thank Sebin for growing well and healthy, and Jeongran for sharing the happiness of our daily lives. My relationship with and memories of them are one of the big inspirations for this book about Ozu's cinema, which in itself is about family. Thank you, and I would like to dedicate this small piece of work to you all.

Introduction: Ozu, History and the Everyday

Among Japanese filmmakers, Ozu Yasujiro (1903–63) has long occupied a particular status. Generally recognised as one of the three most representative masters of Japanese cinema – along with Kurosawa Akira and Mizoguchi Kenji – he is best known as 'the most Japanese' director who, 'as a kind of spokesman', represents 'the Japanese flavour' with his films.[1] But no other term describing Ozu's cinema is as much misrepresented and misunderstood as this 'Japaneseness'. Ozu was initially introduced to Western countries as something 'foreign' that required a special effort to be understood. Legend has it that the Japanese film industry was reluctant to export Ozu's films to the West for fear that they would not be understood by Western audiences. In retrospect, this is absolute nonsense, if not an inverse form of Orientalism. It might be true that the real intention of Japanese producers was to continue the initial success of such *jidaigeki* (period drama) films as *Rashōmon/Rashomon* (Kurosawa Akira, Daiei, 1950), *Ugetsu monogatari/Ugetsu* (Mizoguchi Kenji, Daiei, 1953), or *Jigokumon/Gate of Hell* (Kinugasa Teinosuke, Daiei, 1953) in the West in the early 1950s.[2] But even so, I think it is very unlikely that contemporary Western audiences would have struggled any harder to understand Ozu's urban family drama *Tōkyō monogatari/Tokyo Story* (1953) than Kurosawa or Mizoguchi's period films. In fact, Japanese film companies began to realise the limitations of *jidaigeki*, and attempted to introduce *gendaigeki* (contemporary drama) to the West. The first such event held in Los Angeles in 1956 showed the films of Gosho Heinosuke, Naruse Mikio, Toyoda Shirō as well as those of Ozu, whose 'treatment of modern Japanese life' was appreciated for being 'truly international in its universal human appeal'.[3]

The studies of Ozu that followed in the West also contributed to the mystification of the meaning of Japaneseness. Donald Richie argued that Ozu's cinema was Japanese because it actualised on screen 'traditional virtues of [Japan]', for example, the 'quality of restraint', which was expressed through a strictly low-height and static camera work that produces the famous 'tatami shot'.[4] Richie's aesthetic approach was too arbitrary when he tried to locate the concept of *mono no aware* ('sympathetic sadness ... caused by the contemplation of this world') in Ozu and connect the director's restricted style to Japanese traditions of Noh, tea ceremony, haiku, and Buddhism.[5] Richie's traditionalism would be later denied by David Bordwell and Kristin Thompson in the 1980s, whose formalistic approach articulated the influence of the classical Hollywood narrative system on Ozu. However, they still positioned Ozu as a 'relative concept' to the West. Ozu's unique formal style was the result of the director's aberrant playfulness with Hollywood norms after he first learned them faithfully.[6] Thus Bordwell and Thompson's perspective was as much confined to the matter of Ozu's peculiar aesthetic form as Richie's, and left aside the issue of what Ozu's cinema meant to Japanese audiences.

I do not intend to argue here that Ozu's works are devoid of Japanese flavour. Even Ozu himself seemed to regard his films as being of a particular kind, which had not yet been properly understood by foreigners. What I want to argue is that the meaning of that 'Japaneseness' should be looked for in the context of Japan's modern history rather than only from the formal aspects of Ozu's films. It should not be underestimated that Ozu was a *gendaigeki* (contemporary drama) director, who was always conscious of contemporary Japanese society. What primarily mattered to most of the Japanese critics was also this social consciousness of Ozu, which was often disputed to be disassociated from reality, rather than his already proven aesthetic style and technical meticulousness. Thus Ozu's Japaneseness cannot be identified with tradition, but should be re-examined as a modern concept related to everyday life in the present tense. Bordwell was in fact aware of this point when he mentioned the 'referential and thematic dimensions' of Ozu, which he summarised as 'the modernized, urbanized life of the contemporary Japanese' with a sense of 'a lost past and a fleeting present'.[7] Recognising in the late 1980s that the 'social category of everyday life [was] only now beginning to receive intensive scholarly analysis', Bordwell anticipated that the very concept of the everyday, 'upon which Ozu's work concentrates', would be a significant academic subject to explore.[8] The starting point of this book is to share such a perspective, which was suggested nearly thirty years ago but has not yet been sufficiently investigated.

Thus firstly, this book will be an effort to draw our attention back to the 'life in Japan' that Ozu not only dealt with as his primary subject matter but also himself considered essential in order to understand his works. Such an approach requires a socio-historical perspective with regards to the phenomena and changes in everyday life in Japan, and I will investigate and present wide contextual evidences from Ozu's biographical records to modern Japanese history in order to support my arguments. But this does not mean that discussion of visual forms and styles will be disregarded. Rather, stylistic issues will often become a central point in my analysis in order to examine how effectively cinematic expression on screen can represent the concept of the everyday on a social level. Cautioning against what Bordwell calls 'reflectionism' – a belief that cinema can be a 'barometer of broad-scale social changes' by assuming 'spurious and far-fetched correlations between films and social or political events' – I will nevertheless aim to prove that Ozu's cinema is a case that actually requires that 'correlation' between film and society because of the director's continuous involvement with the everyday.[9]

Studying the Everyday

The everyday, as an academic subject, is a confusing concept. If there is one thing that can be agreed upon in studies of the everyday, it is the difficulty involved in presenting a definition of the concept that can satisfactorily explain its various different aspects. Henri Lefebvre has thus declared that 'ambiguity is a category of everyday life, and perhaps an essential category'.[10] Maurice Blanchot has said, 'the everyday . . . always escapes the clear decision of the law'.[11] This difficulty seems even more disturbing if the concept's naturalness ('transparency' in Highmore's term) is considered.[12] The everyday is quite naturally 'every' 'day', the life we, as human beings, live on a daily (that is, repetitive) basis, which can be found all around us, and at an intimate proximity. In this sense, the everyday is also universal; all human activities and institutions contain aspects of the everyday. War – actual combat and triumphant heroism – cannot be 'everyday', but 'the army has its everyday life: life in barracks and . . . among the troops'.[13] Such universality thus leads us to ask whether the study of the everyday should encompass 'everything' that we experience in our lives.

The ambiguity and multiplicity of the everyday that these questions suggest can only be resolved when our perspective and scope are transformed to the extent that we do not see it as a fixed concept but as a *modal* concept. The problem of the everyday lies less in the difficulty inherent in finding its general concept, one that would be valid in the East or the West, or in the past or the present, than in observing and analysing its variation according to differing geographical entities and historical phases. Lefebvre explains this point by saying that the goal of a critique of everyday life should not simply be 'describing, comparing and discovering what might be identical or analogous in Teheran, in Paris, in Timbuktu or in Moscow', but rather 'discovering what must and can change and be transformed in people's lives in [such diverse places]'.[14] Thus the eyes of the researcher of the everyday focus on actual life, practice and concrete methodology in order to recognise and interpret the variations, rather than maintaining critical distance and focusing on theory and abstraction in order to generalise the concept. But this does not mean that the critique of the everyday stops at the phenomenological stage of describing lived experiences; it also includes the process of abstraction that makes the everyday meaningful within a 'structure', and ultimately strives for a 'totality'.[15] Without this metamorphosis of level from the everyday into the totality, 'structure' itself (for example, religion, philosophy, history, science, politics, the state, art and culture) cannot achieve its aspiration to universality.

The everyday that Ozu dealt with in his films reflects this dynamic between phenomenon and structure. It is an ambiguous yet ubiquitous entity that appeals throughout different spaces and times. Thus we have to pay attention to the specificity of the everyday in Ozu; both temporally and spatially demarcated, it signifies a plural number of possibilities. For example, eating in a family in good peace and harmony epitomises Ozu's everyday as it appears in the breakfast scene in *Bakushū/Early Summer* (1951). For viewers familiar with this kind of image, however, similar family dining scenes in such films as *Nani ga kanojo o sō saseta ka/What Made Her Do It?* (Suzuki Shigeyoshi, Teikoku Kinema, 1930) or *Dokkoi ikiteru/And Yet We Live* (Imai Tadashi, Shinsei Eiga, 1951) come as a great shock in their realistic depictions of poverty-ridden family life. Closely related to the contemporary cinematic trends in the nation (leftist tendency films in the case of *What Made Her Do It?*, and postwar Italian neorealism in the case of *And Yet We Live*), each film (and its everyday life inside) not only represents an unstable social atmosphere during the Great Depression and the US Occupation era respectively, but also reveals how much proletarian experience of the everyday can differ from that of the suburban upper-middle classes in Ozu's films. Such criteria of the everyday are not limited to historical period and economic class but expand to other categories such as gender, generation and geographical location. This is also related to genre and studio because, in Japan, major film studios usually specialised in a certain stylistic flavour and subject matter for a specific target audience. For instance, the drastic difference of Ozu's everyday from that of *What Made Her Do It?* can be attributable to the production policy of Shochiku, the studio Ozu worked for, which was 'more oriented toward the female audience' and hence 'found little reason to inject politics into tear-jerkers' as found in other studios' tendency films.[16]

These kinds of differences inevitably raise the significant question of realism with regard to the interpretation of the everyday. As mentioned, Ozu was always subject to harsh criticism from Japanese critics of a progressive political tendency, who saw him as a conservative director, avoiding or distorting the reality of Japanese people's life. Ozu actively responded to this condemnation, defending his stylistic position that consistently emphasised the encouragement of warm humanity. The famous reference of tofu – 'I can make only tofu [and nothing else]' – came out of this exact situation, where he strongly defended the kind of everyday that he always depicted.[17] Whether he avoided (or could ever avoid) reality will be an important issue to be discussed throughout the following chapters. I would just like to articulate here a slightly different point, that this tofu reference is another example underlining the importance of properly placing Ozu within a social context. Tofu does not merely indicate Ozu's idiosyncratic formal style, but is more related to his subject matter and thematic concerns, which cannot be properly understood without considering the long history of the debate between Ozu and Japanese critics over what reality cinematic art should pursue and in what way this should be done.

It should not be forgotten that Ozu's tofu was not a single kind but had variations of its own. His corpus of a total of fifty-four films spanned thirty-five years from the 1920s to the 1960s, reacting to the changing historical conditions of modern Japan throughout the prewar, war and the postwar eras. His typical characters were generally known to be middle class, but there were many other cases where the director moved higher or lower within the social stratum to present different sides of everyday life. The contrasts or conflicts among males and females, and the young and the old were also a fundamental element of Ozu's films, varying the face of his everyday that has been simply understood as a repetitive (and thus oppressive) entity. Thus the everyday this book will investigate is not so much a contemplative, detached observation of a static, external world as an active rendezvous with the real, lived experiences of various characters and their surrounding society. Paul Schrader once said, 'In the everyday nothing is expressive, all is coldness'; this book's major position will be the complete opposite, that is, 'In the everyday, nothing is cold, all is expressive'.[18]

Several Western thinkers provide some basic theoretical frameworks and concepts applicable to the analysis of Ozu's everyday as a social phenomenon. Firstly, Lefebvre approaches the issue from a Marxist's standpoint, as implied in his use of such terms as structure and dialectics, and the key critical issues including work, alienation and money. His critique aims to elucidate 'everydayness (*la quotidienneté*)', the 'modality of capital's administration of atomisation and repetition' inherent in these issues, and to differentiate it from the possibility of 'the everyday (*le quotidien*)', which means the 'modality of social transformation and class resistance'.[19] However, Lefebvre also distances himself from dogmatic Marxism, which distinguishes the everyday of the proletariat from that of the bourgeoisie and tends to reduce every problematic to labour and class struggle. Rather, the working classes are subject to 'needs and desires' as much as the bourgeoisie are.[20] The need (for a specific thing) and desire (for totality) exist in a dialectical relationship: 'the transition from need to desire and the vital return of desire back to need, in order to reabsorb itself within it'.[21] However, this movement is interrupted in a consumer society, the expansion of which Lefebvre witnessed in postwar France. There, 'the consumer does not desire. He submits . . . He obeys the suggestions and the orders given to him by advertising, sales agencies or the demands of social prestige'.[22] In this way, everyday life becomes 'alienated' or 'colonised' by consumerism.[23]

Although Ozu's rendition of everyday life is hardly Marxist, Lefebvre's critique suggests a few points to consider with regard to the director's political position. As mentioned, Ozu was consistently criticised by Japanese progressive (if not Marxist) critics throughout his career owing to the thematic ambiguity of his films, which 'never reached the essence of a matter but remained a superficial phenomenon'.[24] This criticism focused especially on the petit-bourgeois characteristics of his so-called prewar *shōshimin* films (see Chapter 1), which dealt with white-collar middle-class life with 'humour' and 'pathos' instead of articulating 'class struggle'. With its apparently complacent approach to reality, Ozu's everyday can be regarded as an object of Lefebvre's critique, which is fundamentally a search for the possibility of change. However, Ozu's approach is not without consideration of the 'dialectical movement' between the everyday and the structure at the upper levels (namely, various social institutions such as school or company), and in this sense, does not necessarily champion a private life segregated from society. This point becomes even clearer in Ozu's later films about the postwar middle classes (see Chapter 5), where he, as Lefebvre does, closely analyses contemporary Japanese society from the viewpoint of technological development, consumerism and urbanisation.

If Lefebvre's critique pays attention to the possibility of transforming the everyday from its alienated state, de Certeau's interest is drawn more to the actual practices of everyday life and their variety. These 'practices', contrasted with 'systems of production' that impose rational order, construct another order of production, which is more creative, individualised and devious. They can subvert the system 'not by rejecting or altering [it], but by *using* [it] with respect to ends and references foreign to [it]'.[25] De Certeau's perspective is thus both optimistic – he admits the possibility of change within a system – and pessimistic – the everyday cannot fundamentally escape the rule of the system. He conceptualises the essential characteristics of the two contrasting notions of systematic control and the everyday practice with the terms 'strategy' and 'tactic'. The former denotes the effort to secure a proper 'place' by separating the area inside the reach of its power from the outside, and to establish a rational system with its powers of panoptic sight and knowledge to control foreign forces. Strategy also detests temporal variation; it pursues a universality that operates regardless of time, and hence is 'a triumph of place over time'. Such is the 'typical attitude of modern science, politics and military strategy'.[26] In contrast, 'tactic' is 'determined by the absence of a proper locus'; it instead has 'space', a different spatiality from 'place', composed of 'intersections of mobile elements' with 'vectors of direction, velocities and time variables'.[27] Thus it waits for an opportunity to infiltrate the 'cracks ... open in the surveillance of the proprietary powers' and to 'play on and with a terrain imposed on it and organised by the law of a foreign power'.[28]

This relationship between strategy and tactic (or place and space) can be verified and illustrated in various actual circumstances. In terms of speaking, strategy corresponds to 'an established vocabulary and syntax' (that is, 'scientific practices'), which are consistently modified and adjusted by the actual 'enunciation' of individuals (that is, 'everyday linguistic practices').[29] If applied to a capitalistic society, commodity production is the realm of scientific, rational knowledge controlled by a system. However, its cultural meaning is not directly transferred to consumers but rather reinterpreted through their 'tactical' behaviours of consumption. In urban geography, there is a difference between mapping and touring, where the former's 'totalising eye', which creates a 'transparent text' or 'theoretical ... simulacrum', is counterbalanced by the latter's 'contradictory movements', a 'process of appropriation of the topographical system on the part of the pedestrian'.[30] As Baudelaire noted, such walking practices within tactical space became the key methodology of the *flâneur*, a modern subject who, strolling the streets of nineteenth-century Paris, extracted 'the eternal' out of 'the transitory'.[31]

De Certeau's conception of space versus place is adopted in Wada-Marciano's analysis of national identity appearing in Japan's underworld genre films. She differentiates an 'actual geographical location' (i.e. 'place') from a 'specific space as one's recognition of locale'; for example, Yokohama Bay, a geographical place in Japan, was encountered by audiences as a 'de-Japanised', 'foreign experience', the kind that they had seen in Hollywood gangster films, as a result of various foreign elements being used to depict the place.[32] This kind of 'dis-place-ment' also performs an important function in Ozu's films, the best example of which is the empty field in the Tokyo suburb of *I Was Born But . . .* (see Chapter 1), which becomes a liberated space for the children who investigate and subvert the capitalistic order that originally contributed to the construction of such suburbs. Throughout this book, I will expand upon this theory in order to develop a concept I call 'deviation' – a variation on de Certeau's notion of 'trickery' or 'deception' in the practice of everyday life set against the operation of a system. Ozu's everyday never escapes from the constrictions of the order imposed upon it by society, but it deviates from it in order to exhibit alternative possibilities of modern life. Tokyo's Shitamachi district (Chapter 2), the middle-class residences of Kamakura (Chapter 4) and the 'new salaryman films' (Chapter 5) will be analysed from the perspective of deviation from an enforced spatiality.

Deviation, however, is not confined to the spatial alone; rather, this concept cannot be complete without consideration of its temporal aspects. If explained in Lefebvre's terminology, deviation is a movement from 'linear rhythm' – the product of 'homogeneous' and 'quantified' time characterised by 'brutal repetitions' and subordinated to the logic of capitalistic labour – towards 'cyclical rhythm', that is, 'great cosmic and vital rhythms: day and night, the months and the seasons, and still more precisely biological rhythms'.[33] Although de Certeau does not assume any temporality in his conception of 'strategy', to which Lefebvre might have assigned 'linear rhythm', he recognises that 'tactics', composed of rapid movements through different points of a space, are essentially 'procedures', 'durations' and 'heterogeneous rhythms'.[34] Moreover, unlike Lefebvre's analysis, that of de Certeau notices that the rhythm generated by the practice of the everyday necessarily accompanies a historical perspective. He thus notes, 'Objects and words . . . have hollow places in which a past sleeps, as in the everyday acts of walking, eating, going to bed'; for example, while engaged in everyday walking, people often notice the 'presences of diverse absences' and say, 'here, there used to be . . .'.[35] Various everyday practices are thus 'an exploration of the deserted places of [one's] memory', a 'detour' for the 'discovery of relics and legends'.[36]

The discovery of lost time in the present everyday becomes the central issue for Walter Benjamin. Influenced by studies of modern urbanity by both Baudelaire and Simmel, Benjamin pays attention to the incessant shocks of modern urban everyday life, which make the sensory system of city-dwellers unresponsive or 'silent'.[37] He calls such instantaneous but fleeting experiences 'isolated experience' or '*Erlebnis*'.[38] *Erlebnis* elicits an explicit and conscious response from the human mind; it registers information at the level of consciousness, and generates '*mémoire volontaire*' (voluntary memory) in Proust's terminology.[39] However, consciousness cannot filter out all the threatening shocks of modern lives; some experiences (called '*Erfahrung*') penetrate into the unconscious to shake up dormant memory ('*mémoire involontaire*'), which is historically registered and accumulated. When *Erfahrung* occurs in the appreciation of art, it creates an 'aura' – the authenticity that endows a work of art with a 'unique existence' through the 'data of *mémoire involontaire*' or the 'mark of the history'.[40] Such involuntary memory is not merely a private phenomenon; what is restored is a 'tradition, in collective existence as well as private life'.[41] Such experience rooted in the collective unconscious is, by its nature, communicable between and amongst constituents of society.

Benjamin's conception of memory and history, however, is different from nostalgia, a passive reflection on time passed; it is rather based upon the dialectical and critical relationship between the past and the present. The way these two temporalities dialectically react is through an 'image' that 'flashes up at the moment of [the past's] recognisability'.[42] Thus the past and the present, whose relationship is a 'purely temporal, continuous one', should be differentiated from 'the Then [or What-Has-Been] and the Now' that are in dialectical relation.[43] History is born out of this 'dialectical image', rather than a mere accumulated set of knowledge of the past.[44] Conversely, it is also important that the temporal site upon which this historical rebirth is attempted is the 'Now' of the present, not the future or the past. In other words, history can be constituted only when it is critically read through the 'historical index' that the Then carries for the Now of the present, which should be a particular 'Now' among the plural, distinguishable 'Nows'. (Hence, 'each now is the Now of a particular recognisability' or 'legibility'.)[45] The everyday, then, is not a routine repetition ('everydayness' in Lefebvre's term), but serves as a catalysis of multilayered temporalisation among the past, present and future, and during this process the role of historical materialism that Benjamin advocates is essential.

Studies so far tend to regard the fleeting instantaneity of the cinematic image as an epitome of Benjamin's theory. Leo Charney, for example, emphasises the fact that it is the fleeting, fragmentary and shocking effects of images that lead modern subjects into 'tangible reawareness of the presence of the present'.[46] The present tends to constantly drift away, leaving behind an empty, wasted space, but there are many artistic efforts to overcome this 'absence of presence' through the 'perceptual extension of the single moment', and Benjamin's proposed method of achieving this is the shock effect (that is, *Erlebnis*).[47] But it is also important to understand that for Benjamin, the key issue is not the fragmentary experience of modernity *per se*, but the historical consciousness that it brings from the past to generate the 'dialectical image' in the present. *Erlebnis* should not stand alone without the experience of *Erfahrung*. Benjamin makes this point clear in his critique of modern art forms that have the characteristic of reproducibility (above all, cinema), where the 'decay of the aura' is predominant.[48] After all, what he desires is that the dialectical image can 'criticise modernity [the forgetting of the aura] through an act of memory and, at the same time, ... criticise archaism [nostalgia for the aura] through an act of essentially modern invention, substitution and de-signification'.[49]

In this sense, Ozu offers an interesting counterproof to the 'decay of the aura' Benjamin witnesses in cinema. The process I would call 'permeation' of the past into the present in the form of memory becomes the central issue of the director's postwar films (Chapter 4), where the two temporalities intersect with each other in terms of space, gender and generation, to construct a sense of continuous history from the previous wartime experiences (Chapter 3) as well as the spatial notion of Shitamachi articulated in the prewar period (Chapter 2). This temporal permeation may not be presented in a 'dialectical' form, affecting viewers with a 'momentary shock', but it essentially demonstrates the same critique of modernity through history as Benjamin attempted. The way that Ozu deals with it, however, is not necessarily by slowing down the passage of time and emphasising the inertia of stilled objects as generally considered. The everyday in Ozu rather exists in the form of conflicts, negotiations and deviations among different temporal and spatial elements; there is hardly an empty time and space in Ozu's everyday.

The Everyday and Japan's Modernity

Applying Western theory to the case of Ozu's cinema inevitably raises an issue about weighing the particularities of Japan's experience within the context of more general discourses of the modern everyday. If 'everyday life ... came into being only with the rise of the masses', as Ross explains with an example of the development of European cities, then Japan shared a similar experience in the 1920s when 'many of the hallmarks of modernity – urbanisation, the experience of simultaneity, the proliferation of new media [such as film, radio and popular music], the transformation of gender roles – occupied the centre of national attention'.[50] According to Lefebvre, the diversity of everyday lives became an even weaker tendency in the postwar, because 'technological or industrial civilization tends to narrow the gaps between lifestyles ... in the world as a whole'.[51] On the other hand, Harry Harootunian thinks that 'each society ... differed according to specific times and places', even if 'all societies shared a common reference provided by global capital and its requirements'.[52] Thus, according to a subject's cultural and historical experience, there existed 'coeval modernities' (not 'alternative modernities'), which challenged the 'universalising and homogenising claims of the Western example'.[53] What in fact makes these heterogeneous modernities possible is the everyday, which does not consist simply of routine and repetition, but 'negotiate[s] the compelling demands of homogeneity through the mediations of a past that constantly stood in a tense, often antagonistic, relationship to the present of the new'.[54]

In Japan's case, the fundamental difference of its modernity (*kindai*) and modernisation process (*kindaika* or *modanaizeishon*) comes from the nation's complicated historical relationship with the West, which firstly made a shocking impact on the former, and afterwards became the ideal model to emulate. These 'mimetic processes of non-Western modernities' had the dual effects of 'reifying the West as the site of seamless and fully realised modernity . . . and of ensuring that modernity in the non-West [was] regarded as deficient'.[55] On the other hand, as Takeuchi Yoshimi acknowledges, this self-humiliating consciousness was accompanied by the continuous resistance of the Japanese to the European 'instinct for self-expansion', which was 'deeply intertwined with the essence of what is called "modernity"'.[56] In the end, Japanese modernisation was made possible in the course of these resistances. Thus the struggle for maintaining the nation's identity whilst obsessively pursuing Western ways made the fundamental nature of the Japanese modern contradictory, as explainable in a phrase, 'tradition within modernity' or 'modernity through tradition'. Such contradiction can be verified in the fact that a significant part of the Japanese modern – such as modern family system *ie* or the ideal image of womanhood *ryōsai kenbo* (good wife, wise mother) – owed its ideological basis to traditional ideas and values that constituted a reconstruction of Tokugawa ideologies. Therefore, the conflict between Westernisation and traditionalism was a predetermined consequence, as can be found in Ozu's prewar *shōshimin* films (Chapter 1). Takeuchi, however, had a more pessimistic view; as far as Japan's modernisation meant Westernisation (that is, adopting the West's belief in historical progress, scientific quantification, positivism and empiricism), the eventual fate of the resistance was nothing other than defeat.[57] This deeply disturbing sense of defeatism (and frustration) should be understood in a historical context: Takeuchi wrote on this in 1948 when Japan was under US Occupation after being devastated by the recent war (see Chapter 4). The postwar in Japan thus has a very different historical and cultural dimension to, for instance, that of France, not only in terms of the experience of nationalism and militarism ended by the defeat in war, but also with the more fundamental problem that the nation's history of modernisation has been established through the contradictory relationship with the West.

In a similar sense, 'reprivatisation', which became a central concept for analysing the everyday life of postwar French society, also can have a different connotation in the context of Japan. As a critical term for a growing tendency towards consumerist society, Lefebvre suggests that reprivatisation of everyday life from the 1950s onwards consisted of 'an escape from the nuclear threat and from the setbacks of history', accompanied by the 'growth of needs, alienation of desire', the satisfaction of which was possible through objects, mediated through advertising.[58] Building upon this perspective, Kristin Ross's study on the ideology of domestic hygiene and cleanliness, disseminated by the women's magazines to French housewives in the form of commodity fetish, identifies the 'state-led modernisation effort' in postwar France, which resulted in the 'movement of retreat, or *repliement*' from history and society, characterising the phenomenon of 'reprivatisation'.[59] The similar critique of reprivatisation arose in Japan as well with the advancement of the new leftists in the 1960s, who rejected the privatised everyday as a bourgeois ideology serving to stabilise the establishment, and attempted to overcome it through 'non-everyday' methods such as theory and revolution. However, as Takabatake Michitoshi acutely points out, this is an attitude of 'enlightening the commons from above', while ignoring the fact that those theories from Marx to Lefebvre were actually a product of the everyday life of Western society.[60] Takabatake thus argues that the self-contradiction assumed in the leftists' thought can be resolved through the return to the everyday by 'plac[ing] more weight on the process of developing relations with actuality over theory or systems'.[61] Seen from this perspective, it is essential to recognise that, in the specific context of Japanese history, a 'return to private life' after war was a natural reaction to the nationalistic ideological excess that had long dominated the country, and a progress towards an idealised form of liberated individualism. Wartime slogans such as *taibōseikatsu* (life in austerity) or *messhihōkō* (devoting one's self for the sake of the public) were finally replaced by a respect for people's everyday life established on the foundation of a new political democracy.[62] In the end, reprivatisation, when applied to Japan's actuality, can have more critical layers of meaning than a unilateral process towards isolated individualism.

A study of Ozu's cinema then should accompany a due consideration of the particularities of the everyday that are distinctively applied to the historical and social context of Japan. It can be obtained, for instance, through a detailed analysis of customs, manners and lifestyles on screen, the exhibition of which is 'the principal condition of cinema' as argued by Tosaka Jun.[63] Inversely, from the audiences' point of view, their moral consciousness is confirmed and affected by the customs and manners depicted on screen. It goes without saying that Ozu's cinema builds on a keen observation of Japanese way of everyday life, but attention should be paid to the question of how it is related to the construction of Japanese viewers' national as well as personal identity, which is closely interrelated with the changing phases of modern Japanese history, as will be discussed in the cases of the *shōshimin* film (Chapter 1) or national policy film (Chapter 3). It is also significant that this close focus on the actual everyday life of the

Japanese is not Ozu's personal invention, but a variation of the basic production principle of Shochiku's Kamata studio and of its head Kido Shirō. Chapter 1 will discuss their desire for the faithful representation of reality to ultimately create a unique form of modernism, albeit its ideal was continually modulated according to the changing historical condition of Japanese society.

Another key particular aspect in the study of the Japanese everyday is the role of women. As suggested in the discussion of 'reprivatisation', women can act as a central agent in domestic everyday life, shaping and leading the commodity consumption culture. The sociologist Dorothy E. Smith shows a critical view of this phenomenon since women, in the end, become the primary victims of the 'interior colonialism' of everyday life in the course of modernisation and consumerism. In Smith's terms, it means a domination of the female everyday by the 'relations of ruling', a complex of power institutions (such as 'government, law, business and financial management, professional organisation and educational institutions') that manage to operate male-centric society.[64] It is, however, important to note that the meaning of modern consumerism and the nature of female subjectivity may vary greatly according to specific socio-historical context. For instance, the discourses around Japanese women's experiences of the modern everyday in the 1920s and 1930s, which have drawn the interest of many academics, including Barbara Sato and Miriam Silverberg, display complex layers of meaning, with the issues of feminine subjectivity bound up with the intricate workings of Japanese modernity. Studies so far have tended to acknowledge the role of the modern Japanese woman as an active subject in the construction of a new femininity – a radical example is *modan gāru* (modern girl) – which was placed in tension with the premodern, patriarchal norms of traditional Japanese society. This more positive view of women's autonomy (compared to the French case) not only reflects the historical difference between the interwar and the postwar period, but also articulates the particularity of the problem of modernity that each society had to deal with in its own way.

Ozu's representation of modern femininity reflects such socio-historical specificity, but in a convoluted way as it changes with time. Most of his early films do not directly articulate consumerism culture at the level of domestic everyday life, but rather deploy it within the narrative of sensationalism and moral melodrama as found in his depiction of modern girl characters, which works to reassure patriarchal social conventions (Chapter 2). However, the tendency takes a dramatic turn during the wartime when he begins to foreground the female characters of bourgeois class (Chapter 3), to which his conceptualisation of the postwar everyday as well as the construction of postwar femininity owes much. Ozu's cinema, especially that of his postwar years, can be largely characterised by this advancement of female subjectivity as a counter-identity against masculinity – though its method is less direct confrontation than deviation and temporal mediation in Benjamin's sense – as will be discussed in the following chapters.

Methods in Ozu Studies: Texts and Contexts

As mentioned, if calculated from the 1950s when postwar *gendaigeki* films began to be introduced in the US, Western critical writing on Ozu now has more than half a century worth of history, and has played a key role in the development of Japanese cinema studies. Mitsuhiro Yoshimoto has summarised the history of Ozu studies up to the early 1990s into four categories according to the combination of two different paradigms: Ozu's aesthetic style (traditional or modern) and its political implications (reactionary or radical).[65] The traditional-reactionary group, which includes critics such as David Desser, reads traditional Japanese elements (for example, Zen Buddhism) into Ozu's films, and interprets them as evidence of the director's conservative political stance. In contrast, for Noel Burch, such traditional Japanese aesthetics imply a radical political instrument used to deconstruct what he calls the 'institutional mode of representation' as found in classical Hollywood cinema, which serves to solidify Western bourgeois ideology. The third group corresponds to Japan's new wave cinema directors of the late 1950s and early 1960s, who saw in Ozu a 'total indifference to contemporary social reality' hidden behind 'restrained aestheticism and a skilful formal exercise' – hence aesthetically modern but politically reactionary.[66] For so-called 'neo-formalists' such as David Bordwell and Kristin Thompson, Ozu's modern formal experiments, especially in narrative mode (which they call 'parametric'), contrast with the narrative mode of classical Hollywood films, which concentrate on story construction. They are thus in line with Burch's critique of Hollywood cinema, but they attribute Ozu's style to the influences of modern Western culture rather than to Japanese aesthetic traditions as Burch does. Yoshimoto also separately classifies the fifth group, 'apolitical culturalists' (such as Donald Richie and Paul Schrader), who, at the beginning stage of Ozu studies, resorted to the concepts of quintessential Japaneseness and universal humanity to present Ozu as an 'auteur'.[67]

Though not without simplification, this categorisation encompasses all the major tendencies in Ozu studies up until Bordwell's work in the late 1980s, and still remains a valid framework for understanding the general topography of the history of Ozu scholarship (and its problems) in the West. In his introduction to Yoshida Kiju's book *Ozu's Anti-Cinema* (2003), Daisuke Miyao almost directly adopts Yoshimoto's categories to review Ozu scholarship up until that point, although he rightly points out that 'Bordwell and Thompson do not share

Burch's political position that poses Japanese cinema as a challenger to capitalism'.[68] More recently, Abé Mark Nornes also repeats a similar historiography of Ozu studies with regard to the criticism of *Late Spring*.[69] Nornes suggests that what characterises the post-Bordwell phase is a socio-historical approach – for example, paying attention to the social conditions of the US Occupation era in an analysis of *Late Spring* – as found in Eric Cazdyn's *The Flash of Capital* (2003).

The real importance of Yoshimoto's theory, however, is that he presents his historiography of Ozu studies as a broad critique of Japanese film studies as it has been practised by Western academics. In fact, the framework he has described – the 'binary oppositions as modern/traditional and reactionary/radical' – is intrinsically flawed; Ozu is never *either* modern *or* traditional, or *either* reactionary *or* radical. For instance, the dichotomy between the modern and the traditional ignores the actual circumstances of modern Japanese history, where tradition coexisted with modernity as relative concepts for each other. Yoshimoto thus argues that designating Ozu as modern, traditional, reactionary or radical is a 'discursive practice' (i.e. more ideological than textual), and asks the question 'why the West/Japan dichotomy plays such a hegemonic role in the discussion of modern Japan; and why this dichotomy has been dominating the discussions of Ozu's films in particular'.[70]

Agreeing that Ozu studies so far have largely been a discursive construction of the Western academic, I do, however, think that the meaning of the constructed discourse can be more refined through reconsidering Ozu's actual text as well as context. It should not be overlooked that Ozu intentionally deployed Japanese iconography in order to evoke a feeling of Japaneseness, the purpose of which may be related to the specific historical conditions of the immediate postwar (Chapter 4). In other words, it cannot be asserted that Ozu is traditional or not traditional; only a certain part of a certain film from a specific period is *traditional*, and for a specific reason. Most studies so far, their scope confined to a few representative films by the director, miss this important point about Ozu's cinema: that it is not a homogeneous corpus detached from historical specificity. The discursive field thus has a valid connection with Ozu's actual filmmaking practice, which in turn corresponds to specific historical conditions. Ultimately, the study of the everyday should be more about actuality than hermeneutics.

In terms of the principal methodology, this book will mainly adopt the positions and approaches of the recent socio-historical studies that pay attention to the historical specificity. Bordwell in fact had already anticipated and suggested this new path in his late 1980s work *Ozu and the Poetics of Cinema* (1988). Using close shot-to-shot analyses to demonstrate Ozu's formal deviations from the Hollywood standard, Bordwell's 'poetics' nevertheless attempts to find 'norms arising from formal principles, conventional practices of film production and consumption, and proximate features of the social context'.[71] Thus it is not correct to criticise that Bordwell disregards a contextual dimension on behalf of his formalistic purpose in his study. In several chapters of the book (especially chapter 3) and in analyses of individual films, he deals with the socio-cultural conditions surrounding Ozu's cinema, mentioning the director's relationship with the Japanese film industry, the influences of Westernised urban mass culture and the everyday life of different social classes (for example, salarymen, college students and proletariat). The problem is rather an ambiguous and mechanical way that Bordwell's theory postulates in interrelating formal norms with social, industrial contexts. What would Ozu's following (or violating) of Hollywood's formal norms – for instance, 180-degree rule, eyeline and graphic matching, low-height camera etc. – have to do with the proliferation of urban mass culture or the advancement of militarism during the war? Without confronting this issue, there is a danger of isolating the textual level of analysis from the contextual one, or forming an arbitrary connection between them, even though this does not mean that every textual element contains a meaning that can directly correspond to a certain contextual background.

The same problematic can be applied to the studies on the opposite side of methodological position. Some of them are designed as macro-scale historical studies, dealing with Ozu's films within the specific context of the history of Japanese cinema, including discussions of industrial foundations, the star system, genre conventions and audience responses, as well as broader political influences. For instance, Isolde Standish's *A New History of Japanese Cinema* (2005) takes the position that '[i]mages and cinema should be understood as part of the social process of the creation of meaning', but argues that the social process must be understood and described in relation to local terms, specific to Japan's historical experiences.[72] She thus reconstructs the national cinema according to changes of the predominant discourses in Japanese society, for example modernism in the interwar period, nationalism during wartime, and humanism (or democracy) in the 1950s, and so on. Among them, the period of the fifteen years' war from 1931 to 1945 becomes the focus of interest in Peter High's *Imperial Screen* (2003). It examines the transformations in the Japanese film industry at the time of the advancement, reign and decline of Japanese nationalism, which appeared in the form of the media policies and censorship of the militarist government. High does not present a simple, unidirectional model of influence of politics upon cinema; in fact the big picture he suggests is much more complex, with the 'commercial instincts' of film entrepreneurs and the 'liberalism' or 'humanism' of filmmakers together interacting with the state's ideological control. Above all, this approach offers a great deal of information about Ozu during wartime, as will be discussed in Chapter 3. However, the issue here is again how to interrelate the extensive contextual information with the concrete filmic text without reducing every event in the latter to the reference of the former. This would be a potential problem for any study predicated on a historical methodology, the grand scope of which tends to be oblivious to the actual form of individual text.

Many Ozu studies written in Japanese exhibit the same kind of division between textual and contextual approaches. Some of them contain extensively detailed factual information, notably the works of Tanaka Masasumi, which will be frequently referred to as primary sources. Most Japanese publications on Ozu, however, can be positioned in between biographical writing and academic research, the intention and structure usually oriented more towards describing background information than raising and resolving particular research questions. There are, however, some exceptions, such as Hasumi Shigehiko's *Kantoku Ozu Yasujirō/The Director Ozu Yasujiro* (1983) and Yoshida Kiju's *Ozu Yasujirō no haneiga/Ozu's Anti-Cinema* (1998), which focus on detailed analysis of Ozu's texts, especially in terms of narrative and style. Hasumi pays attention to Ozu's playful aberrations that are not integral to narrative construction, and groups them according to particular themes (or 'thematic system' in his term) – such as eating outside, changing clothes, or watching together in one direction – that recur throughout Ozu's films.[73] These non-narrative tropes are all closely related to everyday experience, though Hasumi does not explicitly foreground the word 'eveyrday' in his discussion. However, unlike Bordwell, Hasumi does not attempt to correlate the pure textual concept of the thematic system with context; in fact, the thematic system itself 'is introduced to affirm the [textual] details that may be regarded as surplus seen from the [social reality's] point of view'.[74] Yoshida Kiju's interest is also placed on the role of the everyday at the textual level as a factor antithetical to narrative order. The everyday as such betrays the viewers' anticipation of drama and reveals the 'artificiality of the film narrative' by defamiliarising it; thus Ozu's cinema is 'anti-cinema', where essentially nothing happens.[75] Paralleling Schrader's aforementioned expression of 'cold everyday', these attempts to purify the everyday seem to end up in another excess bent towards text, apart from Ozu's rich *dramatic* tradition, not to mention the context of Japanese society and history. Nevertheless, as Ozu himself clarified in his last words to Yoshida on his deathbed, 'Cinema is drama, not accident'.[76]

In this book, the socio-historical method aims to both properly situate the textual experience of the everyday within its contextual field and, in reverse, to recognise the textual evidence, especially at narrative level, in the discussion of social and historical issues. There are several exemplary studies from the past decade or so that suggest a model for this bilateral investigation. Mitsuyo Wada-Marciano's *Nippon Modern: Japanese Cinema of the 1920s and 30s* examines the specific issue of Japanese modernity, including city space, the Japanese urban middle classes, female subjectivity and national identity, as represented in the style of Shochiku's Kamata studio (where Ozu also worked). The effect of the Kamata style, however, was a complicated one, for the ideology it conveyed to Japanese audiences reflected the unstable interactions of Western influence and traditional Japaneseness, or modernism and nationalism. Wada-Marciano finds textual examples of this duality in modern girl figures appearing in the woman's film, or in liminal cinematic urban spaces.[77]

Alastair Phillips' major concern is also the 'contested' nature of Japanese modernity expressed in the form of everyday life, which he analyses with the case of the middle-class suburban space in Ozu's *I Was Born But...*[78] For Phillips, however, the contestation in modernity is not only spatial but also temporal, between tradition and progress, which results in a 'more consensual version of continuity, a sense of the past within the present'.[79] Ozu, Phillips argues, appropriates this temporal sensitivity in the construction of femininity, as exemplified by the representative postwar character Noriko, who, involved with the narrative of marriage and death, 'is literally embodied as the important link between one generation and the other'.[80] If Wada-Marciano conceptualises female subjectivity as an ultimately ideological construct subordinate to the patriarchal order, Phillips' position is more accepting of the possibility of a woman's independent subject formation, which can lead to intergenerational 'camaraderie' among females, beyond the segregation of traditional and modern femininity.

The formation of female subjectivity within a specific historical context of Japanese modernity also becomes the central issue in Catherine Russell's study of Naruse Mikio's works. Her broad investigation of modern mass culture in interwar Japan provides a useful framework for interpreting Naruse's female characters, who, often as working women such as barmaids or waitresses, are able to 'negotiate [their] own terms' in the midst of a materialistic urban environment.[81] Even domesticity, the site of patriarchal oppression from Wada-Marciano's viewpoint, is a 'complex site of femininity', becoming 'at once the site of [women's] repression and their only token of identity'.[82] What also distinguishes Russell's work is her close attention to textual analysis, which delves into the effects of details such as everyday domestic objects and Naruse's flamboyant camera work and editing. Along with a wide array of contextual knowledge, this comprehensive perspective on a director suggests a new possibility for auteurism, which Russell believes can become 'a method of *historical* research that takes the author's work as a case study or sample of a complex historical-cultural formation' (italics added).[83]

Ozu, as an object of a socio-historical study, presents a rewarding as well as intriguing case, for his filmmaking career spans a long enough time – from the prewar, through the wartime, and until the postwar – to trace its historical change in comparison with the transition of modern everyday life in Japan. This will require a discussion of the way in which Japanese modernity provided the major historical impetus to Japanese people, and also an investigation of Shochiku Kamata studio, which primarily produced the films about urban modern life, but at the same time negotiated older cinematic styles and subject matter. The middle classes (discussed in Chapters 1 and 5), the working class (Chapter 2) and female characters (Chapters 2 to 4) will be focused on as the major subjects of the everyday, while avoiding a kind of determinism or reductionism that considers their representations to be direct reflections of a social ideology, whether it be patriarchy or consumerism. The complexity of the relationship between modern subjectivity and society will be fully explored, using the concept of deviation drawn from de Certeau's theory. A key point of doing this is to return to Ozu's texts and discover their richness in the actual, concrete expression of the everyday, as Tosaka advocates. This 'return to the text', emphasised in Russell's work as well, will demand a more sophisticated examination of Ozu's films in order to identify minute yet meaningful effects, not only at the level of pure visual/aural experience, as seen in Hasumi and Yoshida's studies, but also in relation to narrative and drama. The contextual study in this book is presented in order to aid this process of developing textual ambiguity (and our understanding of it) into a more concrete form, not just to verify its applicability in the text.

Another important methodological issue is the temporal aspect of the everyday, which has not yet been thoroughly investigated in other studies. The historical imagination that Benjamin engaged with can be compared with the recognition of the past in the present in Ozu's films, as Phillips has noted. In order to capitalise on this historicity, the following chapters are structured around a chronological order. Chapter 1 sets the founding stone with the issue of the Japanese modernity in the early 1930s, when the goal of modernisation confronted a crisis out of economic depression, the fear of which became the major subject in Ozu's successful generic variation of the *shōshimin* film. In the mid-1930s, the director began to expand to a new thematic territory of retrospective sensitivity by using the nostalgic space of Shitamachi that connoted the disappearing past in modern Tokyo, as will be discussed in Chapter 2. Chapter 3 will introduce an issue of gender division and conflict as Ozu's new allegorical device to delve more into the matter of dialectical temporality, contrasting the everyday of female characters against the male-driven militarism that prevailed during wartime. Ozu's following postwar years are largely an extension of these prewar problematics. Chapter 4, roughly corresponding to the US Occupation period, will articulate the stark historical consciousness that Ozu developed after the war in both temporal and spatial dimensions, resulting in his canonical works such as *Late Spring* and *Tokyo Story*. The last chapter will examine the director's late years which produced stable (or conventional) genre dramas against the backdrop of radical change of political and economic environments as a new young generation (and their 'reprivatised' life) gradually emerged to the front of Japanese society. The history, in summary, will be confronted with the deviations of the actual subjects of the everyday, the complex morphology of which is what essentially differentiates this study from others that are only about any of the three issues here: Ozu *or* history *or* the everyday.

Chapter 1
Early Ozu: *Shōshimin* Film and Everyday Realism

For Ozu, the cinema and the earthquake came together. It was in August 1923 when, having spent ten years outside of Tokyo for his education, Ozu finally returned to his hometown to take up a job as an assistant cameraman in Shochiku's Kamata studio. Only a month later, the Great Kantō Earthquake occurred, devastating everything, not only buildings and houses but also the memory of Edo (Tokyo's old name) that was already dying out. Tokyo's old Shitamachi district would disappear, many people would leave, and the film studios (all except Shochiku) would find their new home in Kyoto. Meanwhile, from the heap of rubble, the energy to create a new world was slowly growing. This is the apocalyptic Tokyo that Tanizaki Jun'ichiro gazed at and then exclaimed, 'Tokyo will be better for this!'[1] The commercial centre of the city would soon move from Nihonbashi to Ginza, where several department stores, offering goods for everyday living rather than only expensive speciality or imported items, would lure Tokyo citizens to partake in the new commodity culture. This was the beginning of a new world called 'the modern', and Ozu's filmmaking incidentally (but meaningfully) corresponded with this important phase of transformation in the early twentieth-century history of Japan.[2]

Needless to say, the modern did not begin the day the earthquake happened. Studies have shown that the modern of the 1920s, the period which saw the enthronement of the new emperor Shōwa as well as the earthquake, owed much to what the previous Taishō era (1912–26) had been experiencing under such mottoes as '*bunka* (culture)', the concept of which was itself a reaction to the previous Meiji period's (1868–1912) national agenda dubbed '*bunmei* (civilisation)'. According to Minami Hiroshi, what distinguished *bunka* from *bunmei* was the former's 'individualism and consumerism', which contrasted with the latter's emphasis upon 'national enrichment, security, and industrial production'.[3] If *bunka* concentrated on such an individual, everyday life, the modern for artists and intellectuals meant a new spirit of the age expressed through various movements in literature, fine arts, architecture, photography, theatre and cinema that could be summarised with the term *modanizumu*, a Japanese counterpart of Western modernism in the early twentieth century. The chronology of *modanizumu* also implied continuity between Taishō and Shōwa, disproving its sudden appearance in history; although the earthquake in 1923 is 'invariably cited as the metaphorical marker for the eruption of a modernist consciousness in Japan, such stirrings predated the earthquake by a decade or more'.[4]

In cinema, most film historians agree that a meaningful turning point can be identified in the late 1910s (whether it was 1916, 1917 or during World War I), moving from sound to vision, from perceptive openness to narrative closure, and from theatricality to cinematicity. Standish recognises this period as the second phase in the national cinema history, characterised by the 'emergence of an "intellectual" approach to filmmaking symbolized by the "Pure Film Movement" (*jun'eiga undō*)', and Gerow agrees that a 'paradigm shift' occurred between 1916 and 1924 that transformed '*katsudō shashin* (moving pictures)' into '*eiga* (film)' and '*benshi*' to '*setsumeisha* (explainer)' through the 'large scale effort to import American and Hollywood filmmaking techniques'.[5] The groups that actively advocated this shift were critics, intellectuals, reformers of the Pure Film Movement, and new production studios such as Tenkatsu and Shochiku, which aimed for a 'system of self-sufficient, realist narration' that Western films were achieving, while simultaneously problematising older non-cinematic practices such as the *benshi*.[6] It is undeniable that the cinema of Ozu, who began his filmmaking career in Shochiku (and would continue there until he died), owed a large part of its formation to the studio's position in the Japanese film industry of the 1920s as a cultural agent, which, extending the attempts of the previous decade, addressed modernity by dealing with modern everyday life through its artistic style of realism.

This chapter will examine the early phase of Ozu's cinema, from 1927 to 1932, in the context of this transformation and development of Japanese cinema into an artistic vehicle to represent Japanese modernity. A key concept I will probe here is *Kamata-chō*, or Kamata style, named after the place where Shochiku's *gendaigeki* studio was located, and used as a metonym for the unique form of realism and subject matter of urban everyday life commonly found in the studio's films. *Kamata-chō* then can be understood as the basic tenet of Shochiku's *modanizumu*, resulting from the company's conscious effort to adopt Western style filmmaking and actualise it through the cinematic depiction of the modern everyday. I will thus discuss the birth and development of *Kamata-chō*, focusing on such key figures as Kido Shirō, the head of Kamata studio, and Shimazu Yasujiro, a Shochiku director who is known to have most faithfully fulfilled Kido's idea of Kamata style on screen. It is undeniable that the genre pictures of early Ozu, which culminate in the form of *shōshimin* film (petit-bourgeois film), are also within the reach of *Kamata-chō*'s stylistic influence. However, I will also pay attention to the contradictory nature of *Kamata-chō*, whose goal of Westernisation was in fact always under constant tension with a retrogressive tendency towards Shochiku's theatrical tradition and non-Western style as established in the pre-Kido era. This complexity, I will argue, can be identified as a symptom of the Japanese modern in a larger context, which is essentially a compromise between a progress of Westernisation and an appeal to more indigenous history and culture. Ozu's films, even the early ones generally regarded as having the strongest affinity with Western mass culture, are, for various reasons, not entirely free from this contradiction (and ensuing process of negotiation). In the later part of this chapter, I will confirm this point by closely analysing Ozu's *shōshimin* film genre films from this period.

The Birth of Shochiku: Osanai and Nomura

On a page of the *Tōkyō nichinichi shinbun* (*Tokyo Daily News*) published on 26 February 1920, the following advertisement appeared:

> ... Here Shochiku Partnership establishes Shochiku Kinema Partnership, and commences shooting new motion picture films. The main purpose of this Kinema Partnership is to endeavour to improve the quality of Japan's motion pictures by producing artistic films that are currently actively advocated in the West and releasing them at home and abroad. It is also to contribute to harmonious international relationship among Japan and other countries by introducing the true state of our people's lives . . .[7]

In this small notice, which announced the beginning of one of the major film studios in Japan, Shochiku clarified its vision of filmmaking and summarised it in two essential points. Firstly, there was an issue of Westernisation: as a latecomer in the industry, the company recognised that the primary issue of Japanese cinema was to 'improve' its standard to that of 'artistic films' from the West. Secondly, it aimed at the faithful representation of the '[Japanese] people's lives'. From the start, therefore, Shochiku clearly understood that what was demanded of Japanese cinema at that time was Western modernity and the 'true' (that is, realistic) depiction of everyday life in Japan, which are interrelated but, at the same time, can be contradictory with each other. Shochiku's history itself, from the beginning, exhibits this kind of complexity.

Shochiku began as a cooperative theatre business between the twin brothers Shirai Matsujirō and Ōtani Takejirō in 1902. The early twentieth century, when Shochiku was growing, was a transitional moment for the Japanese theatre industry. As the whole nation transformed into a new modern state modelled after Western civilisation, Japanese theatre, represented by *kabuki* (on which Shochiku also concentrated), accordingly faced the same social pressure to reform old traditions. Shirai and Ōtani, in their twenties, were very conscious of this tendency and maintained a progressive attitude to changing conventions in the theatre business.[8] Thus, they formed the Engeki kairyō kai (Association of Theatre Improvement) after opening their first theatre in Kyoto, which emphasised the performance art's sociality as a mass edifying tool.[9] Shochiku also made an effort to adopt *shinpa* (meaning 'new school') style dramas, which, 'after the end of Sino-Japanese War (1895), had developed to the status where it rivalled *kabuki*'.[10] A revolt against '*kabuki*'s inability to present plays in contemporary settings', *shinpa* dramas were often based on political novels, the theme of which often dealt with 'the idea of the individual making a success of his life in the new Japan in spite of the hurdles of low birth or misfortune'.[11]

The installation of a film branch in Shochiku in 1920 was thus an extension of its business strategy to actively respond to new entertainment trends. Japanese cinema in the first two decades or so up until Shochiku's arrival had already experienced the coexistence of two contradictory tendencies. On the one hand, cinema was mainly an imported cultural property, a symbol of Western civilisation. After it was first introduced in 1896 with Edison's Kinetoscope, the Japanese film industry, favouring stable profitability, chose to depend upon importing foreign films rather than investing in domestic production, and the ratio of imported films eventually rose to 70 per cent of all films released in cinemas.[12] Production was also led by import traders such as Yoshizawa Shōten and Yokota Shōkai. The early period of Shochiku can thus be interpreted as a history of nationalising cinematic resources and techniques by observing and learning how the role models, America and European countries, were doing. For several months in 1919, Shiroi Shintarō, the younger brother of Ōtani, was sent to the West to test the feasibility of the film business. Shiroi stayed for a long time in Hollywood and was impressed by Universal City Studios, then the largest 'city made of studios' in the world, which became the model for Shochiku's Kamata studio. The next step was to find appropriate employees and Shochiku tried many new approaches to finding the right personnel both in and out of the industry. It abandoned the tradition of *onnagata* (or *oyama*, an actor who impersonates a female role) from the start, and gave birth to the first star actress in Japan, Kurishima Sumiko. It also established an acting school so that the studio could supply performers on its own. Those technicians that could not be found in Japan were sought in America, such as Henry Kotani, one of the earliest directors in Japanese film history, who greatly contributed to the transfer of Hollywood's director system as well as technological knowledge.

On the other hand, the traces of old entertainment industry conventions persisted in early filmmaking practice. For instance, the early star system, which created the 'first idol' Onoe Matsunosuke in the 1910s, relied largely on the theatre industry (*kabuki* or *shinpa*) for its supply of new actors.[13] Lower-class players, who could not succeed in 'legitimate' *kabuki* theatres and thus worked in touring troupes or *shinpa* theatres, also often transferred to the film industry, landing a job as not only actors but also production staff. With this movement of personnel from one medium to another, performance and production styles followed accordingly. The *onnagata* tradition in *kabuki*, for instance, made the transition. Another indigenous element of Japanese cinema in this early period was the existence of the *benshi*, the explainer of narratives as well as the narrator of intertitles during exhibition.[14] At its highest peak, the *benshi*'s power superseded even the intention of the director or producer in that he could intervene and reconstruct the story of a film during exhibition. The theatrical convention persisted in Shochiku's filmmaking as well. The style of *shinpa* especially, as a theatrical form that emphasised excessive emotions, proved commercially viable in film, and competed with the tendency toward Westernisation within the studio. Shochiku thus experienced a tension between the desire for a new Western form of expression and the reality of cultural assimilation, both of which coexisted in the progress towards the modernism it had originally dreamed of.

Two of the most influential figures in Shochiku at this period, whose different origins and opposing artistic tendencies directly reflected the internal contradiction of the company, were Nomura Hōtei and Osanai Kaoru. Nomura, originally a stage artist from Kyoto and later the head of a theatre called Hongōza in Tokyo, joined Shochiku as the head of Kamata Studio and immediately started to direct films such as *Futari no yūkanbai/A Couple Selling Evening Papers* and *Hō no namida/Tears of Law* (both in 1921). By bringing in the influence of *shinpa*, he thus represented the commercialism of mass appeal, appropriately mixing 'fashionable (*haikara*) American style expressions' with '*shinpa* tragedy's contents'.[15] His motto was, 'High is the ideal, low are the hands', of which the mild compromise explained the essence of 'Nomura-ism'.[16] This pragmatic line, which was effective in the box office, was of great importance in the early history of Shochiku, whose business, in contrast with the original ambition of developing an 'art' cinema, was actually being directed towards 'popular-taste *kyūgeki* (old theatre, e.g. *kabuki*) or *shinpa*' style moving pictures that could be produced 'cheap and fast'.[17] It is also an important point that Japanese audiences, regardless of the Americanism pursued by some Shochiku staff, were not so content with the experiments, and rather preferred (and felt comfortable with) the theatrical, *shinpa*-style movies, as well as the *benshi*'s existence.[18]

If Nomura Hōtei, leading the Kamata Studio, represented the *kabuki* or *shinpa* group in Shochiku along with directors such as Kawaguchi Yoshitarō and Kako Zanmu, Osanai Kaoru, the principal of Shochiku's school for actors, represented the opposite position. Contrary to Nomura's career based on *shinpa*, Osanai came from the *shingeki* ('New Drama') movement, which emerged after the turn of the century.[19] In contrast with *shinpa*, which grew out of *kabuki* and maintained a mutually influential relationship with it, *shingeki* was a much more Westernised form of theatre, backed by college students, intellectuals and writers, who were familiar with the grammar of Western drama. *Shingeki* was thus active in adopting 'the paradigm of Western realist theatre' and forms such as naturalism, which opposed theatrical 'artifice' and instead emphasised 'the representation of the real'.[20] Coming from this modern background, Osanai was therefore against Shochiku's growing tendency towards commercialism built on *shinpa*-flavoured theatricality as exemplified in the works of Nomura and other directors. He eventually left Kamata studio and, with his students from the Shochiku actors' school, established an independent institute called Shochiku Cinema Institute (Shōchiku Kinema Kenkyūsho) in November 1920. Among the staff who followed him were important future directors such as Murata Minoru (*Rojō no reikon/Souls on the Road*, 1921; *Nichirin/The Sun*, 1926), Ushihara Kiyohiko (*Kare to jinsei/He and Life*, 1929; *Shingun/The March*, 1930), and Shimazu Yasujirō (*Tonari no yae chan/Our Neighbour Miss Yae*, 1934; *Ani to sono imoto/A Brother and His Younger Sister*, 1939). Their efforts resulted in *Souls on the Road* (1921), which, featuring cross-cutting editing as well as Western thematic issues (the story was partly based on Gorki's *The Lower Depths*), demonstrated the direction that Osanai and his colleagues were inclined toward.

Osanai's experiment, however, did not last long. Owing to financial limitations and internal controversy over the future direction, the Institute was dissolved in August 1921. During this time, Kamata studio was occupied by ex-*kabuki* and ex-*shinpa* staff, whose productions constituted 'really a strange sight' to the young filmmakers who had already been baptised by Osanai's modern methods.[21] Their idealism had to wait a few more years before blooming, when the coming of the Great Kantō Earthquake and the appearance of Kido Shirō, who, under the name of *Kamata-chō*, would deny theatrical influences and reaffirm Shochiku's original goal of Westernisation through the realistic depiction of the everyday life of Japanese people.

Kamata-chō and the Realism of the Everyday

Kido Shirō entered Shochiku in 1922 at the age of twenty-eight. Assigned to the accounting department in the beginning, he had an opportunity to manage Kamata after the studio had been destroyed by the earthquake in 1923, when he was (at first temporarily) sent to supervise its reconstruction. During this time, he endeavoured above all to reinstate production activities, which, with the director Shimazu Yasujiro, resulted in such films as *Otōsan/Father* (1923) and *Nichiyōbi/Sunday* (1924), which will be discussed in the next section. Kido's appearance at Shochiku implied another important swing of the pendulum towards the modern, Western and cinematic way of filmmaking and away from the old, theatrical style. An elite university graduate with a good command of English, he was active in learning and adopting Western practices of filmmaking, especially emphasising the director system (instead of the star system) and scriptwriting. His inclination towards the West can be exemplified by his long visit to several Western countries (the USSR, Germany, Spain and the US) from July 1928 to April 1929, which made him realise the importance of sound technology, leading to an effort to develop Shochiku's own talkie system. It is thus a symbolic occurrence that Kido replaced Nomura Hōtei as the head of Kamata studio in July 1924.[22] In the turbulent mood of the post-earthquake society, Nomura's *shinpa* tragedies did not reflect the urban masses' desire to watch 'bright films rather than dark ones', which Kido well understood and developed into his concept of *Kamata-chō*.[23]

What did *Kamata-chō* mean then? As a loose tendency in style, subject and resulting atmosphere, it is hard to define it simply, but according to Kido's own words, it can be equated with Shochiku's original vision of depicting the everyday life of ordinary people in a realistic way.

> We should make films that are directly linked to the life of the masses, not ones that attempt to transcend their understanding. Our job is to discover what the masses experience, what they subconsciously feel, and provide it [in film]. Such an attitude is connected to realism in description [on screen]. This is the foundation of *Kamata-chō*.[24]

Other interpretations also agree that *Kamata-chō* was about realism in style, a methodology of showing 'life as it is' and thereby appealing to mass audiences; and in terms of subject matter, it dealt with the things happening around us, everyday (*nichijō*), all of which I would summarise with the term 'everyday realism'. Yoshimura Kōzaburō, a director who worked in Shochiku, mentions 'simple human relationships, frequent use of everyday conversation, and emphasis on lifestyle and custom' as the key features of *Kamata-chō*.[25]

Another Shochiku director Yamada Yōji also explains that what was important in *Kamata-chō* was 'necessarily the detailed depiction of everyday life'; such trivial aspects as a house that was 'located in a Tokyo suburb, with a small garden', accommodating the 'life of a salaryman', were all decisive details of the everyday that constructed the realism of *Kamata-chō*.[26] In addition to tangible objects, a nonchalant (*sarigenai*) performance style is a part of *Kamata-chō*'s everyday realism. Yamada, referring to Ozu's advice for actors – 'Don't try your best. Do it moderately' – characterises *Kamata-chō* by its natural performance style, which emphasises '*shigusa*' (subtle change in expression or the movement of body)', instead of theatrical *ōgesa* or *kochō* (exaggeration).[27] This natural style was also well suited to the urban modernity that Kamata was pursuing at the time. Most of the adherents of *Kamata-chō*, from leaders such as Kido, Shimazu, Gosho and Ozu to other staff and actors, came from Tokyo, and were thus familiar with the light and buoyant tempo of big city life that formed the basic atmosphere of Kamata films. The urban nature of the Kamata studio can also be connected to its symbolic image as the only major studio that decided to remain in Tokyo after the Kantō Earthquake.

Kamata-chō's concern with everyday realism can be compared to Tosaka Jun's theorisation of the everyday. As an antithetical reaction to the conservative tendencies of contemporary Japanese intellectuals in the 1930s, who, facing the impending war, tried to grasp the problem of the everyday from a metaphysical and ethnocentric stance, Tosaka's thoughts strongly objected to such an abstract, non-scientific and 'philistine' approach, and 'redefine[d] the task of philosophy as the problem of the present, the now (*ima*) of everyday life' in its 'totality' and 'actuality'.[28] Thus he rejects any kind of methodology which, lacking the key step of observation of actual reality, allows 'hermeneutic' manipulation – be it political, economic, historic, literary or philological – that deploys 'the order of *meaning* in place of the order of *reality*'.[29] In a similar way, the 'common sense' that pervades the everyday life of a society became the object of Tosaka's criticism, if it meant just a quantitative average of the majority's opinions (the 'bourgeois-democratic concept of common sense'). He rather advocated a common sense that is based upon the '*jissaisei* (act-uality, Wirklichkeit in German, where wirk- means to act)' of the everyday.[30] An idea can be common sense not because many people (a vague quantity) agree (or believe) but because it reflects the actual reality of our everyday lives.

Thus for Tosaka, the 'principle of everyday life' is 'actuality'.[31] And actuality is closely linked to current affairs and the problems of an ever-changing society. He thus evaluated the role of journalism more highly than philosophy or literature as a practice of actuality. The emphasis on actuality is also present in his theory of film, which he regards as 'the most realistic art form that can visually represent the actual existence'.[32] This 'actual reality (*shajitsusei*)' of film, which can show the everyday of society as well as nature in 'live action', is what grants the medium its high artistic value. Tosaka thus speaks highly of documentary or news film as the genre that actualises this quality of cinema. At the social level, reality can be experienced through customs, manners and lifestyles, the exhibition of which is 'the principal condition of cinema'.[33] Customs and manners in cinema, such as clothing, architecture, behaviour and facial expression, are not only a material and sensory experience but the representation of the moral consciousness that defines and distinguishes a society from others. Thus Japanese cinema, by showing Japanese customs and manners, may become the 'concrete expression of Japanese people's thoughts'.[34] Or from the audiences' point of view, their moral consciousness is confronted and affected by the customs and manners depicted on screen.

However, the everyday realism was only one aspect of *Kamata-chō*'s identity; since the everyday is plural in reality, the question of which 'life' and 'realism' Kido was talking about should be raised. According to him, life should be optimistic, and reality should be grasped from such a point of view.

> Humans are not god, and cannot become divine until the end . . . This permanent defect is the essence of humanity . . . The mission of art is to contemplate this truth and deal with it in as warm and cheerful way as possible. There is a way of seeing the humanity with dark sentiments, as exemplified by religion, which searches for salvation, or by [political] revolution. Shochiku is the opposite, trying to look at life from a *warm, cheerful and hopeful* point of view. In conclusion, the fundamental purpose of film should be nothing but *relief*. It shall never disappoint audiences. This is the basis of what they call *Kamata-chō*.[35] [Italics added]

In this statement, we can identify Kido's unique secular humanism, one that was supported by a 'warm, cheerful and hopeful' view of life. Here he also implies *Kamata-chō*'s non-ideological and non-political nature by distancing it from 'religion' and 'revolution', concepts that hinge on a pessimistic vision of humanity and hence 'disappoint' audiences. *Kamata-chō*'s realism was thus ironically a 'political' one, refusing to confront those realities of everyday life that required a more critical perspective on humanity.

The ideological naivety of *Kamata-chō* has caused much controversy amongst critics. Though they did not question Shochiku's stylistic deftness in delicately depicting life 'as is', such achievement was not acknowledged beyond the level of formal realism. In his analysis of the everydayness of Kamata films, the Japanese critic Sawamura Tsutomu asserted that Kamata's everyday was nothing more than 'subordination to the visual' (i.e. obsession with the faithful representation of the visible), lacking the ideology required for 'true cinematic realism'.[36] Jeong Suwan, calling Kamata's realism 'hypocritical', has argued that the everyday of *Kamata-chō* (or 'Kido-ism' in her terminology) 'does not represent the truth but deludes viewers into believing that they are seeing a represented reality'.[37] This constructed realism was also related to the issue of class; the everyday that *Kamata-chō* presented on screen was not a generic one, but a specific kind applicable only to the urban middle classes. As Satō Tadao argues, *Kamata-chō* 'adopted the *shomin's* (lower middle class's) point of view, dealing with the things happening close to their social life'.[38] And again, it was not only the text but also the context of filmmaking that was 'middle class'; most of the filmmakers working in Kamata were of 'petit bourgeois origins'.[39] This does not mean that Kamata's films appealed only to urban middle-class audiences. Rather, as will be discussed later in this chapter, while remaining faithful to the middle-class reality, they could create a 'fantasy of the real' that audiences from other classes could enjoy (or even criticise) together.

The everyday realism of *Kamata-chō* can be more clearly understood by comparing it with the style of *shinpa*, the antithesis of what Osanai and Kido had pursued. As mentioned, *shinpa* began as a reformation movement in response to *kabuki*, but gradually became conservative itself, becoming more like a 'purveyor of repetitious melodrama'.[40] By the time Kido appeared, it was criticised for going overboard, with narratives becoming 'too predictable' and depending too much on exaggerated emotions and performances, resulting in 'false reality' or 'pseudo realism' as the Japanese critic Honma Shigeo criticised.[41] Thus it was an important matter for Kido to articulate *Kamata-chō*'s realism as distinct from *shinpa*'s emotional excessiveness. This naturally led to an emphasis on comic (or more precisely, carefree and light) elements in Kamata films, which clearly contrasted with *shinpa*'s serious, tragic mood. Kido explained:

> It is good to take a handkerchief to cinema to see a tragedy, but it is not that interesting to make all the films for those 'ready-to-weep' audiences. Entertainment must be a bright and healthy product, and we can learn something about life when we can discover and laugh about the irony or contradiction of society.[42]

> The reason *jidaigeki*'s *chanbara* (sword fighting) is popular is because it is interesting to see the stimuli of the various movements coming out of such scenes. Tragedy is more theatrical than cinematic. I believe, to win over *jidaigeki*, [Kamata's *gendaigeki* should concentrate on] comedy that has the similar ability [to *chanbara*] to attract audiences by evoking *interests in visuals*.[43] [Italics added]

It is interesting to see that Kido, as with his predecessors in the Pure Film Movement, was well aware of the significance of separating cinematicity from theatricality; he believed that the former should be based on visual elements such as those found in comedy and sword-fighting spectacles rather than the verbal elements of the latter.[44] Thus comedy, with all its movements and visual rhythms, was an important genre vehicle with which to oppose *shinpa*'s theatrical influence, and became the emblem of *Kamata-chō*. Satō Tadao summarises the three most conspicuous characteristics of *Kamata-chō* as 'cheerfulness', 'freshness' and 'speed', which are, after all, the typical stylistic features of a good comedy.[45]

The disparity between *Kamata-chō* and *shinpa* could also be found in their different thematic perspectives. As mentioned, Kido's humanism and secularism were based upon an optimistic attitude, which avoided from the old biases of a teleological and ethical view of humanity and society. He thus objected to *shinpa*'s emphasis on morals.

> As for *shinpa-chō* (*shinpa* style), ... although touching on some truth, it did not deal with the essence of humanity. [*Shinpa*] takes the morality of the times for granted, and develops a character who is only governed by it, moving within that boundary. We are not interested in such a narrative ... Until now, morality first existed, and humans were to be wrapped inside it. From now, morality will be criticised and its value judged through the gauge of essential humanity.[46]

Satō Tadao, mentioning the popular *shinpa* film *Kago no tori/A Bird in a Cage* (Matsumoto Eiichi, Teikoku Kinema, 1924), also points out that the morality in the film was based on an idea that romance is a 'guilty thing', even though it was a romance film. It was around the late Taishō and early Shōwa, simultaneously with the rise of *Kamata-chō*, when the theme of romance started to be dealt with in a 'freer and easier' attitude, as something that could be 'cheerful and bright'.[47] *Kamata-chō* was thus comparatively free from socially imposed morals that often misled narrative into a predestined tragic end as was often seen in the *shinpa* style films. In other words, the characters in *Kamata-chō* films were supposed to be more multifaceted and variable in relation to fate, as human beings in real life usually are, and can be differentiated from *shinpa* characters, who are rather flat and predictable in their behaviour.

Taking all these *shinpa* elements into consideration, it becomes clear that what was really essential in *Kamata-chō*, as an oppositional form, was less the pathos or sorrowful mood that has been regarded as a representative characteristic of Shochiku films, than a light tempo and cheerfulness (or composure) that, facing emotional crisis, effectively redirects and vents the tragic elements concealed underneath. Ozu was definitely a part of this tradition, especially in his early comedies, but he also grew further and further away from the influence of *Kamata-chō* to construct his unique world of the everyday. In that sense, and in contrast with the popular understanding of his work, Ozu cannot be accepted as the key exemplar of the original *Kamata-chō* as it was envisioned by Kido. That honour should rather be attributed to the director Shimazu Yasujirō.

Born in 1897 in the Kanda district of Tokyo, Shimazu was one of the first employees in Kamata who responded to Shochiku's newspaper advertisement mentioned above. He began work under Osanai Kaoru, who at this time established the Shochiku Cinema Institute, where Shimazu would continue writing scripts and participate in the making of *Souls on the Road*. After the disbandment of the Institute, Shimazu returned to Kamata and became one of the studio's most prolific directors, making twenty-nine films in the period between 1922 and the Kantō Earthquake of the next year. In this early period, most of Shimazu's films were regarded as 'Shitamachi-*mono* (story of Shitamachi)' or '*rakugoshu* (a *rakugo* style genre) that dealt with the life of *shomin*. His directing style was already evaluated as a sensible, skilful and, most of all, '*shajitsuteki* (realistic)' rendition of '*nichijōsei* (the everyday)'.[48] Shimazu's tendency toward everyday realism was a perfect match with the new direction that Kido was considering for Shochiku. Shimazu was, so to speak, the first director who actualised what Kido wanted, that is, not a 'meandering, unrefined play' but 'a work with a simple plot and subject matter based on familiar life, seizing the truth of humanity by realistically depicting daily practices (*nichijōsahanji*)'.[49] Shimazu also 'greatly contributed to the establishment of the director system', which Kido was pursuing as an alternative to the then prevailing 'star system'.[50] Kido thus valued Shimazu highly, designating him without hesitation as his favourite director.[51] In the confrontational structure within Shochiku, between Osanai (and Kido)'s faction pursuing artistic, experimental, cinematic and American tendencies, and Nomura's line holding on to the conventional, popular, theatrical and Japanese style of filmmaking, Shimazu was the hope of the former, who rose in rebellion against Nomura-ism.

Most critics agree that Shimazu's realistic style began with the two post-earthquake films, *Father* and *Sunday*. Although neither of the films exists today, the summaries of the narratives indicate that the basic tenets of the *Kamata-chō* are present in good form. Neither strays from the spatial and personal boundaries 'around (*mijikana*)' the protagonists, and the plots are constructed from an episodic structure, full of the small and comic occurrences of urban daily life. In *Father*, for example, there appear such scenes as a baseball game (the protagonist is a player at school), student-*geisha* relations, and car driving. In *Sunday*, the modern urban atmosphere is conveyed through the protagonist, whose preparations for going out – wearing a fashionable suit, trimming hair and perfuming himself – are depicted in detail. A light and carefree mood – as exemplified by the protagonists' whimsical attitude to affairs – suggests these are clever romantic comedies emancipated from the moral restraints of *shinpa* melodrama. Not only did post-earthquake audiences react positively to the lightness of the two Shimazu films, but contemporary Japanese critics also acclaimed the achievement; *Father* was called a 'cheerful masterpiece', and *Sunday* demonstrated 'still more refining of Shimazu's skills'.[52] Their main point concentrated on the films' 'taste of comedy', the 'bright and optimistic element that had been principally lacking in Japanese cinema'.[53]

The making of *Father* and *Sunday*, however, shows that Shimazu's choice of genre and style should also be considered from a broader contextual perspective. Labouring in the midst of a Kamata studio reconstructing itself after the earthquake, the production of the films suffered great limitation of resources, and only two studio sets were allowed for each film. Since *shinpa*'s tragic melodrama, with frequent scene changes, needed a substantial number of sets, Shimazu instead turned to making the more simplistic 'home drama', which emphasised 'an elaborate and realistic expression of life and manners'.[54] This anecdote does not mean that *Kamata-chō* was merely a fortuitous outcome; the concept, as discussed, should be understood as a phenomenon within a more general tendency towards modern, cinematic filmmaking in the late 1910s and early 1920s, and as such, was a necessary development regardless of the earthquake. Nevertheless, it should also be noted that *Kamata-chō* was exposed to various conditions – such as studio environment, finances, and a range of production options – that constantly adjusted its practical shape. It could be argued that, if other conditions had been met, Shimazu might have continued to produce *shinpa* melodrama. Indeed, while experimenting with such films as *Father* and *Sunday*, Shimazu did not totally abandon making films closer in style to *shinpa* (possibly for commercial reasons). Such films as *Cha o tsukuru ie/Tea Making Family*, *Fukōsha/A Bad Son* and *Norowaretaru misao/Damned Chastity* (all released in 1924, the same year as *Sunday*) dealt with self-sacrificing parents and a love triangle relationship entangled with pecuniary matters, which are typical tragic elements of the *shinpa* style.[55]

Thus even if *Kamata-chō* opened an important new phase for Shochiku, it was not the only option the company persisted with. The tradition of *shinpa*, as Oda Takashi (the scriptwriter of *Tea Making Family*) argues, was practically an inevitable element of Japanese cinema, and this applied just as well in Shochiku.[56] In fact, *shinpa* prospered in a sense because, as Kido himself often emphasised, Shochiku publicly declared that its films were intended for female audiences, and the tearjerking melodrama about a troubled family life was one of the easiest ways to guarantee a gendered spectatorship. Nomura

Hōtei, for example, regardless of his relegation to Kyoto in 1924 and death in 1934, remained the most commercially successful director in Shochiku in the 1920s with *Haha/Mother* (1923) and another *Haha* (1929, not a remake), the latter of which was 'one of the biggest hits from Kamata Studio'.[57] These films, with a common narrative of multiple mothers who sacrifice their lives for the sake of a single child, can be classified in the prewar genre of *kateigeki* (home drama), which retained the tradition of the *kateishōsetsu* (home novel) as well as *shinpa*, and anticipated the postwar variation of *hahamono* ('mother films') or *chichimono* ('father films'). In narrative, the *kateigeki*, which Shochiku excelled in, depicted 'unstable family' with 'complex and often confrontational relationships', and it was female characters who, under 'unquestionable patriarchy', were supposed to 'endure fate and wait' in order to maintain the family. Such a suffering female character developed into the devoted mother of the postwar *hahamono* films, where the mother was typically involved in a *shinpa*-flavoured melodramatic relationship with her child, full of 'dramatic action, self-sacrifice, and [emotional] confession'.[58] Even Ozu could not be free from this melodramatic tradition, as his filmmaking career progressed in the mid-1930s and onwards. As will be discussed in the following chapters, the virtue of parental devotion and emotional intimacy was a major subject in Ozu's films such as *Haha o kowazuya/A Mother Should Be Loved* (1934), *Hitori musuko/The Only Son* (1936), *Todake no kyōdai/The Brothers and Sisters of the Toda Family* (1941) and *Chichi ariki/There Was a Father* (1942), which can be regarded as the precursors of more sophisticated postwar classics such as *Banshun/Late Spring* (1949) and *Tōkyō monogatari/Tokyo Story* (1953). Sakamoto Kazue thus summarises that, surrounding the hegemony of style and narrative in Shochiku's films, there coexisted two competing lines, each of which consisted of related genres connected in a chronological order of appearance; one was the *shinpa* tragedy – *kateigeki* – *hahamono*, and the other was the *Kamata-chō* comedy – *shōshimin* film – *hōmudorama*.[59]

The division, however, should be accepted as a general tendency, which, in reality, existed within a more complex relationship. As we have seen in Shimazu's case, both *shinpa* and *Kamata-chō* styles intermingled in a director's career, and in this regard, Shimazu's representative film, *Our Neighbour Miss Yae* (1934), suggests an intriguing example of the point at which the growing influence of *Kamata-chō*'s everyday realism meets the archaic remains of *shinpa*. Sasaki Yoriaki, referring to Kishi Matsuo's review at the time of the film's release, argues that the narrative of *Our Neighbour Miss Yae* can be divided in two by the appearance of the character Kyōko (Okada Yoshiko).[60] In the first part of the film, the narrative concentrates on the realistic depiction of the everyday life of two suburban middle-class families

(Yaeko's and Keitarō's) residing in perfect peace. Nothing really happens in this world of the everyday except for trivialities – breaking a window while catching a baseball, going to the public bath, mending socks, as well as eating and drinking – and as such it becomes the epitome of the *Kamata-chō* (or in Kishi's expression, 'sketch'). In order to visualise this suburban everydayness, Shimazu builds a sheltered space with two houses and an empty patch of land between them, from which the characters rarely escape before Kyōko arrives in the narrative. In terms of time, the film's earlier part sticks to the afternoon and evening, a sluggish or 'empty' part of a day when nothing significant seems to happen. The sudden appearance of Kyōko, Yaeko's elder sister who returns home to divorce her husband, is an intrusion by foreign elements into this stable everyday life, and marks the ending of the 'sketch' and the beginning of the 'drama'. This latter part of the film, through the character of Kyōko, brings to the fore serious and fatal life-issues such as divorce, woman's labour, unrequited love and suicide.[61] Thus Kyōko's existence belongs to the '*shinpa* tragedy', as opposed to Yaeko and others' 'innocent' everyday world that gazes at the former with 'displeasure' and a sense of 'vague anxiety'.[62] As such *Our Neighbour Miss Yae* displays the 'intermingling of the *shinpa* and the everyday elements' within its narrative, the 'disharmony' of which, Sasaki argues, is a result of Shimazu's gradual progress from the former into the latter.[63]

The film concludes in favour of the everyday of Yaeko. By exposing Kyōko's 'impure' behaviours – she actively seduces Keitarō – Shimazu succeeds in provoking an uncomfortable emotional reaction against her morality from viewers, which is re-affirmed by her abrupt disappearance from the narrative at the end.[64] However, it is also important to notice that there is an ideological emptiness in the realism of suburban middle-class everyday life, a vacuum where Yaeko and others are deprived of the social concerns embedded in Kyōko's turbulent life. If Kyōko's world is (over)loaded with painful meanings, Yaeko's and Keitarō's suburban home is a sterilised space, where nothing should happen and nothing actually happens. The film thus reconfirms the apolitical or innocent nature of *Kamata-chō*'s everyday realism that 'does not have a logical relation with the external world, and is ruled by the principle of pleasure/displeasure'.[65] Kyōko and her 'female autonomy and individualism' as a divorcee mean only a 'threat' to this stabilised social order.[66] By juxtaposing two different worlds based upon two different perspectives on style, genre and (ultimately) filmmaking in general, *Our Neighbour Miss Yae* reveals the awkward tension that *Kamata-chō* bore when mixed with *shinpa*, revealing its limitations as a specific middle-class realism against *other* realisms that might disrupt the stability of the everyday.

The Japanese Middle Class and Ozu's *Shōshimin* (Petit-bourgeois) Film

As discussed, the everyday realism of *Kamata-chō* was not an ahistorical and objective reality, but a very specific kind, emerging from post-earthquake Tokyo, produced by people of particular geographical, educational and economic backgrounds, with the concerns of the urban middle classes in mind (even though it eventually appealed to audiences of varied classes). This particularity of the everyday in Kamata films has generated controversy regarding its ideological nature in critical discourses in Japan, as suggested in the case of *Our Neighbour Miss Yae*. Such an urban middle class's drama centring on their everyday life was called *shōshimin* (petit-bourgeois) film. It became a staple of Shochiku studio in the late 1920s and early 1930s, but in fact, the genre's success is mostly attributable to Ozu's effort as a director. Even though the economic background of a protagonist's family in his films varies widely, the middle-class family life in *shōshimin* films became the most typical prototype of Ozu's home drama. The first sign of his interest in middle-class everyday life can be found in *Hikkoshi fūfu/A Couple on the Move* and *Nikutaibi/Body Beautiful*, both released in 1928. In the next year, he developed the format into a more refined form in *Daigaku wa detakeredo/I Graduated But...* and *Kaishain seikatsu/The Life of an Office Worker*, which drew a strong attention from critics. Two later films, *Tōkyō kōrasu/Tokyo Chorus* (1931) and *Otona no miru ehon: Umarete wa mita keredo/I Was Born But...* (1932), were especially highly praised as major works of the genre, and can be regarded as an initiating point of Ozu as an auteur, with his characteristic styles and themes firmly set in place.[67] His established auteurship can be proved by an Ozu special issue of the Japanese film magazine *Eiga hyōron/Film Criticism* published in July 1930, which analysed the director's recent films and the boom in the *shōshimin* film genre.

However, it should be noted that the *shōshimin* film Ozu created somewhat deviated from the genre norms that Kamata (and Kido) defined. Putting more emphasis on the sorrow and pathos of middle-class families under economic hardship, as if to reconfirm the destabilising effect of *shinpa*-esque element in Kamata films, Ozu drew a line between his *shōshimin* film and more typical *Kamata-chō* films with cheerful mood and happy ending. Kido, whose first concern was always commerciality of a film that he produced, did not entirely consent to Ozu's style, arguing that the thicker the pathos in a film gets, the less it appeals to wide audiences. Kido's idea can be supported by the fact that Ozu's *shōshimin* films generally did not do well at the box office, whereas the less serious ones – such as *Shukujo to hige/The Lady and the Beard* (1931) – that dealt with the *shōshimin* life with comic touch enjoyed good commercial success.[68] It is, then, not surprising that Shochiku was reluctant to release *I Was Born But...* when completed because the tone of the film felt too bleak. Kido even seemed to regard Ozu's *shōshimin* film as the director's own invention set against the studio's creed, *Kamata-chō*. In his autobiographical writing, he recollected:

> [Ozu] started to do so-called *shōshimin* films from around *Body Beautiful*... When I returned from the US [in April 1929], he became better skilled at it... It had been the basic strategy of Shochiku to favorably deal with contemporary *shōshimin* people. However, Ozu did not think petit-bourgeois life a wholly cheerful one [as in other Shochiku films], if not necessarily a desperate one... For him, the *Kamata-chō* films until that time could have seemed cheap. I could sense from his [stubborn] attitude that he, finding too much easy compromise with society [in Shochiku's filmmaking], decided to overcome it with all his might.[69]

On the other hand, Japanese critics criticised Ozu's *shōshimin* film for a different reason from Kido's. There was little disagreement regarding the argument that Ozu had reached a certain artistic level with *Tokyo Chorus* and *I Was Born But*.... The point of debate, however, was the middle-class consciousness in *shōshimin* film, and its political conservatism, which caused much controversy amongst leftist film critics. The petit-bourgeois origin of Shochiku employees has drawn the attention of several critics and academics, from Ikeda in the 1930s to Wada-Marciano in the 2000s, who argue that the studio, comprised of middle-class employees, was faithful to class ideology, avoiding politically progressive tendency film (*keikō eiga*) and instead choosing ideologically ambiguous *shōshimin* film in order to evade the state's political control.[70] More recent academic studies have also paid attention to *shōshimin* film's ideological stance in order to criticise the conservative ideas (such as patriarchy and nationalism) embedded in the genre.

These critical views on Ozu's *shōshimin* film reveal an ambiguous position it occupies in between apolitical *Kamata-chō* and social realism as found in leftist tendency film. On the one hand, this reconfirms the complexity of Kamata films, which were the negotiated output of both *Kamata-chō* and *shinpa* style as discussed. From leftist critics' point of view, however, Ozu's *shōshimin* films lack some requirements necessary for the genre to be accepted as truthful analysis of social reality. Without disavowing these contradictory viewpoints, the following discussion will examine whether and how Ozu's *shōshimin* film can be evaluated as a meaningful critique of contemporary society, which would both place the genre in an uncomfortable relationship with *Kamata-chō* as Kido acknowledged, and distinguish its critical stance from that of leftist films charged with more direct political activism. The validity of this intermediate position can be found in Ozu's detailed examination of the middle-class everyday, which, I will argue, eventually functions as his own way of criticising Japan's modernity and the nation's history of modernisation.

The typical subject matter of *shōshimin* film is the plight of contemporary urban white-collar workers who were going through Japan's depression era in the late 1920s and early 1930s. The Japanese term *shōshimin* can be literally translated into 'petit-bourgeois', which, as in European history, originally indicated 'shopkeepers, wholesalers, petty manufacturers, and their ill-paid employees' (called 'the old middle class'), but later in the twentieth century came to mean 'educated salaried employees of corporations and government bureaus and their families'.[71] *Shōshimin* (小市民) may have to be distinguished from a similar word *shomin* (庶民), a vaguely defined term translatable as the common people, designating a broad range of economic groups including both middle classes (especially the old middle class) and working classes. There is a dramatic genre for *shomin* called *shomingeki* – typically set in lower middle-class districts such as Tokyo's Shitamachi – for which Ozu left many notable films such as *Deki gokoro/Passing Fancy* (1933), as will be discussed in the next chapter. In contrast, the major subject of *shōshimin* films is the new middle class – salaried, urban, white-collar employees – whose appearance in Japan is specifically related to the rapid transformation of the Japanese economy into industrial capitalism. The national economy's growth during World War I (1914–18) was great enough to provide young university graduates with an unprecedented opportunity to find office-based jobs in metropolitan centres, and the term '*sararīman*' ('salaryman', meaning salaried man) was first coined in the 1920s to identify this new group.[72] It was the life and crisis of this salaryman and his family that became the main subject matter of *shōshimin* film. For instance, in *Tokyo Chorus*, the salaryman husband/father, Okajima, is actually dismissed from the insurance company where he works and struggles to survive for most of the film. In *I Was Born But . . .*, the husband/father, Yoshii, maintains his company position, but only at the expense of toadying to his boss.

Japanese contemporary critics appropriately paid attention to the specific middle-class consciousness inherent in the *shōshimin* film. In 1932, when *I Was Born But . . .* was released, a Japanese critic Ikeda Hisao asserted that 'almost 90 percent of contemporary commercial films' dealt with *shōshimin* as a subject matter.[73] Ikeda, however, emphasised that not all of them could be categorised as authentic *shōshimin* film, which, by his own definition, should contain '*shōshimin*'s ideological viewpoint' appearing in the form of three basic elements: 'cheerfulness', 'humour' and 'pathos'.[74] Another critic, Shimizu Shunji, also distinguished the films that merely deployed petit-bourgeois life as 'subject matter' ('*puchi buru mono* [petit-bourgeois genre]' in his term) from the real *shōshimin* film that possessed an attitude towards *shōshimin* as a class.[75] The appeal of the former, however, was more universal; Shimizu appropriately pointed out that even in the cinemas in rural regions, where the number of white-collar *shōshimin* people was expected to be low, the films dealing with *shōshimin* life were still more popular than other genres.[76] Such superficial *shōshimin* 'life' films served as a form of cinematic voyeurism by non-*shōshimin* audiences, who wanted to 'forget present life' by consuming the 'most progressive and chic' image of the urban petit-bourgeois.[77] On the other hand, as a critic Ōtsuka Kyōichi indicated, such a masterpiece as *Tokyo Chorus* could be a 'completely meaningless and boring film' to ordinary audiences except a small group of real urban middle-class people who could 'understand the sophisticated flavour of the film and sympathise with the state of mind of petit-bourgeois filmmakers [in Shochiku]'.[78] From this point of view, it can be deducted that there was a subtle gap between Ozu's *shōshimin* films that Japanese critics approved of and other films that Kamata studio was selling to general audiences.

However, even a critically approved *shōshimin* film such as *Tokyo Chorus* or *I Was Born But . . .* was an object of criticism for other critics. For instance, the critics of the magazine *Eiga hyōron/Film Criticism*, such as Ōtsuka Kyōichi, Ikeda Hisao and Sekino Yoshio, problematised the petit-bourgeois ideology that the *shōshimin* film disseminated. While the films were open to socioeconomic issues that the salaryman group was facing and the pathos that ensued, they fundamentally suffered from an apolitical position that ignored socio-structural causes and attributed everything to individual cases. The *shōshimin* film was thus criticised for 'never attempting to touch the essence of the situation but stopping at an extremely superficial phenomenon'.[79] In terms of the aforementioned Ikeda's three elements of *shōshimin* film, 'cheerfulness' is regarded as an unrealistic 'escape', 'humour' a 'light stimulant', and 'pathos' is close to 'nihilistic sentiment', leading one into 'lethargic, decadent resignation'.[80] *Shōshimin* films, as a Shochiku product, may possess the virtue of *shajitsu*, a spirit of 'formal' realism in order to depict life as it is, but it could not deliver the 'ideological' realism that critics wanted. What they required was less 'romantic, warm tears of sympathy' than acute social consciousness, as in films such as *What Made Her Do It?*.[81]

In order to reach the more structural analysis of the *shōshimin* film, it is imperative to perceive the emergence and failure of the *shōshimin* class, and its constituent salaryman, in the longer historical context of Japan's modernisation process, which had been planned and expedited by the state since the Meiji Restoration in 1868. The key means for this goal was higher education, through which the Japanese government, under the banner of 'civilisation and enlightenment', infused young people with a dream of secular success, as summarised in the phrase *risshin shusse shugi* (careerism; literally meaning 'ideology of standing and advancing in the world'). During the Meiji era (1868–1912), when the salaryman was not yet born, this dream was realistic as 'the demand for trained people far outran their production by the universities'.[82] However, as the number of college graduates increased their career prospects grew more limited. Jobs in government, which had been exclusively intended for the graduates, started to decrease, pushing them into the private sector from the mid-1910s onwards. And the situation got even worse in the 1920s, which started with a postwar recession, followed by the Great Kantō Earthquake of 1923 and successive financial collapses in 1927 and 1929.[83] 'Intellectual unemployment' became a ubiquitous phenomenon. The salaryman class, therefore, enjoyed a self-contradictory existence from its beginning, caught between expectation and frustration, perseverance often rewarded with dissatisfaction, upon which the pathos of the *shōshimin* film was based.

It is worth noting that the purpose of the higher education that the salaryman group received was also essentially contradictory. While many of the students were motivated by the dream of *risshin shusse* to climb the social ladder, for the state of Japan, it was essentially a 'national initiative, installed almost like conscription' to produce an educated labour force for building a modern nation.[84] Thus the salaryman was a product of two opposite and competing tendencies in Japanese modernity – modern individualism and more traditional collectivism, the balance between which alternated throughout the nation's modern history. As Carol Gluck explains, the 'official' ideology that emphasised 'collective cooperation within the family and the community' could not completely exclude the 'alternative' one that articulated individual success through the chain of 'education, employment, and rising in the world'; if 'moral conduct' was necessary, 'economic goals' were legitimised as well.[85] The salaryman was expected to resolve this dilemma in his everyday life; on the one hand, he was not only producer but also consumer within a capitalist society where 'modern individual consciousness' was rewarded; but at the same time, in social relations, he had to abide by the rule of 'more solid values of feudal morality' such as patriarchy.[86] A salaryman and his family could exist as long as the tension between these two different requirements was resolved through his stable employment and income to support the family's consumption, and in addition, the patriarchal order at home that justifies the existence of a housewife and the reproduction of the next generation. The innate contradiction, however, could not be sustained when one side of the balance, the salaryman's economic independence, was seriously threatened by unemployment in the Depression era of the 1920s and early 1930s. The *shōshimin* film was the genre that specifically capitalised on this decline of the fundaments of modernity in Japan.

The Japanese middle class's contradictory nature is represented in Ozu's *shōshimin* film through two contrasting (but interrelated) ways: urban materialistic culture and patriarchy in crisis, both commonly based on their everyday life. As mentioned, the 1920s when the salaryman emerged as the middle class in Japan overlapped with the peak of Western-influenced high culture, or *modanizumu*, which, unlike the more political and economic connotations of *kindaika* (modernisation), designated a cultural aspect of modernity, ranging from art and literature to street fashion and domestic life.[87] For the middle class, such a cultural transformation was happening at the level of everyday life in the post-earthquake urban space after 1923, making them more and more recognised as the consuming masses. *Modan raifu* (modern life) and *bunka seikatsu* (cultured life) became the catchphrase of the new consumerism for middle-class families, whose materialistic desire was appropriated by capitalistic interests to be transformed into a cliché of various domestic *bunka*-commodities purchased in urban department stores. And at the other end of this urban consumption lay the suburban home, a domestic space where the actual 'cultured life' would be practised. A significant element that spatially maximised this bifurcated system was the development of the railway, which provided salaryman families in the suburbs with a means of transportation to Tokyo's city centre. It was actually private railway companies that not only constructed the new suburban lines but also developed 'culture houses' and shopping centres in the suburbs to attract middle-class people out of the city. A railway transfer point such as Shinjuku accordingly became a commuters' hub, full of shopping and entertainment facilities such as department stores, cinemas, music and dance halls, cafes, bars and restaurants.[88] The figure that stood at the centre of all these life activities – city centre and suburb, production and consumption, commuting and entertainment – was the salaryman, upon whose salaried labour the life of his family was dependent.

Between these two spatial nodes of modern life, Ozu's emphasis in his *shōshimin* films lies more on the suburban space. What characterises this space in both *Tokyo Chorus* and *I Was Born But . . .* is a long road, which, punctuated by rows of electricity poles, disappears into an endless horizon, obscuring its

Figure 1.1 A road that connects city and suburb in *I Was Born But...*

ultimate destination – the city centre (see Figure 1.1). The barren indifference visible in the lost horizon implies the failure of modernity to deliver on promises that the middle-class families in both films have invested in. It is on this deserted road that the son in *Tokyo Chorus* encounters his father Okajima who, just dismissed from his job, is returning home with a scooter for his son in his hand. Disappointed that it is not a bicycle – a more expensive commodity that the son originally asked for – the son bursts into a fit of tears against the backdrop of the ever-receding, quiet road, the end of which – the city – is left incomprehensible to viewers.

In *I Was Born But...* a similar road appears in the first scene. The protagonist family has moved into a suburb because of the father's belief in the benefit of living near his boss. However, as the first shot of a wheel stuck in the mud implies, it is only a futile hope that reconfirms the helpless destiny of the salaryman in a capitalist society. The sense of a loss – there is little but two parallel lines of electricity poles on this road – strengthens the sense of pity for the life of this struggling family, whose households are seen 'on the move' in the back of a truck.

Compare this isolated vision of a suburb with the more concrete and confident linkage to the centre in Ozu's postwar film *Late Spring*, where Ozu deliberately builds up a train ride sequence with a clear sense of direction and progress from Kitakamakura station in Tokyo's suburbs towards Ginza, the centre of the modern. The more pleasant and upbeat mood, punctuated by rhythmical train sounds along with cheerful music, is hardly found in the two prewar *shōshimin* films; even a commuting scene of the salaryman father character is elided. This displacement from the centre is, however, compensated for by the endless passing of trains *inside* the suburban space of *I Was Born But . . . .* In fact the passing trains are featured so frequently and so close to everyday situations that, if the film had had sound, the railway noise would have drowned out any other sounds including conversations. With its intimidating speed and black body, along with (inaudible) sound, the train in *I Was Born But . . .* becomes a visual metaphor for the threatening impact of modern civilisation encroaching on middle-class suburban life, which, ironically, is founded upon that modernity.

Lacking an array of active consuming activities thriving in the city centre, Ozu's treatment of urban modernity can be evaluated as a moderated kind in comparison with other contemporary films. For example, there are no detailed investigations of the urban street in Ozu's *shōshimin* film, as in Naruse Mikio's *Kagiri naki hodō/Street without End* (1934), the opening sequence of which features a series of juxtaposed shots of store displays, various passers-by, signboards and street vendors in Ginza, followed by an interior scene of a *kissaten* (coffee house) that is filled with the bustle of cooks, waitresses and customers.[89] Nor are there housewife characters who incline towards excessive commodity consumption, as in Gosho Heinosuke's *Madamu to nyōbō/The Neighbour's Wife and Mine* (1931) and *Jinsei no onimotsu/Burden of Life* (1935), played in both cases by Tanaka Kinuyo. Jeong Su-wan notes the peculiar lifestyle of Tanaka's character in the two Gosho films – she either asks her husband for money to buy an expensive Western-style dress (*The Neighbour's Wife and Mine*) or enjoys a free '*modan gāru* (modern girl)' lifestyle, wearing Western suits, having a short hairstyle, and engaged in smoking (*Burden of Life*) – and argues that such a female character produces a crisis in the traditional order of the middle-class family, which the films suggest can be overcome by the return to the patriarchal domestic order.[90] In Ozu's case, however, domestic consumption is depicted as a very rational, prudent activity, limited by the salaryman father's income, as demonstrated in the aforementioned bicycle episode in *Tokyo Chorus* or the housewife's delayed purchase of a pack of beer until the next payday in *I Was Born But . . . .* Housewife characters in both films do not freely leave home to visit the city centre, let alone a department store.[91] Even the salaryman fathers who commute to the centre are not exempt, for there is an almost complete omission of such leisure spaces as the restaurant, cafe or bar in their everyday lives, which are prevalent in Ozu's postwar salaryman films (as will be discussed in Chapter 5). Alastair Phillips notices this substantial distance from consumerist life in Ozu's *shōshimin* film, and attributes it to 'the commonsensical repository of governmental values increasingly being urged upon ordinary Japanese citizens in the early years of the 1930s'.[92] I, however, think that, by the 1930s, the economic reality confronting the middle class was already harsh enough that rationalising consumption became a matter of necessity for survival rather than assent to a governmental agenda. This point importantly suggests that the critique of modernity Ozu addresses with his *shōshimin* films is less directed towards consumption culture than the whole modern capitalist system whose fundamental contradiction produces the social ills of depression and unemployment.

Patriarchy and its accompanying moral values, as a part of Japanese modernity, face the same crisis and criticism in Ozu's *shōshimin* films. The life of the salaryman, as a father, husband and office worker, not only becomes the centre of narrative, but also reflects the hierarchical system of a capitalist society. In *I Was Born But . . .*, father Yoshii has to curry favour with his boss at work, but back at home, he changes into an authoritative patriarch. The interconnected father's role between society and home is comparable to Japan's political ideal of *kazoku kokka* (family state), through which the relation between emperor and his subjects is equated to that of father and son. As a symbolic acknowledgement of this interrelated authority, Yoshii asks his boss to write his family name on the new doorplate for his new house, and receives it from him. The hierarchical power structure is also re-enacted by his children in their own way; at school, they are subject to the authority of a teacher as much as they are to their father at home, but in the playground with their friends they recreate what they learned in an amusing game of 'order-and-submission' – if the stronger raises his fingers, the weaker will lie on the ground. In addition, there is another unequal relationship assumed in the domesticity between a husband and a wife. Based on the principle of segregation of labour according to gender, a wife is supposed to stay at home to support the wage-earning role of her counterpart.

Though not as authoritative a type of patriarch as Yoshii, the father Okajima in *Tokyo Chorus* also takes a strong leading role in his family. In the scene of his daughter's hospitalisation, he exhibits a gentle, caring side of his character by attending to her and also reading a book and giving a piggyback to his son. When the daughter fully recovers and returns home with the family, a delighted Okajima 'wakens' his house by opening every closed door and window and leads the rest of the family into sitting and singing together in a circle. His wife is startled to find that Okajima has sold off her kimono to pay the hospital bill, but Okajima persuades her by saying, 'Miyoko (the daughter) became healthy, instead'. Domestic crisis is thus resolved through the ideal of unified family under Okajima's leadership. The chorus, as a symbol of unification, reappears at the ending sequence of a class reunion party, where the more fundamental crisis of the film – Okajima's unemployment – is similarly resolved through help from his former schoolteacher Ōmura, a patriarchal figure for Okajima. The virtue of collectivism as the antidote to harsh reality cannot be more clearly articulated than in this last restaurant sequence. Not only Ōmura and his wife, but also Okajima's wife join in preparing dishes of curry and rice for the party. Then a notice of Okajima's employment arrives in timely manner during the party, which Ōmura hands to Okajima to the latter's great joy. After rounds of communal drinking and eating, the film ends with everyone singing an old dormitory song in chorus. *Tokyo Chorus* thus strongly signals a conclusion that even the social ills of modern capitalism can be overcome by appealing to collectivism under the guidance of a patriarchal leadership.

Recent studies on *shōshimin* film have argued that the emphasis on patriarchal character in the genre is a reaction to the overdevelopment of Western modernity, and an attempt at returning to Japan's traditional value system. *Shōshimin* films, on the one hand, 'create a new modern subject, the middle class, and promote the idea that Japan has already reached a level of modernisation on par with the West'.[93] However, on the other hand, the development of 'materialism in modernisation' and the loss of 'Japan's traditional spirit' became the cause of the economic hardship that the middle-class characters had to suffer.[94] What the genre accordingly suggests to viewers as an alternative is to 'enter a nationalist discourse, with which they paradoxically resist modernisation . . . while evoking a lost "traditional" past'.[95] Such a 'call' to the traditional order was most conspicuously revealed through the character of the patriarch. In the *shōshimin* film, the 'modern material culture that permeated the family weakened paternal authority', and the repercussions of this were suggested in the end through the 'longing for an elegiac old Japan and its social mores'.[96] The genre thus operates as a critique of modernity that advocates such a traditional value as patriarchy, and eventually restructures the subjectivity of Japanese people for the nationalistic concern.

The crisis and restoration of patriarchy is a central theme in one of the earliest (and the most unconventional) *shōshimin* films of Ozu, *Body Beautiful* (film non-existent). In the script, the usual conjugal hierarchy in the genre is presented in a reversed form: the wife and painter Ritsuko (Iida Chōko) is the breadwinner of the household, who has her husband Takai (Saitō Tatsuo) pose nude for her work.[97] Not only unemployed but also physically weak, Takai represents a castrated salaryman in a more humiliating way than the patriarchal characters in other *shōshimin* films. Though his body is being used as a model, what Ritsuko actually paints is a picture of a woman, which is sold to a rich old man who flirts with her before powerless Takai's eyes. Moreover, Ritsuko also falls for a student athlete of a muscular build, the symbol of authentic masculinity that Takai lacks. At the end of the script, however, Takai turns out to be the more talented painter, and re-reverses the gender role, now ordering his wife to pose nude. Though with a satirical tone, the narrative clearly reveals the middle-class male's obsession with power (as expressed through sexuality), and anxiety about a subverted domestic hierarchical relationship, which should be rectified. Such a patriarchal morality is prevalent in the very early Ozu films, as will be further discussed in the next chapter. It is, however, important to understand that patriarchy was a part of the whole 'modern' system – consisting of home, office and school among others – and cannot be considered separately from the general notion of modernisation in Japan. It was thus not 'traditional' even if it came from 'a tradition'. Just as in the field of education, patriarchy was a modern concept constructed by the Meiji government which had a pivotal role in legitimising this change into a modern family system of *ie* by establishing such principal laws as the Meiji Civil Code (1898). As such, the Japanese family became 'suitable for the purpose of a modern nation-state', and the nation-state was reciprocally shaped to become 'suitable for the purpose of the family model'.[98] The segregation of labour based on gender was as much a new phenomenon in twentieth-century Japan as patriarchal family was. Women in Japan, except for a small number who belonged to the samurai class, were traditionally a part of the productive labour force in the agricultural and domestic industrial economy. The ideology of *ryōsai kenbo* originated from the samurai class's view on womanhood and became the cornerstone of women's education from the 1900s.[99] Not only each household but also the capitalist state of Japan operated upon these constructed traditions that justified the hierarchical authority and the segregation of gender roles. This means that if patriarchy was shown to be facing a crisis, it indicated a failure of the whole modernisation process rather than a weakening of traditional Japanese values, a symptom of which I think Ozu was well aware.

The doubt in and failure of the patriarchal character is thus a prevailing narrative element in the *shōshimin* film. Because of the contradictory subjectivity that the salaryman is destined to have – an authoritative father at home and a weak employee in his workplace, which Wada-Marciano calls 'the illusory division between public and private realms'[100] – Ozu's films typically have a moment when this tension between the two worlds is resolved through the revelation of the father's double identity to his family. In *Tokyo Chorus*, the strong sense of responsibility that the father Okajima holds for the rest of the family is significantly damaged when he loses his job. In the aforementioned scooter sequence on the day of his dismissal, Okajima tries to mollify the crying son, but finally resorts to violence, possibly out of desperation as well as anger towards the

Figure 1.2 Unemployed Okajima is seen alienated from his family

powerless self. This domestic disaster confirms his alienation from the rest of the family, visualised as the distance between the exhausted father and the others in the frame, which depicts Okajima as an 'existence without wholeness, never fully understood, only to be gazed at, detached with awe'[101] (see Figure 1.2). The alienation of the father figure later reappears as the film's moment of revelation. It is a tram ride scene where Okajima's wife, along with her children, happens to see through the tram window Okajima carrying an ad banner on the street, making her amazed and ashamed because she cannot imagine her husband doing such menial work. Her view of the unemployed patriarch is presented as a cinematic image, with a black window frame filling the left side of the shot, so that it augments the un-everydayness of the sight (see Figure 1.3).

Although Yoshii in *I Was Born But...* is a much sterner type of father than Okajima, faithful to the traditional image of a patriarch, he is still subject to the alienation and eventual revelation of his true subjectivity. The decisive moment comes in the 'home movie' sequence of the film, when Yoshii's sons, watching an amateur film his boss made, find their father performing silly facial expressions and gestures in order to please the boss and his colleagues. There is both irony and insight in the fact that the fundamental contradiction of modernity – the

Figure 1.3 The moment of revelation in *Tokyo Chorus*

father's double identity in private and public space – is revealed through one of the most modern technologies of the day, a 16mm camera. Consisting of three reels, the home movie explores and summarises what film can do as a document of modern everyday life. The surprise and enjoyment of an attraction (exotic animals in a zoo) in the first reel is followed by the revelation of an uncomfortable truth in the maze of modern life (the boss's flirting with geishas on the street being watched by his wife) in the next reel, and the third one combines these two main functions of cinema into the character of Yoshii who is depicted as both a funny clown and a sorrowful salaryman (see Figure 1.4).

Cinema, however, is not the direct cause that weakens Yoshii's domestic authority (rather, it can be attributed to the structural contradiction of the capitalist society to which he is bound), but a 'medium' that works to record and represent a slice of modern life. In effect, what is destroyed here are not merely the traditional values of patriarchy but the Japanese modernity that originally reinvented those values, a system through which work, school and home are combined in the service of capitalist production and consumption. What Yoshii's children despair at is not merely the fact that their father is not as great as they had believed, but a fearful realisation that such a pitiful salaryman will be their future again in this society. Thus the poignant challenge of the elder

Figure 1.4 Yoshii clowns in his boss's amateur film (compare with Figure 1.3)

son after watching the movie is less the declaration that he is not afraid of his father anymore than the acute question, 'what would be the point of going to school, if I am only destined to be worse off than my bourgeois friend (the boss's son)?' It is not a coincidence, then, that his gesture of resistance to his father is to throw away books, a negation of the system that he is destined to internalise.

Deviation in the Everyday

At this point, it becomes clearer that Ozu's critical view goes beyond the matter of patriarchy and is more broadly concerned with the fundamental dilemma of Japan's modern experience, that is, the desire for material success as a middle class in a capitalistic society, as encouraged by the nation, and the despair coming from the failure of that vision despite the sacrifices made in the course of modernisation. Ozu's critical approach to the issue, however, neither analyses the structural cause of the problem nor suggests a radical change of the system as his contemporary leftist critics desired. Instead, his way of critique is to find an alternative possibility within the everyday, which sets itself apart from both the uncritical everyday realism of *Kamata-chō* and the fatal emotionalism of *shinpa*. Humour, for instance, is an important stylistic tool to this end. In *Tokyo Chorus*, Okajima's defiant attitude to the established social order is depicted through comic gestures and behaviours in the opening sequence of his school days. Here, the PE class Ōmura leads is totalitarian in nature, corresponding to the collectivity of the last reunion party sequence. The teacher not only disciplines the body of the students with his commands, but also appropriately deploys his punitive power with a markbook to keep an orderly state.[102] His efforts, however, are constantly foiled by the students' clever and timely actions, which deviate from his order. If Ōmura adjusts a student's hat, it will soon be returned to the original position, and if he opens the markbook the students will peek from behind to see who's being checked. Young Okajima, with insolent and playful attitude, is ordered to stand alone on the ground, but he is soon found sitting by a stall bar, striking a match to smoke a cigarette. Such a character later becomes the basis of his resistance to the boss at work over the sudden dismissal of his colleague, resulting in his lay-off. But, as in the school sequence, the conflict here is still expressed in the form of a rhythmic gag of Okajima and the boss touching or pushing each other's bodies. Thus, as Satō Tadao notes, Ozu's comedy is 'not a bizarre and extraordinary kind', but 'comes from the occurrences of everyday life'.[103] As such, it does not remain a means of laughter, but becomes a physical form of confrontation with and distortion of the everyday order in modern life.

Ozu often uses a variation of this tactic of loosening the confinement of the everyday order, which I conceptualise as a device of 'deviation'. It not only means comic gesture, movement and attitude, but also includes an attempt to step outside of the usual rhythm of everyday life and search for a different space, time and sensibility. As 'practices' do in de Certeau's theory, deviation can disrupt the everyday order 'not by rejecting or altering [it], but by using [it] with respect to ends and references foreign to [it]'.[104] A good example of this diverted space and time can be found in the empty field scene in *I Was Born But . . .*, where Yoshii's two sons skip school and spend a peaceful day in a field free from the woes of being bullied. The scene is actually split into two parts, the first one showing the children having an early lunch in the field and a later one in which they forge a grade for a calligraphy class they missed that day. What is importantly inserted between these two moments are scenes of a usual boring day at school and office, which is ingeniously connected with the empty field scenes by Ozu's tracking camera work (see Figures 1.5–1.7), which many critics have noted.[105] The juxtaposition of the empty field and the school/office in editing articulates the contrast in temporality and spatiality between them, which epitomises the Ozuesque moment of the deviated everyday. Hasumi Shigehiko pays attention to the reversal of the spatial relation implied in the empty field scene, where a lunch that is supposed to be eaten 'inside' is taken 'outside'.[106] I think the meaning of such spatial transposition can be more broadly interpreted through the concept of deviation – as exhibited by the children's arbitrary usage of time and activities (including having lunch outside its spatio-temporal context) – and the resulting sense of freedom provides a sharp contrast to the collectivistic and capitalistic order of modern everyday life as administered in school and workplace.

Early Ozu 51

Figure 1.5 A day in the life in an empty field

Figure 1.6 A day in the life at school

Figure 1.7 A day in the life at a workplace

In terms of spatiality, Ozu's deviations have an intermediate quality that is distinct from the operation of public or private space. The salaryman father's predicament, as Wada-Marciano notes, lies in the 'modern capitalist strategy of creating an imagined separation between the public and private spheres', which accordingly requires his doubled identity set between subordination at work and domination at home.[107] A tiny step aside from that structure, however, can change the order of public or private daily life into an ambiguous space and time, introducing a new understanding of the everyday. Intermediate space thus becomes available through the act of exploration, an everyday practice comparable to de Certeau's concept of 'touring', which appears in the form of arbitrary and contradictory spatial movements, articulating a 'process of appropriation of the topographical system on the part of the pedestrian'. Such arbitrary movements of a pedestrian include sudden turns, detours, crossings, wanderings and avoidings, making the consequential paths opaque and invisible to the panoptic viewer's attempt at 'mapping', an effort to create a 'transparent text' or 'theoretical . . . simulacrum' with a surveying and 'totalizing eye' upon urban space.[108]

In this regard, the empty field in *I Was Born But . . .*, detached from the boys' home and school, is an example of an intermediate space. The long, empty road that links the city centre and the suburban town is a similar example. Such a spatial ambiguity can also be found in the dark screening room for the boss's home movie in *I Was Born But* . . . . Cinema in fact has always been a space for everyday diversion that blurs the border between the public and private, where spectators are provided with a chance to ponder the essence of modernity, as Yoshii's two sons do with regard to their father. Such a critical function of the intermediate space can also be found in the public park scene in *Tokyo Chorus*. This park space, though a few steps away from a busy main street and intended for a public purpose (hence a 'mapped place'), is 'appropriated' by the unemployed males as a congregating point, and is thus private in essence. The characteristic of deviation is signalled through relaxed mood and slow rhythm as found in the empty field scene in *I Was Born But* . . . . While Okajima shares sympathy with his former colleague who was dismissed on the same day as him, some bored (and possibly unemployed) male adults are seen in the background see-sawing right beside a group of children on swings (see Figure 1.8). This unlikely scenery not only makes another Ozu-esque gag point, but also turns into a critical vision of 'Tokyo, the city of unemployment' as a preceding intertitle declares. The tension with society, however, does not exist on the street in the form of resistance, but still resides in the intermediate space as humour and deviation.

Figure 1.8 A public park, a deviated everyday space for adults as well as children

From this point of view, Ōmura's restaurant in the last reunion party sequence in *Tokyo Chorus* can also be interpreted as a deviated intermediated space. As with the urban park discussed above, the restaurant has both public and private spatiality; though open to the public, it is located on a desolate street, and throughout the film there is no customer seen except Okajima and his friends. There is no bustling urban mood as seen in the aforementioned coffeehouse scene in Naruse's *Street without End*, but the fraternal and joyful atmosphere of the communal meal can be compared to the relaxed rhythm of a day in the empty field or the public park, which implies that this is a kind of shelter from the harsh outside world for the salaryman friends. But Ozu here falls into sentimentalism by resorting to a collective nostalgia for the past through the old dormitory song Okajima and friends sing together, instead of maintaining his acute sense of humour and critique. as the Japanese critic Okamoto Susumu argues, this emotive denouement can be interpreted as 'fortuitous . . . [and] imperfect redemption', indicating 'Ozu's self-deception'.[109]

In contrast, *I Was Born But . . .* leads to a more ambiguous conclusion. The final morning sequence of the film is a start of another ordinary day after the brawl between Yoshii and his two sons on the night of the home movie viewing. As an intertitle, 'And so, as usual', indicates, everyday order is resumed to normal as if nothing had happened. Yoshii will bow to his boss, pupils will bow to their teacher, and the 'order and submission' game will continue among the children. The sons even accept the reality that their father is not the greatest, and allow him to go and bow to his boss as if they had finally understood the necessity of compromise. But on the other hand, this seeming resignation comes not without residual doubt on such social relations, which remain dormant inside the everyday. Yoshii's children thus engage in a hunger strike in the morning, and on their way to school with Yoshii walk 'in front of' the father for the first time, not 'behind' or 'beside' him as before. The intense conflict between the resignation and the resistance is not eventually resolved in the film, as metaphorised by an entangled wire puzzle (called *chie no wa*, meaning ring of wisdom) that the children play with. Ozu instead hints at an existential dilemma that the middle class is destined to suffer in another scene of the deviated everyday. Coaxed by both parents, the children stop the hunger strike and eat a rice ball with Yoshii in the front yard, an intermediate space between their house and the outside world. The three-shot of the father and the sons, sitting side by side in contemplation, and the relaxed mood with bright sunlight and gentle breeze faithfully reproduce the similar deviated space – the public park in *Tokyo Chorus*, where two unemployed salarymen share their anxiety and sympathy (see Figure 1.9). This is the moment of reluctant realisation that the burden of life as a member of the middle class will last until they die, as Yoshii emphasised to his

Figure 1.9 A breakfast of contemplation (compare with Figures 1.5 and 1.8)

wife the previous night. However, in spite of the despair, the everyday will also continue as symbolised by the rice ball the family grab and eat. The breakfast scene thus implies a metaphoric truth that their everyday life will be in an ever-deferred future tense, as an ever-repeated fluctuation between resistance to and acceptance of their middle-classness, with an ever-failing effort of deviation.

Such negotiated pessimism later turns into a much bleaker reality in the film *Daigaku yoi toko/College Is a Nice Place* (1936, film non-existent), in which Ozu seems to have wanted to examine the issue of *shōshimin* identity to an extreme degree. The script sketches the lethargic everyday lives of college students, who, lacking both money and career opportunities, idle their time away outside the classroom. One of them, Amano (Ryū Chishu), finally decides to drop out without being able to secure financial aid from his family. Towards other friends who try to dissuade him, Amano rather asks back in anger, 'What will I get in return if I graduate? Isn't it endurance for nothing?', an acerbic criticism that resonates with the elder son's challenge to his father in *I Was Born But . . . .* Fujiki, Amano's best friend, despairs of the same reality only to face an outcry from his wife, 'No need to go to college then. Quit it right now!'[110] Through these straightforward voices, instead of the allegory of a children's story in *I Was Born But* . . ., Ozu clarifies the loosening connection between the aspiration and achievement of the middle class, which once became the grounds for modernisation in Japan. Not only *College Is a Nice Place* but even other student comedies of Ozu (such as *Gakusei romansu*, *Wakaki hi/Days of Youth* (1929) and *Rakudai wa shitakeredo/I Flunked But* . . . (1930)) imply this predicament under the superficial narrative of romance and cheerful college life, and therefore can be understood as a prelude to the salaryman tragedies of the *shōshimin* film genre.

College Is a Nice Place, however, is distinguished from other *shōshimin* films, not to mention student comedies, with its strong nihilistic sentiment. Ozu's typical humour, albeit present here and there, works more as cynical satire than as a deviating device that would have prevented the film from falling into monolithic seriousness. For instance, Ozu juxtaposes the everyday of the classroom and the off-campus locations through moving camera work and parallel editing, just as he does in the lunch in the field sequence of *I Was Born But* . . ., but the emphasis in the former (at least in the script) is put on criticising meaningless college education rather than playfully exploring an alternative possibility of the everyday.[111] The student characters are in fact stuck for an escape without finding any shelter to retreat from the oppressive everyday order. Ozu, interestingly, connects the background of this deadlock to the stiffening current political situation in the mid-1930s. The script begins (and ends) with a scene of military drill by college students at Toyamagahara in Shinjuku, where there actually existed a training ground. The scuffle in the PE class at the beginning of *Tokyo Chorus* reappears almost exactly in this scene, with the teacher Ōmura replaced by a nameless drill instructor, confirming Ozu's view to equate school with the military in terms of their sharing essentially the same collectivistic culture. However, in contrast to Okajima, who is able to deviate from Ōmura's order, Amano and Fujiki are strictly disciplined by the instructor, who emphasises the importance of 'military spirit' in a 'state of emergency that Japan is going through at the moment'.[112] After all the dramatic conflicts of Amano's leaving and Fujiki's despair, a brief reprise of the military drill appears as the final scene, where the instructor orders the students to 'march to the right', suggesting the ultimate direction that Japan is heading for to find a solution to the social crises that the middle classes suffer from. Here, Ozu-esque deviation within the realm of the everyday is not of help anymore. Thus the last shot of the film ('The unit, changing the direction to the right, marches on in solumn silence' as in the script) could have looked like Ozu's gesture of farewell to the *shōshimin* film genre, of which the fundamentals ceased operating with the change of social conditions.[113] Ozu in the rest of the 1930s would instead turn to *shinpa*-flavoured lower-class dramas, dark melodramas and bourgeois domestic dramas, as will be discussed in the following chapters.

What Ozu achieves in his *shōshimin* film with his unique style – the combination of satirical humour and spatio-temporal use of deviation – is a critical view of the modern everyday life of the Japanese urban middle class, which transcends the generic boundary between the depoliticised *Kamata-chō* comedies and emotionalised *shinpa* melodramas that Kamata studio was producing. Although sharing the same principle with *Kamata-chō* films of avoiding *shinpa*'s exaggerated style and pursuing a realistic depiction of the everyday, Ozu's *shōshimin* film revises *Kamata-chō*'s tendency to interpret Western realism only in a technical sense, and attempts a critique of Japanese modernity through detailed investigation of the urban middle class's everyday life. By confronting the failures in Japan's modernisation process into an industrial and capitalistic state – from authoritative and collectivistic social system to salaryman family's fear of unemployment during the Depression era – the modernity in Ozu's *shōshimin* film achieves a historical dimension as well. Upon that historical perspective, the director constructs a realm of the everyday that not only delineates the contour of middle-class life, but also provides relief and an alternative possibility through the deviated use of space and time. I think this critical stance – though varying in degree and effect in each film – is worth due notice, despite the criticism from contemporary leftist critics regarding its ideological thoroughness. Far from adopting the proactive strategy of tendency films, Ozu retains a critical position by suggesting deviations in the everyday, which makes his *shōshimin* films more genuinely middle-class in nature.

The early 1930s for Ozu can be regarded as a period when the director already succeeded in establishing a position as an auteur within the Japanese studio system. As Kido himself acknowledges, Ozu is almost solely responsible for the creation and completion of the *shōshimin* film genre, and, with a possible exception of visual style, largely maintains its basic structure (urban setting, middle-class everyday life as subject matter, mixture of humour and pathos in tone) throughout his career. Upon that widely approved assumption, however, the following chapters will focus on the historical variation in Ozu's auteurship in later stages. Ozu's cinema had always been in constant negotiation with the commercial ends and means of Kamata studio, which itself had a complex position set between modern and more retrospective styles of filmmaking. As *Our Neighbour Miss Yae* shows, this coexistence did not necessarily result in hybridisation in form and style; rather, *shinpa* developed along its own path, retaining a competing relationship with *Kamata-chō*. Thus Shochiku was a contradiction; a company producing film *and* theatre, its ideal of modernisation and internationalism in constant negotiation with the reality of commercialism. In this regard, I come to a similar conclusion to what Aaron Gerow argues in his study of the Pure Film Movement, that is, the transformations in Japanese cinema were 'not simply instances of "Americanisation" [or reactionary "Japanisation"] so much as a complex set of discursive enunciations and influences that cannot be reduced to an East/West binary'.[114] But I reach that point from the opposite direction to Gerow; if he emphasises the Pure Film Movement's role in modernising Japanese cinema, I attend to *shinpa*'s enduring influence on audiences as well as film texts. The next chapter, which deals with the period of the mid-1930s – the great transition era not only for Ozu but also for Japanese cinema in general – will discuss how Ozu, as a studio director, began to reinforce *shinpa*-esque elements in his films, a decision that I argue was closely related to the rapidly changing filmmaking environment of the time.

Chapter 2
Ozu in Transition: The Coming of Sound and Family Melodrama

Ozu's mid-1930s – after the culmination of the *shōshimin* film genre with the critical success of *Tokyo Chorus* and *I Was Born But . . .*, and before his first talkie film, *Hitori musuko/The Only Son* (1936) – can be described as following two different paths. One deals with female-oriented melodrama, such as *Tōkyō no onna/Woman of Tokyo* (1933) and *Haha o kowazuya/A Mother Should Be Loved* (1934). The other is a series of films dealing with the lives of lower-class people, which is called the 'Kihachi series' after the name of the reappearing male protagonist (consistently performed by the same actor, Sakamoto Takeshi). Ozu made four Kihachi films in this period – *Passing Fancy* (1933), *Ukigusa monogatari/A Story of Floating Weeds* (1934), *Hakoiri musume/An Innocent Maid* (1935, the film does not exist today), and *Tōkyō no yado/An Inn in Tokyo* (1935), the latter two of which may overlap with the female-oriented melodrama genre as well. None of these films has received as much critical interest as his *shōshimin* films did; lacking the latter's sophisticated social commentary, the former were mostly underrated either as tearjerkers or carefree comedies. For instance, the Japanese critic Iwasaki Akira remembers when he first saw *Passing Fancy* and *A Story of Floating Weeds*; 'Many of us were deeply disappointed to find that Ozu had abandoned serious social themes'.[1] As will be discussed, Ozu himself did not regard the Kihachi series as serious work even though it suggested a very new approach in his filmmaking career.

Such a low valuation is also attributable to the fact that these films articulate relatively conservative ideas and values that can easily appeal to mass audiences. Warm familial relationships based on mutual understanding – the typical Ozu theme – replaced the salaryman patriarch's trouble and conflict with his family in *shōshimin* film. In terms of form and style, the old and stable atmosphere can be understood as Ozu's adoption of *shinpa*-esque elements as represented by the appearance of a suffering mother figure. This compromise would mean that the unique distance Ozu managed to keep between *Kamata-chō* and *shinpa* began to be disrupted, and accordingly he entered a new phase in his filmmaking career. The main goal of this chapter is to trace that changing aspect of Ozu, and to examine whether and how the director maintained his critical view of Japanese modernity in the established and mass-oriented genre format. This firstly requires a detailed investigation of the transition in the Japanese film industry of the period, especially regarding the conversion to sound cinema, which greatly influenced Ozu's filmmaking. A discussion of the Kihachi series and female melodrama will entail a review of the genres that became the basis of those films – that is, *shomin ninjōgeki* (humane drama of the common people) and *josei eiga* (woman's film) – as well as a re-examination of *shinpa* as a fundamental cinematic style behind those generic structures. The generic terms will be finally confirmed through textual analysis of Ozu's films and their comparison with other contemporary Japanese films to examine how Ozu's everyday realism, formed through his *shōshimin* film, worked within the context of established generic formats, or how it interacted with the conservative ideologies embedded within the genre films to remain as a critical view of Japanese modernity.

Ozu and the Talkie

If we see the history of the conversion to sound cinema in Japan, it becomes clearer that the transition process is an outcome of complex interactions among various business factors existing in the industry. On the positive side, the transition to talkie films was regarded as an impending future, and Kamata Studio began to prepare for it in the late 1920s. Its chief Kido Shirō was first impressed by talkie films in the US during his extended observation tour around the West from July 1928 to April 1929. It was still the early period of sound film production even in the States, and the talkie films that Kido saw were only Warner Brother's sound-on-disc system, but he was assured that sound would be the future of cinema, along with colour and three-dimensionality.[2] Meanwhile, during his stay in the US, the rumour of the talkie arrived in Japan and became a big issue for Japanese media as well as film industry. Around the time he returned home, *Shingun/Marching On* (dir. Marcel Silver) became the first American talkie film to be released in cinemas in Japan (May 1929), and its success accelerated both the import of foreign talkie films and the race for the development of a Japanese sound film system. Although arguing in public that the talkie was premature in Japan, Kido actually was the only executive in Shochiku to argue for the talkie, and he secretly embarked on developing Shochiku's own sound system, called Tsuchihashi Shiki Shōchiku Fōn, which would be used in making Japan's first commercially successful all-talkie feature film, *Madamu to nyōbō/The Neighbour's Wife and Mine* (1931).[3]

On the other hand, there were negative elements that impeded the process toward the talkie, for example financial ability, which required almost triple-sized budgets for production in addition to the investment in new sound equipment in cinemas, risking low marginal profits from the box office.[4] In consequence, the Japanese film industry went through a restructuring process that forced small independent productions to be merged into larger studios such as Shochiku or Nikattsu, which were able to capitalise on the new production system and renovate their theatres.[5] Of course, there was also the problem of *benshi*, who fiercely resisted the advancement of the new technology, which obviously looked harmful to the prospect of their career. In consequence, it took another five years or so after 1931 for the Japanese film industry to produce talkie films in full scale, and silent films continued to be produced in 1937.[6] Kido was well aware of this peculiar circumstance of the Japanese film industry, and thus pursued a gradual transition in Shochiku, by producing such intermediary formats as '*saundoban*' (sound films with only background music and sound effects) and '*pātō tōkī*' ('part-talkie', films with partially inserted dialogues).

Japanese directors also took a cautious approach towards making talkie films. In January 1933, Shochiku's fan magazine *Kamata* published a special section titled 'A Plan for Shochiku's Talkie Production in 1933', including the articles of four representative directors of the studio about their thoughts on talkies. Although the titles of the articles – such as '1933, the Year of Talkie' and 'Desire for Talkie Production' – suggest the ambitious expectations of the directors, the actual contents rather reveal the hesitation, or even fear, that they were feeling at the time regarding talkie production. Between the lines, it can be read that the passive attitude largely comes from their worry about the quality of the end product and ensuing problem of commerciality. For example, Shimazu Yasujiro was all for the talkie only a few months previously in 1932, encouraged by the success of his talkie film *Arashi no naka no shojo/Maiden in the Storm*. He even declared that he was not able to return to make a silent film anymore and actually implored Kido to allow him to keep making talkies. But having experienced a disastrous failure with his next talkie, *Kanki no ichiya/A Night of Joy*, Shimazu's tone in his article in *Kamata* is greatly down, confessing 'the more I make talkie the more difficult it becomes'.[7] This word '*muzukashisa*/difficulty' aptly summarises the mood of other directors' articles too. For them, the fundamental barrier for the transition to sound was less an artistic belief in silent form than the fear of being a scapegoat in adapting to the new technology.

In consequence, the principal strategy they had in mind in the face of the coming of sound was to evade or reduce commercial failure and ensuing financial burden. Nomura Hōtei's idea was to 'remake' his own silent *shinpa* film *Mother* (1929), which had proved to be very popular a few years previously. Ikeda Yoshinobu decided to concentrate on small-scale production, less than eight reels in length. But, as Ikeda importantly points out, whether or not to produce talkies is not up to directors but the studio's decision. He says, 'As far as I'm working in a mainstream film studio, I can't imagine at all that I'm free to make a film as I want. In case there's an order from the company, I might have to be involved in a big production regardless of my intention'.[8] On the contrary, in some other cases, directors had to yield to a studio's demand that they give up on an idea to produce a talkie film. According to Masumoto Kinen, Shimazu was originally interested in directing *The Neighbour's Wife and Mine*, and sounded out Kido's opinion on that, who however declined the suggestion. Gosho, who was eventually given the role of making the film, was not an exception to the studio's strict control; after his second talkie film, *Wakaki hi no kangeki/Excitement of a Young Day* (1931), ended up in commercial failure, Kido did not allow him to make a talkie film; for the next one and a half years, Gosho had to be content with directing part-talkie and *saundoban* films until his third all-talkie film, *Satsueijo romansu: renai annai/A Studio Romance*, came out in mid-1932.[9]

Partly due to this passive position of directors, and partly out of executives' decision to test the water without risking large investments, part-talkie and *saundoban* formats thrived in the mid-1930s. In the case of Kamata, during the years between 1932 and 1935, *saundoban* and part-talkie films always outnumbered all-talkie films (see Table 2.1). Seen from a director's point of view, this also means that during the mid-1930s, there was a long interim period when talkie works (all or part) were being released side by side with *saundoban* or even silent films.[10] As seen in Table 2.2, most Shochiku directors continued to make silent films until 1933, while already beginning to make *saundoban* in 1932, which continued largely until 1935. It was a rare case not to have an experience of *saundoban*; Shimazu Yasujirō,

Table 2.1 The number of all-talkie versus part-talkie and *saundoban* from Kamata studio (compiled from Nagayama (ed.), *Shōchiku hyakunenshi, honshi, eizō shiryō*, pp. 66–81)

	1931	1932	1933	1934	1935
All-talkie	2	5	4	13	16
Part-talkie and *saundoban*		15	19	22	33

Table 2.2 Key Shochiku directors' transition to talkie films (compiled from Nagayama (ed.), *Shōchiku hyakunenshi, honshi, eizō shiryō*, and Jacoby, *A Critical Handbook*)

	Last silent	First *saundoban*	Last *saundoban*	First partial or non-feature-length talkie	First feature-length talkie
Ozu Yasujirō	Haha o kowazuya/A Mother Should Be Loved (1934)	Mata au hi made/Until the Day We Meet Again (1932)	Tōkyō no yado/An Inn in Tokyo (1935)	Kikugoro no kagamijishi/Kakamijishi (1935)	Hitori musuko/The Only Son (1936)
Shimazu Yasujirō	Seikatsusen ABC/Lifeline ABC (1931)	Jōen no toshi/City of Passion (1934)	Kanojo wa iya to iimashita/She Said, No (1935)	Shōbai/Win or Lose (1932)	Joriku daiippo/First Steps Ashore (1932)
Kinugasa Teinosuke	Nezumikozō Jirokichi/Jirokichi the Ratkid (1932)			Ikinokotta Shinsengumi/The Surviving Shinsengumi (1932)	Chushingura/The Loyal 47 Ronin (1932)
Gosho Heinosuke	Ramūru/L'Amour (1933)	Ginza no yanagi/Willows of Ginza (1932)	Akogare/Yearning (1935)	Nisan no baka/My Stupid Brother (1932)	Madamu to nyōbō/The Neighbour's Wife and Mine (1931)
Ikeda Yoshinobu	Nyonin airaku/A Woman's Grief and Joy (1933)	Koi no shōbai/Winning or Losing Love (1933)	Eikyū no ai/The Eternal Love (1935)		Jyōjin/Lover (1932)
Shimizu Hiroshi	Tabine no yume/A Traveller's Dream (1933)	Rikugun daikoshin/The Army's Big March (1932)	Kare to kanojo to shōnentachi/The Man and the Woman and the Boys (1935)	Manshū kyōshinkyoku/Manchurian Marching Song (1932)	Nakimureta haru no omayo/The Lady Who Wept in Spring (1933)
Nomura Hiromasa	Jogakusei to yotamono/The Girl Student and Layabout (1933)	Senso to yotamono/War and the Layabout (1932)	Yotamono to komachi musume/The Layabout and the Town Belle (1935)		Ōendancho no koi/Love of a Cheerleader (1933)
Nomura Hōtei	Seidon/Fine and Cloudy Weather (1933)	Shin yotsuya kaidan/The New Yotsuya Ghost Story (1932)	Machi no bōfu/Storm in Town (1934)	Shin yotsuya kaidan/The New Yotsuya Ghost Story (1932)	Onna keizu/The Geneology of Women (1934)
Naruse Mikio	Kagiri naki hodō/Street Without End (1934)	Mushibameru haru/Moth-Eaten Spring (1932)	Mushibameru haru/Moth-Eaten Spring (1932)		Otomegokoro sannin musume/Three Sisters with Maiden Hearts (PCL, 1935)

who was able to quit silent film and quickly convert to talkie film in 1932, had to step back and direct *saundoban* films in 1934 and 1935. Only Kinugasa Teinosuke could directly jump from silent to sound cinema and never go back into the old or intermediate format. The early talkie in Japanese cinema thus hardly provided an environment for auteurism to bloom. As far as circumstance allows, directors grabbed a chance to experiment with the new sound technology, but at the same time, they suffered fear of failure in the quality of the end product and became reluctant to face the challenge given the big production budgets. Moreover, the decision whether to advance to talkie film, or remain in silent or intermediate form was often made by the studio in accordance with the logic of profit. A famous anecdote regarding Naruse Mikio – not having a chance to make a talkie in Shochiku, he transferred to PCL (Photo Chemical Laboratory) Studio – proves this point.

In this regard, Ozu was an exceptional case. It is a well-known legend that among the key Japanese film directors, Ozu was the last one who continued to make silent films. His first feature-length all-talkie film, *Hitori musuko/The Only Son*, came out in 1936, fairly late timing compared with other Shochiku directors, as confirmed in Table 2.2. In fact, though released as an '*Ōfuna eiga* (Ofuna film)' after Kamata studio moved to the sound recording-friendly studio of Ofuna, *The Only Son* was originally planned as a silent film, and literally became the last film shot in the empty, 'silent' Kamata studio. Thus symbolically speaking, Ozu closed the door of Kamata, taking the last fade-out shot of silent cinema as he himself used to jokingly wish. Because he rejected sound and continued directing silent films throughout the first half of the 1930s, Ozu was hailed as the 'master of the silent cinema'. The first-generation Japanese film scholars such as Anderson, Richie and Burch interpreted Ozu's tenacity to the silent cinema from a purely aesthetic perspective, as a declaration to refine and complete the old form. Anderson and Richie argue, 'Some, like Ozu, felt that they were finally on the verge of reaching the summit of a new art form and that sound was a most unwelcome interruption'.[11] Burch also advanced this point to support his argument that Ozu's peculiar form constituted an aesthetic alternative to classical Hollywood cinema.[12]

Historical evidence, however, strongly suggests that Ozu's long delay was not so much an aesthetic resolution as an inevitable choice out of a personal situation, which could have changed if the circumstance had been different. Since 1928, Shigehara Hideo, who was Ozu's close friend as well as the exclusive cinematographer of *Ozu-gumi* (Ozu's production staff) at that time, had been individually developing a sound system that would be later called Super Mohara Sound System, and Ozu promised Shigehara that he would make his first talkie film using this system. The completion of the system, however, was delayed until the end of 1935, and in the meantime, in order to keep his promise, Ozu adamantly refused to make a sound film. The anecdote may sound almost unbelievable in the professional filmmaking field, but it seems Ozu was quite serious about the promise; he once wrote in his diary, 'I gave my word to Shigehara a few years ago. If I cannot keep it, I'd rather quit this job. I wouldn't mind it'.[13] This strong resistance of course indicates that Ozu and Shochiku were in a difficult relationship over the talkie matter. In June 1935, when the diary was written, it seems the disharmony reached a critical point; Ozu was appointed to make a short documentary about a kabuki drama in talkie, entitled *Kikugoro no kagamijishi/Lion Dance of Onoe Kikugoro*. Since this was to be his first talkie film, Ozu insisted on using Shigehara's system that had not been completed yet, and had to visit Kido's home several times in order to consult with the studio chief, who persuaded the director to use Shochiku's official Tsuchihashi sound system instead. There must have been a very heated argument between them, as inferable from the remark of 'quitting the job'. After all, according to Tanaka Masasumi, *Lion Dance of Onoe Kikugoro* had to be filmed using Tsuchihashi's system, although Ozu's record in his diary only reveals that there was some 'mutual agreement (*dangō*)' among Kido, Shigehara and himself regarding the matter.[14]

Regardless of Ozu's intent, however, seen from Shochiku's perspective, Ozu's persistence must have been a hard position to accept; by 1935, his first talkie film was already being delayed for two to three years compared with other Kamata directors, and the studio, under the motto of '*Shōchiku daiichi shugi* [Shochiku Number One-ism]', had been accelerating its goal to take the lead over other studios, where producing more high-quality sound films was an essential part. Complaints also came from cinema owners who were running Shochiku titles; in a survey of forty-one cinemas around the nation, conducted by the planning department of Kamata, one of the suggestions to improve the studio's marketing activity was letting Ozu make a talkie film; this not only proves Ozu's brand power among the exhibitors, despite his notoriety for poor box-office records, but also reconfirms the symbolic importance of the talkie film as a trendsetter to lead the market.[15] Such a change could be actually felt in box-office results; with regard to the success of Kamata's early 1933 talkie films *Hanayome no negoto/The Bride Talks in Her Sleep* (dir. Gosho Heinosuke) and *Ōendanchō no koi/Romance of a Cheerleader* (dir. Nomura Hiromasa), Shōchikukan, a cinema in Tokyo's Asakusa district, acknowledged the 'strong box-office power of Shochiku's all-talkies', and analysed that 'in *gendaigeki* (if not *jidaigeki*), there is a huge gap between silent and talkie films as far as commercial value concerned, a fact clearly shown by the box-office record of [Asakusa's] Teikokukan and Shōchikukan this year so far'.[16]

Moreover, Ozu's contemporary Japanese critics also strongly objected to Ozu's remaining in silent cinema. In his aptly titled article 'Why Ozu Keeps

Silent?', Ōguro Toyoshi, mentioning Chaplin, who was resisting producing talkies at the time, worried that Ozu had 'such a foolish faith' too.[17] Ōtsuka Kyōichi in *Eiga hyōron* also complained that Ozu's adherence to silent form proved his 'stagnation' after *I Was Born But . . .*, and was 'fatal' to the artistry of his current releases.[18] Having no idea of Ozu's promise with Shigehara, the critics often asked him the reason for insisting on silent production during the period of 1934 and 1935, by which time most other Shochiku directors had made at least one talkie film. A roundtable talk held by *Kinema Junpo* in April 1935 shows how curious they were about this mystery of Ozu's. Hazumi Tsuneo even jokingly said to Ozu, 'On behalf of our readers, I want to receive your promise to make a talkie film within this year', to which Ozu responded, 'I can't say that, because I'm not a producer'.[19] Mostly avoiding the participating critics' persistent question, 'Why are you not making talkie?', Ozu, however, revealed a few significant thoughts of his about talkie film. Firstly, he is not uninterested in making talkie films for 'anyone would want to do it as long as he is a filmmaker'. Secondly, he agrees that talkie film is now more popular than silent film or *saundoban*, but still worries that his talkie might fail at the box office, which Hazumi criticises as a 'cowardly' attitude. Lastly, to Hazumi's question, 'Will you never make a talkie?', Ozu answers, 'Yes, I will, but after I *study* it more', suggesting both his fear and expectations of the new technology, as a perfectionist.[20] Disappointed by this attitude, a reader of the magazine contributed an article in June titled, 'An Open Letter to Mr Ozu', where he figured out six reasons for Ozu's not making talkie films and refuted them one by one. About the possibility that Ozu rejected talkie film in favour of silent film, he simply affirmed, 'It is inevitable that the achievement silent cinema has accumulated so far will be succeeded by talkie'.[21]

Later that year, when Ozu's *An Inn in Tokyo* was released, again only with music and sound effects, the film was harshly criticised for not being full-talkie. One critic said, 'I'm used to talkies, so *saundoban* is hard to watch'.[22] Asked again if there was a particular reason not to have made the film in talkie, Ozu answered that his turn in the studio had not come yet. It is certainly an unconvincing lie, an intentionally ambiguous type of response that only attributed to the creation of the myth of Ozu as a master of the silent cinema, but at least reconfirms the fact that he was recognising the talkie issue in the context of his relationship with Shochiku. When Shigehara's system was finally completed and Ozu started filming *The Only Son*, he rather frankly clarified his true position with the old form: 'It's not that I intentionally didn't make a talkie because I had a lingering affection for silent cinema'.[23]

Two conclusions thus can be drawn from the discussions so far. Firstly, by 1935, non-talkie films were clearly recognised as being out of date in Japan by film industry people and critics, if not audiences, making Ozu's position more difficult. Secondly, making a talkie film was recognised much more as a complex business issue involving various sections of the industry rather than as an artistic matter for a director, and it is very unlikely that Ozu, without the personal promise with Shigehara, had a reason to avoid this reality. Had he had other reasons, it would be more reasonable to imagine that they might not have been that different from other colleagues' concerns, that is, the technological limitations of the new form and resulting quality of the end product, the burden of a big budget and ensuing fear of commercial failure, and the pressure of compromise to make the best of the situation.

On the other hand, there is other evidence to prove that Ozu was actually interested in sound cinema, carefully calculating what benefit or harm the new technology could bring to his cinema. First of all, he was watching and analysing the contemporary talkie films, foreign or Japanese. He was particularly impressed and influenced by King Vidor's 1933 film, *Stranger's Return* (released in Japan with the title, *Minamikaze* [meaning southerly wind]), which he watched four times.[24] Regarding Shimizu Hiroshi's first talkie film, *Naki nureta haru no onna yo/A Lady Crying in Spring* (1933), Ozu rated highly its bold attempt at new expressions with sound, even though it resulted in failure.[25] He also mentioned he was learning from *kabuki* theatre about the usage of sound.[26]

Ozu also noticed the strength inherent in the talkie form. Firstly, sound can free the camera from objects, allowing more long shots than close-ups. Secondly, sound can enrich circumstantial evidence, reducing the number of unnecessary shots. For example, an organ tune from a mansion can explain a setting of high-class life, and a shaky voice can convey a character's emotion without complementing a shot of anxious bodily movement. Thirdly, in silent cinema, an intertitle comes later than facial expression and action to work as prosaic explanation, but in talkie film, a speech comes first or at the same time with a visual, and thus a freer and improvised form of verbal expression (such as ad libs) can be used in a more effective way. After all, Ozu said, intertitle belonged to the realm of scriptwriting rather than director's discretion.[27] It is natural then that Ozu was already receiving influences from talkie's unique techniques, and actually adopted some of those elements in his silent films. Asked how he managed the dilemma between the desire for making a talkie film and his identity as a silent filmmaker, Ozu said, 'I don't despise silent film, but when making it, I inadvertently take an attitude of a talkie filmmaker'.[28] He also confessed that he tended to use long shots, which is a 'talkie technique' according to him, although he regretted that it did not work well in his silent films. Noticing such influences of talkie film in Ozu, Hazumi Tsuneo stated,

'If talkie had not appeared, Ozu's silent cinema would not be completed in the current form'.[29]

Given all these circumstances, it is plausible to think that Ozu was constantly considering and preparing for the conversion to the talkie. His apparent hesitation can be read as a sign of a cautious approach towards the new technological form of which the quality and risk were not yet fully proved, rather than a stern refusal of it as an unwelcome interruption of his art cinema. And in this regard, other Japanese directors' attitudes were not that different, as discussed. Supposing there had not been the promise with Shigehara, I imagine Ozu's transition process could not have been that different from other directors; he would have made the first talkie much earlier, possibly with encouraging pressure from Kido and Kamata studio, but would have been still making silent films and *saundoban* along with talkies throughout the mid-1930s. Chances are the transition period was not the most satisfactory time for the director in terms of the artistry available for him in relation to sound, but the limit in form and style also ironically reveals the negotiating relationship Ozu had to maintain with Kamata studio. It was the time when the logic of filmmaking in mainstream Japanese cinema was rapidly reconfigured through the two contradictory factors of new technology and commerciality, and Ozu, as a studio director who was not making talkie film, could not help but be restricted to this context. This situation exerted influence on the change of subject matter and style with the beginning of the Kihachi series, which I will discuss in detail in the following section.

The Kihachi Series: Journey into/from the Nostalgic World

What distinguishes the Kihachi series from Ozu's *shōshimin* film is its oldness and lowness. The background setting has moved from the latter's newly developed suburbs to Shitamachi (literally, town in low land), Tokyo's lower-middle class district which had existed as a commercial and residential centre since the Tokugawa period (1603–1868). The characters that appear are accordingly working-class or old middle-class people (for instance, small shop owners) whose everyday life presents a striking difference to that of the white-collar middle-class family in *shōshimin* film. The first part of this section will identify and analyse such class-based differences from spatial, temporal and cultural points of view by attending to the characteristics of Shitamachi as an urban community that operates on the various signifiers of Edo traditions. This, however, also leads to another important question about the contextual implications of Ozu's translocation into the old world in a turbulent time of deepening war with China and a growing tendency towards national unity as well as the emergence of the new sound technology. It is difficult to prove how Ozu was reacting with this zeitgeist when he produced the nostalgic vision of Shitamachi in the Kihachi series – four times in three years – but, despite the ostensible impression, Kihachi's retrospective world might not entirely indicate sympathy with the politically reactionary move towards traditional values, but rather constitute the continuation of his commentary on modern society as in the *shōshimin* film. This assumption should be carefully cross-examined with the previous discussion of the film industry background during the production of the series, which constantly put Ozu close to the reality of both commercialism and technological advancement rather than pursuing any aesthetic and thematic principle of his own. I will discuss this point through textual analysis to show how the class-specific everyday, albeit apparently based on nostalgic sentiment, demonstrates an active commentary on modern life.

Shitamachi – the principal geographical background of the Kihachi films – was a district in Edo, 'inhabited by the non-samurai merchant and artisan families' who made their living as 'a tailor or a restaurant-owner, a carpenter or the owner of a small workshop employing one or two workers'.[30] As the composition of the population implies, the district functioned as the supplier of goods for 'feudal nobilities and ... the lesser ranks of samurai class', whose residences gathered in the opposite side of the city called Yamanote.[31] However, as Seidensticker properly explains, Shitamachi was less a 'geographic entity' than an 'idea', where spatial 'borders' were hard to demarcate.[32] It could be better characterised by its unique atmosphere or 'vitality' that originated from the commercial nature of the district's economy and was practised in everyday life by the Shitamachi people, or *chōnin*. The number of *chōnin* was estimated to be half a million, out of Edo's population of over one million, which made it 'probably the largest city in the world' in the late eighteenth and early nineteenth centuries.[33] Shitamachi's *chōnin*, mostly shop employees, servants or artisans, were accommodated in *nagaya* – shabby row houses in the back alley, consisting of 'nine feet by twelve feet' two-room residences – and suffered from 'mud, dust, darkness, foul odours, insects, and epidemics' as well as frequent fire.[34]

These physical conditions of Shitamachi – its compact size, crowding and exclusiveness – largely determined the culture of the *chōnin*'s everyday life. Philipe Pons points out that the collective residential form of *nagaya* resulted in an intimate neighbourhood community and strong solidarity.[35] In order to govern the huge web of human relationships in the community, virtues such as *ninjō* (an emotion containing 'solidarity, sympathy, generosity, and respect towards others') or *giri* (a sense of duty) were encouraged, which also became the major sentiments to lead a narrative in dramas set in Shitamachi. Shitamachi was also characterised by the ambivalent border – both spatial and temporal – between private and public realm, which permeated each other. The street was not merely a transition point between two spaces but a place of living, where various people carried out their private lives and intermingled. Since domestic space overlapped with public space, working time and leisure time were also not clearly separated. Shop owners could be freely diverted to private matters or engaged in chats, leaving their shops unattended. Indeed, the temporal rhythm of Shitamachi was far from the 'coercive' or 'money-making' time divided and delineated by the clock as in the outside world; it was rather sensed through 'various human activities, sounds, and smells' that metaphorically indicated the passage of time.[36]

Shitamachi can be also characterised by the unique personality of its *chōnin* residents, as symbolised by the name *edokko* (the child of Edo), a citizen who was born and raised in Shitamachi. The typical *edokko* was thought to be 'hot-tempered, but warm-hearted, uninhibited in his enjoyment of sensual pleasures, extravagant and with no thought for the morrow'.[37] He also had a challenging and competitive spirit, known as '*hari*', which was fostered by his antagonistic relationship with the ruling samurai class. This resistant attitude encouraged *edokko* to pursue 'softer' values in contrast to the samurai's *bushido* (warrior's code of conduct), blooming into the aesthetic ideal of '*iki*', the very concept that influenced *edokko*'s cultural sensitivity.[38] Thus the *chōnin*'s way of life with *iki* was essentially hedonistic and was in antagonistic relation to the neo-Confucian ethics of the ruling samurai class, who 'tried to restrain [the *chōnin*'s] pursuit of pleasure'.[39] The *Chōnin*'s characteristics – 'derision of the ruling class' and 'tolerance for pleasure' – were expressed in diverse artistic and cultural practices including *kabuki*, *ukiyo-e* (woodblock prints), various kinds of music and popular literature.[40] Amongst them, comic verbal performances such as *rakugo* and *manzai*, which targeted commoner audiences, particularly revealed the spirit of satire and banter. Escaping small, humid, and filthy *nagaya* and going to a nearby *yose* (variety hall) to enjoy these performances was one of the most popular entertainments for the Shitamachi people.

The socio-geographical characteristics of Shitamachi became a decisive background in the production process of the Kihachi films. Being an *edokko* himself from the town of Fukagawa in the Shitamachi district, Ozu based the character of Kihachi upon his own memory of his hometown:

> I grew up in Fukagawa, and at that time there was this nice guy of carefree style often stopping by my house, who roughly became the model of Kihachi. Ikeda Tadao [the scriptwriter of Kihachi films] has also lived in Okachimachi, and seen such a guy himself there, so we created the character together.[41]

The spatiality of Shitamachi adopted in the Kihachi films constructs a very different milieu from the college, urban office or middle-class suburban home that had largely filled his previous works. Thus Ozu at this time said, 'What determines a film's style is . . . background rather than actor', implying that he was conscious of the translocation from a modern city to a pre-modern town in the series.[42] Such a change is evident from the very first scene of the first Kihachi film, *Passing Fancy*. A tracking shot, which Ozu at this period often used, skims through the audience – including Kihachi, his son and his close friend Jirō – listening to a *naniwa-bushi* (story recitation and singing) performance in a *yose*. It is a typical hot and humid summer in Tokyo, which can be inferred from the audience's light attire of *yukata* and their incessant waving of Japanese-style fans. This, along with the physical closeness of the small crowd in the theatre, creates a loosened and intimate atmosphere in the scene. The vibe of connectedness inside the *yose* is shown through two gag elements. One is an empty wallet being thrown around by the audience members, who open it, are disappointed, and throw it away to be picked up by the next; and the other is the sudden invisible appearance of fleas, which, transferring here and there, make itchy people stand up one by one. The theatre space as a metaphor for communal everyday life is expanded to the whole narrative of the next Kihachi film, *A Story of Floating Weeds*, which deals with an itinerant troupe led by none other than Kihachi.

The collective nature of life in Shitamachi is also well represented by Kihachi's everyday space and time. The most conspicuous characteristic of Kihachi's life is that it mostly takes place outside of the domestic. Kihachi's residence is a typical *nagaya*, consisting of two rooms and a kitchen, and facing towards a narrow back alley. But many of the important developments in the narrative occur not in the *nagaya* but in and around the small neighbourhood restaurant run by Iida Chōko, one of the best known of Ozu's supporting performers in the prewar period, whose character Otsune (Otome in *Passing Fancy*) appears in all the Kihachi films as a small neighbourhood restaurant or hair salon owner. Since the Kihachi character is without his wife, Iida plays a maternal role for his son(s) as well as for Kihachi himself, who daily drops by at the restaurant to have meals and to get Iida's help in domestic matters such as sewing. Thus in the Kihachi films, as in the real Shitamachi community, the boundary between the inside and the outside is blurred, and domestic everyday life is extended into public space, where it is shared by other people. In *Passing Fancy*, Kihachi even brushes his teeth and washes his face in the alley in front of Otome's restaurant, but this is not merely Kihachi's aberrant behaviour, for the alley is constantly occupied by neighbours and kids who treat it as an everyday space, where private time overlaps with public time as in the case of typical Shitamachi temporal rhythm.

Otome in *Passing Fancy*, for instance, freely walks out into the alley to join in a conversation with the people outside while her restaurant opens.

From this point of view, Kihachi's world can be contrasted with the ideal of the petit-bourgeois family as discussed in the previous chapter. It should be remembered that there is no such sense of community in the suburbs of *Tokyo Chorus* or *I Was Born But* . . . . Although both *shōshimin* films do depict the notion of neighbourhood through the playing of the children in the field, there is a lack of substantial interaction amongst the adults. The vast desertedness of the road and the threatening passage of trains that I mentioned as being characteristic of the suburban space can be interpreted as contributing to this destruction of communal links. What *shōshimin* films have instead is a stable nuclear family structure that is sheltered inside the domestic boundary. The white fence that demarcates Yoshii's house in *I Was Born But* . . . and protects his children from being bullied by neighbourhood kids is indicative of this separation. Since Kihachi does not belong to the bourgeois ideal, he is accordingly free from the congenital anxiety of the middle class that is represented by the *risshin shusse* ideology. Kihachi as a character is in fact an antithesis of the middle-class patriarch; illiterate, spontaneous, and more interested in drinking and women than money, his personality is closer to the image of the pleasure-seeking Edo *chōnin* than the gloomy salaryman father. The irony that the son in *Passing Fancy* is more knowledgeable and mature than the father proves that the middle-class patriarchal ideology depicted in the *shōshimin* film is not operative at all in the Kihachi series. This contrast between the Kihachi and *shōshimin* films in relation to public space can be compared with that of his postwar films, such as *Sōshun/Early Spring* (1956) and *Ohayo/Good Morning* (1959), which, dealing with middle-class family life but retaining the neighbourhood community in the narrative, should be differentiated from the wealthy family drama of *Higanbana/Equinox Flower* (1958) and *Akibiyori/Late Autumn* (1960), which completely elide the concept of regional communality.

To what degree, then, can Kihachi's world be related to the modern everyday life of the *shōshimin* film? Does its Shitamachi element simply work to avoid the reality of contemporary society and escape into an archaic realm? Japanese critics at that time were in general agreement that the world Ozu dealt with in the Kihachi series was 'old-fashioned (*kofū*)', which was significantly different to what he had achieved with *I Was Born But* . . . . The tone of *Eiga hyōron* was particularly harsh as it had been towards the *shōshimin* film. Ōtsuka Kyōichi regarded the change in the Kihachi series as Ozu's failed gesture of 'compromise' with commercialism to recover from continuing failure at the box office, which, as mentioned, was not untrue.[43] In comparison, *Kinema Junpo* – which put two of the Kihachi films at the top of its annual list – had a more lenient view;

Kitakawa Fuyuhiko wrote in a laudatory voice, only worrying that 'Ozu was slightly indulging in old-fashioned sentiments' and wished the director would 'restore the vision of *I Was Born But* . . .'. Bordwell, whose concern is primarily with formalism, points out that Ozu's experiment with centuries-old 'Japanese iconography' (or in Bordwell's term, 'material') pervasive in *A Story of Floating Weeds* – such as the village street, the landscape, the forlorn café, the decaying theatre – can 'tone down overt formal devices' and cannot 'become completely obedient to Ozu's aesthetic system'.[44] To summarise these critical viewpoints, the Kihachi series becomes Ozu's unsuccessful attempt to resort to oldness (or 'Japaneseness'), risking his already highly developed formal system, in order to create more mass-appealing popularity.

The complex circumstances surrounding the series' production support this view. There is a good possibility that the Shitamachi elements (not only in spatial terms but also in sentiment) were added due to commercial considerations, as Ozu's films had been successively failing at the box office. Many of his interviews with critics in the first half of the 1930s reveal that Ozu was quite sensitive to the box-office results of his films (and Shochiku's response), and knew he had to 'compromise' to satisfy the studio's anticipation to a certain degree. Of course, as Hazumi Tsuneo asserted in defence, Ozu could not be wholly blamed for his commercial failure because Shochiku 'lack[ed] a publicity plan that [could] appeal Ozu or Naruse's films to the intellectual audiences'.[45] Nevertheless, it is not hard to imagine that Ozu's relations with the company, including the negotiation on talkie, must have been complicating his filmmaking during the period. In his interview in 1935, Ozu said,

> Once a subject matter is decided, it would be inevitable to include commercially helpful elements. Among them, there can be something that I don't want to put in, but eventually, it can't be helped . . . So if a film is meant for profit, I want to make sure that [Shochiku] makes money with it. Then sometimes I can be allowed to make something I truly want to. I think this is the best way for both the company and me.[46]

In accordance with this strategy, the first Kihachi film, *Passing Fancy*, was originally conceived as a kind of 'throwaway' film that would 'make money for the company once' before Ozu made what he really wanted to do.[47] After finishing *Dragnet Girl* in early 1933, Ozu was preparing *College Is a Nice Place* as the next film, which, as discussed, was about a disillusioned college student's life with a pessimistic mood (Ozu conceded, 'I wrote about how much meaningless this place called college is')[48] The script was actually finished by June, but after Ozu's meeting with Kido, it was decided to postpone the project because of the film's dark atmosphere and unrelieved ending, and *Passing Fancy* was instead produced.[49] *A Story of Floating Weeds* was also a compromise that was made with an 'intention to generate box-office value'.[50] Here, Ozu clarified that he brought 'fraternal love, maternal love, or paternal love', now known to be the essential elements of Ozu's cinema, for box-office reasons because they were 'easy to understand and commercially promising', at the price of sacrificing 'nihilism' that he wanted to explore more.[51] Ozu even confessed that he was abashed regarding the critical success that the two films achieved.[52]

A retrospective tendency to appeal to a lost memory was indeed in fad in the Japanese cultural scene in the mid-1930s. Ten years or so after the earthquake in 1923, Shitamachi – largely destroyed because of its weak reclaimed ground and its dense cluster of residences which were vulnerable to fire – had rapidly lost its nature as a concrete geographical entity. Large numbers left the district and joined a westward or southward movement into the suburbs where relocation was concentrated. However, the earthquake was really only the final blow in a gradual shift that had already started when Edo transformed into Tokyo after the Meiji Restoration. Many writers, including Nagai Kafū (1879–1959), Hasegawa Shigure (1879–1941), and Kubota Mantarō (1889–1963), had previously lamented the disappearance of the culture as well as the physical landscape of the district and evoked nostalgic feelings towards Edo's past in their works. Kafū, whose writings are 'essentially nostalgic and elegiac', lamented that Tokyo had killed Edo, but also remembered 'how Edo yet survived at this and that date later than ones already assigned to the slaying'.[53] *Sumidagawa/The River Sumida* (1909) and *Bokutō kitan/A Strange Tale from East of the River* (1937) epitomise his longing for the disappearing past. Here, perhaps, we can find Bordwell's 'materials in Ozu' – 'the river, the little houses on the embankment, the bridges, the groves of trees visible in the temple grounds across the river' – which together evoke an atmosphere that is no less important than story or character.[54]

The temporal recollection of Edo also had its parallel phenomenon in a kind of spatial nostalgia for the hometown, both of which provided perspectives of the Tokyo of the here and now. Just as in the Edo period, the modernisation of Japan required the spatial relocation of labour forces from the provinces to Tokyo, a process that was expedited following the Great Kantō Earthquake, as more hands were needed for the reconstruction work. The homesick urban migrants found solace in the pseudo-hometown spaces of Tokyo – notably Asakusa in the pre-earthquake period. To conceptualise such spaces, the Japanese sociologist Yoshimi Shun'ya uses the term '*kakyō kūkan* (hometown space)', which is constructed by the people who share the collective memory of leaving one's hometown. In contrast, post-earthquake Ginza constitutes the modern and cosmopolitan '*mirai kūkan* (future space)', where the 'contemporary life of consumption' is pursued, in opposition to the cultural receptiveness based on 'sympathy of communalism' as championed in the *kakyō kūkan*.[55] Recognising this hometown space as a constructed fantasy, Wada-Marciano analyses various popular cultures that appealed to and integrated the consciousness of the mass audiences who had recently migrated to metropolitan cities. For example, Gosho Heinosuke's *Izu no odoriko/Izu Dancer* (1933), released in the same year as Ozu's *Passing Fancy*, 'invents a country space appealing to the nostalgia of city dwellers'.[56] From this perspective, the protagonist's journey to Izu becomes a 'journey for pleasure' allowing the film's middle-class audiences to consume a 'perfect nostalgic space ... with [Gosho's] well-chosen scenery'.[57] Wada-Marciano suggests that the reason for *Izu Dancer*'s appeal to middle-class audiences was related to the development of the tourism industry in Japan, which resulted in the 'levelling of leisure travel from upper-class recreation to middle-class consumption'.[58] Her following conclusion thus can be interpreted as an answer to Bordwell's question about Ozu's excessive use of 'materials' in the Kihachi series; 'While the shots of mountains, rivers, and country roads in *Izu Dancer* may be considered excessive and inefficient within the narrative practice of classical Hollywood cinema, they supported the economics of popular culture familiar to the 1930s Japanese audience'.[59]

If urban audiences were not fully satisfied with film images, they could go out and dance to a retro-style tune in order to connect with the past. The year 1933 saw the explosion of the craze of *Tōkyō ondo*, an adapted traditional-style song for *Bon Odori*, which is a collective dance performed at the *Bon* festival in summer and one of 'the most beloved popular entertainments in the provinces'.[60] The Japanese record and film industry quickly jumped on the bandwagon to capitalise on the song's success; Shochiku quickly produced an eponymous film, and the following spring, in time for the annual *hanami* (cherry blossom festival) season, four new songs and five films, all with the same title *Sakura ondo*, were released. However, as in *Izu Dancer*'s case, *Tōkyō ondo*'s appeal to a nostalgic sentiment existed within the concrete, realistic context of present-day society. The song originated from a marketing plan of the restaurant owner's guild in Tokyo's Marunouchi district, which intended to revitalise the economy of the district in the Great Depression era by bringing the provincial culture of *Obon* dance into the city of Tokyo.[61] Its popularity was also related to Tokyo's geopolitical transformation: in 1932, Tokyo's territory greatly expanded by absorbing new suburban areas where many new migrants had settled, and there arose a need to 'create a new identity for New Tokyo', under which the new and old citizens could be assimilated together.[62] In other words, *Tōkyō ondo*, with its hypnotically collective nature, was an effective vehicle for reuniting and revitalising Tokyo as a single community with a differentiated geographical character and historical continuity. Such anecdotes clearly show that the nostalgic element found in the popular culture of the 1930s was 'an answer to the shade or anxiety of modernity' that was oppressing the atmosphere of the period.[63]

Would it then be possible to find in the nostalgia of the Kihachi series a similar symptom of contemporary Japanese society as found in the cases of *Izu Dancer* and *Tōkyō ondo*? First of all, as critics so far have noted, the Kihachi series contains a strong Hollywood influence in subject matter and style. Satō Tadao finds a concrete example in the buddy relationship between Kihachi and Jirō in *Passing Fancy* ('vagabond worker style men who, exchanging smart jokes, develop a gallant friendship') and in the plot of *A Story of Floating Weeds*, which he argues is almost an adaptation of *The Barker* (dir. George Fitzmaurice, First National Pictures, 1928).[64] The father-son relationship frequent in the Kihachi films is also strongly influenced by Hollywood films, such as *Kid* (dir. Charles Chaplin, Charles Chaplin Productions, 1921) or *Champ* (dir. King Vidor, MGM, 1931).[65] According to his own evaluation, though in retrospection, Ozu seems to regard the Kihachi films as a peculiar type of project where Western modernity coexists with Japanese tradition:

> *Passing Fancy* was an effort to open up a new stage by developing the *shomin* (commoner) dramas I had been dealing with. I was fed up, so to speak, with Japan's damp (*jimejimeshita*) life [appearing in the *shomin* films] and wanted to broaden my world in a very modern style . . . [I had a] bold intent to draw an *ukiyo-e on a copperplate*.[66] (Italics added)

Ozu raises an example how he brought in small everyday objects imported from the West (such as toothpaste and soap) for props in the film. The scriptwriter Ikeda Tadao also supports Ozu's remembrance in a more personal and detailed way:

> Ozu and I liked the Shitamachi district in Tokyo and used to wander around looking for vestiges of Edo. But at the same time, we often headed to Yokohama as well to breathe modern air in the port or the streets of the city. We spent our last money to buy imported goods such as knife, fountain pen and pipe . . . In the end, we imagined both Edo and San Francisco, or longed for reminiscence and civilization, as if a playwright of Edo attempted to imitate the dandy style of American films.[67]

Therefore, Ozu and Ikeda's vision at that time transcended simple nostalgia and homage to the old world, and was directed towards a more contradictory representation of that disappearing past in the present under heavy influence of modernisation, as conveyed through their own everyday experience from imports to cosmopolitan space of port city.

A more significant aspect of cinematic modernity, however, would be found in its concrete representation of the everyday that can reveal various contradictions in social reality, as suggested in the discussion of the *shōshimin* film's everyday realism. Paying attention to the contemporariness in the Kihachi series, critics have interpreted the films as Ozu's realism work. A Japanese critic Kitakawa Fuyuhiko argues in his review of *Passing Fancy* that the film is 'a song of despair despite the cheerfulness on the surface'; 'at first sight, the scalpel dissecting reality might look blunt . . . but [there is] a delving enquiry of the reality of the working class, a true depiction of it. Such is Ozu's production method as a realist'.[68] In the same vein, another critic Yūda Jun'ichirō also agrees that *Passing Fancy* is 'not *shumi* (refined taste), *kanshō* (sentimentality), or *teikai* (contemplativeness)', the idiomatic rhetoric often attached to Ozu's works with negative nuances.[69] Iwasaki Akira, whose disappointment with the Kihachi films for abandoning social criticism has been mentioned at the beginning of this chapter, actually concludes in the same article that the series, in retrospection, is 'Ozu's first rate form of resistance'.[70] It may not be possible to simply equate this 'resistance' with the more direct and confronting kind of 'social realism' as appearing in tendency films or proletarian cinema. The uniqueness of Ozu's realism style may rather exist in its 'sentimentality' and 'contemplativeness' coming out of the 'true depiction' of the everyday. Therefore, in addition to everyday realism, we may call this style as '*ninjō* (humane) realism' as well (quoting the name of the Shitamachi genre *shomin ninjōgeki*). The fact that the two contradictory words – 'everyday' (a term originally related to *Kamata-chō*) and '*ninjō*' (*shinpa*-esque element) – are used to describe Ozu's realism ironically proves the complexity of his cinema, a body of work historically formed through diverse negotiations between opposite tendencies.

Regarding the realism of the Kihachi series, it is worthwhile to pay attention to the vagrant nature of the protagonist character who, while existing in Shitamachi's 'close and closed' community, does not essentially belong there. Moving into the nostalgic space (and time), he still carries with him a trace of reality, generating a subtle tension with the community, which eventually forces him to leave the space. Such a narrative form is not so strongly established in the first film of the series, *Passing Fancy*, where Kihachi resides in his neighbourhood from the beginning, although he, out of *giri* (duty) to pay back money, briefly leaves and comes back to the town in the ending sequence. In *A Story of Floating Weeds*, the element of vagrancy shapes the whole narrative as it starts and ends with the sequences of Kihachi's visiting and leaving the remote provincial village in which it is set, where he not only stages a show with his troupe but also spends time with his son, who is not aware that Kihachi could be his father. The separation between a Shitamachi-like closed community and the outside world is most vivid in *An Inn in Tokyo*, the narrative of which is divided in two by a meeting between Kihachi and the local woman Otsune, who helps to integrate him into her neighbourhood. Before that, during the first half of the film, he is an unemployed worker with two sons, wandering around a bleak industrial district in Shitamachi looking for a job, and in the end has to leave Otsune's neighbourhood again, this time alone and guilty because he has stolen money to help a woman he is fond of. Thus in both *A Story of Floating Weeds* and *An Inn in Tokyo*, the Shitamachi neighbourhood is presented as a temporary solace for Kihachi, who, however, must return to the real world, leaving his family behind.[71]

The difference between the inside and outside of the community space and time is presented visually in *An Inn in Tokyo*. The early sequences contain images of long empty roads lined with electricity poles, or barren fields of grass and sand dotted with tanks and cable spools, with factory buildings seen in the background. These are the working-class variants of the empty suburban space discussed in the previous chapter, which points towards the urban centre – the middle class's space of production – over the horizon. Kihachi's domestic everyday life, nonexistent at this stage despite his stay in an inn every night, instantly revives after he meets Otsune and finds a job through her. A morning sequence of his *nagaya* and its vicinities (back alley and Otsune's restaurant), as seen in *Passing Fancy*, reappears, and Otsune, as her character always does in the Kihachi series, takes the maternal role for Kihachi's family by serving meals. The intimate closeness of Shitamachi, visually represented by a shot of the narrow *nagaya* alley, generates a stark contrast to the indifferent vastness of the roads and fields outside the town, filled with giant industrial icons in the background.

The deviated space-time discussed in Chapter 1 in relation to *shōshimin* film appears in the Kihachi films as well, especially in *An Inn in Tokyo* that similarly focuses on the everyday life of a working-class protagonist and his family under economic hardship during the Depression. The park scene in *Tokyo Chorus*, for instance, where unemployed Okajima and his former colleague detach themselves from a busy main street and share sympathy, is echoed in an empty field scene in *An Inn in Tokyo*, where Kihachi happens to meet a single mother Otaka (Okada Yoshiko). Watching their children play together in the field, the two jobless characters console each other, which Ozu's camera frames in a similar profile shot to that in the public park scene in *Tokyo Chorus*. Also, the deviated temporality in the outdoor lunch scene in *I Was Born But . . .* is reproduced in another outdoor eating

Figure 2.1 Kihachi drinks imaginary *sake* (compare with Figure 1.5)

scene in *An Inn in Tokyo*, but this time inflected with more direct criticism of industrial society. Here Kihachi, exhausted by walking around all day long looking, to no avail, for a job in a factory area, sits on a grass field with his two sons to have a rest, when, at the elder son's suggestion, he starts to pretend a gesture of drinking *sake* with his bare hands (see Figure 2.1). This moment of fantasised pleasure, obtained through a re-enactment of a daily life practice that the jobless protagonist is robbed of in reality, is juxtaposed with a vague sight of factory buildings and smoking chimneys in the background, generating a visual conflict between this powerless (yet intimate) working-class family and industrialised urban civilisation. This spatial contrast, articulated by the physical distance between the foreground and the background, becomes a foundation of momentary deviation that Kihachi can take in the everyday, comparable to the one in the outdoor lunch scene of *I Was Born But . . .*, though in the latter case, the contrast is presented in a temporal way, that is, by editing the empty field scene with the following shots of school and workplace (see Figure 1.5). Kihachi can fulfil his ardent wish to drink in the latter part of the film after he enters and settles in Otsune's Shitamachi community, where the everyday operates in a different spatiality and temporality from the industrial capitalism looming in the background of the outside world.

Poverty is a decisive force in many parts of the series' narrative. Although a spendthrift in the mode of the mercantile class *chōnin*, Kihachi is essentially a working-class character; he works in a beer factory in *Passing Fancy*, and is looking for lathing work in *An Inn in Tokyo*. In *A Story of Floating Weeds*, Kihachi is a *geinin* (performing entertainer) for a travelling theatre, which is also a lower-class occupation. The narrative of vagrancy pervasive in the series – except in *An Innocent Maid*, where Kihachi runs a *senbei* (rice cracker) shop in Shitamachi – is typically caused by a situation where Kihachi is in need of money. As mentioned, in the ending sequence of *Passing Fancy*, Kihachi goes to work in Hokkaido in order to earn money to pay back a hospital bill of his son's. In *A Story of Floating Weeds*, Kihachi's itinerant troupe goes broke and disbands, and in *An Inn in Tokyo*, Kihachi steals money to help Otaka pay a hospital bill for her daughter, which eventually makes him leave his neighbourhood alone (possibly) to surrender himself to the police. The film's last scene, however, seems to side with Kihachi's morality, with a shot of his gesture of slinging his jacket over his shoulder, thrusting a hand into his pocket and walking towards gas tanks as if he were determined to face up to the giant symbol of industrial society.

These narratives of leaving commonly suggest that Kihachi's neighbourhood, an idyllic nostalgic space, is not free from the contradictions of modern, capitalistic society, to which Kihachi, as a working-class man, is destined to belong. After all, Ozu does not simply tell reminiscences with the Kihachi series; as noticeable from his expression '*ukiyo-e* on copperplate', he rather intends a critical examination of Japanese modernity, which is an outcome of multilateral interactions between Japanese tradition and Western modernity. Old Shitamachi is an allegorical vision of the past upon which that relationship could be reflected. Later in the postwar years, Ozu would further refine this notion of the spatio-temporal multilayered-ness of Japanese modernity in relation to the historical continuity between the wartime and the postwar, which will be discussed in Chapter 4.

Solidarity in Sympathy: Ozu's Woman's Film

In the genres of the *shōshimin* film and the Shitamachi film discussed so far, the role of female characters is minimal, compared to that of male characters such as the salaryman and Kihachi. Women are usually depicted as being inactive, responsive, and supportive if not subordinate. The world of housewife in the *shōshimin* film, for instance, is typically confined to domesticity and her voice is limited in order to restrict the revelation of her subjectivity according to the ideal of *ryōsai kenbo*. There are some exceptional scenes, as when Okajima's wife in *Tokyo Chorus* reproves her unemployed husband for doing menial work or when Yoshii's wife in *I Was Born But . . .* acts as a go-between after the conflict between her husband and children. The most extreme case would be the wife

Machiko (Tanaka Kinuyo) in *I Graduated But . . .*, who, on behalf of her unemployed husband, works as a bar waitress, a scandalous transgression, which shocks the husband to exert himself more to find employment. However, even these cases ultimately reaffirm the status of the middle-class housewife in the genre as a character secondary to her male counterpart, with her primary role defined as a sympathiser, observer or supporter of the suffering patriarch. Such a husband-wife relationship is usually visualised in point-of-view shots from the wife's viewpoint, through which she observes and discovers the true identity of her husband as a powerless patriarch (see Figure 1.3 for example). The character of Otsune (or Otome) in the Kihachi series conforms, for the most part, to this tendency by performing a pseudo-maternal existence for Kihachi's family.

Apart from the housewife, however, there was another type of female character in Ozu's prewar films. The *modan gāru* (modern girl), who, appearing as a more central character than the middle-class housewife or Shitamachi shop owner, is placed in a different context from her counterparts in relation to the domestic everyday life she leads. The modern girl's different stance on the everyday makes her a menace to male-centric ideologies such as patriarchy both on and off screen. The response can be divided in two ways: either discipline a modern girl into the logic of domesticity or, if that is not possible, remove her existence from the everyday entirely. A case of the latter has already been introduced in Chapter 1 with regard to the character of Kyōko in Shimazu Yasujiro's *Our Neighbour Miss Yae*. In this section, both of the two cases will be more thoroughly re-examined and, in addition, re-contextualised from a narrative level to the broader genre convention of the *shinpa* melodrama that largely constituted Shochiku's so-called *josei eiga* (woman's film).

By definition woman's film means films for female spectators, appealing to their sentiments and interests through a particular type of narrative and female protagonist, and, at the same time, contributing to the construction of female subjectivity by raising gender-specific issues. On the other hand, as many critics have argued, the genre has been more or less interpreted as serving male interests because of its implied ideology to support and reinforce a male-dominant system in society. The main question to be addressed here, then, is how to negotiate the contradiction between the dominant male-centric ideology that either reforms or eliminates the spoiled modern girl and the subjectivity formation of the female audiences who are the major consumer of the gender-exclusive genre. As a possible answer, I will assume that there is a more positive function of the domestic everyday, wherein the emotional solidarity between female modern girl characters and more conservative types can build a strong critique of male-centric ideologies, which eventually appeals to female audiences. In the sense that Ozu began to articulate these more complex relationships among female central characters in his films, Ozu's mid-1930s can be reconfirmed as a transition era.

I will examine this point through textual analysis of Ozu's female-oriented melodramas such as *Mata au hi made/Until the Day We Meet Again* (1932), *Tōkyō no onna/Woman of Tokyo* (1933) and *Hijōsen no onna/Dragnet Girl* (1933).

Although the Japanese modern girl has been the theme of many academic studies as well as journalistic writings, her identity is extremely ambiguous. The problem is aggravated by the nature of her existence as a visual, instantaneous image without a substantial socio-economic basis. As Barbara Sato defines, the modern girl was thus a 'voiceless existence surrounded by . . . the ambivalence of class and occupation, [which was] presented and represented through the media'.[72] However, if put in the narrowest terms, the *modan gāru* designates a group of young Japanese females characterised by new fashion styles and a liberal lifestyle expressed through their interest in commodity culture and sexual promiscuity.[73] They began to appear on the streets of urban centres after the Great Kantō Earthquake, making them an icon of post-earthquake Westernisation and modernisation. As the fact that the term was derived from the English phrase 'modern girl' indicates, the phenomenon of *modan gāru* and the social discourse surrounding it originated from and coincided with the emergence of her Western counterpart in the 1920s.[74] Recent studies, in contrast, emphasise 'multidirectional citation' in the global dynamics of the modern girl phenomenon, articulating the 'mutual, though asymmetrical, influences and circuits of exchange'.[75] Nevertheless, it is still undeniable that the phenomenon was a kind of image culture especially conveyed through Hollywood films. The Japanese modern girl modelled her identity on the personae of movie stars such as Colleen Moore, Clara Bow and Louise Brooks, and the image of the flapper was reincarnated by such Japanese actresses as Tatsuta Shizue, Natsukawa Shizue and Irie Takako.[76]

Japan's male-centred media not only engaged in constructing the scandalous image of the modern girl, but also provided the patriarchal critique of it at the same time, transforming this cultural phenomenon into a broader social and political issue. Fujiki argues that the modern girl's economically independent and morally subversive image consequentially 'activate[d] [a form of] reactionary, exclusive, and conciliatory power', including the actions from the Japanese government; by 'inciting anxiety in Monbushō (the Ministry of Education, Science and Culture) or other powerful institutions', the modern girl 'provided an excuse for them to control the new forms of femininity and women's activities'.[77] An important reason why the Japanese government was concerned about the modern girl and wanted to intervene was the tendency of Americanisation inherent in the phenomenon, which might eventually be detrimental to the national identity of Japanese people. Equating the modern girl problem with the cultural rivalry between America and Japan, governmental agencies turned to 'the reactionary sensibility of protecting or justifying the nation against foreign countries'.[78] When this nationalistic concern was applied to cinematic texts, it was often expressed in the form of a 'drama that either excludes a modern girl from the social or familial community, or subsumes her into it' in order to reform her into a part of 'the homogenised Japanese'.[79]

The responses of intellectuals were multifaceted. Some suggested that the outward aspect of the modern girl (for instance, consumption and promiscuity) could not be simply deprecated as a fashion craze or a construct of the patriarchal order, but was itself a productive and liberating element. Such writers as Hirabayashi Hatsunosuke, Chiba Kameo and Nii Itaru 'envisioned an assertive, individualistic woman of the future – a product of consumerism, who demonstrated a previously unknown degree of agency'.[80] Kikuchi Kan also regarded these new women as 'representatives of a new sexual awakening' and 'declared that their appearance announced the beginning of modernity'.[81] More recently, Miriam Silverberg exhibits an optimistic view of the issue, acknowledging the Westernised and sexually liberal behaviour of the modern girl as the sign of a new, autonomous femininity, as exemplified by the character of Naomi, the female protagonist of Tanizaki Jun'Ichirō's novel *Chijin no ai*/*A Fool's Love* (1924).[82] As such, the modern girl, freed from 'ties of filiation, affect, or obligation to lover, father, mother, husband, or children', rejected the patriarchal state ideology that was documented in the Meiji Civil Code and being taught in the schools.[83]

However, other liberal critiques and the older generation of female intellectuals were sceptical of the modern girl's obsession with fashion and commodity culture, regarding it as a 'bourgeois ploy to distract modern women from the more pressing issues of politics and class'.[84] For the journalist Ōya Sōichi, the 'externally observable' characteristics, such as Westernised appearance, straightforward personality and unrestrained behaviour, did not bestow the modern girl with 'hundred per cent' authenticity that could be found in other radical groups of women (for example, '*Atarashii onna*/New Women' of the previous generation), who 'resolutely demolishe[d] conventions that control[led] women's morality, male-female relationship, and lifestyle'.[85] These critics thus recognised a gap between serious, politically conscious young women and the superficial, materialistic *modan gāru*, who was subordinate to prevailing masculine desires. Fujiki thus suggests distinguishing the latter type as '*moga*', with a contemptuous nuance, from the more general concept of the '*modan gāru*', which the liberal or feminist intellectuals preferred and idealised.[86]

It would be more desirable, then, to approach the phenomenon from a broader perspective and reconceptualise the modern girl within the diverse spectrum of women's existence in the modern Japanese society. In this sense, Silverberg's inclusion of the 'working woman (*shokugyō fujin*)' category in her discussion of modern Japanese femininity is important. Defined as 'a single or married Japanese woman wage-earner ... forced into paid employment by financial need following the end of the economic boom of the World War I years', this group of women was not merely a 'passive consumer of middle-class culture' as the image of modern girl suggests, but rather a 'producer' who strived for economic self-sufficiency.[87] Silverberg, in conclusion, regards these two groups as two different aspects (consumption and production) of the same experience for modern Japanese women, whom she characterises as 'militant', fighting against the social, economic and cultural status quo. By being 'placed alongside the history of working, militant Japanese women', the 'free-floating and depoliticised' modern girl is finally able to be 'rescued'.[88]

Silverberg's attribution of militancy, however, might be too optimistic a view in assuming a certain ideal model of femininity while ignoring the reality that Japanese females were facing at the time. Above all, the modern girl was a phenomenon confined to a small number of females, residing and working in urban areas.[89] In this regard, Yoshimi Shun'ya's analysis provides a more realistic view. He argues that most of the young working females, whose image overlapped with that of the modern girl (such as 'office clerks, shop girls, and telephone operators') were of urban lower-middle class origin, with their parents being civil servants or small business owners, and considered their job as an interim career until they got married.[90] These limited opportunities arose not only from economic considerations (the modern girl as a cheap labour resource) but also from the 'cultural politics of sexuality' that deployed the modern girl's erotic attractiveness in order to sell products and services.[91] For example, female bus conductors, who started to appear in Tokyo around 1920, were employed not merely because their labour was necessary and cheap but because they could also provide 'some other kind of services', that is, 'visual, auditory, and tactile enjoyment to satisfy (male) passengers'. Such an employment strategy was similarly applied in the cases of usherettes and petrol station workers.[92] Thus modern femininity – as with other aspects of a capitalistic society – was fundamentally subordinate to the logic of capital and patriarchy, which constructed a 'colonial gaze' towards the working woman, who in return projected and internalised that gaze into a self-image of herself as commodity.

Militant or *moga*, optimist or realist, none of the diverse aforementioned discourses presents the definitive image of the modern girl. Yoshimi's concept of the 'colonial gaze' is effective in explaining the interrelationship among the agents of different genders and power hierarchies, but tends to underestimate the active participation of the female masses in the formation of their new identity, as evidenced by the popularity of women's magazines during the interwar period.[93] Silverberg and Sato's position pays attention to this subjectivity, and, as seen in the positive interpretation of the working woman's experiences, emphasises the 'materiality of everyday existence', which is an important step towards an understanding of the real modern girl.[94] In this regard, the inclusion of the housewife, based on a study of women's magazines, as the third category of modern Japanese female (reproducer) after the modern girl (consumer) and the working woman (producer) broadens the boundary of the everyday into domesticity and thus completes the whole modern experience of Japanese women.

The housewife, socially confined in the household and economically excluded from waged labour, was the most vulnerable and most subject to the patriarchal ideologies of the society. Many intellectuals of the time criticised the socio-political conservatism that pervaded articles in the women's magazines that housewives read, the policy of which, after all, was mainly decided by male editors who were also subject to state-driven ideologies.[95] On the other hand, state-initiated programmes (such as the Everyday Life Reform Movement) propagated in women's magazines resulted in modernisation at a domestic level, by 'urging rationalization (*gōrika*)' of household affairs. Confessional articles (*kokuhaku kiji* – readers' contributions about various quotidian concerns) also contributed to constructing the housewife's modern identity by offering a thoroughfare of communication amongst anonymous readers. Satō thus concludes that women's magazines accomplished at least the 'partial redefinition of femininity' by 'reinforcing and propelling women away from timeworn practices', while Silverberg is even more positive, affirming that the magazines were 'challenging the patriarchal family-state ideology by offering a space for men and women (married or unmarried) in which they could reveal their desires'.[96]

The essential characteristics of the discourses of the modern girl can thus be summarised as multiplicity and relativity. The phantasm of the modern girl on the street finds its grounding in the reality of the working woman at work and the housewife at home, constituting a new, broader picture of the 'Modern Girl', a figure who actually existed through the everyday experiences of the 1920s and 1930s in Japan. However, this trinity of modern Japanese women did not exist in isolation. What made them truly 'modern' was their interrelation with other agents – mutual actions, discourses, and 'gazes' that constantly interpreted, evaluated and affected each other. As mentioned already, the modern girl phenomenon started as a result of such an influence as the gaze – Japanese young women discovering their persona on the silver screen from outside the country and adapting themselves to it – and the same principle continued to be applied on the street, in newspapers and in magazines, where a complex spectrum of gender ideologies was being communicated, emulated and practised among intellectuals as well as among the modern girls themselves.

This multifaceted existence of the modern girl and her relative position in opposition to other agents becomes a fundamental assumption in the formation of the genre of woman's film. Wada-Marciano's study on the subject has added an important historical perspective, defining the woman's film as a 'genre' based not only on 'audience composition' but also on 'the genre's place within the Japanese film industry in the 1920s and 1930s'.[97] Capitalising on the emerging young urban female populations who secured buying power from their salaried employment after World War I, Shochiku strategically concentrated on the woman's film, which 'served both to configure a female identity as consuming subject and to provide material for her consumption'.[98] As discussed in Chapter 1, the change inevitably entailed the acceptance of Hollywood's modernised production style while eschewing the old, theatrical *shinpa* traditions. One of the most significant examples of this was the abolition of *onnagata* and the birth of the actress, with whom the female spectators could identify themselves. The main thrust of Wada-Marciano's argument, however, is to emphasise 'a Japanese vernacular experience' in the woman's film genre that 'negotiated the audience's expectations, becoming at once modern and distinctly Japanese', through merging Hollywood influence with 'a sense of authenticity drawn from the audience's everyday life'.[99] The contestation between the modern and non-modern appearing in the genre was thus often contradictory. For example, while the modern girl images represented the 'spectacle of Japanese women embracing Western style and values', they were also 'contained within alternately patriarchal and national discourses'.[100] Just as the journalistic view of the modern girl was bifurcated, in the woman's film there was a 'subtle play within the strict terms of the dichotomy's separation' between 'transfigurative new women' as bourgeois consumers and the 'desire for control over the threat that the figure represents'.[101]

This view has limitations in that the dichotomy assumes two fixed images of the modern girl as imagined by the patriarchal perspective discussed earlier. Such transformation from one form of femininity to another does not fully explain the relative multiplicity of the modern girl figure I suggested, excluding the subjectivity and mutual gazes of the working woman and the housewife who constituted the Modern Girl. Nevertheless, it is also true that the 'dichotomy [and transformation] between the modern girl and so-called traditional Japanese woman' effectively explains basic narrative formulas prevalent in the woman's films.[102] For instance, Wada-Marciano finds the case of a traditional type of female character traversing the boundary of *ryōsai kenbo* (and becoming a kind of modern girl) in the young wife characters in the two Gosho Heinosuke films, *The Neighbour's Wife and Mine* (1931) and *Burden of Life* (1935) – both, interestingly, performed by Tanaka Kinuyo.[103] However, what is more pervasive and often emphasised in the genre is transformation in the opposite direction, that is, from *modan gāru* to *ryōsai kenbo*, which usually results in patriarchal reformation or the punishment of a modern girl character in the narrative. The typical formula, which I call 'failed *moga*' narrative, contrasts a modern girl with a more traditional female character, the latter's domesticity and chastity always prevailing over the former's extravagance and licentiousness in the end. As Wada-Marciano points out, it reveals a patriarchal symptom of 'appropriation, trivialisation, and subsequent control of such potentially subversive female subjectivities', making them remain as a mere 'commodified figure', a fabricated image that eventually serves to 'refigure and re-establish Japanese national identity'.[104]

There are many examples of the 'failed *moga*' formulae in prewar Japanese cinema. Among the woman's films produced by Shochiku in the 1920s and 1930s, Wada-Marciano mentions *Fue no shiratama/Undying Pearl* (Shimizu Hiroshi, 1929), *Nasanu naka/Not Blood Relations* (Naruse Mikio, 1932) and *Seidon/Sunny Cloud* (Nomura Hōtei, 1933), where the dichotomy between the modern girl and the traditional girl concludes with the former's exclusion.[105] *Our Neighbour Miss Yae*, discussed in the previous chapter, also articulates the contrast between Yaeko, a schoolgirl taking a domestic *ryōsai kenbo*'s role, and Kyōko, a divorcee who takes the role of a modern girl, and eventually disappears from the narrative. As discussed, Shochiku Kamata studio's films were not free from the influence of *shinpa* for commercial purposes, and it is undeniable that the *shinpa* tradition greatly contributed to the woman's film genre. In fact, 'Shochiku's pervasive use of this dichotomy [between modern girl and traditional girl]' was in line with the typical *shinpa*'s melodramatic formulae, rather than an effort to distinguish the woman's film from *shinpa* as Wada-Marciano argues.[106] Sasaki has also clarified that in *Our Neighbour Miss Yae*, contrasting Okada (the not-innocent, '*shinpa*-tragic' world) with Yaeko (the innocent 'world of the everyday') is the 'common method of the *shinpa* melodrama'.[107]

As explained, *shinpa* had its roots in Japanese theatrical tradition, and many *shinpa* films were paired with their theatrical versions, which were often also adaptations of original popular novels including *kateishōsetsu* (home novel), often being serialised in *kateishinbun* (home newspapers). The *kateishōsetsu* was intended to be read by a patriarch to his illiterate wife and daughters, confirming the morally patriarchal nature of the early modern media for females. For this purpose, *kateishōsetsu*'s style was plain to understand and its contents were closely related to practical home life. It often dealt with the 'tragedy of a

Table 2.3 Representative *kateishōsetsu* adapted to *shinpa* melodrama (compiled from McDonald, *From Book to Screen*, pp. 4–16)

Author	Title	Year of publication	First theatre adaptation	First film adaptation (total number of remakes)
Izumi Kyōka	Giketsu kyōketsu/ Blood of Honour (Theatre and film version: Taki no Shiraito/ The Water Magician)	1894	1896	1912 (6)
Ozaki Kōyō	Konjiki yasha/ The Golden Demon	1897–1902	1897	1911 (19)
Tokutomi Roka	Hototogisu/ The Cuckoo	1898–9	1901	1909 (22)
Kikuchi Yūhō	Ono ga tsumi/ My Sin	1899–1900	1900	1908 (25)
Kikuchi Yūhō	Chikyōdai/ Foster Sisters	1903	Unknown	1909 (16)
Ōkura Tōrō	Biwaka/ Lute Song	1905	1905	1910 (15)
Izumi Kyōka	Onna keizu/ A Woman's Pedigree	1907	1908	Unknown (at least 6)
Yanagawa Shun'yō	Nasanu naka/ Not Blood Relations	1912–13	1913	1916 (8)

pitiful high class woman', which 'satisfied vanity or sympathy of female readers' and 'vindicated the good manners and morals [of society]'.[108] Some of the most popular novelists and novels (mostly from the Meiji era) that were repeatedly adapted into *shinpa* theatre and film productions from the 1910s until the 1950s are listed in Table 2.3. All of these works are characterised by the story of a woman's suffering that results in a fateful tragedy; there is a sacrifice for the success of her lover (*Blood of Honour*), unrequited love produced by difference in social status (*A Woman's Pedigree*), the woes of marriage due to illness and conflicts with a mother-in-law (*The Cuckoo*, *Lute Song*), and divorce and the separation from (and eventually death of) a child (*My Sin*). Confrontation between two women is also prominent; it could be between a wife and a former fiancée

(*My Sin*), a birthmother and an adoptive mother (*Not Blood Relations*), or two stepsisters (*Foster Sisters*). Okada Yoshiko appeared in film versions of the last two properties, taking the role of a modern girl just as in *Our Neighbour Miss Yae*: a famous actress returning from America to reclaim her abandoned daughter in *Not Blood Relations* (Naruse Mikio, 1932), and, in *Foster Sisters*, a poor country girl who, pretending to be her stepsister, attempts to seize the wealth and status of the stepsister's family (Nomura Hōtei, 1932). Her characters are not exempt from the destiny of a failed *moga*; in the former, she gives up the child, and in the latter, dies after being stabbed by her former boyfriend who is angered by her betrayal.

The modern girl characters in Ozu's films also follow a similar narrative formula. In *Hogaraka ni ayume/Walk Cheerfully* (1930), Chieko (Date Satoko) competes with a traditional type of girl, Yasue (Kawasaki Hiroko), to win the love of her gangster boyfriend Kenji, who falls in love with Yasue and deserts Chieko. Although both girls are working women in the same office, Chieko's after-work *modan* life marks her with a stereotypically negative image of a debauchee, who is well dressed in the Western style, enjoys golf and billiards, and hangs out with men in bars, not to mention smoking and drinking. Such prodigality is in contrast with Yasue's moral chastity as well as domesticity – Yasue is often seen at home with her family while Chieko's family is never suggested – justifying Chieko's defeat and expulsion from the love triangle relationship. A similar pattern of the 'failed *moga*' narrative is repeated in *Shukujō to hige/The Lady and the Beard* (1931), in which Date Satoko and Kawasaki Hiroko perform the same love rivalry between a modern girl and an ordinary girl character over the male protagonist Okajima.

Without a doubt, there is a strict patriarchal perspective governing the formulaic narrative structure of these modern girl films. For example, *The Lady and the Beard* suggests that the way Date Satoko's modern girl character can win Okajima's love is by repenting of her reckless life and accepting a woman's domestic role, such as helping him to change clothes or sewing. When she witnesses her rival Hiroko excelling at these everyday chores, the modern girl finally admits defeat and leaves Okajima with a promise that she will reform. This acceptance of 'failure' is possible through the modern girl's female gaze at Hiroko as a model of *ryōsai kenbo*, which is presented through Date Satoko's point-of-view shot, followed by a three-shot where the inclusion of a sleeping Okajima in front of a sewing Hiroko reaffirms the proper gender relationship according to the patriarchal order (see Figure 2.2). The modern girl's 'intra-gender' female gaze is also complemented by an 'inter-gender' gaze of Okajima's in an earlier scene, where he brings the modern girl into his apartment and curiously (but disapprovingly) surveys her figure, from her shoes (improperly not taken

Figure 2.2 A failed *moga* observes a *ryōsai kenbo*

off in the tatami room) to her flamboyant dress and hairstyle. His patriarchal look at the wanton modern girl can find a comparable precedent in a similar scene with a point-of-view shot in *I Graduated But . . .*, where the unemployed husband watches in silent frustration and anger the sight of his wife, a bar waitress, lighting a cigarette for her male customer (see Figures 2.3–2.5). The common prevailing ideology in these films entails both the denial of the modern girl and the endorsement of *ryōsai kenbo* from a masculine perspective, faithfully reflecting the view of patriarchal society.[109]

At a more explicit level, patriarchal control is expressed in the form of direct punishment exerted on a modern girl's body by a male character. Chieko in *Walk Cheerfully*, for instance, is thrown onto the floor by Kenji when her plea for love is denied. An even more violent example appears in Ozu's *Woman of Tokyo*, where the female protagonist Chikako (Okada Yoshiko) is severely slapped by her younger brother Ryōichi, who is shocked to learn that his sister works in a bar at night and is also (probably) involved in communist action. According to Wada-Marciano, this patriarchal punishment on screen must have evoked complicated reactions from contemporary spectators, who were familiar with the scandalous personal history of the actress Okada Yoshiko.[110] The dissonance between a

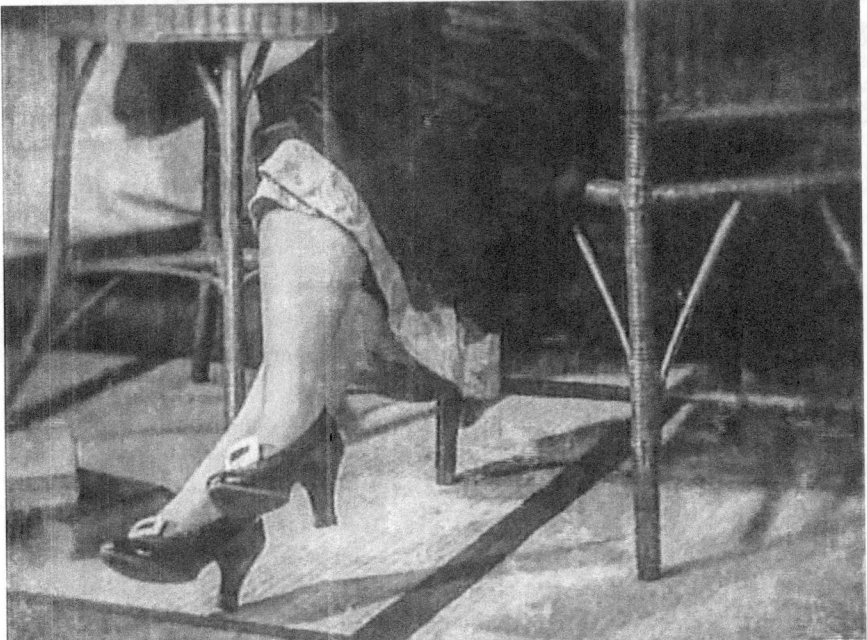

Figures 2.3 (upper) & 2.4 (lower) Okajima surveys Date Satoko's modern girl appearance

Figure 2.5 A moment of revelation for a husband to witness his wife working in a bar (compare with Figure 1.3)

woman of 'sexual autonomy' in reality and her 'unglamorous' on-screen images made the audience 'read other meanings into her performances', as if Okada suffered a 'castigation of her modern girl persona'.[111] While enjoying 'masochistic attraction to the foreign body [of Okada]', the viewers could eventually feel safe with the 'sadistic response toward the chastised modern girl figure'.[112]

However, as mentioned earlier, the dichotomy and transformation between the modern girl and her traditional counterpart pervading the woman's film may not adequately explain the multiplicity of modern Japanese femininity. I thus argue that the genre's text can be re-examined from a different context, one that asks an essential question of the 'woman' for which the woman's films were made. There can be two possible answers regarding how these female spectators actually saw and read the woman's film genre. They could have been passive audiences faithfully responding to the cinematic apparatus, internalising and reproducing patriarchal ideology in themselves. Or the woman's films could have engaged female spectators with a more strongly subjective position to construct their own meaning that deviated from a dominant patriarchal point of view. It would be hard to imagine that weeping female audiences, who were sympathetic enough to identify with the suffering heroine, all failed to catch the ethical and ideological potential of subversion in the genre. In this 'predominantly female', gender-exclusive experience of the text, which 'men tended to mock . . . [as] "boring *shinpa* drama . . . and tearjerkers"', it would not be unreasonable to expect that a certain kind of solidarity or 'sisterhood' was being collectively borne out of the female audiences.[113]

A condition to make that relationship possible is a more multidimensional character who would be more fit to the definition of the modern girl in the wider sense, and therefore could more easily inspire a sympathetic gaze amongst women both on and off screen. The female protagonists appearing in the three consecutive films that Ozu made during 1932 and 1933 – *Until the Day We Meet Again*, *Woman of Tokyo* and *Dragnet Girl* – are good examples, which commonly display more a complex identity beyond the simple dichotomy between a delinquent modern girl and a conventional *ryōsai kenbo*. All three characters have in common that they change their multiple identities according to the everyday space and time they belong to. The protagonist woman (very unusually for Ozu, her character name is not given in the script) in *Until the Day We Meet Again*, played by Okada Yoshiko (her first role for Ozu before *Woman of Tokyo* and *An Inn in Tokyo*), is a prostitute working on the street, but in her apartment takes the role of *ryōsai kenbo* by giving great emotional support to her boyfriend, who is troubled by an estranged relationship with his father. In *Woman of Tokyo*, the protagonist Chikako is the same kind of devoted and caring sister who supports her brother at home, but works as an able office clerk during the day, and then metamorphoses into a bar hostess (and possibly a prostitute) at night. In *Dragnet Girl*, Tokiko (Tanaka Kinuyo) is also an office clerk, but enjoys her exhilarating nightlife with her gangster boyfriend at night. These characters' lives as a chaste and dutiful *ryōsai kenbo*, highly educated and professional working woman, and sensual and seductive streetgirl reflect the multiple identities that contemporary modern Japanese women retained.

What also importantly distinguishes these protagonists from other female characters who fall prey to the failed *moga* narrative is their moral superiority to male counterparts. Firmly standing on the world of the everyday as well as having access to economic resources, they commonly perform a role of 'persuader' for a wandering man they earnestly love. The woman in *Until the Day We Meet Again* strongly persuades her boyfriend to see his estranged father before going to war, even preparing a new suit for him to wear. As such, the scene not only makes a melodramatic climax for itself but also sets a foundation for the following *shinpa*-flavoured narrative of reunion and final separation of the boyfriend and his family. As for Chikako in *Woman of Tokyo*, she is confident of her working life and thus in subjective control of her morality. Although she keeps silent to her brother Ryōichi about her nightlife until it is revealed to him by his girlfriend, Harue (Tanaka Kinuyo), Chikako does not show a penitent attitude as other failed *moga* characters tend to do, considering it as a proud self-sacrifice in exchange for Ryōichi's education – the typical narrative set in *shinpa* melodrama. It is rather Ryōichi who agonises over the truth of his sister, which leads to his sudden suicide on the very night he is informed of it. Desperately trying to win back the love of her boyfriend, Jōji, who falls in love with a *ryōsai kenbo* kind of girl, Kazuko, Tokiko in *Dragnet Girl* might be the least self-determined and self-confident type of character of the three. But on the other hand, in the sense that she finally succeeds in persuading him to join the domestic everyday she dreams of – even by shooting him in the end – rather than being punished as a failed *moga*, she can also be evaluated as a modern girl true to her desire, placed farthest from the norm of self-sacrifice that *shinpa* melodrama tends to impose on female characters.

In order to articulate the female subjectivity and its comparison with masculinity in his woman's films, Ozu pays elaborate attention to domestic everyday objects. In *Woman of Tokyo*, the beginning morning sequence of the film is full of such ordinary objects as dishes on a dining table, socks hanging outside a window, and a smoking chimney and air vent, which strengthens the sense of stable domesticity upon which her life is founded. These objects are the very examples upon which Noël Burch developed his idea of the 'pillow-shot', an intervening visual element composed of inanimate objects, which generates the 'decentring effect' that guides viewers 'outside the diegesis'.[114] While I agree with his argument that this stylistic device of Ozu's had 'reached full development in *Woman of Tokyo*', I do, however, want to emphasise that the essential issue here is more Ozu's *objective* in addressing these objects at the beginning than the *method* he deploys to articulate it.[115] No other previous film (at least among the surviving ones) begins with an emphatic shot of domestic objects as *Woman of Tokyo* does. Even his previous *shōshimin* films are not that interested in the space of the kitchen and its objects, which explains the secondary role of housewife characters in the genre. Faced with the daringly frontal composition of the first shot of bottles, a kettle, a gas stove and a rice cooker, viewers are led to examine the implication of the everydayness that these inanimate objects emanate, which I argue is closely related to Chikako's identity rooted in domestic everyday life *within* the diegesis.

This interpretation is supported by another domestic object: a mirror. Chikako's looking in a mirror is not only a moment of preparing herself for everyday work but also a deviated time for self-examination out of the context of the everyday. There are four mirror scenes in the film: first, in the opening morning sequence when Chikako is preparing to go to work; secondly, while she is putting on heavy makeup in the bar; thirdly, when she returns home from the bar to remove a slight trace of the night work; and lastly, when she checks the bruise on her cheek after being slapped by Ryōichi. In the first three cases, looking in a mirror connects not only three distinct places but also her three different lives (as a housekeeper, a typist and a barmaid), merging them into the identity of a modern girl. Here a mirror, as an everyday object, attests to her busy daily life, supporting Chikako's moral superiority over her brother. The fourth mirror scene is different in that it exists as a moment of introspection, with a definite *shinpa*-esque tragic tone. After being slapped by Ryōichi, Chikako, in tears, persuades him in vain not to care about her night work, and when he leaves home in anger, silently approaches the mirror to examine the trace of the violence on her cheek (see Figure 2.6). What she is feeling could be self-pity for being ignored by the brother in spite of all her sacrifices, but the pity can also transform into a contemplation of the meaning of that sacrifice and a new understanding of herself.

This kind of introspective look clearly distinguishes itself from the 'intra-gender' or 'inter-gender' gazes that appear in failed *moga* narrative to justify and internalise patriarchal order (see Figures 2.2 and 2.3). In fact, Ozu's male characters hardly look into themselves through a mirror; their gaze is typically directed towards the outside, and thus necessitates a space between themselves and the object of the look, including women. This spatial separation can be found in other

Figure 2.6 Chikako examines the bruise on her cheek in a mirror

Figure 2.7 A stove always separates Ryōichi and Harue in *mise en scène*

cases where a visual gaze is not involved. For instance, when Ryōichi has an argument with Chikako or his girlfriend Harue, his body is positioned separately from that of the female characters. In a scene where Harue visits Ryōichi to inform him of her suspicion about Chikako's night work, Ozu deliberately places each character on either side of a stove that sits in the middle of the frame (see Figure 2.7). There are incessant movements of the two characters to and from the background while the conflict between the couple is escalating – Ryōichi is half-confused and half-angered by Harue's story about his sister – but neither of them eventually crosses the dividing line drawn by the stove. On the contrary, Ryōichi's slapping Chikako occurs when she violates this principle of gender segregation and approaches her brother over the stove line to appease his anger (see Figure 2.8).

In contrast to this 'inter-gender' segregation, the relationship between Chikako and Harue suggests a new possibility of female 'intra-gender' relationship that evades the narrative formulae of love rivalry and failed *moga* in the *shinpa* melodrama. Ozu had already tested the possibility of such sisterhood in the final scene of the previous film, *Until the Day We Meet Again*, where the protagonist woman, after sending her boyfriend off to the front at a train station, is consoled by her fellow prostitute, who sits and smokes together with her. The film, which no longer exists today, ends with a shot of the two women walking side by side on the street, the space of their everyday life.[116] This visual

Figure 2.8 Chikako violates the stove line and gets punished

comradeship develops into a lengthier and more sophisticated ending sequence in *Woman of Tokyo*. Throughout the film, Harue is depicted as a typical *ryōsai kenbo* character, without a job other than housekeeping for her older brother. She does not look in a mirror as Chikako does, and instead directs her gaze towards the masculinity of Ryōichi upon whom she can depend. Thus Harue does not understand Chikako's way of life in the outside world that destabilises her relationship with Ryōichi, and blames the couple's discord on the sister's misbehaviour saying, 'I feel sorry for Ryōichi [because you work at a bar]', to Chikako's face. In this regard, Harue's emotion is not that different to the fear, disdain or hostility that other *ryōsai kenbo* characters (such as the role of Kawasaki Hiroko in *Walk Cheerfully*) feel towards modern girl characters. The two women's relationship, however, dramatically changes in the ending sequence after Ryōichi's death. With tears in her eyes and on her cheeks, Chikako utters, 'You died for nothing' and calls Ryōichi a 'coward (*yowamushi*)' in front of his dead body. Then Harue, sitting next to Chikako and herself full of tears, slowly turns her eyes and watches Chikako's profile, which shines with the pure beauty of deepest sorrow. For Harue, this is the moment of revelation to understand and sympathise with Chikako, an intra-gender version of the sympathetic look of a housewife at her salaryman husband, as found in Ozu's *shōshimin* films (see Figures 2.9 and 2.10). The stove, which separated them from Ryōichi, is now

Figures 2.9 (upper) & 2.10 (lower) Harue watches Chikako in sorrow (compare with Figures 2.2 and 2.6)

Figure 2.11 The stove at the side conjoins the two women in one space

placed to the side of the frame in order to group the two women together in one space (see Figure 2.11).

A similar visual trope of female solidarity is found in the relationship between Tokiko and Kazuko in *Dragnet Girl* too. At the beginning, the characterisation of them follows the typical failed *moga* narrative with a sharp contrast between a model *ryōsai kenbo* and a *moga*; Tokiko, for instance, never wears a *kimono* in the film whereas Kazuko always does so. A turning point of this dichotomy appears when Tokiko meets Kazuko in person. The former originally intends to shoot the latter out of hostility towards the love rival, but (possibly) impressed by innocent Kazuko's lack of resistance, begins to like her all of a sudden. The moment of change seems too abrupt and unexplained, but the important point in this scene is that the confrontational line between a *ryōsai kenbo* and a modern girl in woman's film becomes blurred and permeable, as in the case of Chikako and Harue in *Woman of Tokyo*. Their reconciliation and unity is expressed by Tokiko's sudden approach and kiss on Kazuko's cheek, saying 'I hate to admit this, but I like you'. A rare situation in Ozu's films (not to mention between the same sex), the kiss is only indirectly suggested by a low-height camera showing Tokiko's legs approaching and withdrawing from Kazuko, followed by a shot of the latter touching her cheek in confusion. At the moment,

Figure 2.12 A kiss by *moga* and *ryōsai kenbo*

there also appears a direct contact of the two contrasting sets of female dress codes – kimono and Western suit, and *zōri* (Japanese sandals) and heeled shoes (see Figure 2.12). This unusual visual rendezvous represents the birth of the new modern femininity that overcomes the simple division between the traditional and the modern. Tokiko, already a *moga* and working woman, adopts Kazuko's domesticity as another side of her subjectivity to grow into a modern girl with a wider and fuller identity.

Regarding the woman's film, Catherine Russell raises an important argument that the female characters in the genre depict an 'unusual attitude of resistance to . . . oppressive social ills', and their troubles are 'not [theirs] alone, [but] might be in some way symptomatic of [their] station in life'; in this sense, they may not be called *moga*, but their 'behaviour and attitude are very modern'.[117] By elevating the otherwise male-centric sentimentality of the *shinpa* melodrama into a social critique, the genre could work as the true *woman's* film. Compared with the female characters in Naruse Mikio's films that Russell analyses, the ones in Ozu might look less confrontational, lacking the former's excessive emotion expressed through Naruse's flamboyant formal style. However, as seen in the relationship between Chikako and Harue, Ozu's strength lies in articulating self-realisation and mutual understanding among female characters through a slow intra-gender female gaze, which builds up a sense of feminine subjectivity and solidarity outside of the patriarchal order. The three variations of the modern Japanese women – the modern girl, working woman and housewife – discover here a way to acknowledge each other's reality and construct the trinity of modern femininity without depending upon the mediation of masculine existence and the male gaze.

It is also a significant common characteristic that the female protagonists of Ozu's woman's film in this period are all active out on the street against a backdrop of dark night under a strict gaze of surveillance by police officers. Whether they are a prostitute, barmaid or gangster's lover, the space of their everyday life crosses the beat of policemen whose eyes and steps are always in the vicinity. I have mentioned the communist reference in *Woman of Tokyo*, and *Dragnet Girl* ends in a long police chase sequence. *Until the Day We Meet Again* also begins with a night-time street scene of a patrol, where a policeman finds a strange-looking leaflet on a wall, only to realise it is just an extra reporting 'Shanghai Incident' (and he makes an 'extremely satisfied face').[118] These examples reconfirm that Ozu was very conscious of the current repressive political situation in the early 1930s after the Manchurian Incident. As Daisuke Miyao discusses with Ozu's *Sono yo no tsuma/That Night's Wife* (1930), darkness (and lighting) becomes an effective device for evoking a 'sociopolitical referent to indicate technological modernity that illuminates a dark corner on the street under constant police gaze'.[119] In the *shōshimin* films discussed above, such a mood is only alluded to through collective activities in school, but in woman's films, the threat is more visually direct and imminent, against which a melodramatic narrative of woman's sacrifice and love unfolds.

What is interesting here is the fact that Ozu does not avoid adopting *shinpa*-esque elements – suffering, emotional excessiveness and fatalism – into his everyday realism for the effect of articulating feminine subjectivity and solidarity, which eventually broadens the perspective of his cinema. As in the case of Kihachi, this change may be attributable to a commercial issue to attract more general audiences (especially the female ones that Kamata studio was exclusively aiming at) under the limitation of the silent form that Ozu could not but cling to during this period. Regardless of the background, the change constitutes a transitional point for him in the mid-1930s towards a more complete form of family drama based on complex relationships among members of both genders. This approach, along with the unique spatio-temporal sensitivity shown in the depiction of the nostalgic world in the Kihachi series, becomes the basic foundation of Ozu's postwar family dramas as well known today. The time between the late-1930s and the mid-1940s, then, can be recognised as an interim period for Ozu, composed of a long hiatus and intermittent productions due to his participation in the war. However, Ozu actually continued to make further significant developments during wartime founded upon what he had achieved in the mid-1930s, which in turn would exert a quintessential influence on his postwar cinema. The next chapter will discuss this bridging period which seamlessly connected the prewar and the postwar of Ozu.

Chapter 3
Wartime Ozu: Between Bourgeois Drama and National Policy Film

The preceding chapters have discussed the three most important tendencies of Ozu's 1930s films – the *shōshimin* film, the Kihachi film, and the woman's film – that are not merely separable in genre but also can represent three different agents of the everyday, who, distinguished by their social, economic and gender status, lead different kinds of everyday lives. The middle-class family, founded on a salaryman patriarch's waged labour, pursues the modern material life of the 1920s and 1930s, while at the same time, it suffers a fear of failure of that dream and searches for a possibility of deviation in the everyday. In contrast, Kihachi films suggest an image of the alternative everyday (albeit still male-centric) standing against what *shōshimin* film represent; deeply embedded in the nostalgic Shitamachi culture, the *shomin* class display a closed yet public world with a retrospective spatio-temporal sensitivity, in opposition to the salaryman family's 'open (towards city centre) but private' suburb. On the other hand, the female characters in the woman's film exhibit multifaceted identities from liberalised modern girl to conventional housewife, and their unique sense of sympathy and solidarity distinguish them from male characters, and set a basic generic rule of *shinpa* drama.

In the late 1930s, Ozu began to rearrange the aforementioned complex generic elements distinct from each other not only in narrative and style but also in space, class, gender and temporality to advance towards a new direction. Ozu's last two films released before he went to war, *Hitori musuko/The Only Son* (1936) and *Shukujo wa nani wo wasuretaka/What Did the Lady Forget?* (1937) respectively suggest two contrasting tendencies – comedy versus serious drama, Yamanote versus Shitamachi, bourgeois versus *shomin*, and female versus male – that would continue to be referred to in his later works, and thus can be regarded as a turning point in his cinema. This change was, of course, accompanied by the transformation of Shochiku and Japanese cinema against a backdrop of the oppressive political environment of militarism and war. This chapter first investigates a very subtle issue of how the war experience – from joining the Chinese front to enjoying Hollywood films in Singapore – influenced Ozu as an individual as well as a filmmaker; it does so by examining Ozu's biographical materials including his own writings and interviews during the war, which have not been well articulated in Ozu studies so far. That historical background is related to another question: how to position Ozu's wartime works (two films and two scripts) within the contemporary Japanese cinema, which became increasingly engulfed by the logic of wartime nationalism. Just as the relationship of the film industry to national policy was equivocal, so too was that of Ozu's films, requiring multifaceted consideration of textual evidence in conjunction with the impact of political restriction, notably by censorship.

The main focus of this chapter, however, is on finding the consistency of Ozu's wartime works in terms of the director's continuing inquiry into the everyday as having been established through his previous films. In this sense, the comparison with the aforementioned two generic trends – as represented by *The Only Son* and *What Did the Lady Forget?* – is a necessary step not only to confirm how they continued operating in an ideologically conservative environment but also to verify their connection with the director's later works in the postwar period. In particular, Ozu's attempt at dealing with the bourgeois class, which was antithetical to wartime collectivism, and the expansion of the female domestic everyday will be discussed in detail; this attempt, I believe, helped to formulate a distinctive political spectrum of everyday life during the war (and postwar as well) whether Ozu actually intended it or not. Thus the fundamental purpose of my inquiries is to re-evaluate Ozu's wartime period as a connecting bridge (rather than a long career gap and creative hiatus) between the problematics of the prewar and those of the postwar period, so that the latter, generally regarded as the pinnacle of the director's artistry, can be recognised as an 'extended history' of the former.

Coping with Militarism: Ofuna and Ozu's War Years

For both Ozu and Shochiku, the year of 1936 was a big change. In February, Ozu left his hometown Fukagawa and moved to Takanawa, a symbolic advance from a Shitamachi village on the east side of the Sumida River to a high-class residential area on the west side, where historically many *daimyo*'s mansions were located. As Bordwell points out, it may be an unreasonable interpretation to find a correlation between Ozu's moving and a 'shift to an interest in the moneyed classes' in his films; 'Ozu had made films about wealthy families before [this period], and he would make films about less well-off families afterward'.[1] However, in a symbolic sense, the move represents a shift towards bourgeois everyday life that would become an increasingly prominent theme in Ozu's films from then on. On the other hand, about a month before Ozu moved, there was another important move that marked the end of one period and the beginning of a new one; Shochiku's Kamata studio transferred to Ofuna, a ten-day undertaking that ended with a grand parade by all the employees down to the new studio.[2] It was the fruition of eighteen months of effort that had begun in 1934, when Kido, convinced that the future of Shochiku was dependent on the successful switch to the talkie, launched a plan to produce every Shochiku film with sound.[3] Meanwhile, the theatres owned by Shochiku had completed installing sound systems for exhibiting talkie films, and from April 1935, this left no *benshi* in Shochiku's cinema.[4] Shochiku also continued to expand its power in the industry by taking control of Nikkatsu as well as independent studios such as Kyokutō, and Zenshō, in order to compete with the new rival in the industry, Toho.[5] Overall, in the history of Shochiku, the second half of the 1930s marked both an end and a beginning of an era, not merely in the sense of the technological transformation but rather as a wholesale change in physical space, working staff and production policy.

This period however also corresponded with the advancement of nationalism in Japan, with the beginning of a full-scale war against China in 1937, although the war had begun in 1931 when Japan invaded Manchuria, prompting its labelling as the 'fifteen-year war' until 1945. In 1940, the front was expanded to Vietnam. America, concerned about Japan's increasing power in East Asia, responded with economic sanctions. The Pearl Harbor attack, an attempt to 'neutralize' the American forces before Japan advanced south, was only nine months away.[6] Throughout the 1930s, domestic politics in Japan had been gradually encroached upon by the influence of military expansionists. Parliamentary power waned, and in 1940, all the parties were forced to disband. Fervent patriotism based on the principle of *kokutai* and *kazoku kokka* was encouraged and became more popular. Literally translatable as 'national body', *kokutai* indicates the lineage of Japanese emperors that has descended eternally without a break. The concept was incorporated into the Meiji Constitution in 1880s, when the government tried to establish the 'sacred and inviolable' sovereignty of the emperor, and later became the basis of all kinds of ideological discourse, from *shinto* to 'moral education, patriotism, nationalism, and imperialism'.[7] When *kokutai* is applied to the concept of *kazoku kokka* (family state), all Japanese subjects are connected to the origin of the imperial family through their parent-child relationship with the emperor.

Along with the rise of nationalism, there came an attempt to re-examine and redefine the meaning of modernity in the Japanese context. The epitome of such attempts during the war is the symposium on Overcoming Modernity (*Kindai no chōkoku*) held in 1942, which was serialised in the literary magazine *Bungakukai* (*Literary Society*) and then also published as a book in 1943.[8] Prominent Japanese intellectuals from various fields participated in the symposium and discussed the issue of modernity that had been the primary agenda of the nation since its adoption from the West in the Meiji era. The discussion had not reached any meaningful, concrete conclusion, which, as Sun Ge argues, could be due to the oppositional position between the two major groups of participants, namely, literary critics (such as Kobayashi Hideo and Kamei Katsuichirō) and historians/philosophers of the Kyoto School (such as Nishitani Keiji and Suzuki Shigetaka).[9] The symposium nonetheless occupies a significant position in the intellectual history of Japan as it was the first organised effort of intellectuals to raise any serious doubt about the modernisation process after the Meiji Restoration. It thus can be understood as a self-examination and confession by Japanese intellectuals who were 'certainly at a loss [at the time of the Pacific War], for [their] Japanese blood that had previously been the true driving force behind [their] intellectual activity was now in conflict with [their] Europeanised intellects'.[10]

During the symposium, some of the participants displayed strong convictions about the detrimental results of Japan's modernisation on the Western model. Kamei Katsuichirō, the literary critic active in *Bungakukai*, who also first proposed the idea of the symposium, characterised the modern history of the nation after the Meiji period with the words 'vulgarisation', 'standardisation' and the 'decline of sensitivity [towards subtleties that traditional culture had retained]'.[11] For another critic Hayashi Fusao, the contemporary civilisation meant the 'emergence of utilitarian bureaucratism, functional specialisation, and mass production and consumerism'.[12] Kamei thus concluded: 'I believe that our greatest enemy is that swiftly changing mode of civilisation that, ever since the influx of the West's dying culture of "modernity", has steadily violated the deepest recesses of spirit while producing all manner of daydreams and garrulity'.[13]

It is not difficult to see how the interest in reviving the Japanese 'blood' and 'spirit' could be extended to the Japanese intellectuals' view on the recent beginning of the war against the West. The war thus was double-sided, against the enemy both outside and within. In Kamei's own words, 'externally, the war that we are currently fighting represents the overthrow of British and American power, while internally it represents the basic cure for the spiritual disease brought about by modern civilisation'.[14] And the two fronts justified each other; the encroached state of the Japanese spirit explained the need to fight against the Western enemies, while the outbreak of the war clarified the problems of Japanese modernity that had been harassing intellectuals. Even those who had not been able to easily persuade themselves of the case for war with China could accept the reason for war with the US. For example, Takasugi Ichirō, the writer and critic who despised Japan's invasion of China, understood Japan's attack on the United States as a 'defensive' one, identical to the Soviet Union's attack on Germany in World War II, and he thus could support the Pacific War without hesitation.[15] The same resolution of moral dilemma can be felt in an article by Kawakami Tetsutarō, written two days after the beginning of the war and published in *Bungakukai* in 1942 before he took the role of moderator in the Overcoming Modernity symposium later in the same year: 'I can say I'm feeling so clear. How vague and unpleasant a chaotic, gloomy peace is, compared to the purity of war!'[16]

In politics, the re-evaluation of Japanese identity over Western modernity became the ideological basis of the Japanese wartime government, which began to apply it to regulating broader sections of society including not only the economy but also cultural spheres such as education and media. Ofuna, along with other studios, was largely influenced by this historical change. The Japanese government's intention to maintain control over the film industry had already emerged by the mid-1930s, and culminated in the establishment of the Film Law (*eigahō*) in 1939 which stipulated rules such as pre-production censorship, a licence system for film business, and the registration of actors, directors and cinematographers.[17] In the next year, these rules were followed by a limit on the number of films that could be produced (forty-eight a year for each major studio). These efforts to control the industry eventually reached their climax in 1941 with the enforced merger of ten film studios into three (Shochiku, Toho and the newly established Daiei), each of which was allowed to produce two films a month. Such a severe measure was passed by the Information Bureau (Jōhōkyoku), which also took on the power of sponsoring as well as prohibiting certain materials. The Information Bureau's apparent reason for restricting the film industry was the limited supply of negative film; as addressed by a division manager in the office, 'Since raw film for filmmaking is munitions, a mere one foot cannot be transferred for civilian use'[18]

Films that advocated individualism and Western culture were discouraged while an essential Japaneseness, which could persuasively justify national unity under the emperor, was pursued by the government. According to Davis, the ardent desire to search for the 'authentic Japanese essence' was 'never higher' than in the 1930s. The attempt could be characterised by its institutional and 'prescriptive' nature; various kinds of organisations and mass media were devoted to the pursuit of the Japaneseness as the government contrived. Cinema, the recipient of a particular interest due to its visual accessibility and propagandist nature, gradually found a unique way to depict more traditional Japan, which Davis named 'monumental style'.[19] A related term in contemporary Japanese cinema was 'spiritist film', which prioritises the unique Japanese spirit that an individual should realise for oneself through a spiritual voyage in narrative. Essentially a masculine genre, the spiritist film features 'fiery determination, fanatical devotion to duty, and martial valor' in the male characters, often expressed in the form of military training, while their female counterparts, largely devoid of independence and individuality, act a subsidiary role as 'observers of the spiritual dramas'.[20] The 'prophet and high priest' of this genre was the critic Sawamura Tsutomu, who also wrote the scripts for two spiritist films, *Shanhai rikusentai/The Naval Brigade at Shanghai* (1939) and *Shidō monogatari/A Story of Leadership* (1941), both directed by Kumagai Hisatora.[21] According to Sawamura, the mission of cinema is 'not simply to be "fun" or even "artistically excellent"' but to 'serve the state and the lives of its people', and to that end, 'lethargic hedonism' or 'purely escapist fare' in *shōshimin* films and comedies should be avoided.[22]

In this regard, Shochiku was in a more disadvantaged position than other studios in terms of handling ideological surveillance and regulation. In July 1938 and again in August 1940, the authorities in charge of film censorship at the Ministry of Home Affairs decided upon a list of guidelines for filmmaking, which could be summarised as the 'exaltation of Japanese spirit' while excluding the 'infiltration of individualistic tendencies influenced by Western films'.[23] This was a clear obstacle for Shochiku, whose *Kamata-chō* (or *Ōfuna-chō* as it was called after the move to Ofuna) had been advocating a Western style in line with modern trends. For instance, the themes, content and imagery that the Ministry of Home Affairs specifically prohibited – 'female smoking', 'drinking in cafés', 'frivolous language and action' and '*shōshimin eiga* [that] depicts only the happiness of the individual' – were on the list of Shochiku's specialties as revealed in the studio's subject matter, style, genre and targeted audiences.[24] The Ministry of Home Affairs' view, however, also confirms the nature of the *Ōfuna-chō* film as an advocate of individualism and urban everyday life in opposition to the totalitarianism and industrial production activities that the government was encouraging.

Shochiku's crisis – the confrontation between its identity and the state's ideology – can be more precisely understood when the situation of the other studios is taken into account. In the late 1930s, when the government-controlled system went into top gear, Shochiku enjoyed a short period of success – its revenue in 1939 reached 19,875,000 Yen, a 50 per cent increase on the previous fiscal year – largely helped by the success of a series of melodramatic films that were 'removed as far as possible from the political arena'.[25] Kido himself mentioned that he had intended to give wartime audiences 'consolation' and 'relaxation' with Shochiku-style entertainments.[26] Represented by such popular films as *Kon'yaku sanba garasu/The Trio's Engagement* (Shimazu Yasujirō, 1937), *Aizen katsura/The Love-Troth Tree* (Nomura Hiromasa, 1938), *Shin josei mondō/New Woman's Dialogue* (Sasaki Yasushi, 1939), *Junjō nijūso/Naïve Duet* (Sasaki Yasushi, 1939), and *Danryū/Warm Current* (Yoshimura Kōzaburō, 1939), this late 1930s 'Shochiku boom' benefitted from the fact that 'other studios' films that were reflecting wartime circumstances' more or less excluded female audiences.[27] Among these, *The Love-Troth Tree*, directed by Nomura Hiromasa ('Shochiku's best entertainment director') and its leading role played by Tanaka Kinuyo, was Shochiku's representative melodrama in this period, which became 'the greatest box-office sensation in prewar and wartime Japanese film history'.[28] Standish presents this film as an example of the studio's rendition of the 'modern woman', a 'move away from the "pathetic" *shinpa*-derived melodramas chronicling women's suffering towards an alternative conception of womanhood'.[29] Although still retaining *shinpa*'s elements, such as a single mother's struggle to raise her daughter, the film does not fall into the trap of emotionalism, and emphasises the female protagonist's independent identity as a working woman, closer to the model of modern Japanese woman I discussed in the previous chapter.

In contrast, while Shochiku was releasing a series of melodramas, Nikkatsu produced such war movie classics as *Gonin no sekkōhei/Five Scouts* (1938) and *Tsuchi to heitai/Mud and Soldiers* (1939) both directed by Tasaka Tomotaka. Toho was also very quick to 'cooperate with the military and government in [its] production policy' and release 'films with a sense of the current situation' such as *The Naval Brigade at Shanghai* and *Moyuru ōzora/Flaming Sky* (Abe Yutaka, 1940).[30] As the war in China developed into the Pacific War and governmental control became accordingly stricter, Shochiku's ongoing 'feminine' and 'entertainment-centred' policy became more awkward and 'irritating (*jirettai*)' to the authorities, and was criticised as 'cartilage cinema, almost lacking social sensibility'.[31] Among film critics, Tsumura Hideo, who argued for active state control over the film industry, was critical of *Ōfuna-chō*'s effeminacy. One of the participants of the Overcoming Modernity symposium, he advocated a 'war of culture' against Americanism which he defined as 'our greatest enemy'.[32] What he therefore demanded of Japanese cinema was 'spirit' or 'the will of the man who lives by ideal or faith', and thus most entertainment films that lacked this willpower became the target of his criticism.[33] For the sake of national unity in the era of total war, Tsumura also emphasised the importance of films set in the provinces dealing with provincial people, such as *Bakuon/Airplane Drone* (Tasaka Tomotaka, 1939), *Tsuchi/Earth* (Uchida Tomu, 1939) and *Kojima no haru/Spring on Leper's Island* (Toyoda Shiro, 1940), contrasting them with Shochiku's 'contemporary urban life' films.[34] Such a stance reflected governmental policy as well; the Ministry of Home Affairs actually suggested that, instead of *shōshimin* film, Shochiku should produce 'films dealing with rural life' that could visualise the labour of farmers.[35] In light of this situation, it can be reconfirmed that Shochiku's tenet, whether it is high Western modernity or more *shinpa*-flavoured, feminine emotionalism, was founded upon private and everyday interests that could not but bear an uncomfortable relationship with the greater social initiatives during the wartime.

After 1940, Shochiku finally turned to making war movies, starting with Yoshimura Kōzaburō's *Nishizumi senshachōden/Legend of Tank Commander Nishizumi* (1940). Its *jidaigeki* division in Kyoto also established a new company, Kōaeiga, and produced historical materials with nationalistic ideas such as Mizoguchi Kenji's *Genroku chūshingura/The Loyal Forty-seven Ronin* (1941-2). However, such a transition in policy was not without trouble, as seen in an anecdote about the difficulty of finding the director for *Legend of Tank Commander Nishizumi*. After all, Yoshimura Kōzaburō's direction of the film was closer to 'Ōfuna-chō's home drama style' than 'war spirit exaltation' with the depiction of the protagonist in the battlefield as an 'ordinary young man' rather than a war hero.[36] High includes the film within the 'genre of "humanist" war films' along with Tosaka's *Five Scouts* and *Mud and Soldiers*, where the individuality of soldiers is articulated in harmony with the group. The 'humanism' in the genre supposes 'a continuity of personality stretching from the character's life at home to his actions, thoughts, and sensations at the front'.[37] Thus 'some pathetic aspect of the human condition: mortality, fallibility, or frailty' is stressed and frankly acknowledged through an individual character faced with war.[38] However, according to High, this 'humanist' tradition in Japanese war films would gradually transform into other perceptions of humanity such as 'nonhumanness', which negated humane feelings involved in war as found in 'spiritist' films, and 'new humanism', which, instead of promoting the universality of humanism, promoted a regionalised version of it centring on the relationship between Japan and the surrounding East Asian community.[39]

Overall, during the 1940s until the end of the war, 'most Shochiku movies suffered confusion and dullness', making the company look like a 'straggler behind the times'.[40] The slump would have felt even more bitter by comparison with Toho's continuing success with such a big budget, grand-scale war movie as *Hawai marei-oki kaisen/The War at Sea from Hawaii to Malaya* (Yamamoto Kajirō, 1942), the enormous popularity of which signalled 'the new round of spiritist films of the Pacific War period'.[41] After all, as Masumoto points out, the nature of filmmaking in Shochiku hardly left space for the 'manliness of the "state" or the enormity of the "government"'.[42] That discrepancy or distance between the studio and politics was both a strength and a weakness for Shochiku, a state which would persist even after the war, as discussed in the following chapters.

Ozu occupied a very peculiar position in this turbulent war period. Along with Yoshimura Kōzaburō, Shima Kōji, Yamamoto Satsuo and Koishi Eiichi, he was one of a handful of Japanese directors at that time who actually experienced the front as a soldier and returned alive. Furthermore, Ozu went to war twice; once conscripted as an infantryman in China in 1937 and the second time in 1943 to make a propaganda film in Singapore for the military. What has been mainly referred to (and mythologised) by Ozu scholars in the West so far is the days in Singapore (Shōnan under Japanese occupation), where Ozu spent a more relaxed time than in China, an unexpected piece of luck in the circumstances of war. The role he was given was to make a semi-documentary that dealt with the activities of the Indian National Army led by Subhas Chandra Bose. Its purpose was to encourage the anti-British movement among southeast Asian people, in a similar way to other films advocating the ideal of *Daitōa Kyōeiken* (the Greater East Asia Co-prosperity Sphere) such as *Ano hata o ute/The Dawn of Freedom* (1944). However, due to the worsening war situation in Malay where the filming was originally planned to take place, Ozu had to remain in Singapore and, being unable to progress the project, spent days reading, playing tennis and watching Hollywood films.

In contrast, Ozu participated in real action on the Chinese front. He received a draft note in September 1937, and consequently landed in Shanghai later in the same month to be assigned to the Second Company for Field Gas Operation belonging to the Shanghai Expeditionary Army (see Figure 3.1). His rank was initially corporal but he was later promoted to sergeant, leading a squad of his own. His main duty was transport and communication.[43] A newspaper report thus described him as waving the Japanese national flag to control the passage of trucks, and Ozu himself left records of transporting the remains of Japanese soldiers in a truck, which would later be used as a motif in his wartime films, as will be discussed.[44] Therefore it is more likely that he was not directly involved in actual battles, even though the company he belonged

Figure 3.1 Ozu, an imperial soldier, in Jiujiang, China (owned by the Ozu family and provided by the Kamakura Museum of Literature)

to was responsible for poison gas warfare. Nevertheless, it is also true that his company took part in most of the major operations in the Central China region including Shanghai, Nanjing, Hankou and Wuchang. It is especially intriguing that Ozu's unit was stationed around Nanjing at the time of the city's fall and ensuing massacre, although it is not certain whether Ozu himself entered the city and observed what was happening. The most severe warfare he endured was the Xiu River Crossing Operation in March 1939, when Ozu took a role of digging trenches in front of the enemy, followed by long marches suffering from thirst and lack of sleep.[45] But the bitterest experience he had at the Chinese front could possibly be the loss of his close fellow filmmaker Yamanaka Sadao, who was also drafted and died of acute enteritis in September 1938 at the age of just twenty-eight.[46] His untimely death had a great impact on Ozu, who, reading Yamanaka's will, 'was utterly struck by [the deceased's] ardent passion about film even during war' and 'since then, regretting [his] indolence, began studying again'.[47] However, after returning, Ozu admitted that the days in China had made him 'almost alienated from the world of cinema', leaving only 'the self as a soldier'.[48]

In what way the war experience exerted an influence on Ozu – both as a human being and a filmmaker – is not an easy question to answer definitively. Surely, as discussed in the previous chapters, war itself had already begun to appear in Ozu's films even before he went to war, as a minor narrative motif to imply a contemporary socio-political atmosphere; putting aside the collectivistic school class scenes in *shōshimin* films, the male protagonist in *Until the Day We Meet Again* is about to leave for the front, and in *College Is a Nice Place*, there appear students being disciplined in a military drill. Ozu, however, would never complete a war film that directly dealt with the subject matter whether during wartime or after the war, even though he attempted a few times. Nevertheless, it is still possible to conjecture his thoughts on war through quite a number of interviews he did on returning home from China in 1939, and through his own writings including diary and personal notes. In the interviews, Ozu repeatedly emphasised that the most important change during the war was that he came to possess a 'positive spirit' to accept the horror of war as it is, and to get used to it. Such a positive spirit, though recalling the spiritist film, is not so much related to the spirit of Japaneseness as to an ability to remain calm amidst the extremely precarious conditions of war, as explained in the following remark of his.

> The battlefield is not scary at all. Sometimes bullets are literally showering. There was once an occasion when the bridge for retreat was cut off and our troops were surrounded by a gang of bandits. But I didn't feel that frightened because, after all, a soldier has already got used to such a reality . . . The battlefield [thus] becomes a place for everyday occurrences for soldier.[49]

Such familiarisation with the reality of war (or 'quotidianisation of war'), however, can also imply a danger of apathy towards the atrocities encountered in everyday situations, a state of 'nonhumanness' in High's term. Ozu left some frank impressions of carnage and destruction of war, which could have made him reach a conclusion that war is about having the positive spirit to accept any phenomenon as it is.

> War seems to mean demolishing houses. You somehow get to feel that it is alright to do that at war.[50]

> Killing people with sword looks just like in *jidaigeki*. You swing, and the body remains still for a while before finally falling down . . . I became able to keep calm enough to notice such a minute detail.[51]

It may have something to do with my experiencing the Great Kanto Earthquake, but when I first saw the deserted dead bodies of the enemy, it was nothing. I didn't feel anything... A soldier always has to face a reality [of life and death] and all the other matters are unnecessary.[52]

Ozu, however, further develops this idea of the quotidianisation of war. What actually draws his attention is less the positive spirit itself than the 'psychological process' for the soldier to have such a mindset. For Ozu, the 'soldier is originally a complex being', in the sense that they bring diverse social and personal backgrounds – education, occupation, wealth and social group (especially family) – when enlisted.[53] The military is a place where these complex backgrounds are enforcedly simplified through rules and disciplines. This simplification process requires from soldiers a 'great psychological leap' between that original complexity and well-disciplined martialism. Ozu argues that war films or literature should focus on this deep individual psychology and the way in which it is *incompletely* transformed into a simplified, 'positive spirit' at war:

> [A soldier] retains deep psychological [conflict] until the end without being able to completely getting rid of it. Even the one who immediately cleared it off returns to it again when he feels the final end is near. [War literature] should write on this psychological depth and the process through which the depth is abandoned and becomes simplified.[54]

He thus criticises popular literature and reportage on war – Hino Ashihei's novel *Tsuchi to heitai/Mud and Soldiers* (1939) being a representative example – which fail to deal with the psychological transformation of soldier characters and instead depict them in too simplistic a way – as either heroic or humanistic, comparable to a 'brave samurai appearing in children's books'.[55] This problem is due to the fact that such writers have merely superficial knowledge on war obtained through short visits to the front before writing, yet without actually participating in war as a soldier under strict discipline.[56]

Ozu's perspective on war can thus be summarised as a continuing process of balancing individual psychology, which is complicated by one's past background and experiences, and the apparent quotidianness of battles and life in barracks, which is formulated and governed by military rules and disciplines. A soldier can struggle with horror or homesickness but these personal conflicts eventually subordinate to the everyday reality of war and the need to fight and survive. The reverse may apply too: behind the well-disciplined everyday activities, there still exist anxieties and pain encroaching on soldiers' psychology. This bidirectional switching process differs from a unidirectional narrative of 'growing up' through one's spiritual pursuit in the spiritist films. It is also distinguishable from the naïve heroism of humanist films; as High points out, Ozu emphasised 'the radical *dis*-continuity separating the psychology of the civilian from that of the soldier' in opposition to the humanist film's emphasis on continuity of personality.[57] As mentioned, his main interest was rather in tracing the changing process from psychological continuity to discontinuity. Ozu's view thus can be situated between the two major tendencies in the Japanese war film, more in line with his typical position of everyday realism and deviation.

Such a focus on the individual psychology of Japanese soldiers, however, leaves unexplored and disregarded a huge issue regarding war: the enemy, namely the Chinese people including the soldiers whom Ozu encountered at the front. As the contemporary Japanese cinema tended to elide the existence of the enemy, Ozu's view of China was more or less a superficial one lacking deep knowledge of its history and culture, hence his attitude could not but remain one of objectifying the country and people at a distance. This does not mean that he was entirely uninterested in the first Asian, not to mention foreign, country he ever visited. Ozu was particularly drawn to writings in Chinese characters; whenever an occasion offered, he transcribed them in detail into his notes. An extreme example is a lengthy Chinese pamphlet for propaganda guidelines (対敵士兵宣伝標語集), published by the Nationalist Government and written in both Japanese and Chinese, to be used for propaganda manoeuvres as well as Japanese-language education for Chinese soldiers.[58] Going around Chinese towns, Ozu also witnessed anti-Japanese slogans and drawings attached to walls and doors, which he recorded in his diary.[59] It is not certain why Ozu carefully transcribed these Chinese writings, but he at least had an interest in (and was aware of) the opposite perspective of the war from the Chinese point of view. This experience of the 'other', however, did not seem to lead to a change of his own idea about the war; counter-examined with his writings and interviews, there is little possibility that Ozu sympathised with any form of anti-Japanese or anti-imperialistic discourse of the war. In an interview in 1939, he introduced an anecdote about Chinese prisoners who were brainwashed by the Chinese government's anti-Japanese propaganda to believe that China was winning the war and would soon invade Japan. Utterly dumbfounded, Ozu showed a pitiful, if not contemptuous, reaction, saying 'nothing is as dreadful as ignorance'.[60] In fact, compared to Japanese soldiers, Chinese soldiers were hardly characterised as human beings with a voice in Ozu's accounts, their existence often being replaced by flying bullets and grenades that threatened the lives of Japanese soldiers. Under this circumstance, it is unimaginable that Chinese anti-war leaflets could ever be effective for Japanese soldiers, whose only concern was about fighting and surviving in battle.[61] It can be inferred then that Ozu was faithful to his position and role as an imperial soldier, and in that respect, I agree with Peter High's argument that Ozu was 'patriotically convinced of the essential rightness of his nation's cause during the war', even though he was not a 'craven, undiscerning collaborator with the proto-fascist regime of the Fifteen Years' War era'.[62]

Ozu's stance on Chinese soldiers can be extended to his view of Chinese civilians as well. According to his diary, Ozu's troop often approached the Chinese to do barter or requisition foods, which must have given him a chance to contact local people and experience local cultures.[63] But lack of background knowledge and language proficiency seems to have eventually worked as an obstacle to his having a deeper understanding of them. In an interview, Ozu confessed that although he came across many famous temples and historical sites in China, he could not help feeling at a loss viewing them without knowing the historical context behind them.[64] His diary, though recording occasional meetings with civilians, also keeps silent about their real voices. Among them, the most intriguing one would be when Ozu encountered comfort women (*ianfu*) in several places; his diary describes in great detail who the women were (in Yingcheng, there were three Koreans and twelve Chinese), and the rules for Japanese soldiers to use the service (no alcohol, keeping sanitary, admission times, prices and so on).[65] It is, however, unlikely that Ozu actually approached those women in person, as can be presumed from an anecdote that unable to go to sleep one night owing to the noises from such a facility, he yelled out to them to keep it quiet.[66] Ozu's attitude, after all, still remains that of objective observer from a distanced position, just as when he recorded Chinese propaganda writings.

Therefore, setting aside his personal curiosity about China and Chinese culture, it would be reasonable to conclude that Ozu in China had a limited perspective in terms of reducing the distance between himself and the East Asian sphere beyond a necessary boundary required for an imperial soldier. It is a revealing fact, especially considering that this war was a rare opportunity allowed to few Japanese directors to leave their home country and contact a massive number of other East Asian people. This does not mean that China was not an influence on Ozu and his cinema. Ozu studies so far have noted the appearance of China (or Manchuria) as a narrative element in Ozu's wartime and postwar films. *The Brothers and Sisters of the Toda Family* (1941) is a notable example, where China is suggested as a land of a promising future, which some critics have argued implies an imperialistic justification of Japan's invasion into the country.[67] More recently, a Japanese scholar Yonaha Jun argues for a more active interpretation of the Chinese element in Ozu's cinema as a trope of transnationality, which would question the long established tendency of attaching the myth of pure Japaneseness and stable family to Ozu's films. For instance, Yonaha aptly points out that the colonial cities mentioned in Ozu's wartime and postwar films – Tenshin in *The Toda Family*, Dalian in *Munekata kyōdai/The Munekata Sisters* (1950) and Keijō (Seoul) in *Tōkyō boshoku/Tokyo Twilight* (1957) – can commonly represent a postcolonial space where 'the afterimage of empire' lingers on, and as such present a setting for a more precarious type of familial relationship distinguished from the mythologised harmonious family spatially situated within mainland Japan.[68] However, the use of transnational space *per se*, albeit expanding the scope of narrative and theme, is not necessarily connected to a transnational consciousness that would include a concern for 'others' beyond national boundary. In this regard, mentioning China in Ozu's postwar films is related more closely to postcolonial nostalgia from the imperial centre's perspective than transnational imagination, mostly narrated through male characters who remember war experiences, as will be discussed in the next chapter.

As mentioned, since Ozu never made a film that deals with war as a central subject matter, it is not easy to investigate how his experience of war – whether individual psychology or encounter with the enemy – influenced his filmmaking. During the war – more exactly, the intermediate period of repatriation from 1939 to 1943 – Ozu directed two films, the aforementioned *The Toda Family* (1941) and *There Was a Father* (1942) – and wrote two scripts, *Ochazuke no aji/The Flavour of Green Tea over Rice* (1940) and *Biruma sakusen: Harukanari fubo no kuni/Burma Campaign: Far away from Motherland* (1942), neither of which could be made into films due to the military government's pre-production censorship. Among these four, *Burma Campaign* is the only project that can be defined within the generic term of war film, which thus can be examined in the context of Ozu's war experiences discussed so far. It is, however, an interesting fact that *Burma Campaign* is also Ozu's last work before his being re-drafted and leaving for Singapore, that is, he was delaying making war films for a substantial period of time after coming back from China. The first project he worked on, *The Flavour of Green Tea over Rice*, was hardly a war film but a typical Ozu-style family drama with a comic tone, focusing on the everyday life of a bourgeois family with the depiction of trouble and reconciliation between a husband and a wife. As in the case of the talkie, it was certain technical issues in production that seem to have contributed to Ozu's hesitation in making a war film.[69] Nevertheless, the move suggests that everyday realism was still operating as the fundamental of Ozu's cinema even during wartime, in a continuous form connecting the time immediately before he went to war and the postwar period when bourgeois drama would repeatedly appear. The next section will explore this continuity of the everyday in *The Flavour of Green Tea over Rice* before moving on to a discussion of *Burma Campaign* and other films in the final part.

Bourgeois Ladies and the Gender Politics of the Everyday

It was towards the end of the year he returned from China in 1939 when Ozu began work on *The Flavour of Green Tea over Rice* (working title: *Kare shi Nankin e iku/He Goes to Nanking*) with his long-time collaborative writer Ikeda Tadao. As mentioned, Ozu's original intention with the project was to make a comedy (*kigeki*). According to Ozu, the choice of the comedy genre was not irrelevant to his experience of war and resulting belief in the 'positive spirit', an attitude of accepting everything about war and continuing one's everyday life as it is in order to survive. It seems such a wartime philosophy even demanded self-criticism and revision of his former critical consciousness in themes that had distinguished his everyday realism from that of *Kamata-chō*. Ozu thus said:

> There is a need of relief and hope for the future in cinema, and in that sense, my works so far can be strictly criticized by myself before anyone else. For example, such films as *The Only Son* and *I Was Born But . . .* were an unfinished sort, and I think those have been made so far by another Ozu Yasujiro [different from who I am now]. After all, 'I was born but . . .' is not an essential emotion for a human being; we should rather appreciate the fact that we are born to this world.[70]

It can be inferred, then, that the experience of war ironically made the director decide to return to the early *Kamata-chō* style, even denying his past achievement in *shōshimin* films. It is not certain whether this was a result of compromise and complacency, or if he intended a satire on and allusion to political reality, but it is at least true that the new project would be placed out of the context of contemporary Japanese cinema. As Bordwell points out, 'the Ofuna comedy of manners was rare now, and the film's humorous aspects were out of keeping with the aims of war films and home-front women's pictures'.[71]

The concern turned out to be a reality; the completed script was rejected by the censorship board, resulting in the unusual cessation of the project in early 1940. Overall, *The Flavour of Green Tea over Rice* deals with a conflict and reconciliation between a husband (Mokichi) and wife (Ayako) of a bourgeois family. Ayako, who was reluctantly married to Mokichi through *omiai* (arranged marriage), is not fond of Mokichi's plain personality and simple lifestyle. (While the former is from Tokyo's high-class Kōjimachi district, the latter comes from rural Nagano.) As if to resist her unwanted fate, Ayako does not care for her home, and enjoys leisured life outside with her female friends, dining out in Ginza or going on a trip to a hot spring. However, on the night when Mokichi receives a draft notice, his calm attitude deeply impresses Ayako, and the couple finally reconcile with each other while eating a bowl of *ochazuke* (green tea over rice). It is known that this *ochazuke* eating was the scene that the censors frowned upon because the dish was too humble in style to encourage a man who goes to war; instead, *sekihan* (red rice) was to be served. However, in a retrospective reading of it, the more serious problem of the script that must have made the censors uncomfortable is the female protagonist Ayako, who not only ignores her role as a housewife of a bourgeois family, but also shows an insolent and recalcitrant attitude towards Mokichi. There appear such scenes as her smoking or leaving home without telling her husband, not to mention her frivolous behaviour and luxurious lifestyle with her friends throughout the script, which, as Satō Tadao points out, look antithetic to the aforementioned guidelines for filmmaking implemented by the Ministry of Home Affairs, which wanted to restrict the 'infiltration of individual tendency' on screen.[72] Tanaka Masasumi also agrees that the conduct of the bourgeois ladies in the script was 'too realistically depicted to fit the morals of the times'.[73]

In contrast, this view of the censors is the opposite to the interpretation of Bordwell, who sees the script as an 'ideal piece of home-front morale-boosting', and thus finds it 'surprising' that the script could not pass censorship.[74] His position is based on an interpretation that Ayako and Mokichi's reconciliation comes as a result of the latter imposing his patriarchal power on the former. The key evidence Bordwell suggests for this argument is a moment when Mokichi abruptly slaps Ayako 'criticis[ing] her selfishness', which Bordwell reads as a 'reminder of her patriotic duty'.[75] In the last sequence of the script, where Ayako tells her friends about the night of the slapping, she reveals an apologetic and repentant feeling towards her husband, and as such, the domestic violence can fit in the 'failed *moga*' narrative discussed in the previous chapter. However, even if the narrative eventually ends up with a moral lesson that (intentionally or inadvertently) acknowledges the recuperation of masculinity in domesticity, the process is still far from being oppressive; not only is no actual slapping shown – the incident is only verbally 'told' during a lengthy conversation among females – but it only happens in the context of the couple's mutual reconfirmation of their love for each other when faced with the husband's impending departure for the battlefield.[76] Moreover, Mokichi himself is not a patriarchal figure – he shows a consistently gentle and generous attitude towards Ayako's misbehaviour – not to mention the fact that he is hardly patriotic. He has an easy-going personality and leads a simple lifestyle, keeping his stance unshaken by the changing world, as exemplified in the scene where Ayako, hearing about Mokichi's receiving the draft notice, hurriedly returns home from her trip to find that the husband is sound asleep and snoring, as if nothing had happened. An incarnation of the 'positive spirit' that Ozu advocated, Mokichi's equanimity and carefreeness in the face of war deeply moves Ayako's heart, leading to the couple's final reconciliation. The story is then less about the moral edification of a spoiled wife to serve a nationalistic concern, than a family melodrama, the narrative of which is constructed around a domestic conflict between man and woman, with 'going to war' becoming a motive for recovering the troubled relationship.

The Flavour of Green Tea over Rice is a *bourgeois* family drama as well, and Ozu is not reserved in revealing the fact and exploring the everyday details of bourgeois domesticity. The primary setting of the script is mansions in Tokyo's upscale areas such as Akasaka and Sendagaya, where characters live a comfortable life attended by housemaids, who move around separate rooms and long corridors. Other spatial signs of affluence abound such as a private bathroom, which could have been the only such scene in Ozu if it had been made into a film, and a golf course, which would reappear in postwar salaryman dramas. In terms of characterisation, Mokichi is a hardworking businessman in a trading company, whose recent concern is securing a sufficient number of shipping vessels, which is becoming more and more difficult under wartime regulation. In opposition, Ayako is depicted as a spendthrift, still receiving subsidies from her wealthy father, and hanging out in the city until late at night. This bourgeois lifestyle and its gender differences are the particular subject matter of Ozu in this period, a new tendency that began from his previous film *What Did the Lady Forget?*, released before Ozu went to China, and continued to be partially adopted in the next film, *The Toda Family*.[77]

What Did the Lady Forget?, as the first instalment of this 'bourgeois trilogy', marks a significant turning point in Ozu's filmography. A 'wry, affectionate, and ironic domestic comedy' showing a strong sense of urban modernity, the film was actually not the first time the director had dealt with a high-class family as his subject matter (*Shukujo to hige/The Lady and the Beard*, 1931; *Seishun no yume ima izuko/Where Are the Dreams of Youth?*, 1932; and *Haha o kowazuya/A Mother Should Be Loved*, 1934, are such precedents). However, as Ozu remembered, it could be the first time he articulated a wealthy Yamanote district as a setting being conscious of its contrast to the working-class Shitamachi district that had largely become the geographical background of his films from the mid-1930s.[78] Bordwell argued that such 'a shift to a bourgeois milieu was a general Shochiku trend around 1937' as Kido Shiro, 'always alert for a fad that would attract a female audience, probably sensed that public interest had drifted from *ero-guro-nansensu* to melodrama and satire involving the privileged classes'.[79] Sawamura Tsutomu also regarded *What Did the Lady Forget?* as a new turn for the director in that it combined the three separate genre branches in the previous Ozu's films, namely Kihachi film, student or salaryman dramas, and other 'romanticism' films.[80] Therefore it can be evaluated that Ozu, backed by the trend shift in the industry and having fully explored various genre types, began to actively pursue the detailed picture of the bourgeois and female everyday through the generic form of comedy, a new perspective on class and gender that anticipates one of the quintessential narratives of his later postwar films. In this sense, *What Did the Lady Forget?*, along with the other wartime bourgeois films, becomes a prototype of Ozu's late salaryman dramas such as *Equinox Flower* (1958) and *Late Autumn* (1960), not to mention *Ochazuke no aji/The Flavour of Green Tea over Rice* (1952), the postwar remake based on the wartime script of the same title. Even the very last work of Ozu, a script of the television drama *Seishun hōkago/Youth after School* (1963) is within the sphere of *What Did the Lady Forget?*'s influence, with the same basic narrative of a young female protagonist visiting a wealthy family of relatives in Tokyo.[81]

The subject matter of the urban bourgeoisie, which presents a proof of continuity in Ozu's cinema between wartime and the postwar, can be contrasted with another continuous meta-subject of the life of *shomin* and *shōshimin*, which runs through various genres from the *shōshimin* film to the Kihachi series discussed in previous chapters. The contrast can be roughly paraphrased by a generic term of comedy and melodrama, or in a stylistic term of *Kamata-chō* and *shinpa*, the two contradictory yet coexisting elements of Ozu's films. If *What Did the Lady Forget?* marked a new beginning of the former tendency, it was *Hitori musuko/The Only Son* (1936) that summed up the latter while suggesting a newer direction. Ozu's first feature film in talkie, *The Only Son*, tells a story about a white-collar salaryman, who comes to Tokyo from a rural village to graduate from college and pursue a successful career, only to find himself struggling to survive as a poorly paid night school teacher. As such, the narrative seems to capitalise on the same *risshin shusse* ideology (and its failure in Showa period) as already exploited in the *shōshimin* films. The film, however, is distinguishable in its articulation of the hometown where the protagonist is from, the temporal origin of the salaryman drama as well as a spatial counterpart of Tokyo. In other words, *The Only Son* narrativises the pre-history of the salaryman that Ozu's previous salaryman films failed to suture.

The hometown in the film is, as in Kihachi's Shitamachi neighbourhood, based on a multilayered spatiality, not only a real space that incessantly changes through time, but also an imagined, nostalgic one retaining the proto-vision of the past. According to Narita Ryūichi, hometown, for migrated workers in Japan, is not an 'actuality' but a 'constituted' space based upon an assumed commonality in the 'time called history, space called landscape ... and emotion called language', which is repetitively told and confirmed through stories, poems, songs and images.[82] An example of the real-life replacement of this imaginary hometown is the Asakusa district in Tokyo, which, as mentioned in

Chapter 2, constitutes a hometown space that symbolises receptive communalism. Physically located in Tokyo, the migrants endlessly yearn for their place of origin, which, however, was more an illusion than a reality.[83] In Narita Ryūichi's term, they thus begin to develop a 'compound identity' formed in the 'relation' between things rural and urban.[84] For Ozu, such a distance between city and hometown, and the schizophrenic conflict between the real and imaginary were first suggested in *The Only Son* through a combination of the *shōshimin* film and the Kihachi series. This new approach would develop into a much more complex form with historical connotations in the postwar years after going through the destruction of the urban environment and resulting affinity to the nostalgic past, as will be discussed in detail in the next chapter.

In comparison with the contradictory temporality and spatiality implied in *The Only Son*, *What Did the Lady Forget?* and *The Flavour of Green Tea over Rice* champion present time and space, largely conveyed through the trivial everyday life of female characters. Enjoyment of urban contemporary culture such as dining out in restaurants, chatting in cafés, walking in Ginza, watching a *kabuki* play in Kabuki-za and a baseball game in Kōrakuen stadium (newly built in 1937) is an essential element of both film/script to characterise the life of the bourgeois ladies. In spatial terms, a tatami-style living room is articulated as a place for female gathering, punctuated by a long domestic corridor in a bourgeois mansion shot in Ozu's low height camera, which all began to appear in *What Did the Lady Forget?*. In this sense, both film/script can be called a 'woman's film' in a quite different meaning from Ozu's previous works in the genre, which showed, though with variations, a more or less *shinpa*-esque tone that defines women as a passive victim of tragic fate, whether explicitly through failed *moga* narratives and *ryōsai kenbo* ideology, or through more complex modern girl characters with stronger subjectivity and solidarity as discussed in the case of *Woman of Tokyo*. In comparison, the female characters in the wartime bourgeois comedies are more lighthearted, assertive and *everyday*, freely expressing their existence and desire through seemingly never-ending chatter, puns and complaints. Even though compromised by patriarchal ideology, they can be regarded as the first female characters in Ozu who make their voices clearly heard.

Take the example of the beginning part of *What Did the Lady Forget?*, which foregrounds a lengthy conversation among ladies who gather together for enjoyment (see Figure 3.2). Enabled by synchronous sound technology, the whole conversation scene hardly has a moment of silence or interruption. The resulting effect is the actualisation of the speedy and uncontrollable female conversation, an unusual case in Ozu's silent films so far. What the ladies talk about is also limited to female interests – beauty, fashion, children's education, and delicious

Figure 3.2 Bourgeois ladies in close conversation

foods – that are expressed through nonsensical jokes, mostly making fun of the unattractive face of one of the ladies, and her desperate effort to overcome it. What should be also importantly noticed in their talk is the full acceptance of commodity consumerism, as noticeable in such topics as 'shopping in Mitsukoshi Department Store' or 'eating biscuits'. Their appearance, with fine clothing and accessories, also indicates the consumption-oriented attitude of these bourgeois females. This certainly implies the economic affluence the high-class ladies can afford, but it is still an interesting contrast to the subdued consumption that characterises the life of the salaryman's housewife in Ozu's *shōshimin* films as discussed in Chapter 1. As in the case of *The Flavour of Green Tea over Rice*, this tendency of revealing liberated women rang an uncomfortable echo within the contemporary ideological sphere. Sawamura Tsutomu, for instance, understood the femininity in *What Did the Lady Forget?* as an interruption of, and impediment to, the nationalistic mission of cinema that he supported. The leisured class's life in the film, where 'neither sad nor joyful things happen' except for the continuation of the everyday, was antagonistic to his historical consciousness as revealed in the quote, 'We, confronting the world outside, must recognise our self-identity as Japanese'.[85]

The ultimate form of modern femininity in the film is represented through the character of Setsuko (played by Kuwana Michiko), who is the modern girl in its most generic meaning of the term, and, as such, can be differentiated from her earlier counterparts. Carefree in personality and defiant in behaviour, she somewhat resembles Date Satoko's modern girl characters in *Hogaraka ni ayume/ Walk Cheerfully* (1930) and *The Lady and the Beard*, but not only is Setsuko far from being a juvenile delinquent but also she never repents her fault or converts to the patriarchal order as Date's character does. She is also not a working woman in an office as Okada Yoshiko in *Woman of Tokyo* and Tanaka Kinuyo in *Dragnet Girl* are, but nor does her life set foot in sensational areas such as prostitution or dissolute nightlife. In other words, she is the most 'ordinary' kind of modern girl Ozu has ever created; though indulging in smoking and drinking, she is just a niece from Osaka, a cheerful but self-assertive young girl. As such, her most important role in the film is to urge her uncle Komiya to stand out against his henpecking wife, Tokiko, insisting on her belief that 'husband should have more dignity'. Because of this attitude, Bordwell, in his discussion of the gender relationship in the film, argues that 'this *moga* turns out to be more old-fashioned than her elders'.[86] On the surface, Setsuko does seem to play a role of acknowledging male supremacy in domesticity, but her strong visual image that overwhelms weakling Komiya, along with the comic tone attached to her immature patriarchal ideology, also makes an ironically opposite interpretation of her character possible, as representable by her own statement: 'I am as dignified as men are'. The objects she keeps close to her – cigarettes, whisky, fencing foil – all support her 'reversed' gender identity that converts her patriarchal remarks into a twisted satire rather than a truthful argument.

On the other hand, Setsuko's performed masculinity is balanced by her feminine sensitivity, as revealed when she takes side with Tokiko during the conflict between her uncle and aunt. The film includes a scene of domestic violence – fed up with his wife's nagging, Komiya slaps Tokiko's face saying, 'You're the insolent one. I treat you well and you walk all over me' – which, compared with the one in *The Flavour of Green Tea over Rice*, is obviously a patronising kind that could have functioned well for audience 'morale boosting'. The husband soon gently apologises for the violence, thinking he is playing with an invisible hand to keep control over his wife. Tokiko, however, accepts his apology without resistance because her shock has been already pacified by the sincere talk with Setsuko, who, after Tokiko is slapped, approaches the aunt and makes an excuse on behalf of Komiya. Later Setsuko tells Komiya that this was her 'play (*shibai*)' contrived to make Tokiko voluntarily apologise to him, and restore his patriarchal domestic order, which she believes righteous. However, if Setsuko's double identity – feminine towards Tokiko and masculine towards Komiya – is considered, the message here is more complicated than its literal meaning. Ozu rather makes Setsuko behave as an extreme sexist before Komiya as an ironic satire on male-centric society, while comparing it with her surprisingly persuasive and compassionate attitude when talking with Tokiko, thus implying the superiority of the latter over the former.

The spatial configuration in both scenes also supports this viewpoint. While in Komiya's reading room, Setsuko stands over the uncle sitting on a sofa, visualising the relation of dominance-subordination (though ironically reversed in gender), but in Tokiko's living room, she sits beside her aunt, sharing an equal space and thus generating an intimate atmosphere. This reminds viewers of the conversation scene at the beginning of the film, where the bourgeois ladies, detached from the interruptions of men, enjoy their own space and time. Its spatial rapport can also be compared with the sympathetic gaze and female solidarity established between the two saddened women in *Woman of Tokyo*, as discussed in the previous chapter, even though the latter lacks the former's more everyday situation presented in a more syncretic form with the sound of chatting. The gathering of women thus can be regarded as having an active and universal function, not merely as a form of leisured-class ladies' useless pastime, but as a representation of gendered communication that makes mutual understanding among female characters possible. It is important that Ozu began to adopt this kind of communicative form around this period, which would expand and be applied to various situations in his following films. The two Ginza café scenes towards the end of *What Did the Lady Forget?* – though one of them depicts a man-and-woman conversation – are such examples, showing that the spatial background of female character is not confined to the domestic space anymore but is now expanding towards the ordinary, everyday space outside. This is a different kind of space from the bar, dance hall and café where Ozu's modern girls previously hung out (or worked), in the sense that the situation does not suppose a female character as an object to be seen but rather as a subject of expression, mainly through a verbal form. Surrounded by the modern-style interior and furniture, the chatting time in a café exists only in a fleeting moment of urban daily life. Such a representation of the everyday soon reappears in a café scene in *The Toda Family*, where a female protagonist's career is the topic of conversation, which will be later varied into a trope of female friendship in such postwar films as *Late Spring* (1949) and *Early Summer* (1951).

The Flavour of Green Tea over Rice, though only in written form, continues exhibiting Ozu's new tendency of foregrounding gendered space and time through extensive exchanges of female conversation. Just as in *What Did the Lady Forget?*, a women's gathering is the essential element that both begins and ends the script (though not in the extra-domestic space of a café but in Ayako's house). As discussed, Ozu seems to intend a thematically ambiguous ending by showing the change of Ayako's feeling towards her husband after the night of the slap, as if to accept patriarchal order. The story of the couple's reconciliation softens other ladies' disrespectful attitude towards men as well, leading into their acknowledgement that 'men are complex beings', whose true face away from home is unknown to wives at home. A significant point of the sequence, however, lies in the fact that the apparent understanding of and identification with men is being achieved in the course of a lengthy ladies' conversation, where trivial jokes, diversions and sympathetic exclamations coexist with the words of regret and reflection. It is thus an important narrative device for Ozu to present the situation of slapping in the form of Ayako's personal 'story' told through her heart as well as her lips, instead of visually showing it in a scene or conveying it through the husband's words. As noticeable in the following line of Ayako's, the focus of the story about the domestic violence is put more on how she experienced it and was *affected* than the act of the violence itself:

> He said [after slapping], 'no, I'm not being sad at my going to war. I'm weeping tears of joy. I've never been happier than today since I married you.' So I replied, 'I'm sorry, I was foolish too. Isn't it too late to understand this today for the first time?' and burst into tears . . . And then, my heart felt relieved and my body refreshed.[87]

From a different perspective, the conversation in the ending sequence can be understood as a verbal process through which Ayako justifies her affection for her husband to her friends. Recalling the day when Mokichi received the draft notice, and remembering how he stayed calm in the face of impending departure, Ayako seems quite delighted and satisfied that she finally finds him a worthy husband to be adored. In other words, it would be appropriate to regard Ayako's change as a result of her subjective desire to choose the right man rather than a submissive move caused by Mokichi's violence. This can be a more consistent interpretation of the female characters who, throughout the script before the ending, have exhibited an antagonistic attitude towards men.

The female subjectivity set against male-centric society in fact occupies a primary theme of *The Flavour of Green Tea over Rice*, even though the conflict is eventually resolved through Ayako and Mokichi's reconciliation. For the bourgeois ladies, men are absurd beings, who need to be taken care of in every detail of domesticity, while in the outside world, enjoy secret affairs. (In the baseball game scene, one of Ayako's friends happens to see her husband having an affair at the stadium; the same situation reappears in the postwar version of the film.) The frequent trips that the ladies capriciously set out upon – one of them says,

'I feel like riding on a train again' – can be a paradoxical proof of the spatial restriction the women have to endure in their domestic everyday life. However free they may seem, these bourgeois ladies are still housewives who are 'supposed to stay home with their husbands after the time when lights are on', as Ayako's father reprimands.[88]

The distrust of men is most emphatically represented through a narrative of arranged marriage. *Omiai* (meeting between marriage partners) is Ozu's well-known narrative motif, which he had already used as a subplot in such early films as *The Lady and the Beard* (1931) and *Where Are the Dreams of Youth?* (1932). Later in *Hakoiri musume/An Innocent Maid* (1935), the only non-existent Kihachi film, the conflict between arranged and love marriage – the female protagonist (played by Tanaka Kinuyo) is forced by her mother to marry a wealthy man in town – became a more central subject matter. *The Flavour of Green Tea over Rice* revisits the theme through a story of a young female character, Setsuko, who encounters her father's pressure to marry although she does not like the *omiai* partner she has been introduced to. In despair, she meets Ayako, her senior schoolmate, to find consolation and ask advice in tears. Learning that the marriage has already been arranged, Ayako however advises Setsuko to marry the man, saying, 'It's the best way to follow what your father has decided'.[89] Her cold rejection of the request for help is not without careful consideration, for Ayako went through the same experience as Setsuko but could not escape the fate of unwanted marriage with Mokichi, as revealed in the next scene of conversation with her friends, explaining the fundamental cause of her dissatisfaction with her husband. After all, what Ayako learned from her unhappy marriage is the wisdom of resignation and acceptance ('Back then, I was weeping too. But how about today? Look at me, I'm laughing. Although I'm not sure whether it's because I like my husband or not, I wouldn't care. Whatever will be will be, isn't it?'), and she merely applies that cynical realisation to Setsuko's case.[90] That this sequence about Setsuko's *omiai* and marriage directly follows the scene of the secret affair at the baseball stadium confirms a certain consistent narrative flow where Ozu successfully delivers his critical view on the discriminative gender relationship prevalent in Japanese society.

Such a representation of confrontational gender politics, conveyed through a very gendered form of verbal communication based on the everyday, indicates a new thematic concern that Ozu began to adopt around this period in the late 1930s, through a successive attempt – even leaping the gap of his draft – to deal with bourgeois female characters in *What Did the Lady Forget?* and *The Flavour of Green Tea over Rice*. This new direction is surely not without limitations at the time, as the two films are basically comedy with a tendency to exaggerate characters' behaviours, and as such the conclusion seems too incomplete and inconsistent with what has been presented throughout the film/script. (For example, in the very last scene of *The Flavour of Green Tea over Rice*, Ayako meets Setsuko once again, this time, however, advising in a more positive way regarding marriage, out of her experience of recent reconciliation with Mokichi.) It is, however, still important that Ozu's female characters finally became able to make their voices heard in the context of the everyday without a need to sensationalise their image, which can be connected to the further development in the director's postwar films with regard to feminine issues, most representatively the marriage of young women, as will be discussed in detail in the next chapter.

On the other hand, Ozu in this period also shows deliberate reflection on masculinity, which occupies the other axis of gender relationships, with a different perspective from the class-based complexes of the middle-class salaryman or archetypal model put into a generic convention of nostalgic Shitamachi drama. It can rather be defined as a man caught in a dilemma of duty, not only to family (as in *shōshimin* films) but also to nation. This new representation of males is without doubt related to the newly developing spiritist film tradition as well as the contemporary political topography of war in Asia and the Pacific region, and as such cannot be appropriately understood without considering the state of Japan's interest in constructing and maintaining a new masculinity that can rightfully serve the concern of the nation. Ozu's rendition of this issue is, however, expressed in diverse forms, from a continuing variation of bourgeois drama to an explicit war film, as will be discussed in the following section.

Absent Fathers and Ozu's Humanistic War Drama

The production of Ozu's two wartime films – *The Brothers and Sisters of the Toda Family* and *There Was a Father* – are inevitably interwoven with the contemporary militaristic political situation. The former was an output of the director's effort to offset the rejection of *The Flavour of Green Tea over Rice* by the censorship board, and accordingly, was made with a 'safety-first principle' in order not to arouse the same trouble again. He thus had to give up an idea of making it a comedy film, thinking that 'sarcasm or satire would not work [this time]'.[91] The film eventually received a warm response from the government, and also became the first commercially successful Ozu film, even leading to a plan for a sequel set in China. *There Was a Father*, as a representative of Shochiku, also participated (and won a prize) in the '*kokumin eiga* (national film)' competition in May 1941 held by the Information Bureau (*Jyōhōkyoku*), then a newly established (in December 1940) intelligence agency with the purpose of governing wartime propaganda activities.[92] However, even acknowledging these circumstances in production, it is not clear whether Ozu himself intended, or regarded, the two wartime films as national policy (*kokusaku*) genre projects that articulated purely nationalistic ideas. In addition to the fact that the script of *There Was a Father* had already been written in complete form in 1937 before Ozu went to China, a period when national policy film was not yet set in place, it also seems Ozu personally did not agree with the idea of making a hard-line ideological film. In his interviews in the early 1940s, he repeatedly argued that cinema should be entertainment for people before art or preaching; 'increasing demand or regulation [from government] has made productions badly shrink ... The worse the situation gets, the more proper entertainments must be provided'.[93] This is clearly an opposite view to that of the advocates of national policy film such as Sawamura Tsutomu, who, as mentioned, thought the mission of cinema was not for providing entertainment but for serving the state. Although clarifying that he was not against producing *kokusaku* films, Ozu was cautious of the tendency that the genre 'forgot entertainment and put only preaching to no purpose', which explained the lukewarm records of such films at the box office.[94] He instead emphasised that his wartime films were essentially family drama as usual, with an aim to depict 'maternal love' (*The Toda Family*) and 'paternal love' (*There Was a Father*).[95]

Nevertheless, the two films have been largely understood in the context of the national policy films genre that was becoming the central issue of Japanese cinema in the 1940s. Western critics especially interpreted them as the director's gesture of representing traditional Japanese values or 'Japaneseness', which the military government encouraged as a principal cinematic subject matter. Darrel William Davis, for instance, argued that such an idea is incarnated in Japanese wartime films as unique formal characteristics, named 'monumentalism', which he summarises as long takes, slow pace, austere look and epic spectacle.[96] According to Davis, *The Toda Family* is an example of this rigorous style, as noticeable in the depiction of the life of an extended family, through which the film eventually advocates a nationalistic ideology that aims to glorify the Japan's past and mythologise the traditional *ie* system. Supporting evidence for this conclusion is the fact that favourable characters in the film lead a traditional lifestyle such as wearing the *kimono*, while unfavourable ones tend to adopt a Western lifestyle such as playing the piano, hence prioritising the idea of Japaneseness.[97] In a similar vein, Isolde Standish understands *There Was a Father* as a representation of 'patriarchal authority and responsibility', interpreting that the father and son relationship of this film stands for the relation between the nation and individual, which together constitute *kokutai*.[98]

Such an ideology is incorporated into the two films through a form of family drama, Ozu's usual generic specialty. The narrative is led by the existence of a solemn patriarchal figure (*There Was a Father*) or an extended family system

(*The Toda Family*). One of the only two Ozu films that has the name of a family in the title, *The Toda Family* deals with the conflicts among siblings in a big, affluent *ie* over how to take care of their mother who is left alone after the death of her husband.[99] The married children (the eldest son and two eldest sisters) consider the mother and their unmarried youngest sister (Setsuko) as a nuisance, and the two women have to move from one place to another until they voluntarily retreat to an old, remote family villa. The youngest son (Shōjirō), who has left for China to work, returns to find the situation and severely criticises his siblings for their lack of filial duty. Such a familial duty expands into a matter of allegiance to country in *There Was a Father*. Horikawa, a single father who raises his only son, Ryōhei, is an austere type of patriarch with a strong sense of responsibility. Due to his job as well as the son's education, Horikawa suggests to Ryōhei that he live separately, which the son, though feeling reluctant, accepts in a docile manner. The situation, however, continues until the son fully grows up, when Horikawa rejects Ryōhei's suggestion to live together because it means the son has to quit his teaching job, a vocation of great responsibility. They eventually never have a chance to get together as one day, when the son is visiting him in Tokyo, Horikawa suddenly falls ill and dies.

At the heart of this family drama is the existence of a father figure, who acts as an advocate of a masculine ideal to serve one's familial and vocational duties, even at the cost of personal suffering. In *The Toda Family*, such a role is given to the character of Shōjirō, who can be interpreted as a returned (substitute) father who gets enraged by the fact that his endurance at the war front is not justly compensated at home, and tries to regain domestic order. Thus, as in the case of *The Flavour of Green Tea over Rice*, Bordwell understands the film as a moral drama in the sense that it 'attack[s] on a decadent bourgeois lifestyle' at the home front, reflecting the suspicious view of the military government on the selfish and unpatriotic class.[100] The basic strategy that *The Toda Family* takes to convey the moral message is also the same gender politics as in other bourgeois domestic dramas: by showing the luxurious and spendthrift life of the female characters. A scene of the social gathering of bourgeois ladies appears again, but this time their vanity, expressed through expensive leftovers on the dinner table, is more explicitly criticised by Setsuko, portending the anger of Shōjirō towards the other siblings in the later part of the film.

Horikawa in *There Was a Father* is an even more traditional type with a solemn and abstinent lifestyle. His teaching to his son, 'no pain, no gain' and 'those who endure can enjoy luck longer', attests to his stoic belief, in line with contemporary social values. Rather than explicitly mentioning war or inserting propagandistic message, Ozu chooses to convey the idea through the depiction of the father-son relationship. The only moment when the war circumstance is implied is in the scene where Horikawa and Ryōhei briefly talk about the son passing the physical examination for the draft.[101] Delighted by the news, the father instantly asks the son, whose head is already shaved, to report it to the dead mother's altar, one of the few occasions when the absent character is referred to. Horikawa watches Ryōhei offering a service in the background, and then compliments the son ('Now I'm relieved. You were a weak child, but have grown up splendidly') patting him on his shoulder, a rare gesture of physical contact between the two through which the father's approval for the son's masculine adulthood is given. An equivalent approval of masculinity can be found in other national policy films as well. *The War at Sea from Hawaii to Malaya*, for instance, includes a scene of two male characters (brotherly instead of father-son) diving. The scene, in fact, works as a resolution of a preceding dialogue between the two boys, where the elder one, being told of the younger one's dream of becoming a fighter pilot, asks the latter to follow him to dive into the water below a cliff. A test of courage, the diving accompanies an attractive visual of the boys' manly naked bodies shining under the sun and moving in an athletic way, as emphasised in lower angle. The scene ends with a two-shot of swimming where the elder compliments the younger on his success in diving (thus, giving his approval of him joining an aviation school).

It should be noted that Horikawa's paternal acknowledgement is only given when the son accepts his duty to serve the country. In other words, a patriarchal figure adopts a role to resolve the fundamental dilemma of the modern young Japanese who are caught between the filial duty to their parents and the social role to work and fight for the state. The film thus can be said to be in line with other national policy films, including *The War at Sea from Hawaii to Malaya*, which were 'designed to boost recruitment and allay the fears of parents who might have been hesitant in allowing their young sons to transfer to the various military academies after graduating from middle school'.[102] In this 'spiritist' narrative, female characters – mothers and daughters – retain a passive role to send and greet their sons/brothers, read letters from the front, and try to understand and accept the reality of war. Such a typified narrative has its origin in Japanese history. The construction of the modern state that the Meiji Restoration pursued was dependent on the relocation of a large population of young people from the countryside into major cities as the labour force in factories and offices. Therefore the Confucian ideal to live with one's parents had to be sacrificed for the sake of the modern idea of serving the nation. Such precedence of loyalty over filial duty was designated in the Imperial Rescript for Public Education (1890), the fundamental law regarding modern education in Japan, and the 'Japanese patriarch . . . act[ed] as an agent of the state' to make this policy run inside a family.[103]

It is an intriguing fact that Ryū Chishū – the representative Ozu actor who shapes the image of postwar fathers in such films as *Late Spring* and *Tokyo Story* – plays Horikawa's character in this film. Besides the work of Ozu, Ryū's role as a conservative, strict and didactic father and teacher was also being exploited in other Shochiku films of the era such as Shimizu Hiroshi's *Mikaeri no tō/The Inspection Tower* (1941) and Kinoshita Keisuke's *Rikugun/Army* (1944). In the latter film, especially, Ryū's character represents a pro-war ideologue who, regretting his failure to be a great soldier, encourages his son to succeed in his dream. Himself studying a book titled 'A History of Great Japan' and teaching his students the story of *genkō* (the failed Mongolian invasion in the thirteenth century), Ryū in this film actively supports the notion of the Japaneseness that would serve to justify the war.

However, close examination of Ozu's wartime films, their narrative as well as style, reveals multilateral aspects of the text that defy a simplistic interpretation to define them within the generic term of national policy film. For instance, even though the narrative is centred around a father figure, it is actually more about an *absence* of such a figure, especially in the present everyday where it is supposed to exist, evoking anxiety and obsessive longing in the family, and eventually weakening patriarchal authority and his role as an intermediary between the home and the state. A repetitively appearing motif that implies this obsession is the act of watching a portrait of the father. In *The Toda Family*, the youngest daughter Setsuko, whenever humiliated by her selfish sister-in-law with whom she is living, walks to her dead father's portrait hanging on the wall and looks up at it for a while. The intention of the scene seems clear; Setsusko's tearful look appeals to the ideal father figure, under whose leadership the whole family could have led a harmonious life. In the film, Setsuko's wish is fulfilled to a certain degree through the existence of a substitute father, Shōjirō, but in the case of *There Was a Father*, the paternal absence leads to a deep psychological trouble and eventually a tragic end. A scene of watching the father's portrait appears when the son Ryōhei, looking forward to a short reunion with his father after a long separation, gazes with a smile at a picture of Horikawa that he keeps in a book (see Figure 3.3). Borrowing Stella Bruzzi's term regarding wartime fatherless households in Hollywood cinema, the absent father in the photograph becomes 'imaginary evocation, a fantasy figure who fills an emotional and psychological lack' of the son.[104] Such a longing out of personal absence is connected to a strong wish for homecoming as well. In the previous scene, Ryōhei's students, who are away from home for schooling, watch a passing train and talk about visiting home. One of them requests a leave of absence from Ryōhei, who, giving approval, asks out of concern whether the student's family is in trouble without his elder brother who went to war. Ryōhei's longing for his father thus

Figure 3.3 A picture of his father that Ryōhei observes

can be put within a more universal context of sympathy felt toward other broken families in contemporary Japan due to war.

Watching a portrait of an absent father then conceals a personal emotional conflict out of unfulfilled desire to be with him, which disrupts the original purpose of a national policy film to encourage and naturalise the break-up of family. Instead of solidifying paternal authority, which would connect to the loyalty to *tenno* (Japanese emperor) by *kazoku kokka* theory, Ozu rather reveals its limitation through showing the ongoing failure of restoring an intact family unit and relationship, resulting in seriously undermining the moral effect of the narrative of the stable patriarchal family. This is ironically the point that made Tsumura Hideo severely criticise the film *The Brothers and Sisters of the Toda Family*. For him, the self-indulgence and extravagance of the Toda brothers and sisters, with the sole exception of the youngest, Setsuko, is a proof that Ozu ignores the changing social climate of contemporary Japan and, in that sense, 'has not changed at all in essence' in spite of two years' hard service at the Chinese front.[105] Even the character of Shōjirō, who is given the role to correct the familial order, is not without a problem, for he once irresponsibly leaves home without taking care of his mother and Setsuko but then suddenly returns home to denounce his siblings.[106] It is also worth noting that Shōjirō, despite his role as a substitute, has a distanced relationship with the dead father. The only good memory he can bring up regarding the father is the day when the two had a meal in a restaurant, which remains as extremely fragmented everyday images – the sunshine falling in the room, the cup the father was holding, and a fly that kept sitting on the father's ear – making Shōjirō become instantly saddened. This lack of an authentic paternal relationship contrasts with the fuller one with his mother, on whom Shōjirō's affection seems to lie.

In the case of *There Was a Father*, Ryōhei looks forward in vain to a chance of reunion with Horikawa throughout the narrative, leaving him in great distress and pain. For instance, the famous scene of fishing, where the father and the son swing their fishing rods in an exactly synchronous way, has been interpreted to represent the seamless relationship between the two, where the son's 'rite of passage to manhood' is accomplished by modelling the 'idealised masculinity' of his father.[107] However, Ryōhei in the scene actually stops swinging when he learns that he has to live in the dormitory apart from his father. A moment of his despondency at such news is repeated several times throughout the film whenever his hope of living together is thwarted until the father eventually dies. The whole narrative is a chronicle of this successive cycle between young Ryōhei's hope and despair, where each brief moment of getting together (such as in the fishing scene) becomes a nostalgic (but painful) memory of the lost everyday that was only momentarily allowed to Ryōhei. Ryōhei's last words in the film, 'He was a good father', thus ring as a paradoxical echo.

Seen from this perspective, Ozu's wartime films can be read as less a national policy genre than a *shinpa*-flavoured family tragedy, which he had been playing with throughout the prewar period. It is another proof that the director actually recognised these two films as his *hahamono* and *chichimono* placed within the *shinpa*-esque family drama tradition. Or put in the generic term of Japanese war films, they are attached with strong humanist sensitivity (such as longing for an absent father), which naturally leads to great conflict with the tenet of spiritist films (such as endurance or abstinence) demanded of an individual. As discussed earlier, Ozu understood war as an incomplete transformation process between complex individual psychology, including personal memory and inner conflicts, and simplified and quotidianised activities on the battlefield, including murder and destruction. His goal in filmmaking could have been showing both realms, but the actual result I believe is focused more on the individual psychological conflicts that remain under the seemingly steady, well-disciplined everyday life, making Ozu's wartime works closer to the genre of humanist war films.

Burma Campaign, the only war film project of Ozu in its truest sense, retains the same conflict structure between individual psychology and the military everyday. Ozu wrote this script in 1942 after completing *There Was a Father*. It was a project initially planned and commissioned by the Army press section of the Imperial General Headquarters, but Ozu as well as Shochiku must have considered it a serious work, given the complete quality of the script.[108] The main cast (Ryū Chishū and Sano Shūji took the starring roles) had been decided, and Shochiku even released a teaser poster. According to High, although the reason remains uncertain why the project was aborted even without being submitted to the censorship board, there are possibilities that either Shochiku decided not to proceed after informal discussions with the board or Home Ministry, or Ozu, required to revise the script, personally abandoned the project.[109] If it is true that the military did not like the script, it can be possibly due to 'a subtly comic intrusion of home drama into the inviolable precinct of the *kokusaku* war films', as High argues, or in contrast, a depressive mood generated by such narrative elements as the death of comrade or family at home.[110] Such would be a characteristic Ozu style as the two contrasting aspects coexist in a single work.

The narrative of *Burma Campaign* is constructed around a unidirectional advance of Japanese troops from Rangoon in Burma's coastal region toward Mandalay in the inland area. The earlier part focuses on the seemingly endless marches of Japanese soldiers with occasional depictions of their everyday life in barracks, reminding readers of Ozu's own experience in China. Tired of long marches, the Japanese soldier characters in the script keep asking each other, 'How far is Mandalay from here?' Tension gradually rises in the middle as there appear episodes regarding a death notice from a family and an injury of a scout who ends up being evacuated. Finally, there is a battle sequence, followed by Japanese troops entering the city of Mandalay, which is juxtaposed with the hospitalisation and death of a protagonist, sergeant Adachi (Ryū Chishū). The script ends with a train ride scene – a variation on the endings of *A Story of Floating Weeds* and *There Was a Father*, which also anticipates the train scenes in postwar films such as *Tokyo Story* and *Equinox Flower* – where corporal Aihara carries Adachi's remains to Rangoon.

Writing this script, Ozu seems to have greatly referred to his film ideas notebook that he kept at the Chinese front.[111] The subjects most frequently appearing in the notes can be summarised into a few categories. First, there is longing for family, which is depicted through letters or photographs from home, especially from children, making soldiers wonder how much they have grown up. This can be interpreted as a typical Ozu subject, as discussed in the case of the absent father's picture, but its meaning now adds another contextual layer of war, for such longing would bring up the complex psychological backgrounds of individual soldiers operating (in deviation) behind the everyday on the battleground. Secondly, there are hospital and death scenes: soldiers are depicted to suffer from injury, and there appears a funeral scene as well. However, the most heartbreaking death would be the one of a child at the home front, which is indirectly communicated to a soldier through his senior officer. Thirdly, a motif of eating and drinking repeatedly appears as soldiers' sensory experience of the everyday. Various kinds of foods are eaten, usually in a festive mood, even including stray dogs and cats, which may not be that surprising for it is expected that Japanese soldiers at the front were suffering from chronic hunger. In the idea note, they are depicted to fantasise about eating as well. For instance, there is an episode about watching a picture of shortcake papered on the ceiling and dreaming about having it all, which is very likely based on the real experience that Ozu himself had in China.[112]

Most of the narrative motifs mentioned above are directly adopted in *Burma Campaign*, such as the scenes of corresponding letters with family, Aihara's hearing about the death of his son, and Adachi's sickbed and deathbed. The two main characters on the battlefield and their homes are connected through a photograph of a child or a letter from a child, the affective role of which must have been visually emphasised as the absent father's photograph is in *There Was a Father* and *The Toda Family*. In this regard, *Burma Campaign* is firmly grounded in the genre tradition of humanist war films of Japan, even more faithful to its definition of emphasising the 'continuity' between home and war front in terms of character personality than other humanist films, which Ozu criticised as falling short of depicting the psychological dilemma of individual soldiers. I thus agree with High that the script can be read as 'anachronistic' in the context of the early 1940s, when spiritualism had already replaced humanism in the Japanese war film genre, and, rather, should be comparable with the representative 'humanism' film of the late 1930s, *Five Scouts*.[113] Unanimously acclaimed by the government and military as well as by audiences and critics, the film was considered by Ozu as an important role model for making a war film of his own, as epitomised by the insertion of the similar scouting sequence in the script of *Burma Campaign*. He watched *Five Scouts* in Dong-ya cinema in Nanking with other soldiers around, who Ozu witnessed showing excited responses, some sobbing and others jeering at the screen.[114] Ozu himself valued the film's achievement, but not without reserve, for instance, regarding the reality of everyday life depicted in the film. For him, the characters in *Five Scouts* looked as if they 'were yet at war for only about a month'; after a certain period of time, soldiers at war would 'do various kinds of things such as picking up a dirty bowl on the ground to wash and have a meal with it or taking a trouble to make a *geta* (clog shoes) to wear it'.[115] The brotherly relationship among soldiers in *Five Scouts* can be also distinguished from that in *Burma Campaign*. As High noted, *Burma Campaign* emphasises 'the idiosyncrasies of the individual soldiers' more than 'the rhapsodic synaesthesia which seems to meld the soldiers in *Five Scouts* into a veritable single organism'.[116] *Five Scouts* reaches its climactic moment when all the Japanese soldiers, high or low in rank, sing *kimigayo* (Japan's national anthem) together in tears after an emotional celebration of the safe return of a scout, who fell behind others during his duty. Such an existential unity under the totalitarian ideal of *kokutai* that transcends mere patriotic sentiment is almost lacking in *Burma Campaign*; even though the script articulates a fraternal relationship among the soldiers and their idealised benevolent type of leaders, it also pays great attention to individual conflicts and the way in which they are internalised and digested in the context of war.

The prominent example that reveals this personal dilemma is the narrative of death. In contrast to *Five Scouts*, which can be described as a film about surviving (and fighting on), *Burma Campaign* is more about mourning and overcoming death. Corporal Aihara, hearing from his commander about the death of his son, becomes utterly speechless, a paradoxical expression of extreme shock and turmoil. Nevertheless, he eventually never reveals his true emotion, accepting the commander's advice, 'Endure it. This is war' (an echo of the father Horikawa's teaching in *There Was a Father*), and Adachi's consolation, 'You will have another child'.[117] Aihara later has to witness another death – the one of Adachi, whose deathbed sequence marks the emotional climax of the script. At the moment of Adachi's passing in the dawn, Ozu intends more complex sentiments – glory overlapping sorrow – than the patriotic ecstacy of the *kimigayo* scene in *Five Scouts*, by repeatedly inserting scenes of pagodas shining with the rising sun – two contrasting symbols of Buddhism and Japanese imperialism. Such ambiguity continues in the last scene of carrying Adachi's ash on a train. As mentioned, it is a varied repetition of the previous work, *There Was a Father*, which also ends with a train scene where the son Ryōhei returns home with his father's remains. The connection between the two endings is reinforced by the casting of the same actors – Sano Shūji for both Ryōhei and Aihara, and Ryū Chishū for both Horikawa and Adachi. However, if the ending of *There Was a Father*, with the profile shots of Ryōhei in deep silence and contemplation, suggests a doubtful look at the break-up of the family caused by the absence of the father, *Burma Campaign*, as a war film, ends in a comparably more positive tone with the sorrow for a comrade's death being exchanged with a hopeful interpretation of the death's role in liberating Burma. It is confirmed in the line of Aihara, who, watching outside scenery from the train, says, 'No one is dead . . . Look at those *hinomaru* flags here and there', and makes a resolution to an accompanying soldier, 'Let's do the best we can. Sergeant Adachi must be looking down on us from somewhere'.[118] The scene, if filmed, could have left a vaguer mood through Aihara's performance, but in the script at least, exemplifies the process of how the deep emotional conflict of the individual soldier is transformed into an acceptance of the logic of war.

It is, then, possible to infer that the humanism in *Burma Campaign* is grounded upon a sense of victim consciousness, a perception that innocent lives have been sacrificed for a greater national cause and thus deserve to be remembered. Buddhist images such as pagodas and incense that are frequent in the script support this view, providing a significant clue for the similar religious images that abound in Ozu's early postwar films, as will be discussed in the next chapter. However, it is also imperative to understand that the victim consciousness exists in an indivisible form with nationalistic thought depending on the context a narrative or an image of mourning is placed in. In other words, it depends on the plausibility of the transformation process from individual suffering to the consciousness of collective duty. After all, this process of mental change into the everyday of war, or 'positive spirit', as expressed by Ozu himself, would be an essential problematic of Ozu's wartime works. The imagery of a *hinomaru* flag waving on a pagoda, which Adachi watches on his deathbed, well represents the complex contradiction, conflict and negotiation inherent between the mourning of the individual and the duty to the nation.

Another aspect of war inadvertently missing in the transformation process is the existence of the other, namely, the enemy and the local people. Whether humanistic depiction of individual psychology or realistic everyday life at barracks, Ozu's concern is almost exclusively related to the perspective of Japanese soldiers rather than their interaction with the Chinese, British, American or Burmese. In *Burma Campaign*, there are a few scenes where Japanese troops meet Burmese people during their march from Rangoon to Mandalay, but Ozu's representation of the locals looks superficial in that the Burmese are unanimously cooperative with the Japanese; they bring water, collect boats for crossing a river, help transport military supplies, and join the action together as a voluntary army. The Japanese commanding officer thus enthuses, 'Wherever we go, they treat us so well'. The Burmese goodwill culminates in the scene where Mandalay citizens welcome with happy faces the Japanese troops to their city. What reappears in cross-cut with this celebration is the image of the *hinomaru* waving over pagoda. Considering the fact that the pagoda is the spiritual as well as national symbol of Burma, the shot can be interpreted not only as the victory of Japan but also as the assimilation of the two countries and eventual peace under Japan's rule. The shot, if filmed as such, would not have looked that different from other contemporary visual images produced for promoting the Greater East Asian Co-prosperity Sphere that advocated the ideas of obedience, cooperation and assimilation of other Asian people.

In this regard, it can be reconfirmed that Ozu's grip on the reality of war is a limited kind demarcated by his political as well as professional stance as a Japanese soldier and director. Ozu, in the end, remained in practical silence about the subject of Asia; the references in his diary to encountering the other at the Chinese front – through requisition, bartering, sightseeing and observing comfort women – are scarcely transferred to his postwar films as well as the script of *Burma Campaign*, distinguishing his cinema from the postwar works of such directors as Kobayashi Masaki and Okamoto Kihachi, who all served in the military during the war just as Ozu did. Even when Asian colonial cities are referred to in his postwar films, as discussed by Yonaha, the perspective is essentially a Japanese one for the purpose of examining the crisis of the postwar Japanese society, rather than seriously delving into the subject matter of Asia in relation to his personal experience of it.

Wartime Ozu then can be largely summarised as a period when the director continued to practise and refine the particular type of everyday realism that he had been working on from before the war. As in the case of the *shōshimin* film, the goal was not simply re-presenting reality as it is on screen; rather the reality was selectively reconstructed – whether Yamanote bourgeois family or Japanese troops on the march – in accordance to Ozu's intent. In fact, Ozu's vivid experience of the horror of war seems to have made him quite dubious about cinema's ability to reproduce the reality as it is, even though he himself criticised unrealistic depictions of war found in other contemporary films. In his interview with Tasaka Tomotaka right after he returned from China in 1939, Ozu confessed, 'I have become to feel that I cannot trust film anymore. Facing frightful reality has made me anxious [about filmmaking]'.[119] As Tsumura Hideo, who was also present at the interview, speculated, it might have been this anxiety of realism that prevented Ozu from making a war film.[120] What Ozu attempted instead was widening and deepening the boundary and extent of his everyday realism by, for instance, dealing with bourgeois everyday life and articulating gender conflicts. Deviation from the everyday is also used as an essential tool for interrupting the dominant spatial order and temporal rhythm; not only comic elements (bourgeois ladies' conversations) but also humanistic aspects (mourning of death or longing for family and home) constitute an antithetical relationship with the world of duty and perseverance imposed by paternal character or military activities. As such, Ozu's everyday realism continues to operate as a critique of the quotidianness even during wartime, albeit in a muted form.

Gender politics, spatial and temporal deviation, and everyday life are all central issues in Ozu's postwar works. Furthermore, the memory of war provides an additional layer of historical context, against which each different gender and generation reveals contrasting attitudes in terms of the temporal past and the present, resulting in a complex array of allegorical relationships in narrative. For example, eating and drinking, one of the frequently appearing everyday activities that articulate both female subjectivity and male fraternity in Ozu's wartime works, evolve in the postwar into a quintessential trope to allude to gender difference in the epistemological attitude towards the temporal past of the recent war. The next chapter on Ozu's early postwar years will investigate this historicisation of the everyday appearing in the director's films of the late 1940s and early 1950s, the phenomenon of which, however, is largely based on Ozu's wartime works as well as his real-life experience at war as discussed in this chapter.

Chapter 4
Postwar Ozu: Ozu's Occupation-era Film and Tokyo Regained

In the preceding chapters, I discussed Ozu's prewar and wartime films from the perspective of modern everyday life in Japan. After suggesting three different subjects of the modern everyday – the middle-class salaryman, the lower-middle classes in Shitamachi, and the modern girl – which can also correspond to the three major genres – the *shōshimin* films, the Shitamachi films, and the woman's films – I traced their development during the war into two contrasting styles as well as subject matters – family melodrama with *shinpa*'s influence or light comedy based on modern life, each of which represents Ozu's way of personalising different tendencies in production pursued by Shochiku.

In this chapter, I will continue to examine the issue of modernity and the everyday in Ozu's films after the war. I have emphasised the way his wartime works suggest the prototypic styles and subject matters of his later films, but can the connection between the two periods be proven from the postwar's viewpoint as well? In order to answer this question, it is first necessary to examine how the war and the postwar as a historical concept can be inter-related with each other, which will be the main goal of the first part of this chapter. I will discuss the two significant concepts that have defined postwar Japanese history, *sensō* (war) and *sengo* (postwar), under the single framework of modernity, and re-examine the controversy over the continuity/discontinuity of modernisation during the chronological process of the prewar – war – postwar. This leads into an investigation of the changing nature of everyday life in postwar society, which was not only greatly influenced by political democracy and economic development, but at the same time balanced by an unchanging aspect of continuity with the past. A retrospective sentiment had already been appearing in Ozu's previous works (as exemplified by the wartime films as well as the Kihachi films), but postwar, it became to reflect a more pervasive social symptom due to the additional context of the recent war. This requires a discussion of the memory (or amnesia) of the prewar and war as an operating mechanism of the collective psychology of the past, which, along with the sense of the changing present, dominated the postwar everyday life of Japanese people.

In Ozu's postwar films, the contradiction between lingering memory and the changing present is often presented in the form of spatial disintegration and gender relationship. Ozu's perspective on the relations between female subjectivity and the everyday has been discussed with such examples as the modern girl in Chapter 2 and the bourgeois lady in Chapter 3, which, along with the shift in historical context of the postwar, develops into a further complex form where contrasting space and time as well as gender confront each other. The second part of this chapter will investigate this tendency with such key narrative elements as 'tradition' and 'marriage' that mostly dominate Ozu's works during the period of US Occupation after the war. This would present a chance to re-examine and rethink such characters as Noriko (played by Hara Setsuko), whose role in Ozu's films from this era has been intensively studied, but would still require more consideration with regard to the historical context of her marriage. The last section will then return to the issue of the everyday as the present temporality, upon which I argue Ozu's cinema eventually has to be placed. The process, however, was not without a dilemma for the director in terms of preserving his retrospective sensitivity while catching up with the reality of contemporary post-Occupation society. The two examples of *The Flavour of Green Tea over Rice* and *Tokyo Story* suggest that Ozu dealt with this problem by bringing in (and differentiating the degree of) the contrasting aspects of his cinema so far, not only in subject matter but also in generic convention, as he had been long doing during the prewar and wartime period. This point again will redirect us back to the issue of the historical continuity in Ozu's cinema, which will be discussed in the following section.

War, Postwar and Modernity

Conceptualising Japan's postwar (*sengo*) has long been a controversial subject. It involves complex issues of temporal compartmentalisation related to the beginning and end, and more refined periodisation of the time in between, all of which are concerned with contrasting political views. The 'end' of the postwar, for instance, became a subject of controversy in academia, in relation to the question of whether the era had finally moved onto post-postwar after the 1990s, when the enthronement of a new emperor coupled with an extended economic downturn finally raised doubts about the continuation of the postwar, or whether it was still in present progressive form in the twenty-first century. More than fifty years ago in 1956, the Japanese government's White Paper on the Economy had declared, 'Already, the postwar is over (*mohaya sengo dewa nai*)', advocating the end of Japan's postwar restoration and the start of a new high-growth era that would redefine the nation's position and role in the world in the coming decades. Nevertheless, *sengo* remained a valid concept to stipulate what Japan and the Japanese were, and obsessively dominated the psyche of Japanese people as well as intellectuals throughout the latter half of the twentieth century. As Carol Gluck and Kang Sangjung point out, this prolonged, stagnant postwar in Japan may be due to the Japanese wishful 'contentment with the status quo', a way of thinking that 'things are fine the way they are'.[1]

Not only had *sengo* been obsessively long, but it was also heterogeneous, composed of several junctures that divided the era into periods of different political and economic agendas; the instability of the Occupation era was not the same as the recuperation of the 1950s, which was also different from the optimism of the high-growth period of the 1960s and after. Gluck categorises these different aspects of the Japanese postwar experience into five distinct postwars.[2] The first two of them – the 'mythistoric postwar' and the 'inverted postwar' – perceive *sengo* as a departure from the wartime, though with little difference between the absolute non-existence of the past in the former and the recognition of it followed by negation and oblivion in the latter.[3] The other three postwars are the 'cold-war postwar', the 'progressive postwar' and 'the middle-class postwar', each of which focuses on the different aspects of postwar Japan, that is, Japan's position in the new international political order under American imperium, social and political reformation advocated by intellectuals and the Left, and the advent of private life made possible by technological innovation and economic development. These aspects, though varying in perspective, commonly reflect the new political, economic and social conditions established in the postwar, and thus can be understood as supporting the historical discontinuity from the wartime past, on which the amnesiac effect of the 'inverted postwar' and the 'new Japan' slogan of the 'mythistoric postwar' are also based.

The argument that Japan's postwar is different (or should be differentiated) from the wartime became the theoretical foundation of not only American administrators in the Supreme Commander for the Allied Powers (SCAP) government in the early Occupation period, who attempted various progressive legal reformations according to the New Deal idealism, but also Japanese intellectuals such as Maruyama Masao, who believed that Japan, coming out of the dark past oppressed by militarism and totalitarianism, should be democratised based upon rationalism and individualism. After the defeat in war, the

Japanese people, whose subjectivity had been dominated by 'ultra-nationalistic' ideas of *kokutai* and *tennōsei* (emperor system) during the war, found an opportunity to restore the individuality as a free political agent. For Maruyama, 15 August is, then, a symbol of a critical turning point to construct an epistemological discontinuity in Japanese history, the point of which is shared by other academics such as Miyazawa Toshiyoshi, whose 'Theory of the August Revolution' distinguishes popular sovereignty in the postwar from wartime theocratic monarchism as the principle of the national system.[4] On the other hand, there is a contrasting argument for historical continuity between wartime and postwar Japan as seen in the works of Tsuji Kiyoaki, Noguchi Yukio and Yamanouchi Yasushi.[5] Tsuji, under the new political environment of the 1950s, when the democratic reformations attempted during the early Occupation period shifted towards reactionary policies based on the Cold War international order – the so-called 'Reverse Course' (*gyaku kōsu*) – argues that the conservative swing was based upon Japan's bureaucratic system, which had supported *tennōsei* during war and continued to be 'retained and reinforced' in the postwar.[6] Noguchi's point is on the continuity of Japan's economic system, called the '1940 system', which, originally planned for conducting total war, continued to define Japan's postwar economy with its emphasis on productivity and cooperativeness.[7] Yamanouchi's 'total war paradigm' generalises Japan's wartime within a wider perspective of a worldwide mobilised economic system during World War II, the experience of which made the world progress into a more equalised and systemised economy in the postwar, suggesting continuity throughout the period from the 1930s to 1970s.[8]

The matter of continuity/discontinuity, however, may not be a dichotomous question in reality, and requires a multifaceted consideration of a complex socio-cultural as well as political and economic system called the postwar. In the debates over the postwar economy, as Bai Gao points out, 'the continuity arguments always emphasise *institutions*, while the discontinuity arguments focus on economic *structures*' (italics added); if the latter pay attention to democratic reforms and industrial restructuring in the postwar economy, resulting in a great change from its prewar state, the former articulate the ongoing role of the Japanese government as a driving force in economic development as it had been before and during the war.[9] On the other hand, Eduard Klopfenstein distinguishes the cultural section from other political and economic spheres, and attributes continuity to the former and discontinuity to the latter. Although the segregation can seem too schematic, Klopfenstein's model suggests an important point that the analysis of the individual subject – including the political ideology at personal level – is integral in the study of continuity/discontinuity theory, especially in regard to the cultural and intellectual field. The issue of ideological conversion, both during and after the war, is a key example of such an approach to investigate the complexity of continuity/discontinuity at the level of personal history. In literature, for instance, writers such as Tanizaki Jun'ichiro and Kawabata Yasunari spent the wartime as a period of 'internal exile', sequestering themselves but keeping writing privately without losing their identities until the war was over, when they 'resumed their writing activities from the point it was interrupted as if nothing had happened'.[10] In contrast, in the Japanese film industry, many continued to work throughout the war, while, at the same time, suffering restrictions imposed by the military government. As Mitsuhiro Yoshimoto mentions with regard to Kurosawa Akira's career during the war years, many filmmakers 'did not actively resist militarism' even if they did not purposefully collaborate with the government.[11] Moreover, in the case of Kurosawa, some of the narrative motifs in his wartime films reappear in the postwar ones, confirming the continuity that 'problematises any facile differentiation of so-called postwar humanism and the wartime militarism' of the director.[12]

On the other hand, the US Occupation from 1945 offers a discontinuous side of the Japanese film industry. This foreign occupancy, the first in Japanese history, largely meant the democratisation (in the American sense) of Japanese society as well as the film industry. Led by staff members who were young New Dealers, early Occupation policies reflected their 'inherent optimism'; they expected that the Japanese 'general public', once liberated from their 'military rulers', could be 're-educated according to the new democratic values'.[13] And film was one of the most important communication vehicles for promoting this new political concept to the Japanese. The regulation of the film industry was undertaken by the Civil Information and Education Section (CIE) of the Occupation government, which, led by David Conde, controlled the media through both encouragement and censorship. Thus, as early as 22 September 1945, addressing a gathering of representatives from the film industry, it presented three core principles for filmmaking under the Occupation – 'abolishing nationalistic militarism', 'promoting individualistic tendencies and activities', and 'guaranteeing that Japan will not be a threat to world peace and safety' – followed by ten recommended subjects such as the 'resettlement of Japanese soldiers into civilian life' and 'developing political consciousness and responsibility amongst the people'.[14] Later in November of the same year, Conde also notified the industry of thirteen prohibited subjects, including feudalistic themes such as 'vengeance' and 'suicide'.[15]

This social experiment expedited the release of the film companies from the militaristic suppression they had suffered throughout the war years. However, the abrupt social transformation from wartime nationalism to Western democracy also caused confusion and frustration amongst Japanese filmmakers, who, until just a few months previously, had been making films laden with the opposite political messages. And the Occupation government was no less enthusiastic or assertive about its vision for Japanese film. While most filmmakers wanted to produce 'escapist entertainment movies, musicals, or comedies', Conde did not approve of such a tendency, arguing that 'this was completely avoiding the mission given to film to democratise Japan'.[16] As a result, just as in the war years, there were conflicts between the government and the filmmaker over the contents of scripts and the visualisations of them in completed films.[17] The Occupation government accepted this uncooperativeness as a form of 'quiet sabotage against the purpose of the Occupation', while for Japanese filmmakers, it was simply a new form of the same authoritarianism, with 'GHQ's censorship replacing that of Naimushō (the Ministry of the Internal Affairs)'.[18]

What does postwar mean for Ozu and Ozu's cinema, then? In terms of his career, the postwar years were extremely successful. Based upon what he had been achieving prewar and in wartime, Ozu was now undoubtedly recognised as a *kyoshō* (great master) of cinematic art in Japan, and marketed as such. It is a general myth that Ozu's films were not as much commercially successful as admired by critics, but such was not the case for his postwar works: as will be discussed, many of his important films in this era – including the prodigious *Tokyo Story* – were big hits occupying the top sales lists of Shochiku releases if not all of Japanese cinema. It was also during the postwar period that Ozu's names began to be introduced to Western countries. Even though the legend goes that the Japanese film industry was reluctant to export this 'too Japanese' film director to be properly understood by the West, it seems that already in the mid-1950s Ozu's urban dramas were being introduced to the art cinemas or academic circles in the US along with other *gendaigeki* films, an effort by Japanese film companies to diversify the foreign market in addition to the popular *jidaigeki* genre. Ozu's postwar, however, is also a multivalent period, with the director's changing focus and achievements under constant influence from rapidly changing social and industrial environments that encompass both the devastation of war and restoration from it.

As in the case of history, the beginning of the postwar for Ozu as an individual is a complex matter. His first postwar film, *Nagaya shinshiroku/Record of a Tenement Gentleman*, came out in May 1947 after a five-year hiatus from *There Was a Father* in 1942, but it is often believed that his true postwar cinema began with *Late Spring* in 1949. This two-year period can be understood as an interim period when he, realising that 'already, the prewar is over', strived for a new, 'postwar' schema applicable to his filmmaking. There is also another two-year gap before *Record of a Tenement Gentleman* was released, that is, the period between August 1945 and 1947. As mentioned in Chapter 3, on 15 August 1945, Ozu was in Singapore as a member of the Japanese military information service with the duty to make a war film. Until he returned to Japan on 12 February 1946, he had been detained along with other Japanese at a camp in Jurong district in Singapore, and while working in a rubber forest, participated in publishing a newspaper called *Jiyūtsūshin/The Liberty Report*.[19] Therefore the beginning of Ozu's postwar was a laborious process to come out of war as experienced by the people in mainland Japan.

However, possibly the most significant moment that signalled the end of war and the beginning of a new era for Ozu could be when he burnt the script and stocks of a film that he had filmed during his stay in Singapore, an unthinkable act that had never happened and would not ever happen in the filmmaker's life. In an interview after the war, Ozu mentioned that the film 'was not suitable for [him], that [he] did not want to make it'.[20] Nevertheless, the event indirectly demonstrates that Ozu was conscious enough that what he had filmed could be potentially dangerous in the immediate postwar situation in Singapore. Therefore for Ozu, as for many other contemporary Japanese people, *sengo* had begun with confusion, which required them to deal with many contradictory feelings – a sense of fear, betrayal and self-denial as well as liberation and hope – at the same time. Above all, as the burning symbolises, it accompanied the dual process of oblivion and memory of the war past, which would best represent the main theme of Ozu's films in the coming years as well as the psyche of the postwar Japanese.

The connection between the war and the postwar is also related to a major historical issue of Japanese modernisation, of which the re-examination and re-definition began during the wartime, as seen in the case of the symposium on Overcoming Modernity. The problematics raised in the symposium show that the wartime experience of the Japanese was a complex one, accompanying a full-scale reconsideration of the modernity that had long obsessed the nation. Thus, in the postwar years, even though the immediate feeling tended towards censure of the intellectuals' move during the wartime, which had in effect bolstered fascist ideology and justified the war, 'gradually ... this censure provoked an interest in returning to the rationale behind the symposium'.[21] Takeuchi Yoshimi, for example, was a representative figure who, in the postwar period, attempted to recuperate the legacy of the symposium as a critical discourse on modernity. His basic view on the Overcoming Modernity symposium was that its meaning and implications had 'layers of complexity' that blurred the boundary between a 'war of aggression' and a 'war of resistance', and led wartime intellectuals into confusion and eventually ideological conversion to support for the war.[22] Harootunian seems to understand this 'complexity' as being 'empty of substance', and thus criticises Takeuchi for underestimating the ideological 'utility' of the symposium for producing 'complicity with fascism'.[23] However, as Sun and Calichman both argue, Takeuchi's contribution lay less in his clarification of the relation between the symposium and the war than in suggesting a new critical field in which Japanese modernity, as a general historical problem, could be constantly re-examined as the issue of the present. Thus with his discussion of the symposium, Takeuchi 'reminds us that history can never be reduced to a thing of the past, since the present takes its shape entirely on the basis of this past'.[24] By resuscitating the wartime experience in the present of the postwar, Takeuchi's work exemplified the historical continuity between the two periods that were mostly regarded as being segregated and unrelated. Modernity, being an unresolved legacy from the war, became another haunting ghost of the postwar, but within a very different context from what it had been in the prewar years.

Ozu's postwar began with the same historical consciousness. His interviews and writings in the immediate postwar era after he returned from the front in 1946 reveal that the notion of 'Japan' or 'Japanese cinema' had become a major concern of his in the midst of the triumphant advancement of American culture. As a filmmaker, Ozu's most significant wartime experience would be his encounter with recent Hollywood films in the late 1930s and early 1940s while he was stationed in Singapore, the impression of which he often mentioned with admiration after the war. Donald Richie was right when he pointed out that the direct influence of those foreign films on Ozu was minor, at least in terms of his style, but he missed the implication of the anecdote within the wider picture, that is, that the experience of Hollywood cinema during the war was set against the notion of Western modernity that endorsed it as well as the nation that produced it.[25] Ozu in the immediate postwar period thus tended to perceive the matter of Japanese cinema in terms of a dichotomy with Hollywood cinema, weighing the possibility of the former through the gauge of the latter. In his first article published in the postwar period, aptly titled 'Kongo no Nihon eiga/Japanese Cinema, From Now On', Ozu analysed the tendencies of the Hollywood films he saw in Singapore and anticipated that postwar Japanese cinema would adopt them.[26] But he was also well aware that the two national cinemas could not be the same, comparing the Japanese film industry to 'handicraft', in contrast to the authentically 'industrial' Hollywood, which was systemically provided with new technologies and talented human resources. This realisation of his was not only expressed in the form of criticism of production practices in Japan but also as self-reflection on what he could do as a 'Japanese' director.[27]

These differences (or restrictions) led him to the conclusion that Japanese cinema, in order to survive the competition in the market, had to 'discover a unique taste' of its own with, for example, displays of Japanese customs and manners, or traditional backgrounds such as Kyoto and Nara.[28] It is probably unreasonable to think that Ozu actually hoped for worldwide marketability with the images of old Japanese cities such as Kamakura, Kyoto and Nara while making the three consecutive postwar films – *Late Spring* (1949), *Munekata kyōdai/The Munekata Sisters* (Shintoho, 1950) and *Early Summer* (1951). However, the contrast between traditional spaces and war-torn Tokyo under reconstruction is very prominent, which I will argue was intentionally conceived by the director for a clear thematic reason to reflect on the postwar Japan as a defeated nation and critique her state of modernity.

My discussion so far has elucidated the new conditions and challenges that Ozu faced at the start of the postwar period, which were closely related to the Japanese experience of the war against the US. However, I would like to emphasise that this does not indicate that Ozu (and his rendition of the everyday) finally retreated from modernism into traditionalism. As I have argued, Ozu's quintessence lies in his analysis of an ever-changing contemporary Japanese society, and tradition or Japaneseness only served as a mirror upon which to reflect this contemporaneity, rather than as the ultimate purpose *per se*. Such an argument is not without controversy, for Ozu's cinema was situated in a marginal position between the two contrasting worlds of modernity and tradition, as the Kihachi series proves, and whether he took sides with either of them remains an ambiguous and often contradictory question. For instance, Edward Fowler argues that Ozu in the immediate postwar period presented 'a profoundly conservative worldview' by ignoring Japan's desperate search for a 'new social order', but also mentions that 'this is not to say that Ozu favoured a wholesale return to prewar or wartime life and ideology ... There is no evidence that he was enthusiastic about the military regime or about Japan's imperialist mission'.[29] However, his final conclusion, though still maintaining neutrality, puts more weight on the director's reactive political stance saying, 'Ozu distanced himself as much or more from SCAP's agenda as he did from the militarists', at a time when distancing of any sort was not that much easier than during the wartime years'.[30]

How then can we negotiate this tension between Ozu and the postwar? Had he really decided to reject change and adhere solely to the past? My answer, bearing in mind Ozu's ambiguity and marginality, is that he maintained his position rather than jumped into the chaos, but still recognised *and* approved of the changes induced by the postwar. This paradox of 'the change within the unchanged' can be compared with the Japanese philosopher Nishitani Keiji's argument in the Overcoming Modernity symposium that 'change' and 'changelessness' are not separable but rather work in a dialectical way. Even the works of the greatest thinkers and artists, which are thought to be 'eternal' or transcendental, are 'a product of history' born out of the context of their own era. Thus Nishitani concludes, '[H]istory necessarily changes while remaining permanence itself . . . [T]he mutable always emerges from out of the immutable'.[31]

In Ozu's postwar films, 'changelessness' is appreciated but always accepts 'change' in the end, as Nishitani's idea of 'change within permanence' suggests. There are two ways in which Ozu realises this thematic point in his films. One is from the viewpoint of 'changelessness', namely, older generations (more specifically, fathers) who observe 'change' and lament their powerlessness to oppose it. On the other hand, there is another way to grasp change, from 'change's own point of view', that is, from the viewpoint of the younger generation, especially female characters. What they seek is to live within the present everyday as it is, which should be differentiated from the notion of always chasing after change. In Nishitani's words, this corresponds to a 'struggle . . . with the present day', from which something eternal, unchanging or traditional could also emerge.[32] With such an active attitude towards the present, I find a new possibility of negotiating the tension between changelessness and change, between tradition and modernity.

For that purpose of negotiation, what Ozu's postwar cinema actively adopts is a temporal device of history and memory. Just as Takeuchi attempted to revive the problem of Japanese modernity within the context of the postwar, Ozu re-examined his critique of modernity, which he had been dealing with in shōshimin films and the Kihachi series, in the form of memory that resurrected the unchanging past as an unresolved issue in the ever-changing present. Even though the postwar moved on regardless of the prewar and the war, it was unable to completely wipe out traces of the past that lingered on in the form of memory. Identifying the concrete object and objective of the memory, however, remains a complicated task, especially when considered within a historical context. Harootunian notices a series of recent retrospective tendencies amongst conservative critics (or 'revisionist historians') in Japan, who argue that postwar Japan – in all its individualism as well as prosperity – was 'long and interminable' because 'Americanism . . . destroyed memory and encouraged social forgetfulness' and thus 'obliterated Japan's prewar "traditional" past in order to establish a "postwar without an end"'.[33] They argue that this loss of true identity has caused the 'self-loathing of Japanese people', who are in need of 'redemption from this awful, unending fate'.[34] As a historian of modernity, Harootunian objects to this idea of returning Japan to the memory of the forgotten past (as the Overcoming Modernity symposium aimed for), which was 'fuelled by nostalgia for a loss that never existed'.[35] He thus concludes that 'history is not memory, the conservation of the archive'; history instead should be 'the history of the present', and thus 'necessarily politicised'.[36]

In contrast, Yoshikuni Igarashi greatly diverges from Harootunian's view of history in terms of his active acknowledgement of the role of memory in not only suturing (i.e. forgetting) but also exuding (i.e. remembering) the painful truth buried under Japan's postwar history. Declaring that 'memory does not exist outside of the boundaries of history', Igarashi defines his work as an attempt that 'problematises the concept of history by claiming memory as an integral part of historical production'.[37] Igarashi thus pays attention to the tendency of the Japanese postwar to obliterate the wartime past in the course of the nation's effort to justify the new relationship with the US after the war. He explains the unbalanced political and military relationship between the two countries with the term 'foundational narrative', a melodramatic form where 'through the bomb, the United States, gendered as male, rescued and converted Japan, [which was] figured as a desperate woman'.[38] Under this system, a faithful reconstruction of memory cannot be easily achieved within the realm of politics – 'asserting Japan's political sovereignty in international politics' would mean the annulment of the 'foundational narrative' and hence the complete denial of the postwar system – and instead, the working of memory has been channelled through cultural media.[39] Igarashi thus analyses such postwar films as the *Kimi no na wa/What Is Your Name?* trilogy (Ōba Hideo, Shochiku, 1953–4) and the original instalment of *Gojira/Godzilla* (Honda Ishirō, Toho, 1954). Both films are heavily imbued with the memory of the past, which is repressed for the sake of the 'fundamental narrative' of the postwar politics, but still lingers on and can suddenly re-emerge to haunt the minds of the post-Occupation age Japanese.

The difference between Harootunian's and Igarashi's points of view represents the two temporal aspects – the present everyday and the past memory – that became the main subject of Ozu's postwar films, as will be discussed in the following sections. However, owing to the multivalent position that Japan occupies in twentieth-century history, the memory she retains (and invokes) cannot be defined in a simplistic way. I thus believe that memory in the Japanese context functions in at least three different dimensions: (1) a nostalgia for prewar tradition and wartime militarism, as revisionists have imagined and Harootunian has criticised; (2) a victim consciousness as represented in the film *What Is Your Name?* or *Gojira*, which Igarashi has articulated; and (3) guilt as victimiser, which has not yet been fully articulated in Japanese narratives. These triple faces of victor, victim and victimiser work together, each interfering with (and interrupted by) the other. Some of Ozu's postwar works, with their close interest in traditional images, may look supportive of the first type of memory among the three, but it is rather the second one – the victim consciousness – that is mostly in operation in Ozu's films. Moreover, there exists in the case of Ozu another temporal dimension, the present everyday, which, with the memory of the past, makes Ozu's cinema a much more complex presentation of history than Igarashi or Harootunian conceptualise.

The Everyday and Gender Relationships in Ozu's Occupation-era Films

As mentioned, there is a consensus in Ozu studies that the true beginning of his postwar period is the film *Late Spring*, actually the third film the director made after *Record of a Tenement Gentleman* and *Kaze no naka no mendori/A Hen in the Wind* (1948) after he returned from war. Such a distinction between pre- and post-*Late Spring* films is based on some of the most common-sense features of Ozu's cinema; with serene images of old traditional Japan in the background, the film focuses on the quiet and stable suburban life of a middle-class family, and the question of a daughter's marriage – the quintessential Ozu set-up – in contrast to its two predecessors, which are more explicitly concerned with the struggle to get by in Occupation-era Tokyo. Tanaka Masasumi, affirming that the film 'established the postwar line of Ozu cinema', argues that the success of *Late Spring* 'not only reconfirmed the trust in Ozu as a master of Japanese cinema but also stabilised his position at Ofuna studio'.[40] When the film was being produced in 1949, Ofuna was headed by Takamura Kiyoshi, who maintained a somewhat unfavourable relationship with Ozu. The commercial response to *Record of a Tenement Gentleman* and *A Hen in the Wind* was lukewarm (they ranked at twenty-first and fifteenth in the box-office records among Shochiku films, even though both were included in *Kinema Junpo*'s annual top ten list).[41] There was even a rumour that the discontented director would resign from the studio after the failure to cast Takamine Hideko for his aborted film project *Tsuki wa noborinu/The Moon Has Risen*. *Late Spring* was not only a critical success (the top film in *Kinema Junpo*'s annual list) but also a popular success (seventh among Shochiku's releases in 1949), which discharged this unstable situation and revitalised Ozu's status as the representative Shochiku director, who could compete with new postwar generation directors such as Kinoshita, Yoshimura and Toho's Kurosawa.

One of the most important factors behind this change and success is the inclusion of Noda Kōgo as a co-scriptwriter with Ozu. The collaboration was the first time in fourteen years since *An Innocent Maid* (the non-existent final Kihachi film) that the two had worked together, and also eleven years after Noda had had a huge success with the script for *The Love-Troth Tree*. It seems the compatibility and synergy of the duo was perfect. Ozu mentioned that he and Noda were 'well matched in [their liking of] *sake* as well as in the time to rise and go to bed', which was a 'very important thing'.[42] Noda's most significant contribution, however, is said to be the change in subject matter and theme, which, as mentioned, distinguished *Late Spring* from the first two postwar films. According to Noda, it was in fact his (critical) suggestion that *A Hen in the Wind* 'dealt with the world of phenomena', and Ozu's admittance of this, that led to their collaboration on *Late Spring*.[43] By the word 'phenomena', I believe Noda referred to a more direct approach to social issues, especially with regard to the political and economic chaos of the Occupation era. Such a vivid, frank image of postwar reality was evident in other contemporary films such as Kurosawa's *Nora inu/Stray Dog* (Eiga Geijutsu Kyōkai, 1949) and Imai's *And Yet We Live*, where everyday life consisted of poverty, unemployment, rationing and the black market. As Satō Tadao points out, *Late Spring* 'completely wiped out all these postwar phenomena from the screen' as if 'there had never been a war', only leaving the 'middle class life and ethos of the most stable prewar era'.[44]

Of course, stable middle-class life was not Noda's own invention, but rather a basic formula that Ozu had already been polishing for a long time, especially from the 'bourgeois trilogy (*What Did the Lady Forget?*, *The Flavour of Green Tea over Rice*, and *The Brothers and Sisters of the Toda Family*)' mentioned in the previous chapter. The fact that Ozu had already been considering revisiting this wartime tendency *before* Noda's participation in *Late Spring* can be supported by the aforementioned script *The Moon Has Risen*. Although written with Saitō Ryōsuke in 1947 between *Record of a Tenement Gentleman* and *A Hen in the Wind*, the script deals with the life of an affluent family of Yamanote origin, anticipating the change in *Late Spring*.[45] It would thus be more appropriate to conclude that Ozu, stimulated by the critical failure of *A Hen in the Wind*, decided to return to and concentrate on the stable middle-class everyday he had established, as opposed to the idea that he passively followed Noda's suggestions.

What is actually new in *Late Spring* would rather be the ideal image of traditional Japaneseness – landscape, architecture, religious icons and so on – that functioned antagonistically to the *invisible* image of war-torn Tokyo. Very unusually for Ozu, *Late Spring* starts with an explicit sign that clarifies that the film is set outside Tokyo, in the old capital city of Kitakamakura. Throughout the film, viewers are also introduced to Buddhist temples, Buddha statues and pictures located around the protagonist Somiya's house, a tea ceremony, a Noh performance and, most of all, a trip to Kyoto, where Somiya utters the definitive thematic line, 'Kyoto is nice, so tranquil. There's no such place as this in Tokyo.

Figure 4.1 Somiya (Ryū Chishū) utters the 'Kyoto versus Tokyo' remark when looking at the scenery at Kyoto's Kiyomizudera temple

It's full of dust there' (see Figure 4.1). As Lars-Martin Sorensen argues, the line is charged with a criticism of the reality of postwar Occupation by contrasting 'dusty Tokyo' with 'peaceful Kyoto', the implication of which the US censors did not miss.[46] He also notes that the same traditionalism was already evident in the script of *The Moon Has Risen*, which is full of elements such as the old capital (Nara), Buddhist temples, and Zen practice.[47] And a similar formula using 'traditional Japaneseness' is repeated in the two successive films after *Late Spring* (that is, *The Munekata Sisters* and *Early Summer*) with scenes set in Nara and Kamakura respectively. Thus this tendency towards tradition expressed through spatial displacement allows the three films and one script to be grouped together and seen as Ozu's peculiar period that constituted a particular response to the socio-historic condition of the Occupation era.

The problem is then how to properly interpret the meaning of this successive (but historically demarcated) homage to traditional images and ideas. There have been three predominant approaches to this issue (except in the aesthetic tendency prevalent in early Ozu studies). The first approach is to criticise Ozu for avoiding facing social reality by escaping into old traditions, a position largely adopted by Ozu's contemporary Japanese critics; the second is to emphasise

Ozu's recognition of Western values (such as democracy and free marriage) in the Occupation era, as Thompson and Wood do; and the third approach is to admit the traditionalism prevalent in Ozu in this period as the director's active statement of his conservative views on society, as Sorensen and Tanaka do. I believe that none of these positions fully explains the real scope of Ozu's Occupation-era work, which, immediately after the war, attempted a very sophisticated work of negotiating between modernity and tradition.

First of all, Ozu never avoided social reality. As mentioned so far, this kind of criticism had long existed amongst Japanese critics. I have argued that it is not an appropriate accusation because Ozu's films always touch on contemporary everyday life, even if not in the more obvious manner of social realism or leftism. But the films of the Occupation era raise the issue more seriously because they seem to reveal concrete evidence of the director's evasion of contemporariness through spatial detachment and obsession with traditional images.[48] What was unique for Ozu and Noda in this period was that they actively defended themselves against this criticism, often using riddle-like metaphors rather than simple explanations. The most famous one must be Ozu's comparison of himself to a tofu maker, who can make no other food apart from tofu, or, more exactly put, who can make different 'kinds' of tofu but never *tonkatsu* or steak. The remark has been interpreted as an expression of the director's will to pursue his own unique aesthetic style, but the tofu discourse actually came out of the context of Ozu's adamant refusal of a postwar realism that was being demanded by critics.[49] During the Occupation period, Ozu repeatedly stated his position against showing reality as it is – for example, by depicting violence or destitution – because it threatened his fundamental tenet of humanism, which was compared to tofu making in his expression. Ultimately, Ozu's cinema is rooted in the world of the virtuous, not the villainous. But he believed that this does not imply a distortion of reality. 'Lotus in mud' is another expression he used in order to clarify the relationship between reality and *his* method of realism:

> If mud is reality, the lotus is reality, too. The former is dirty, while the latter is beautiful . . . I know there is a way of expressing the lotus flower by depicting mud and roots. But I also think it is possible to realise mud and roots by depicting the flower. Postwar society is impure. It is messy and dirty. I do not like such things, but it is a reality. On the other hand, there is also a life that humbly, beautifully and purely blooms, which is another reality.[50]

I think that this riddle of the flower and dirt, and its ironic position that 'what you see is not what you get', have not been properly understood, and thus caused great confusion in Ozu studies to date. In the 1980s and 1990s, Western academics attempted to redefine the director as a 'modernist', as a counteraction against the aesthetic approach to Ozu in the previous decade. For example, Kristin Thompson rejected the interpretation of Ozu as a conservative who championed traditional Japanese culture, and argued that '[his] ideology tallies closely with the new, liberalised ideas that were introduced from the West'.[51] This eventually supported her main point that Ozu's form was a reaction to classical Hollywood cinema. Her primary textual evidence for this 'liberalism' was the representation of the family relationship in *Late Spring*, which reflects contemporary democratic social reforms including marriage laws. Wood took a similar position, though he sought to free Ozu's modernity from Bordwell and Thompson's formal perspective. For him, the key issue was still Noriko's marriage, which works as a 'brutal curtailment of her growth', which subdues her under 'the rigorous indoctrination of feudal tradition'.[52] The film is thus a family tragedy, where both father and daughter must abandon their freedom and yield to tradition.

In postwar Ozu, the relationship between woman and marriage is an important issue, and also a complicated one, particularly in the case of *Late Spring*. I will discuss this in more detail later in this chapter, but would like to mention here that it is too simplistic an approach to connect the theme of marriage in Ozu with either tradition or modernity per se. To see Noriko's marriage in *Late Spring* as a reflection of the forces of Westernisation in society at that time tends to miss the whole point of Ozu's confronting of modernity with tradition, which became the consistent thematic element of his Occupation-era films. In other words, Ozu in this period was seriously contemplating the matter of 'what Japan could be after war', which naturally led him to pursue traditional elements in the four films and a script made during that time. In *A Hen in the Wind*, such concerns were expressed in a more direct way through the character of the repatriated husband Shūichi, who is tormented by jazz music from a nearby cabaret. In the post-*Late Spring* films, that confrontational line between Japan and the West is moved from Tokyo to the old capital cities, where the meaning of the Japanese postwar is re-examined against the backdrop of traditional images. In this regard, I believe there is an overlapping point between Ozu in the Occupation era and the intellectuals at the Overcoming Modernity symposium, who attempted to reconsider the meaning of modernity in a Japanese context.

In a similar sense, Tanaka Masasumi has a point when he says that when reading the script of *The Moon Has Risen*, he was reminded of Kawabata Yasunari's eulogy on the death of Yokomitsu Riichi in 1947, which included the famous line, 'I will live on, thinking Japan's mountains and rivers as my spirit'.[53] Arguing that Ozu in this period was 'less inclined towards modernism or American democracy than Kawabata's "nature of Japan as spirit"', Tanaka asserts that what lay in the background of this tendency was the 'deep sense of loss' at the nation's defeat in war, and hope for 'emotional healing in the lasting stability of tradition'.[54] Sorensen also focuses on Ozu's articulation of tradition through 'feudalistic images' (as the US censors understood), which played an 'instrumental role' in inspiring 'awe and respect for the treasures of ancient Japan in contrast to the impurity of the present'.[55] He further argues that Ozu's presentation of Kyoto, Nara and Kamakura 'harks back to the use of the nation's sacred places as utilised by wartime propagandists', and thus concludes that the 'exaltation of Japanese tradition ... must have brought remembrances of the good old days when ... nationalism reached its peak'.[56] In fact, Ozu's recognition of historic sites in this era differed from the viewpoint found in other contemporary films. For example, the spatial characterisation in Yoshimura Kōzaburō's *Itsuwareru seisō/Clothes of Deception* (Daiei, 1951) is practically the opposite of that in *Late Spring*: Kyoto represented the feudal residue that would better be discharged from Japanese society, while Tokyo was the place to go to fulfil individual freedom.

However, I disagree with arguments that designate Ozu as a conservative, traditionalist or even feudalist as much as I disagree with the attempt to present him as a simple moderniser. It is another failure that confuses phenomenon with intent, as comparable to the metaphor of flower and mud. Even though the traditional landscapes and icons are eulogised, Ozu never suggests that the beautified world of the past should replace the present in order to construct a utopian future. An excursion away from reality implies an eventual return to reality, the distance from which only makes it more perceptible. Thus the old capitals are in fact a fantasy for a temporary retreat from the everyday, by which the everyday is ironically re-recognised. As discussed, Ozu had already used this strategy of displacement in the prewar films. There were small-scale moments of deviation, as in the lunch in a field scene in *I Was Born But...*, which disrupt normal everyday rhythm, and large-scale constructs such as the Shitamachi village in the Kihachi series, which functioned as a nostalgic destination, one that the protagonist was destined to leave. Ozu's Occupation-era films offer another variation on the subtle reaction between the everyday and the non-everyday, between the present and the past, using traditional images as 'instruments', but never endorsing the tradition itself. The way in which they differ from the prewar films is that the everyday – as the counterpart of tradition – is presented as a more substantial entity, and its operation is based upon gender-specific differentiation.

Take the example of the tea ceremony in *Late Spring*. As mentioned, the film begins by informing viewers of the traditional place of Kitakamakura. The following shots – gently moving trees at the station and the grand tiled roof of

Engakuji accompanied by chirping sounds and slowly soaring string music – work to strengthen this idea of traditionalism, which continues seamlessly into the following tea ceremony sequence with its solemn quietness and slow movements. It should, however, be noticed that this idea of traditional Japaneseness is permeated by the everydayness inherent in this 'monthly gathering' of ladies acquainted with each other.[57] Thompson thus makes a good point when she mentions that after the war, 'the tea ceremony was regarded more as a social event than as a private aesthetic experience', and that 'Ozu avoids a completely reverential treatment [of the ceremony] by introducing humorous touches' as in the conversation between Noriko and her aunt, Masa.[58] Agreeing with her argument, I would like to add that the tea ceremony in *Late Spring* is essentially a 'woman's hour' for upper-middle-class ladies with time and money to spend on themselves, a tendency in narrative that Ozu began to experiment with during the war, as discussed in the previous chapter. As the beginning sequence of the bourgeois ladies' gathering in *What Did the Lady Forget?*, the tea ceremony in *Late Spring* functions in essentially the same way to articulate the female everyday space-time. And as the former's articulation of the female everyday led to a conflict with the then dominant mail-centric ideologies, culminating in criticism and censorship, a subtle tension seems to be felt in the trivial female conversation set against a backdrop of solemn traditional Japaneseness.

The oppositional nature of femininity is also evident in its relationship with surrounding spaces – especially domestic ones – and the movement of females within these spheres. The houses of Kamakura appearing in *Late Spring* and *Early Summer* are spacious and elaborate enough to generate a sense of stable middle-class domesticity, with their various subsections including the entrance, kitchen, *engawa* (surrounding corridor), washing room, staircase and upper floor. Ozu supplements this stability with his low height and fixed camera, which creates deep perspective with multilayered walls and sliding doors overlapping on both sides. This typical domestic landscape of Ozu, which would dominate his post-*Late Spring* films, originates from the bourgeois mansions of *What Did the Lady Forget?* and *The Toda Family*, affirming the stylistic and thematic connections between them.

However, what differentiates *Late Spring* (and also *Early Summer*) from the wartime predecessors is Noriko's cheerful movement around the house, which enlivens the otherwise static and precisely framed domestic space. She ceaselessly walks from kitchen through corridor to living room, going upstairs and downstairs, whilst busily doing various household chores. The impact of such movement is emphasised by the structure of Ozu's domestic space. Since characters suddenly appear/disappear through the layers of sliding doors and staircase on either side, their movements appear more active and rapid. The best example of these comes from an evening scene in *Late Spring*, where Noriko walks around the house while arranging laundry, setting the table and attending to her father. Ozu designs the timing and direction of Noriko's (and her father Somiya's) movement so deliberately that it almost looks like a choreographed dance. He also uses the invisible space of a back corridor behind a living/dining room (*chanoma*) to amplify the syncopated effect of the sudden (dis)appearance of movement. Focusing on its 'spacing of time' through the shots, Eric Cazdyn praises this scene highly, saying, 'I cannot think of a more perfect scene in all of cinema'.[59] Agreeing with him, I would also add that the element of movement not only makes this scene a true cinematic pleasure, but more importantly is fundamentally related to the articulation of femininity in the film. This kind of female movement can be distinguished from Ross's more pessimistic view on postwar French housewives, whose domestic movement was reorganised for producing maximum effect in managing the household. A housewife 'should be able to proceed from one [appliance] to another in assembly-line fashion without retracing her footsteps'.[60]

Female movement plays another significant role in connecting the spatiality of Tokyo to the everyday of the old capitals. Thanks to the female 'movers' who frequently come and go between the two spaces carrying something, the two terminals are in constant communication, physically detached but not completely segregated. *Late Spring* begins with such an example – the trousers for Noriko's nephew move from her aunt's in Tokyo to Kamakura. We also see a sewing machine at Somiya's, for which Noriko looks for a needle in Ginza. Somiya's gloves are found at the Takigawa restaurant in Tokyo and brought back to Kamakura by Noriko. A supper at home is followed by tea at the Balboa café in Ginza, with the talk of a gift for Hattori's wedding continuing from one site to the other. In *Early Summer*, a female gathering at a Ginza café is connected to Noriko's Kitakamakura home through the shortcake that she brings for her sister-in-law, Fumiko. In *The Munekata Sisters*, the spatial transfer takes the form of continuing trips around the nation, from Tokyo, where the protagonist sisters are living, to Kyoto, Nara, Kobe and Hakone.

The enlivened female movement may well be considered in connection with the change in postwar Japanese society in general. Kano Masanao explains that the 'defeat in the war and the resulting loss of national authority' became an opportunity for the transition into the everyday, which was an expression of Japanese determination 'never to become a prisoner of nationalism'.[61] This tendency towards the everyday also reflected the different realities that Japanese men and women were facing in the postwar situation; while the life of the former was 'damaged hard by defeat', for the latter there remained 'the achievement that during the war they had defended the everyday in the absence of men'.[62] Thus Japanese women quickly rebounded after the war to demand their political rights that had long been delayed since the prewar years. Guided by SCAP's policy, the first few years of the Occupation era saw successive pro-female legal reformations that included the approval of suffrage (1945), the protection of equal rights with men under the new Constitution (1946), and the abolition of the *ie* and the multigenerational *koseki* (Family Registry) system in the revised Civil Code (1947), which 'eliminated the mandate to continue family lines and primogeniture rules for succession and inheritance'.[63] Most of all, marriage, which had been normally practised in the form of *omiai*, now became more of a personal matter for fulfilling one's pursuit of happiness. Article 24 of the Constitution specifically designated that 'marriage shall be based only on the mutual consent of both sexes', which implied the abolition of the requirement of a family head's consent for all marriages in his *ie*.[64] Japanese housewives also started to interpret their domestic role more actively and progressively, securing their position as a subject of consumer culture in the way they had aspired to in the prewar era. There is some controversy regarding whether and how this 'domestic dominance' – 'in exchange for an inferior position in the public sphere' – could guarantee the female equal status to the male in the family, but at least it is true that postwar Japanese women were now able to exert their 'right of decision making in family finances' to a considerable degree.[65]

Food is another aspect of the domestic everyday that is attached to femininity as opposed to masculinity. Women tend to bring *tabemono* (something to eat) into their domestic boundaries, while a few exceptional cases where men deal with food lead to awkwardness, mistakes and even disharmony. For example, in *Late Spring*, father Somiya brings some bread and tea for Noriko and her friend Aya, but not only does he forget sugar and spoon, but his actions look somewhat awkward. In *Early Summer*, the patriarch Kōichi brings a loaf of bread home, which his son mistakes for toy train rails that the father had promised. Disappointed and angered, the son throws it away and complains to Kōichi, resulting in conflict and the boy's running away from home. In contrast, food tends to bring women together and encourages their solidarity against men (and the traditional values they represent). An example of this relationship appears in a restaurant scene in *Early Summer*, wherein Noriko and Fumiko have dinner with Kōichi, Noriko's elder brother and Fumiko's husband. Kōichi, a strict, patriarchal character, has an argument with the two women about the changing moral attitude of postwar Japanese women, who he thinks are getting more and more 'impudent'. Noriko instantly opposes him saying, 'Now it is becoming just about equal. Man has been too impudent so far'. Kōichi retorts by suggesting that Noriko is still not married because she maintains such an attitude, which she simply refutes, 'It's not that I can't but that I don't want to'.

Both Phillips and Wood interpret this scene as one of 'female bonding' and 'progressive female subjectivity', which 'adds a new dimension to the critique of traditional marriage'.[66] I would like to add two more points. Firstly, as implied in

Noriko's response to Kōichi, there is a female historical consciousness that connects a critique of masculine authority to the recent history of war. I thus think that the gender discourse in the film is not confined to the marriage issue, but assumes a broader criticism of wartime militarism, which was predominantly led by men. The character of Kōichi, played by Ryū Chishū, represents such masculine authority in the face of a challenge by femininity, as mentioned in the previous chapter. Secondly, food and eating in the scene function as a sensuous pleasure that negates wartime stoicism and strengthens feminine solidarity. Whenever Noriko and Fumiko object to Kōichi's conservative idea, they suddenly ask each other whether they should have *tenpura* (deep fried foods) or *gohan* (cooked rice) as if to ignore his admonition. Their comradeship against Kōichi is visually represented by their facing positions around the table, alienating the husband/brother to one side of a three-shot. As such, Kōichi helplessly watches the two women engage in their own conversation – 'Isn't it delicious?' or 'Would you like to have rice now?' – while a bowl of rice is handed between them before his eyes (see Figure 4.2). Fumiko, remembering the days she wore *monpe* (women's trousers for work during wartime), now exclaims in joy, 'How soft and delicious!' Instead of the sympathetic gaze that the prewar modern girl

Figure 4.2 Kōichi sits alienated from his wife and sister, while a bowl of rice is handed between the two women (compare with Figure 3.2)

characters shared, the women in Ozu's postwar films generate female solidarity through a more concrete everyday object of a bowl of cooked rice, and as such, eating food also becomes a ritual for women to celebrate an everyday life regained, which had to be relinquished during war.[67]

Another revealing example of this connection between palatable pleasure and the postwar everyday can be found in a scene in *Early Summer*. One night, Noriko buys a box of shortcake and brings it home. This special treat makes Fumiko startled because of its expensive price, even for the affluent suburban upper-middle class family (Kōichi, the patriarch, is a medical doctor). Although Fumiko, a typical *ryōsai kenbo*, says in regret, 'I don't feel like eating anymore ... I'm so depressed', Noriko looks happy and doesn't seem to mind the price. Fumiko finally concedes saying, 'It could be alright, once in a while'. This scene of 'non-everyday' extravagance aroused great controversies amongst critics over its morality as well as its plausibility at the time of the film's release. Asked whether this could be a realistic situation, given the struggling state of Japanese society, Ozu responded briefly, 'Wouldn't people eat anyway, regretting [that it's too expensive], but thinking it's still delicious?'[68] His response can be understood better with a background fact that the scene was an adoption from the director's own war experience in China, as mentioned in Chapter 3. The shortcake scene in *Early Summer* is then the poorly fed soldier's wish-fulfilment, a reaction to unfulfilled desire for everyday pleasure originating out of an extreme situation. Therefore, extravagance can be a form of reality in Ozu's term, an 'ironic realism' (like the riddle of 'flower and mud') that works through the comparative historical contexts of the war and the postwar.

In the end, the domestic movement and eating scenes function as a presentation of the 'possibility' of everyday life that had been lost for the Japanese in the midst of the long suffering of war. And it is important that the subject of that change is gender exclusive; walks that cut through banal domestic space and enjoyment of tasty food are all contingent upon the female sensitivity to history and the everyday. In comparison, the leading male characters in Ozu's Occupation-era films, most of whom are aged fathers, are depicted as the ones who seem to have lost a concrete linkage to the present everyday, and to be drawn to the past. The retrospective tendency is sometimes revealed through their inclination towards traditional space, as evidenced by father Somiya's preference for Kyoto in *Late Spring*. Their static oldness is also visualised in the profile shots of quiet reading that often appear during this period. This does not mean that there is no reading scene for women, but a certain serious atmosphere exists in the males' reading that is hard to find in females, who prefer to 'move' rather than 'read'. These male readers are intellectual enough to be literate in foreign languages (Mimura in *The Munekata Sisters* reads in German,

Figure 4.3 Father Munekata reads a magazine article called 'Atomic Bomb'

and Somiya in *Late Spring* also reads *Thus Spoke Zarathustra*). It would be natural then that they also take interest in the history of recent war, as Ozu implied in a brief moment in *The Munekata Sisters* wherein the father Munakata is seen reading an English article entitled 'Atomic Bomb' (see Figure 4.3). Played by none other than the actor Ryū Chishū, whose roles as patriarchal characters during the wartime films are discussed in the previous chapter, Munekata is a tender yet reticent old man, whose deep contemplation seems to represent the confusion of postwar Japanese intellectuals who had to struggle with the legacies of Japan's wartime history, including the aforementioned Overcoming Modernity symposium.

Stuck in the past time and space for themselves, the father characters in Ozu's Occupation-era films, however, play a significant intermediary role in the narratives to encourage (and sometimes persuade) their daughters to marry. As discussed in the previous chapter, Ozu already dealt with the conflict surrounding marriage in the script of *The Flavour of Green Tea over Rice* with the character Setsuko, who is reluctant to get married through *omiai*. He began to develop this narrative motif even further in the postwar years, and the first attempt was the script of *The Moon Has Risen*, which was written even before

Late Spring, a very well-known example of the marriage problem in Ozu's films. Although no actual marriage occurs, *The Moon Has Risen* is very much a romance drama about two couples. The protagonist family, a father and three daughters, is originally from Tokyo but is living in Nara after taking refuge there during war. The eldest, Chizuru, is a widow, but the other two, Ayako and Setsuko, are as yet unmarried. The narrative follows the love-matches of the second and third daughter in that order.

What characterises these relationships is that they are commonly based on a temporal sensitivity connected with the past. Ayako and her lover Amemiya first met during a summer vacation spent in her family's seaside cottage more than ten years previously, the remembrance of which is repeatedly mentioned by characters until the two finally confirm their mutual affection. Setsuko and her lover Shōji are also old acquaintances, as the latter remembers when the former was a 'snivelling' child. Moreover, Shōji's character signifies the invisible existence of his dead brother (also Chizuru's husband and Setsuko's brother-in-law). The reason for Shōji's brother's death is not clarified, except that it has been two years since he died (that is, in 1945, given that the script was written in 1947). An early part of the script includes a scene of a memorial service for the dead brother, where a friend of his visits the family to offer incense at the altar and mourn that the year he died will 'always be remembered as a hot year'. Such a linkage between a marriage partner and a dead soldier provides an essential clue for historicising the narrative of marriage in this film. A similar connection reappears in *Early Summer*: a widower whom the protagonist Noriko chooses to marry is a close friend of Noriko's brother, who died at war. Although never appearing in the film, the dead character is deeply remembered by his old parents. Their cryptic murmur in the ending scene of the film, 'Many things have happened ... for a long time', sounds less a mere lamentation of ageing parents than a comment on their inner suffering as victims who are as yet deprived of the chance to make their voices heard, whether by the US or by Japanese militarists.

In parallel with this retrospective aspect, the romance in *The Moon Has Risen* also signifies a new start. Both Ayako and Setsuko move to Tokyo following their partner, which does not merely remain a personal affair, but indicates a symbolic advancement towards the war-stricken space of Tokyo from the traditional city of Nara. Even before her relationship begins, Setsuko, the youngest and the most liberal, repeatedly expresses her desire to go back to her hometown, where the rhythm of everyday life is 'allegro', rather than 'Noh's tempo' in Nara. Her idea greatly contrasts with that of her father Mokichi, who, typically as an aged man, prefers tranquil Nara to 'messy and dusty' Tokyo, where only 'weeds grow'. He thus advises the daughter, 'Tokyo as you are imagining does not exist anymore', a remark that clearly echoes the father Somiya's utterance in *Late Spring*.[69] However, the old father does not enforce his idea on the daughters; rather he accepts the difference and encourages them to marry and leave his side to move to Tokyo.

Both the temporal and spatial points considered together, it can be concluded then that Ozu, with the romance narrative in *The Moon Has Risen*, attempted a historical allegory by complexly interweaving the forgotten past of the prewar and the present postwar. While fathers are complacent about the former, they get bewildered and silenced in front of the reality of the latter that results from the wartime. The role of connecting those two separated realms is placed on the young female characters, who are more responsive to everyday space and pleasure, as discussed. Standing on the traditional ground of Nara, they yearn for, and move towards, Tokyo, a place of the Everyday Regained, where the future of the postwar resides. The old, with whom I think Ozu emotionally sympathises, do not deny the flow, but rather accept it as reality. In reverse, the young, while marrying and leaving, do not forget the memory of the past, on which their romance is actually based. It is the 'sensitivities to the continuities of the past [in the present]', as Alastair Phillips put it in relation to Ozu's postwar female characters, that similarly operate in the making of love relationships.[70] Thus Nara, 'the present disguised in the image of the past . . . will be remembered as another image of the past in the future, in a different space', as Setsuko assures Shōji and herself while watching the moon on the night of their decision to leave together.[71]

The essence of Ozu's Occupation-era films thus lies in the complex process of negotiation between these two contradictory temporal and spatial positions, which involves the contrast between history and the everyday, and also the division according to gender and generation. In this regard, Ozu's Occupation era is a distinct period from the preceding wartime and the following postwar years. Ozu's following Occupation-era films – *Late Spring*, *The Munekata Sisters* and *Early Summer* – basically repeat the same principle of 'advancing ahead while holding back' in their narrative of marriage, albeit in varied forms.[72] However, even though the marriage narrative would continue to be retold until his last film, *Sanma no aji/An Autumn Afternoon* (1962), such late postwar films would slowly begin to lose the same intensity of historical consciousness as can be found in the films of the Occupation era. The change signifies a return to modernity both in space and time, as first signalled by the 1952 film *The Flavour of Green Tea over Rice*, a postwar remake of the wartime script discussed in the previous chapter. The next section will cross-examine that resurrection of the modern everyday with another look at the new postwar modernity from an opposite perspective: *Tokyo Story*.

Two Tales of a City: Tokyo Regained, Tokyo Lost

The postwar version of *The Flavour of Green Tea over Rice* was Ozu's first comedy film in fifteen years since *What Did the Lady Forget?*, a long timespan caused by the troubled history of wartime, including the breaking-off of the production of the same titled film. As such, its existence in Ozu's filmography has been somewhat disregarded; not only was it made in between two of the director's most revered films– *Early Summer* and *Tokyo Story* – but also its dominant mood was pleasantly trivial (just as the light-hearted comedy *What Did the Lady Forget?*). It seems that Ozu may have taken up this old project in a makeshift fashion. In 1955, Ozu remembered in an interview that, '[*The Flavour of Green Tea over Rice* had been] an old material brought in to fill up the year, not properly planned as usual'.[73] Ozu and Noda were actually preparing a different script earlier in 1952. But in dealing with a story of a mother and her five grown-up children, it became a more serious work closer to *The Only Son* than they had wanted (for commercial viability). The project was eventually aborted and they began work on revising the wartime script of *The Flavour of Green Tea over Rice*.[74] Accordingly, his evaluation of the film was unfavourable, calling it 'a film with a terrible aftertaste'.[75]

The general response of critics was not that different. Even though the film continued Ozu's postwar commercial success – in terms of box-office revenue it was the most popular Shochiku film and the second most popular Japanese film released in that year – *The Flavour of Green Tea over Rice* was not included in *Kinema Junpo*'s annual top ten list (which ranked it twelfth), the first time any of Ozu's films had been left off the list since he began to be listed in 1930. A Japanese critic, Shimizu Chiyota, wrote in the magazine, 'Among Ozu's postwar films, none disappointed me as much as this one'.[76] He argued that, unlike the original script which had included 'a critique of society and war, even if only slightly', the final film only articulated 'Ozu's view of the husband and wife relationship and contemporary custom and manners (*fūzoku*)', and as a result 'lost touch with the outside world and became isolated'.[77] The criticism was, as usual, directed towards Ozu's understanding of the real world, which had 'just been liberated from the Occupation', with 'complex undercurrents and torrents' still swirling.[78]

But ironically, this shift of focus onto 'custom and manners' can make the film a very important turning point in the progress of Ozu's postwar cinema. It is true that the war references in the original script had to be removed (for example, the protagonist's going to war became a business trip), diminishing the impact of the narrative. But instead, Ozu's new interpretations, inundated with various signifiers of urban everyday culture, drew a representative (though caricatured) portrait of postwar Tokyo, which would become the prototype of his post-1958 'new salaryman films' that will be discussed in the next chapter. In this sense, I agree with Tanaka Masasumi's opinion that the film, for all its weaknesses, 'ironically reflects the phenomenon called the postwar'.[79] Virtually everything relevant to postwar urban everyday life (except for television) seems to appear here – from cars to planes, from newspapers to radio, from baseball to *pachinko*, and from bars to *ramen* restaurants – the dizzying array of which itself is characteristic of the postwar period. Inclusion of these mass culture signifiers was intentional from the earliest stages of the rewriting of the script, as evidenced by Noda's mention of a weekly magazine article about the *pachinko* phenomenon in his interview in January 1952.[80]

In this sense, the film may be seen as a very early document of recuperated mass culture in Japan, matching the new political environment instituted by the end of the US Occupation (with the signing of the San Francisco Peace Treaty in 1952). Such an interpretation can be supported by the fact that the film's primary setting is entirely based on Tokyo, the director's cinematic hometown. After spending a few years in the old traditional spaces of Kyoto, Nara and Kamakura, Ozu, with this film, marks a symbolic return to the place of the everyday and of the now. This odyssey, however, was a big challenge as well, for Ozu had already declared that the 'prewar Tokyo does not exist anymore'. In an interview in 1951, asked why the typical Shitamachi images in his prewar films – factories, gas tanks, shepherd's purse and the inhabitants – had disappeared in his postwar films, he answered, 'I have become less affectionate towards those people living there than I used to be. In the past, they were not as cold-hearted as now'.[81] Now back in the city where he could find little trace of the past, what would he be able to present to the postwar audiences other than the 'dust' and 'weed' that the old fathers in Occupation-era films expect to exist there? In *The Flavour of Green Tea over Rice*, he seems to have decided to answer the question by showing the high modernity of the city that was moving again in full gear after the Occupation.

Such intent looks obvious from the very first scene, where the female protagonist Taeko and her niece Setsuko take a taxi ride through Miyakezaka to the Ginza district in central Tokyo to visit a luxury boutique run by Taeko's friend Aya. The ladies' talk about eating out and watching *kabuki* theatre confirms that the female everyday emphasised in the original wartime script is being adapted intact. However, if the script's spatial scope is greatly restricted within a domestic boundary, the postwar film broadens it into the cityscape of Tokyo seen through the window of the moving taxi. Forward and side tracking shots, where trams, other cars, buildings and pedestrians are seen, move us through the busy streets towards the Hattori building – the symbol of Ginza. Compared to the stilled image appearing in *Late Spring*, the building in *The Flavour of Green Tea over Rice* is a living object floating on the horizon, slowly growing in size as the taxi approaches it. Never before had Ozu's Tokyo obtained such visual immediacy, such a sense of documenting the here and now. There is a kind of joy at the rediscovery of landscape rising at this moment, which makes this opening scene a welcoming statement of Ozu's return to the city.[82]

This cheerful ride happens on a sunny 'afternoon with a gentle breeze in May', accompanied by light, piano-led chamber music.[83] The sunshine from the side window falls on the laps of the two ladies, while they talk about a Jean Marais movie that Setsuko will see that day. In the next scene we see Aya's boutique in Ginza, which, filled with brightly coloured Western furniture and miscellaneous goods, constitutes one of the most modern spaces Ozu ever created. The image of Aya in her office represents the professional working woman, who, for the first time in Ozu, governs the modern space as a subject. Her black stylish dress harmonises with the immaculate surroundings, and a shiny pearl necklace is juxtaposed with a tape measure around her neck. Meanwhile, Taeko, who has arrived at the shop with Setsuko, casually buys a bottle of perfume before going up to the office to see Aya and begin the ladies' chat. With all this mobility, brightness, capability and leisure, the postwar Tokyo of this Ginza sequence seems to leap off the screen with an unprecedented sense of optimism and confidence. If the wartime script's focus was on the affluence and leisure time of the female characters, which, in relation to the subject matter of forced *omiai*, functions as the basis for female resistance to a male-driven social order, that of the film version is transferred to urban modernity, where females were already a predominant subject of everyday life. Although the question of Setsuko's *omiai* still remains, it does not have sufficient momentum to lead the narrative anymore.

Such changes apply not only to female characters but also to males, especially younger ones. Okada, aged twenty-six and called by his nickname 'Non-chan', was a non-existent character in the wartime script, and represents the new postwar generation. He had an older brother who died at war, the memory of which, however, hardly affects the narrative, in stark contrast with Ozu's Occupation-era films. For him, *omiai* is an enjoyable opportunity to 'meet someone first and see if love grows afterwards'. He is also active in pursuing the pleasures of urban life such as eating out and drinking, playing *pachinko* and going to bicycle races. The scene where he drinks at a bar with Mokichi, a friend of Non-chan's dead brother and Taeko's husband, reminds viewers of the long forgotten world of the salaryman. Drinking after work did not exist in the prewar *shōshimin* films, but would become a typically recurring motif of the postwar white collar's everyday life in Ozu's films a few years on. Ozu's typical *mise en scène* of office interior, such as a long corridor shot by a low-height camera, began to appear in this film as well.

The urban modernity discussed so far is characterised by its openness and accessibility, which more fundamentally presupposes the existence of anonymous masses. Viewers are often presented with shots of crowds in which the main characters are embedded – such as in baseball stadiums, at bicycle racetracks and in airports. *Ramen* restaurants, *pachinko* parlours, and the back alleys that connect such small places of cheap pleasure are also open spaces in which anonymous people can pass without noticing each other. The public nature of urban space is strongly distinguished from the more privately oriented spaces that appeared in Ozu's prewar films. For example, the *ramen* restaurant where Non-chan and Setsuko enjoy a bowl of *ramen* is very different from Iida Chōko's restaurant in the Kihachi films. What fills the gap created by the anonymity is an ardent wish of the masses for sound, speed and thrills. *Ramen* exists as a palatable experience to be admired and exclaimed at. Non-chan and Setsuko's slurping sounds add an auditory sensation to this joie de vivre, supporting the carefree 'simplicity' that he explains to her while eating.

It is a similar sound of the city that defines the atmosphere of the *pachinko* parlour, the baseball stadium and the racetrack, but with the speed of ball and bicycle, the experience comes closer to a momentary thrill. *Pachinko* players, all facing the machine in silence, wait for the tinkling sound of scoring, and the spectators at a bicycle race, watching the final spurt towards the goal, all inadvertently stand up from their seats. Non-chan's remark, 'A bicycle race is like *pachinko* with the ball riding on the saddle', eloquently describes the essential commonality shared between the two cultural activities (see Figures 4.4 and 4.5). I agree with Hasumi Shigehiko's point that there is 'unnatural artificiality' in the 'unidirectional gaze' of these people at such moments, which he interprets as Ozu's intentional visual 'exaggeration', working against otherwise repressed and refined narrative structures.[84] The enormous energy dormant within this visual orderliness also signifies the attraction to the thrill of instantaneity, which is not irrelevant to the regained everyday life after war. The everyday as momentary pleasure, which was not prominently articulated in Ozu's films of the early 1930s when urban culture was at its height, now emerges as the central dominant theme of the film. I believe that this is the most fundamental vision of the New Tokyo that Ozu found on his return to the city.

This does not mean that Ozu himself is actively affirming such a change, even though he does not deny it either. His personal stance is conveyed through the character of Mokichi, the forty-two-year-old salaryman. For example, Mokichi's remark about *pachinko* summarises Ozu's critical view of postwar mass society as well as of the urban culture itself: 'One enters a state of self-annihilation while being with many other people. It is a simple way of becoming alone . . . separated from all the woes of the world. The ball is me, and I am the ball. It is

Figures 4.4 (upper) & 4.5 (lower) An ardent energy is dormant in the unidirectional look of the postwar masses when playing *pachinko* and watching a bicycle race

pure loneliness that enchants the people – happiness in loneliness'.[85] On the other hand, Mokichi has his own life principle, that is, favouring an 'intimate, primitive, and relaxed' way of life in contrast to the 'aloofness and propriety' of his wife Taeko's bourgeois lifestyle. Just as in the original wartime script, the film's narrative is structured as a moral drama of reforming the latter's worldview through the former's values, and rebuilding their relationship. This sounds a trite moral conservatism (as found in the 'failed *moga*' narrative) that attempts to redress all the excesses of urban modernity in the earlier part of the film. In this sense, the *ochazuke* the couple share for reconciliation is a very different signifier from the cooked rice or shortcake in *Early Summer* which articulates female subjectivity. If the wartime original had been released in 1940 as planned, its thematic message, the beauty of the simple everyday, would have had a different connotation in the context of militarism. In 1952, however, it seems to work as an anticlimactic ending to a film that is otherwise full of the vibrant energy of urban modernity.

Ozu, I assume, attempted to reduce the gap between this new Tokyo and his unique world of the everyday through the young male character Non-chan. As the one who introduces *pachinko* and bicycle races to Mokichi, Non-chan seems to incarnate Ozu's ideal of the new postwar generation, who can adapt to the changes while retaining Ozu's fundamental values. However, *The Flavour of Green Tea over Rice* is clearly a film for Mokichi's voice rather than Non-chan's. In contrast with his female characters, Ozu would never seriously develop a major young male character, which I think is part of the reason why the director would be faced with an uncomfortable relationship with the postwar generation a few years later on.

As discussed, Ozu's everyday has a deeper meaning when it constantly violates the border between two different realms, whether they are modernity and tradition or the present and the past. If they do not permeate each other and are segregated, the everyday turns into the mere repetition of mediocrity. Perhaps *The Flavour of Green Tea over Rice* might be the first film where Ozu shows a sign of failing to achieve that sophisticated balance and negotiation. A symptom of this failure is noticeable in the first *pachinko* parlour scene in the film, where Mokichi, along with Non-chan, encounters his war comrade, Hirayama, who happens to run the business. Delighted and surprised, Hirayama invites them into his living area, which is just the inner space adjacent to the parlour. As such, the parlour is supposed to be a recreation of the typical Shitamachi space, where living and working areas are openly combined together as we have seen in Kihachi films. But Hirayama's place loses that complex 'public yet private' spatial nature, and is separated into two very distinguished areas: the bright, noisy and buoyant *pachinko* parlour, and Hirayama's dim, calm and somehow melancholic inner space (see Figure 4.6).

Figure 4.6 Hirayama's room inside his *pachinko* parlour, where the nostalgic memory of war is recounted (compare with the outside *pachinko* parlour in Figure 4.4 and also Figure 3.2)

What Ozu intends with this sheltered inner area is certainly the flickering memory of the past. Hirayama – the role properly given to none other than Ryū Chishū again – clearly misses the wartime. Although agreeing with Mokichi that he is fed up with the war itself, Hirayama longs for the images of natural beauty of Singapore where he fought – palm trees, clear sky and Southern Cross. These exotic visual images present a stark contrast with the sorrow of the death of a comrade expressed in the song *Senyū no ikotsu o daite/ Holding the Ashes of Comrade*, which Hirayama sings while drinking. The scene as such becomes the first direct reference to war experience in a reminiscent form in Ozu's postwar films. In great contrast, Hirayama also reveals without hesitation his negative view of his currently thriving business because 'enjoying [*pachinko*] is [morally] bad'. Ozu's typical device of temporal differentiation is used here between the present, which is despised, and the past, which is missed in nostalgia. When Hirayama's song reaches the climax of the second verse with the lyrics, 'Charging forward, day after day/We watched together Southern Cross', Ozu cuts from the saddened face of the singer to the parlour outside, which, now empty and darkened, finally resonates with the memory of the past that Hirayama is mourning.

Ozu, however, does not pursue resolving the conflict between the past and the present in this film, leaving Hirayama's character with a very minor role. Nor does he succeed in extending Hirayama's alienation and dilemma to Mokichi or Non-chan. That sensitivity for the contrasting temporalities existent in the evanescent everyday rather becomes the central issue again in the next film, *Tokyo Story*. For a film regarded as one of the most influential works in film history, as well as of his career, Ozu left an understatement that this was his most 'melodramatic' film in the sense that he 'wanted to depict how Japan's family system was breaking down by showing the change of parent-children relations'.[86] However, I believe Ozu wanted to suggest with this remark that he did not intend the film as an artistic masterpiece (as it is regarded today), but as a return to the familiar world of the Shitamachi, and the *ninjō* of its people, through the typical subject matter of the parent-child relationship. *Tokyo Story*, in other words, could be seen as Ozu's personal look back on what had been his unique territory, which once had culminated in such films as *The Only Son*, but did not exist anymore. If *The Flavour of Green Tea over Rice* deliberately avoided this truth by focusing on the new, *Tokyo Story* confronts it directly, probably for the last time in Ozu's career.

Ozu aimed to achieve a lot with this film. First of all, he had to recover from the failure he felt he had made with the previous *The Flavour of Green Tea over Rice*. Secondly, he wanted to complete what he had planned but could not have dealt with in *Early Summer*.[87] According to Noda, the original idea of *Early Summer* was to articulate the egoism inherent in family life; 'although every family member seems concerned about [Noriko's] matter . . . they are in fact thinking only of themselves'.[88] In writing a script with this theme, Noda and Ozu found the narrative became more discursive, focusing on all the family rather than just Noriko, whose character they wanted to emphasise in order to make use of Hara Setsuko's star power. After all, *Early Summer* became a story about Noriko's marriage, just as *Late Spring* was, and Ozu wanted to revise this in *Tokyo Story* in order to fully explore the theme of familial relationships. He thus clarified the intent of the production as, 'I would like to depict aversion inherent in blood relationships from the perspective of children'.[89] In this regard, the role of the selfish children in the film, such as the first son Kōichi and the first daughter Shige, should not be underestimated. Thirdly, Ozu nevertheless did not want *Tokyo Story* to be a 'realistic' film that simply acknowledges the rise of individualism and familial disintegration in postwar society, but rather wanted it to offer a hopeful vision of the virtue of filial piety. Ozu thus had in mind another attempt at ironical realism, that is, showing dispassionate familial relationships embedded in urban daily life in order to 'make audiences realise the need for filial duty even if oppressing their feeling [of aversion]'.[90]

The main reason why *Tokyo Story* is an *effective* melodrama lies in this mixture of rationalism and emotionalism. It may well be 'didactic' as Bordwell evaluates; Ozu and Noda's script is sometimes too direct in conveying the theme of filial piety, as is evident in the reference to a Confucian maxim, 'It's too late to mourn over a parent's tomb'.[91] However, by successfully distributing the narrative weight amongst the different characters – from the more realistic Kōichi, Shige and Keizo to the more sympathetic Noriko and Kyōko – Ozu does not easily allow viewers to fall prey to melodramatic sentimentalism for the sake of these moral concerns. Rather he confronts viewers with an acute but frank realisation that there is nothing much that can be done about these situations. None of the children eventually regrets or repents their actions (or inaction) in relation to their parents in the film; just as the married daughters in the Occupation-period films did, they advance towards a future situated in Tokyo, leaving the dead and dying past behind. If the film is melodramatic, the thing that triggers our emotion is that cold realistic rigour of the younger generation, which provokes thought rather than tears in viewers. That is why Ozu argued, 'Neither Noda nor I intended to make audiences cry while watching this film. We only wanted to write the parent-child relationship as it is, neither denying nor affirming it'.[92]

Contradictorily, during the early 1950s when the film came out, Shochiku was experiencing a boost in box-office returns aided by the success of popular melodramas. The signs of recuperation began to appear at the beginning of the 1950s, when Shochiku regained its position as top film company, based on distribution revenues, which it had lost to Toho and Daiei during the late 1940s.[93] The peak of Shochiku's popularity was in 1953 and 1954, when the *What Is Your Name?* trilogy was an unprecedented hit – even bigger than *The Love-Troth Tree* trilogy, the previous record-holder in Japanese cinema – and when it made official the return of *Ōfuna-chō*. The revival of *Ōfuna-chō* meant the principal tenet of the company, Kido-ism, was still in operative mode in the postwar. Giving precedence to public reception over individual statement, Kido's creed in business, however, created disharmony with some Shochiku directors with more artistic ambitions, whose ideals were in constant negotiation with the principles of *Ōfuna-chō*. Tanaka Jun'ichirō noted that Kido even believed that 'Shochiku's filmmakers, who had long grown up by the *Ōfuna-chō*'s home drama [tradition], were not sensitive enough to [deal with] social realities and the spirit of the times'.[94] Such a conflict is well revealed in the example of Kobayashi Masaki's *Kabe atsuki heya/The Thick Walled Room* (made in 1953, released in 1956), which, dealing with the subject of war criminals, was 'put on the shelf (*okura*)' by Kido himself.[95] Similarly, in the case of Yoshimura Kōzaburō, his plan to direct *Itsuwareru seisō/Clothes of Deception* (1951) was not supported by Ofuna, and he finally left the studio with his then scriptwriter Shindō Kaneto to establish an independent production company, Kindai Eiga Kyōkai.[96]

However, in the sense that the success of Shochiku's postwar melodrama was dependent on the genre's appeal to the changing taste of the targeted mass audience group, especially women, it can be also regarded that *Ōfuna-chō* had a very social dramaturgy. Ōba Hideo, having been the target of criticism after the success of his *What Is Your Name?*, honestly acknowledged that the so-called *Ōfuna-chō* melodrama was more a popular than an artistic work. If the latter belonged to the realm of realism, then what melodrama dealt with was fantasy, the 'dreamy part of film'.[97] The issue left was the 'extent of separation' (of the fantasy from the reality in a film), and '*Ōfuna-chō* existed somewhere in between that subtle balance'.[98] It should also be noted that Shochiku was not the exclusive beneficiary of the popularity of melodrama, which rather was a more prevalent phenomenon in Japanese cinema from the late 1940s. It was actually Daiei that revived the boom in the form of the *hahamono* (mother film), a genre that was connected to the tradition of *shinpa* tragedy, with a typically strong mother-and-child relationship and a melodramatic narrative about destiny, self-sacrifice, endurance, chance encounters and emotional exaltation. After all, the postwar *Ōfuna-chō* melodrama, as well as Daiei's *hahamono*, was within the influence of the *shinpa* tradition that I have discussed in Chapter 1.

Ozu's work in the context of Ofuna, then, represents this complexity residing in the name of *Ōfuna-chō*, where the desires for mass popularity and artistic achievement are intertwined, and generic convention confronts newer directions. It is a well-known anecdote that Kido himself often referred to Ozu as an exception within the studio, a director who did not conform to his vision of *Ōfuna-chō*, but was too large a figure in Japanese cinema for him to intervene. Dubbed a *meishō* (master), Ozu was regarded and evaluated as an auteur in the postwar period, and as such found himself in an antagonistic position towards Kido's commercialism. On the other hand, it is still true that Ozu's position never greatly transcended the boundary of *Ōfuna-chō* as in the case of Kobayashi or Yoshimura. With all its deep penetration into postwar reality, *Tokyo Story* is still a continuation of the sympathetic story of child-parent relationships as had been told in the Kihachi series or *The Only Son*. Therefore, it is a symbolic occasion of rendezvous between a master of cinema and popular *Ōfuna-chō* style when both *What Is Your Name?* and *Tokyo Story* were released together in the autumn of 1953 to box-office success. It should be noted that Ozu in this period was continuing the commercial popularity that he first achieved during wartime.

Table 4.1 Top grossing Shochiku films in the early 1950s (compiled from Iwamoto and Makino, *Eiga nenkan, sengo hen*)

	1951	1952	1953
1	Five Men of Edo (Itō Daisuke)	**The Flavour of Green Tea over Rice (Ozu Yasujirō)**	What Is Your Name? Part I (Ōba Hideo)
2	**Early Summer (Ozu Yasujirō)**	Wave (Nakamura Noboru)	What Is Your Name? Part II (Ōba Hideo)
3	School of Freedom (Shibuya Minoru)	The Moderns (Shibuya Minoru)	The Life of a Flower (Ōsone Tatsuo)
4	Crossing That Hill (Mizuho Shunkai)	A Cheerful Migratory Bird (Sasaki Yamushi)	**Tokyo Story (Ozu Yasujirō)**
5		Tsukigata Hanpeita (Uchide Kōkichi)	The Garden of Women (Kinoshita Keisuke)

As seen in Table 4.1, not only *Tokyo Story* but also two previously released films ranked within the top five grossing Shochiku films. In this sense, the dichotomy between art and popularity assumed in Kido's attitude was not applicable to Ozu's case, at least during the postwar period. In fact, along with the films of Kinoshita Keisuke, Ozu's films would provide for Shochiku after 1957, when the company's genre vehicles ceased to work in Japanese box-offices, as will be discussed in the next chapter.

Tokyo Story was also favourably received by contemporary Japanese critics, who generally agreed that the film was the director's greatest achievement so far. Above all, it was a long awaited return (since the Occupation period) to a more realistic rendition of Shitamachi's lower-middle-class struggle and everyday life. Togawa Naoki, distinguishing *The Only Son* from *What Did the Lady Forget?*, designated *Tokyo Story* as 'Ozu's new stage', which, while retaining the 'elaborate [formal] expression' of the latter, attempted to 'depict the emotion in the life of *shomin*' whose existence had been forgotten since the former.[99] Imamura Taihei, declaring this was 'the best among Ozu's postwar works', welcomed that the film 'had returned to the poor life of lower-middle classes', with a 'feel of faithfulness'.[100] For Imamura, Ozu's works from *Late Spring* to *The Flavour of Green Tea over Rice* revealed a tendency to reflect the 'taste of parvenus', who appeared amid the confusion of class shifts caused by the unstable postwar economy. This strategy, Imamura argued, could not succeed because the lives of the wealthy were not a part of Ozu's world, and *Tokyo Story* owed its success to the 'return to the *seikatsu* (everyday life) closer to Ozu himself'.[101]

Compared with the nostalgic vision in the Kihachi series in the prewar, *Tokyo Story*'s Shitamachi focuses more on the here and now of the postwar, where the past is reduced to a bare glimmer of memory in the midst of the present life. Even *The Only Son*, which similarly dealt with the life of Shitamachi's people, was not as contemporary as *Tokyo Story*, for its conclusion was mellowed by the unforeseeable hope for *risshin shusse* in the future as well as the longing for the hometown in the past. In *Tokyo Story*, Ozu discovers the presentness of the Shitamachi through the eyes of old parents, whose generation, in Ozu's Occupation-era films, chose to remain in (or retreat into) the past, refusing to return to the land of the 'dust' and 'weed'. It is thus natural that the narrative of the film is structured around a trip by the parents from their hometown in Onomichi, which 'evaded war damage' as the old capitals did, to the once ruined city of Tokyo, the place of *seikatsu*.

The locality of Shitamachi is mainly depicted through the everyday life of the first son Kōichi and the first daughter Shige. Kōichi's surrounding neighbourhood especially shows the typical visual signifiers of Shitamachi – smoking factory chimneys and the riverbank – which filled the urban landscape of *An Inn in Tokyo*, *The Only Son* and *A Hen in the Wind*, but had largely disappeared from the suburbs in the Occupation-era films. Kōichi's and Shige's work spaces are directly adjacent to their living spaces, which is the typical spatial structure of the Shitamachi. This proximity of work and domesticity, however, does not articulate an intimate relationship between the private and the public as appearing in the Kihachi films, but rather functions to reveal the reality of the busy life that Kōichi and Shige are leading. The dialogue of the film is pervaded by the word *isogashii* (busy), which rarely appears in Ozu's other films. Noriko, for instance, is late to meet her parents-in-law as they arrive at Tokyo Station because she 'was so disordered [at work] as to forget the time'. Later in the film, the busy nature of life results in a more serious situation when the last son Keizō does not arrive on time to keep his mother's deathbed. But once the funeral is over, the children (except for the daughter-in-law Noriko) hurry to return to Tokyo, back to the usual everyday rhythm.

The everyday life in Shitamachi is restricted in terms of space as well. The three houses that the parents visit in Tokyo – Kōichi's, Shige's and Noriko's – are commonly characterised by their compactness, which is implied through the *mise en scène* of domestic shots crowded by various domestic objects on walls or shelves. Domestic movement is also accordingly restricted. In the first Tokyo scene, Kōichi's wife Fumiko cleans the house, moving from room to room to prepare for the parents' visit, which almost repeats Noriko's domestic movement in *Late Spring*. However, as this is a chore that must be finished in time for their arrival (she constantly interrupted by her children as well), Fumiko's movement subtly lacks Noriko's cheerfulness and vitality. Shige's place suffers even more from this spatial restriction as seen in a brief shot of the rooftop of her house, where her father Shūkichi, sitting alone, spends a boring afternoon. With black smoke from factory chimneys in the background filling the grey sky and incessant metallic sounds from nearby machinery on the soundtrack, the depressive scenery can be the most pessimistic vision of the postwar Shitamachi.

The Shitamachi space in *Tokyo Story* is also marginal in relation to the urban centre. Ozu does not specify how the former is spatially linked to the latter, but the distance is inferable from the parents' conversation that 'It took quite a long time by car [from Tokyo station to Kōichi's]'. The parents' visit to the city centre is delayed for more than half an hour after the film begins, a significant contrast with the emphatic beginning of the taxi ride scene in *The Flavour of Green Tea over Rice*. Compared with the taxi ride, *Tokyo Story*'s city sightseeing sequence is less about the enjoyment of the present everyday than an observation and reading of the city from an outsider's point of view on a tourist bus. The text is historical, as indicated by the tour conductor's announcement, 'Let's *read* the history of Great Tokyo together', followed by her explanation that the Imperial Palace is 500 years old. The bus then arrives at Ginza, where none other than the Hattori building reappears at the conclusion of the ride. But if the two women in the taxi in *The Flavour of Green Tea over Rice* have full command of the urban life in terms of both space (Taeko tells the driver where to turn and pull in) and time (they talk about how to spend the day, whether to go to the cinema or visit Aya's Ginza boutique), the tourists (including the parents) on the bus in *Tokyo Story* appear to be totally lacking in such authority and seem alienated from the cityscape flowing past outside the window. All they do is turn their heads left and right according to the conductor's announcements, in absolute reticence and simultaneity.

This passive relationship with the urban centre continues into the next scene set on a Ginza department-store building rooftop, where Shūkichi and his wife Tomi, guided by Noriko, try to figure out where their children's homes are located. Although Noriko indicates approximate directions with her finger, Ozu's camera, showing only the backs of the three characters, refuses to give a clear answer to the parents' (and viewers') doubtful question, 'Where?' (see Figure 4.7). The last shot of the scene finally presents a panoramic point-of-view shot of the cityscape, and it only turns out to be dense clusters of indifferent buildings in Tokyo's city centre aimlessly stretching into the horizon.

Figure 4.7 Looking at Tokyo from a rooftop (compare with Figure 4.1)

At that moment, the city loses its spatial contextuality between the centre and the periphery and becomes an incomprehensible text for the parents to read. The bewilderment of the parents is reaffirmed later in the film when they, watching over the city again, utter their impressions: 'How vast Tokyo is,' and 'If lost, we'll never meet again'. The same applies to the temporal references of the city. Postwar Tokyo, now largely reconstructed both in Ginza and Shitamachi, has already effaced most of the traces of war from its surface.[102] The 'dust' that the father Somiya mentioned in *Late Spring* to describe Tokyo is nowhere to be found. Losing these temporal as well as spatial connections, the city is left only to the care of the present, which is acutely recognised as bizarre artificiality by the parents, who represent the past as well as the spatially remote hometown.[103]

For Shūkichi and Tomi, there are two places in the film where they can make sense of the city. One is Noriko's apartment. In terms of the everyday, the apartment space, though a modern form of residence, retains the restricted nature of Shitamachi, even more than Kōichi's and Shige's homes. Consisting of only a small room and an attached kitchen, it is the most impoverished space in the film. But as such, it also faithfully recreates the old neighbourhood community

Figure 4.8 Shūkichi and Tomi look at a photograph of their dead son, Shōji; this is the only shot in Ozu's postwar films where someone who died in the war is visually referred to (compare with Figures 4.1, 4.7 and 3.3)

of Shitamachi, as evidenced when Noriko goes next door to borrow a bottle of *sake* and cups. Noriko has lived here for a long time, for she remembers that her husband Shōji, who died at war, used to bring his drunken salaryman colleagues home late at night. In other words, this apartment is not a postwar space but a memorial space, where the memory of the prewar still lingers. It is thus unsurprising that the parents, emblems of the prewar existence, feel at home here. In the apartment, they finally find a visual text – Shōji's photograph – that is legible to them (see Figure 4.8).

They are also finally seen to eat and drink here, the first time since the film began. So far in the narrative, food has been an element of denial and restriction. At the first dinner at Kōichi's, *sukiyaki* is served but *sashimi* is omitted, and at Shige's, cheap *senbe* is chosen for their snack instead of expensive bean-jam cake. This is an unusual abstinence in Ozu, if the liberating role of shortcake in *Early Summer* is considered. But the period of 'fast' effectively functions in the narrative to signal the transition into the past in the memorial space of Noriko's apartment. In fact, Noriko's pouring of *sake* and Shūkichi's first sip of it (with an irresistible smile on his face – he has abstained from drinking for a long time) becomes the crucial moment in this change of temporality that suddenly brings old memories back into the minds of the three characters, resulting in the first reference to the dead son/husband.

Later in the film, Shūkichi visits his old hometown friend Hattori and, along with another friend Numata, gives himself over to a night of heavy drinking. The topics that the three drunk old men engage in discussing are exclusively related to temporal sensitivity. They remember their long-gone heyday in Onomichi, lament the deaths of their sons at war, and are disappointed by surviving sons who do not live up to their past expectations. As an extended variation of the drinking scene at the *pachinko* parlour in *The Flavour of Green Tea over Rice*, the drinking sequence of *Tokyo Story* thus deals with the same theme of the disappearing memory of the prewar and wartime, and the powerlessness of the older generation in the face of changing postwar society. Instead of Hirayama's sorrowful elegy for a dead comrade in *The Flavour of Green Tea over Rice*, what is heard in the restaurant scene in *Tokyo Story* is the popular wartime melody of the Gunkan (warship) March, whose cheerful tune contrasts ironically with the men's contemplation of the painful (yet nostalgic) past. As if to express his deep grief for the loss of the time, Shūkichi performs a memorial re-enactment of what his dead son used to do – getting dead drunk and bringing friends to Shige's to spend the last night in Tokyo. This unexpected intrusion completely upsets Shige, which not only makes for the most comic situation in the film but also becomes the clearest moment of permeation of the past into the place of present everyday life (that is, Shige's beauty salon). Shige's angry reactions – volatile bodily movements and high-pitched grumbles – towards her father indicate the opposing natures of the two characters in terms of the temporality that each of them represents in the film.

As a memorial place, the two eating/drinking spaces also portend the death of the parents (literally for Tomi, metaphorically for Shūkichi) in the narrative. Shūkichi's drinking with his friends is a very ritualistic behaviour, a process of mourning the death of his own generation. As if to express this sorrow, a deep shadow frequently falls upon his face throughout the 'last night in Tokyo' sequence, a variation of which turns up later in the form of the white handkerchief on Tomi's face on her deathbed. Tomi's death is also more explicitly implied in the scene of her second visit to Noriko's apartment. When she slowly lies down to sleep at night, her body and face drown in darkness when Noriko turns off a ceiling light and says, '*oyasuminasai* (good night)' as if it were the last farewell to the mother-in-law. The fact that the *futon* Tomi sleeps on once belonged to her dead son Shōji also implies her impending death, as well as the retrospective nature of her character. The next morning, Tomi will indulge her memory of Shōji for the last time by looking at his picture again for a while. Noriko's apartment, in this sense, is a tomb – a tomb for the dying parents, a tomb for the dead husband/son upon whose memory the survivors sleep, and a tomb for the times that have been forgotten and left to dwell in deep shadow. No wonder this space looks so stiflingly tiny.

Ozu does not appeal to pity for the parents to produce a melodramatic effect and draw a thematic conclusion to the film. Rather, his way is, as always, to make the opposing temporal elements confront each other. In this sense, the first daughter Shige (Sugimura Haruko) occupies an important position in the film as the counterpart of her parents. Her character indeed incarnates the concept of *seikatsu* (if slightly exaggerated) from the standpoint of Ozu's postwar femininity, as previously discussed. For example, she is the one who governs the transfer of food and the activity of eating in the film. In the first Tokyo sequence where she visits Kōichi with her parents, Shige brings *senbei* (rice crackers) and *tsukudani* (seafood simmered in soy sauce) as presents to Fumiko, orienting Ozu's camera towards the kitchen. She then reassures Kōichi that *sukiyaki* would be enough for the parents' first dinner in Tokyo. Shige is also seen having breakfast with her husband at her place, the first appearance of actual eating in the film, and later treats herself to the bean-jam cake that her husband brings home for the parents, reproving him with, 'This is too expensive to serve them'. As such, Shige's eating constructs her selfish character in relation to her parents, which is repeatedly confirmed throughout the narrative.

Selfishness, however, is only another expression of resilience for Ozu's female characters. As discussed with the example of the 'expensive but delicious' shortcake, there is always a certain affirmative aspect in women's indulgence in everyday life that transcends a moral value judgement. In this sense, Shige's character may well be interpreted as a petit-bourgeois variation of the extravagant bourgeois ladies in Ozu's previous works, who do not hesitate to pursue their desires. In fact, some of her behaviours that signal her selfish character – preparing a mourning dress on hearing about Tomi's sickness and asking for the mother's fabric as a relic – are taken from the first daughter character Chizuru (Yoshikawa Mitsuko) in *The Toda Family*. Ozu's contemporary critics were also aware of this point. Togawa Naoki for instance defended Shige, saying that she was 'not necessarily malicious' but 'only did her best to protect her own living', and as such, her character played an integral part in Ozu's new direction in *Tokyo Story*, and his project of articulating the everyday life of the lower-middle classes. Togawa even thought that Noriko in the film was too much of an 'idealised type' created through Ozu's 'romanticism', which might underestimate the point that Shige's selfishness could be an 'inevitable result of contemporary life'.[104] After all, Shige's character constitutes a culmination in Ozu's female characters who, firmly grounded in the reality of the everyday, oppose a retrospective tendency of old or male characters.

What epitomises this contrast is a family dining scene. Tomi's funeral has just ended, and Shūkichi expresses his gratitude to all the family for their coming in spite of their 'busy' schedules. Shige, however, suddenly changes the subject of conversation from condolence to lively planning of the 'return to Tokyo'. Her following sharp utterance, 'Can I have a bowl of rice?', confirms the irrevocable transition of the mourning atmosphere in the room, comparable to Noriko and Fumiko's playful joke on Kōichi while exchanging a bowl of rice in *Early Summer*. Shūkichi regrets the fact that the children must leave and continues to drink in reticence, which Shige reproves again by saying, 'Don't drink too much'. With the series of opposing binaries between rice and *sake*, young woman and old man, and enjoyment and remembrance, Ozu here produces another variation of the postwar female subjectivity that chooses to move ahead towards the everyday rather than remain caught up in the past. The final shot of the dining scene – a juxtaposed two-shot of Shūkichi drinking *sake* and Shige eating rice – eloquently summarises the fundamental contradiction and dissonance of the two temporal dimensions as represented by the two characters, which nevertheless always coexist in Ozu's cinema (see Figure 4.9).

Figure 4.9 Coexistence in divergence: Shige eats rice while Shūkichi drinks *sake*

Ozu's early postwar years then can be summarised in terms of their acute sensitivity to distance between separate elements, both spatially and temporally. Tokyo, whether a tale of the 'Lost' or 'Regained', is constantly juxtaposed with its distanced, external counterparts, such as Nara in *The Moon Has Risen*, Kyoto in *Late Spring*, and Yamato in *Early Spring*. In these places, the iconic images of Japanese tradition, once a visual trope that supported Ozu's traditionalism, operate as an allegorical vehicle that does not merely stand for the preserved tradition per se, but rather reflects on the distanced existence of the present Tokyo and its everyday life. As discussed, this *distancing*, which accompanies many kinds of spatial movements from a journey in the literal sense to marriage in metaphor, is closely related to the war and Occupation that interrupted Japan's recent history. It is in fact surprising to see how consistently conscious Ozu was of the question of war throughout this period, albeit its expression was mostly implicative in contrast with melodramatic *What Is Your Name?* or destructive *Godzilla*. And the effort seems inevitable considering his unusual wartime experience and resulting self-doubt and self-examination to re-establish national identity, from which most other Japanese would not have been free at that time. In this sense it would be an inaccurate accusation that Ozu lost touch with the reality of postwar society; rather, the concept of tradition he adopted would be better understood by a more active notion of the historical past and its residual memory.

On the other hand, this period of Ozu can also be characterised by a reformed kind of the everyday, a gender-exclusive and domesticity-oriented version, originating from the life of bourgeois female characters appearing in the director's wartime films. Whether it is the high-spirited urban modernity consumed by the masses, as depicted in *The Flavour of Green Tea over Rice*, or the busy lower-middle class's life of the reconstructed Shitamachi district, as in *Tokyo Story*, the '*seikatsu*' led by women becomes the key motif that raises doubts about the male-centric view of the postwar. That peculiar vitality expressed in the flow of moving, chatting, eating and so on effectively permeates and enlivens the static world of tradition, maintaining a connection with the modern world, namely Tokyo, where postwar progress continues. It is also important that such vitality is shared and mutually supported by female solidarity amongst sisters, sisters-in-law and female friends. When this gender division gains historicity (as in the example of the restaurant scene in *Early Summer*), the female everyday can provide an active revelation of the rigidity and oppressiveness of the male-driven history of war and the postwar.

The main issue for postwar Ozu is, then, how to bridge this gap between the historical past and present, each represented through tradition and the everyday. During the Occupation period, the narrative of marriage seems to have successfully presented a solution to this dilemma between progress and amnesia by suggesting characters who, though burdened by the memory of the past, choose to advance. However, Ozu began to fail to achieve this subtle negotiated balance in narrative from the mid-1950s, when postwar Japanese cinema experienced another change of phase not only in terms of its production environment but also through a rapid transformation of Japanese society into a further privatised form of the everyday, as will be discussed in the next chapter.

Chapter 5
Late Ozu: New Generation and New Salaryman Film

After *Tokyo Story*, Ozu interestingly began to replay the prewar genre of *shōshimin* film, starting with *Sōshun/Early Spring* (1956) and continuing with *Equinox Flower* (1958), *Good Morning* (1959), *Late Autumn* (1960), until his last film *An Autumn Afternoon* (1962). Not only do these films constitute the majority of Ozu's post-*Tokyo Story* works, but they are also some of the most familiar and accessible Ozu films for general viewers today. However, although dealing with the similar subject matter of a salaryman's family life, they are substantially different from the genre of *shōshimin* film, which invariably focused upon the specific historical conditions of the 1930s Depression era. As products of the late 1950s and early 1960s, the aforementioned films thus cannot be called '*shōshimin* film' according to its exact definition. Nor would I directly apply the categorisation of *hōmudorama* (home drama) to these late Ozu films. Calling them instead 'new salaryman films', I will explore in this chapter the potential for differentiating them from any established generic terms and re-situating them within the context of Ozu's postwar films as I have discussed them so far.

This means that the primary problematic of Ozu's postwar oeuvre – the uneasy coexistence of distinct temporal consciousness, where past history and the present everyday overlap – continues to play. Intergenerational conflict already existed in the prewar *shōshimin* film, as seen in *I Was Born But . . .*, but it became much more complex in the postwar period, when the conflict between generations obtained wider historical implications. The younger generation of the post-*Tokyo Story* films, as portended in *The Flavour of Green Tea over Rice*, tended to lose this attitude and to step further away from the memory of war and into the present everyday life. The first section of this chapter will focus on the emergence of this new generation in Japanese society, within the film industry, and in Ozu's films. It will analyse how the director dealt with the ensuing conflict between these young people and their parents' generation. I will also pay attention to whether, and in what way, the possibility of mutual permeation – as successfully manifested through the character of Noriko in *Tokyo Story* – is searched for in the new salaryman films. The second section will move the focus onto the everyday itself, which, regardless of the generational conflict, continues to exist as the reality of present experience. The late 1950s in Japanese society can be characterised by the advent of new consumer commodities and the resulting process of privatisation, which greatly changed the shape of postwar everyday life. I will examine how these changes were reflected in the everyday life of the younger generation in the new salaryman films, and to what extent everyday space and time became de-historicised during the process.

A New Generation

'There is no vitality here that reminds us of the modern "dream factory". The wind that crosses the quiet sky teases the tree branches, and stillness dominates the studio buildings . . . [It is] the same stillness that surrounds the works of Ozu'.[1] So begins the reportage of Noguchi Yūichirō and Satō Tadao after they visited Ofuna studio in 1959. The writers interpreted the awkward silence surrounding the studio buildings as 'lethargy', which reflected the 'appearance of Shochiku driven into a corner'.[2] This article, however, enraged the young Ōshima Nagisa, who had been working in Ofuna as an assistant director, not because it criticised the studio but because the criticism was not harsh enough. Agreeing with the basic viewpoint of the article, Ōshima rebuked, 'You're talking about a sleeping lion when you should be talking about a dead lion'.[3] It was more than five years since this ambitious young man, who 'had never even dreamt of becoming a film director', entered the studio in 1954, a time Ōshima remembered as the 'turning point of Japanese cinema'.[4] This year saw Shochiku's peak with the release of the final part of *What Is Your Name?* and Kinoshita's *Nijyūshi no hitomi/Twenty-four Eyes*, two important (but different) renditions of postwar Japanese history. Ōshima understood that these two films represented the 'pinnacle of the road that Japanese cinema had walked so far', where Shochiku cinema and the 'trend of Japanese style anti-war films that had started with *Mata au hi made/Until We Meet Again* (Imai Tadashi, Toho, 1950)' converged together.[5] What, then, happened during the next five years to make Ōshima so frustrated as to criticise his workplace for being 'dead'?

Regarding Noguchi and Satō's article as 'superficial', Ōshima tried to understand why the simple suggestions they were making to improve the situation – strengthening management, perfecting the mass-production structure, and re-examining the Ofuna style – had not been resolved so far, and found the reason in the continuing reign of the old generation (and their filmmaking style) within the studio. Pointing out that Ofuna's interest only remained in the 'distorted feeling of human relationship', which left an 'impression of seclusion' on audiences, Ōshima argued that the 'establishment of new content and method in film [would] come only with the appearance of a new class of directors, whose inner consciousness [was] not yet completely dominated by the old Ofuna framework'.[6] It was thus an open and bold demand for the relinquishment of power to the postwar generation directors, whose consciousness could resonate with that of the majority of contemporary young audiences filling the cinemas.

Ōshima's fretfulness, even to the point of criticising Noguchi and Satō's otherwise appropriate analysis of the crisis, is understandable if the seriousness of the situation is taken into account. By 1959, Shochiku, long regarded as the most prestigious film studio in the country, was collapsing, and the fall seemed all the more dramatic because it was so sudden and rapid. Its distribution revenue having rapidly increased until 1955, Shochiku started to show signs of fatigue. In 1956, it lost its status as top-grossing company to Toei, and in the next year, fell again to the third spot after Toei and Daiei. By 1958, only three years later, Shochiku had to suffer the dishonour of being the fifth out of the six major film-producing companies in Japan, beating only Shintoho. It was certain that the executives were also embarrassed, as proved by the fact that the head of the company was replaced almost every year after 1958. As a result of this confusion, important company policies, including double feature exhibition (*nihondate*), drifted away. It was the time when, apart from a few exceptions, such as the films of Kinoshita and Ozu, Shochiku films found it difficult to attract the attention of audiences and critics. The company's product suddenly became representative of the old forms that were to be avoided.

Critics generally agreed that there were several factors that contributed to this disastrous outcome. Seen from the outside, Shochiku, 'drunk on the success of *What Is Your Name?*', did not properly respond to the rapidly changing business environment such as double feature screening.[7] The lack of an active or aggressive business strategy, or desire to lead the industry, was directly reflected in conservative approaches at the pre-production stage, an example of which was the somewhat passive attitude to casting. Shochiku's executives, who 'knew too much about film or were too confident that they knew about film', excessively interfered in production, and as a result, young producers lost enthusiasm and tried to avoid responsibility by adhering to already proven genre formats, that is, 'unrealistic melodrama and dispirited *shōshimin* film.[8]

Who were the younger generation then, who suddenly appeared as both the subject and the object of the national cinema? Although there was a wide spectrum of youth in terms of age and social status, it largely gathered into a single group according to the shared and distinct historical experience of the recent war and its aftermath. In the elder range, there was the *shōwa hitoketa* generation, who were born in the single-digit years of Showa (1925–34) and reached their twenties by the end of the US Occupation era.[9] Slightly younger than this was the *shōwa futaketa* (double-digit) or the *yake-ato* (burnt-out ruins) generation, who were born between 1935 and 1944, experienced the war in their early childhood, and grew up to become youths after the mid-1950s. I, however, recognise both of these as the single 'post-Occupation generation', who directly experienced the nation's integration into the magnetic field of postwar US international policy. The San Francisco Peace Treaty, signed in 1951, sanctioned the presence of the US armed forces in the nation, in order 'to contribute to the maintenance of international peace and security in the Far East and to the security of Japan'.[10] The most dramatic resistance to this system would emerge later as the crisis of Anpo in 1960, when the conservative Liberal Democratic Party attempted to renew the Treaty, but the tension should be understood within the broader context of the Cold War politics that had already developed throughout the previous decade.

The disbelief and antipathy of the younger generation were not only politically expressed but also mediated through various cultural forms. In literature, according to Margaret Hillenbrand, there were the writings of Ōe Kenzaburō, whilst in film the epitome of this current of thought can be found in the early works of Ōshima.[11] Japanese film critic Iwasaki Akira, in his history written in the early 1960s, also praised Nikkatsu's *taiyōzoku* (Sun Tribe) films as an expression of youthful resistance, which he believed influenced Ōshima and Shochiku's nouvelle vague movement. Iwasaki understood that the response of Japanese youth to Cold War geopolitics was contradictory. On the one hand, there was a tendency for 'psychological stability and self-contentment' based upon economic recuperation, which Japan earned in return for providing a base for US military action in East Asia since the Korean War. Iwasaki argued this had resulted in 'indifference to social reality' and 'complacency in pleasant individual life'.[12] The phenomenon of *taiyōzoku* – as a 'reckless rush of complete repudiation' – constituted the alternative (and opposite) reaction.[13] The series of *taiyōzoku* films after *Taiyō no kisetsu/The Season of the Sun*

(Furukawa Takumi, Nikkatsu, 1956), notably starring Ishihara Yūjirō, was thus a cinematic form of the 'challenge of youth to the hypocrisy of the older generation and stagnation, corruption, or "reverse course" of conservative politics and culture'.[14] These youth films provided a sharp contrast to the films of Kinugasa Teinosuke, Itō Daisuke or Inagaki Hiroshi, who, old in age and high in status, had 'lost their revolutionary will of the prewar' and exploited the 'carefree mood'.[15]

As Ōshima pointed out, Shochiku's *Ōfuna-chō* also became unfashionable in this new postwar climate, especially for the young audiences who had grown up receiving education in democracy and individualism. The warm humanistic perspective that Kido had always emphasised suddenly seemed to have lost touch with an audience that now wanted more straightforwardly realistic depictions of postwar society. Naïve 'human relationships' thus had to make way for the examination of poignant 'social relationships'.[16] This did not mean that *Ōfuna-chō*'s humanism had always lacked such a critical attitude. In the aforementioned article, Noguchi and Satō paid attention to Ofuna's prewar *shōshimin* films such as Ozu's *I Was Born But . . .* or Gosho's *Burden of Life*, where 'warm sympathy' coexisted with 'a touch of criticism'. In the postwar, in such films as *Anjōke no butōkai/The Ball at the Anjo House* (Yoshimura Kōzaburō, 1947), *Honjitsu Kyūshin/The Doctor's Day Off* (Shibuya Minoru, 1952) and *Nihon no higeki/A Japanese Tragedy* (Kinoshita Keisuke, 1953), this critical stance continued with a 'more modern sensitivity', sometimes accompanying a 'tone of severe accusation'.[17] Even these works of social criticism, however, seldom avoided a 'closed' impression at the ending, lacking a vision of resolution. What Shochiku films encouraged was 'endurance' and 'submission', or, ironically put, 'the resistance [of the weak] through non-resistance'.[18] This also meant that the *Kamata-chō/Ōfuna-chō*, once a symbol of Shochiku's Western modernity with its unique attachment to everyday realism, degenerated into the defender of the 'closed, retrogressive emotion of the Japanese', losing 'modernity and rationalism with critical spirit'.[19] This is why Ōshima argued for more 'vivid desires and actions of people who grapple with the status quo'.[20]

As is well known, Shochiku made efforts to improve the situation, a representative example being the introduction of Shochiku Nouvelle Vague in 1960. Actively planned and promoted by the company, the Shochiku Nouvelle Vague, however, was more of a business vehicle than a youth movement. Ōtani Hiroshi, the post-Kido head of Shochiku, regarded it as a goose that would lay the golden eggs, but once Ōshima's *Nihon no yoru to kiri/Night and Fog in Japan* (1960) failed to be as popular as expected, Shochiku quickly suspended the film from screening, resulting in Ōshima's leaving the company and the end of the

Shochiku Nouvelle Vague. Perhaps, the reformation plan was never to be successful for a stern belief in *Ōfuna-chō* remained intact among mainstream staff as well as businessmen in the company, as suggested by the following quote from Kinoshita Keinosuke:

> Watching what [the nouvelle vague directors] have made, I become intolerable ... I thought they were concerned about how to make audiences unpleasant. They cannot express their intention without resorting to the depiction of sex and violence, which only means their directing skill is immature. *Film is entertainment, after all, and necessitates beauty.* That is what I believe (italics added).[21]

A tension and clash would have been inevitable between this conservatism and the dissatisfaction and radicalism of the Nouvelle Vague directors – Ōshima Nagisa, Yoshida Yoshishige, and Shinoda Masahiro. In Yoshida's words, their works aimed at 'destroying the established morals, custom, and order, ... pursuing new human relationships, and *breaking through the wall of the everydayness*' (italics added).[22]

Where can Ozu's postwar cinema be placed within this context? For the new generation, of which Ōshima was emblematic, Ozu was in fact a symbolic figure who represented the old, incapacitated state of Shochiku and *Ōfuna-chō*. Such a criticism of the director sounds hardly new; Ozu's cinema and its attitude towards realism (that is, how to faithfully reflect society) was a decades-old issue in film criticism stretching back to his *shōshimin* film era, and, as discussed, Ozu's position hardly deviated from his own principle of everyday realism that allows more space for irony and allusion than direct resistance. However, postwar Ozu (especially after the mid-1950s) became more vulnerable to this criticism as his films began to be equated with a new generic term of *hōmudorama*, of which the perspective had been narrowed from large-scale social problems such as the economic instability of the urban middle class to intra-familial matters. Sakamoto Kazue, in her study of the Japanese family drama, argues that both *shōshimin* film and *hōmudorama* – as alternatives to the '*shinpa, hahamono*, and melodrama line' – typically dealt with 'patterned family life in repetition' (namely, the everyday), and adopted a 'quiet' approach without depending too much on storyline, and emphasising 'reality' and 'empathy' rather than 'strong emotion'.[23] However, the postwar *hōmudorama* was different from the prewar *shōshimin* film in that the family in the former was more independent, and more clearly separated from external society and its venues (such as the workplace) than the latter. If the *shōshimin* film, as the name suggests, articulated the desire and frustration of the new middle classes who were economically struggling in the early Showa era, the family in the *hōmudorama* was characterised more by the 'ordinary life that anybody can experience', even though its actual economic status was the same urban white-collar class as the family in the *shōshimin* film.[24]

As a representative example that shows the genre transition from the prewar *shōshimin* film to the postwar *hōmudorama*, Sakamoto discusses Ozu's postwar films.[25] I agree with her that there was a growing tendency towards 'safe and self-contained' family life in Ozu's late postwar films, especially after *Equinox Flower* (1958), which, with its narrative focused on the conflict within a salaryman family over a daughter's marriage, set the tone for Ozu's other 'home-dramatic' films in the following years, such as *Ohayo/Good Morning* (1959). Well known as the postwar sequel to *I Was Born But...*, *Good Morning* demonstrated the difference between the genres of *hōmudorama* and *shōshimin* film quite overtly; while the children in *I Was Born But...* are frustrated by the impossibility of 'becoming bourgeois', their postwar counterparts in *Good Morning* are frustrated by the possibility of 'staying behind social homogenisation' (that is, not having a television set). If the ending of *I Was Born But...* suggests that the dilemma will never be completely resolved, *Good Morning* easily achieves a happy ending by providing the family with a television set (albeit not without a pecuniary burden on the parents).

There are, however, a few points to consider before defining Ozu's postwar work within the framework of *hōmurodama*. First, whether the change of genre was a purely postwar phenomenon is controversial in Ozu's case, given that he had already made a style of family drama distinct from the *shōshimin* film in the late 1930s and early 1940s with the bourgeois dramas such as *What Did the Lady Forget?*, which can be regarded as an early precursor of the 1950s *hōmudorama*.[26] Secondly, 'postwar Ozu' is not a simple entity that can be defined by any specific generic term, whether it is the *hōmudorama* or melodrama, but rather a mixture of different elements, the balance of which actually changes from film to film even though it may appear to be the same. Thirdly, although *Equinox Flower* and *Late Autumn* have 'home-dramatic' styles, *hōmudorama* may still be a too restrictive term to put on these family dramas, compared to the genre's more representative examples on television with a quite narrow scope of interest.

The appearance of television was actually an important challenge to Shochiku, if not to Ozu. There were various factors that contributed to the sudden falling-off of the company's audiences in the 1960s, such as the increased opportunity for outdoor leisure activities, but television was especially detrimental to the *Ōfuna-chō* films, which now had to compete with the new medium for an audience group with similar tastes.[27] Shochiku's vulnerability to television can also be attributable to the medium specificity of their specialty genre *hōmudorama*, which, with its domestic setting and everyday narrative, was more easily adaptable to the small (but less distant) television set than other genres with large-scale backgrounds and actions. The earliest examples of the television *hōmudorama* demonstrate how extensively it adapted the basic principles of *Ōfuna-chō* into its format. According to the playwright Onoda Isamu, who wrote early television dramas such as *Otōsan no kisetsu/Father's Season* (NHK, October 1958-March 1961), the genre of *hōmudorama* has to be 'bright, cheerful, refreshing and harmless' as well as 'simple and easily understandable', and also should express 'complete trust in and affection towards human beings', paying attention to the 'happiness of ordinary common people (*shomin*)', all of which largely overlap the basic tenets of Kido-ism.[28]

Ozu did not live long enough to witness the full bloom of the television *hōmudorama* in the 1960s and 1970s. He also affirmed that he was 'not that interested in television drama', saying that film and television were 'apparently similar but actually different [media]'.[29] It is a meaningful irony, then, that the very last project he completed in his life was a script for a television drama, *Seishun hōkago/Class Dismissed* (NHK, broadcast 21 March 1963).[30] The work was a request from NHK, probably from a producer, Yamauchi Daisuke, who had a connection with Ozu through his father Satomi Ton, whose novels Ozu admired and based his *Equinox Flower* and *Late Autumn* upon.[31] Considering the success of *Equinox Flower* and *Late Autumn* (each was the top-grossing Shochiku film in the year they were released), this rare production suggests that even a television studio was aware of the potential appeal of Ozu's work for mass audiences of the new medium. The resulting script, co-written with none other than Satomi, retained the similar 'home-dramatic' elements of those two films, from abounding domestic scenes of affluent upper-middle-class families to the typical narrative of a young woman's concern over her marriage and old businessmen's remembrance of bygone years, confirming the close relationship between the cinematic and televisual forms of the *hōmudorama* genre. The connection is also reinforced by the regular Ozu cast appearing in the television programme, such as Sugimura Haruko, Miyake Kuniko, Kita Ryūji and Sada Keiji.

Seen from a different angle, the genre of *hōmudorama* can be also understood as a true dramatic incarnation of the postwar ethos such as political democracy, economic equality, and individualism. It naturally developed as a natural reflection of social changes in the mid-1950s, when Japan, declaring that 'the postwar is over', inaugurated the optimistic era of high economic growth. Privatised everyday life was also one of the most prominent characteristics of postwar Japan, where people based their identities on a conscious movement away from the wartime collectivistic tendency. Given these circumstances, it may not be appropriate to overemphasise the chasm between the 'home' of the *hōmudorama* and external society. What was problematic in the *hōmudorama* was less a lack of social concerns than the way that *Ōfuna-chō* drew conclusions from the narrative regarding such issues. Shochiku's typically humanistic approach, with happy endings without resolving (or revealing) anything, obscured the points that could have led to a more meaningful social insight. Such self-deceiving complacency became worse as similar subjects and styles were ever-repeated in variations until audiences finally grew weary.

I agree that Ozu's post-1958 films – those with the stronger home-dramatic tendency – were particularly prone to signs of diffidence and fatigue, as evinced by his repeated resort to lighter-toned comedies. This change can be partly attributed to the failure of *Tokyo Twilight* in 1957, in which Ozu, against his scriptwriting partner Noda Kōgo's wishes, experimented with darker images as well as an unusually serious narrative for him. As a result, from the following year's *Equinox Flower*, Ozu 'could not help being returned to Noda's pace'.[32] But even the banal narrative of marriage – the most strongly 'home-dramatic' element in Ozu's postwar works – was not confined merely to the familial conflict between father and daughter, but reflected a reality of postwar Japanese society in terms of inter-generational relations. As such, marriage in Ozu's films continued to articulate the disappearance of the prewar generation, who still retained the memory of war, and the emergence of the new generation, as in the previous Occupation period. In *Equinox Flower* and *Late Autumn*, such historical consciousness was weakened, but in *An Autumn Afternoon* it was revived again, as if Ozu attempted to revisit the themes of *Tokyo Story*.

Ozu's personal attitude towards the new 'post-Occupation generation' seems not necessarily positive. In an interview from 1958, he clarified, 'I do not particularly favour the young people. If anything, I feel rather for the old . . . It seems the films these days, in order to please the younger generation, acknowledge their eccentricities and allow them to have the idea that old people are useless', which parallels Kinoshita's remark, mentioned above.[33] According to Ozu, *Equinox Flower*, which was being filmed at the time, was also a consolation addressed to the old generation: 'since an author perceives things with the view of his age, it is natural that his contemporaries become the subject matter. Frankly speaking, I cannot understand the feeling of the young'.[34] The conflict between the daughter character in the film and her 'feudal' father regarding her love marriage is thus not intended as a defence of the younger generation's position, but rather as an excuse for the father's behaviour by showing that anyone can sometimes act 'contradictorily' even while being aware of it. 'Through this', Ozu explained, 'I want young audiences to understand [the father's] goodwill as a parent'.[35]

This, however, does not mean that he was indifferent to or critical of the new postwar generation. In fact, in terms of casting, the opposite was the case, as he actively adopted young actresses (if not actors) in his post-*Tokyo Story* films, who would represent the Japanese cinema of the 1950s and 1960s. Starting with Kishi Keiko (born in 1932) in *Early Spring*, many of the most popular younger actresses of the time appeared in Ozu's films. Among them were Arima Ineko (b. 1932) in *Tokyo Twilight* and *Equinox Flower*, Yamamoto Fujiko (b. 1931) in *Equinox Flower*, Kuga Yoshiko (b. 1931) in *Equinox Flower* and *Good Morning*, Wakao Ayako (b. 1933) in *Floating Weeds*, Okada Mariko (b. 1933) in *Late Autumn* and *An Autumn Afternoon*, and Tsukasa Yōko (b. 1934) in *Late Autumn* and *Kohayagawa ke no aki/The End of Summer* (Takarazuka Eiga, 1961).[36] All of these belonged to the aforementioned *shōwa hitoketa* generation, and they certainly provided a fresh atmosphere in Ozu's post-*Tokyo Story* films, in contrast to the female characters of the previous generation, as represented by Hara Setsuko's Noriko. For instance, Ozu's cameraman Atsuta Yūharu remembers that Kishi Keiko was Ozu's 'first "postwar" [generation] actress' who 'was not afraid of appearing in Ozu's film', and 'Ozu, in return, enjoyed such a youthful vigour'.[37]

As for male characters, Ozu did not cast an equivalent number of important young actors. The only exception would be Sada Keiji (b. 1926), who, already a major Shochiku star based on his leading role in *What Is Your Name?* with Kishi Keiko, appeared in several of Ozu's new salaryman films as a young salaryman. His clean-cut, well-behaved image offered a strong contrast to Ishihara's tough, sexy style, visually registering the distance that Ozu maintained from the *taiyōzoku* films. However, Ozu's attitude towards the *taiyōzoku* phenomenon and Ishihara as its icon was not one of total rejection but rather selective adoption. What was new about Ishihara, according to Ozu, was his frank, natural attitude towards acting; if other actors had so far been concerned only with how their 'facial expression' looked on screen, Ishihara acted with his 'whole body', without being conscious of the camera.[38] Ozu paid special attention to *Ubaguruma/The Baby Carriage* (Tasaka Tomotaka, Nikkatsu, 1956), where he saw the actor's unexpected potential in the role of a gentle young man who is 'fond of a carefree, relaxed everyday life'.[39] Thus Ozu, acknowledging Ishihara's novelty, actually understood the possibilities that the actor could offer for his family dramas of generational conflict, rather than approving of the actor's original rebellious image. Even *taiyōzoku*, for Ozu, was just another ingredient to make tofu.

Seen from this point of view, Ozu did not strive for something particularly 'new' with regard to the younger generation in his new salaryman films. As for marriage, for example, generational conflict and resistance had always played a role in Ozu's films. Daughters consistently rebel against *omiai* forced on them by their parents and choose their own partners. In this sense, Setsuko's resistance to her father in *Equinox Flower* is only a variation on Noriko's sudden decision to marry Kenkichi regardless of her family's objection in *Early Summer*. However, the marriage narrative that appears repeatedly in the new salaryman films seems to have lost some of the tense energy that had existed in the Occupation-era films. I think the difference comes mainly from the fact that marriage does not retain the same temporal connotations in relation to the past as the marriages in *The Moon Has Risen* or *Early Summer* did. For example, the daughter Michiko (Iwashita Shima) in *An Autumn Afternoon* refuses an *omiai* offer just as Noriko in *Late Spring* did, but her reason is that she has her eye on someone else, rather than her emotional attachment to her widower father, as with Noriko in *Late Spring*'s case. Once it is revealed that the man she is fond of is interested in another woman, Michiko soon changes her mind and marries the partner that her father introduces to her, during which concern for her father hardly becomes an issue. This 'aloofness' makes the last farewell scene on Michiko's wedding day look fairly dry and composed, compared to the heartbreaking moment of the same parting scene in *Late Spring*. After all, marriage for the new generation is something 'natural' or even 'banal' that accords with one's desire, but is barely related to the temporality of the parent generation. And, as such, the everyday loses its previous quality as an element that permeates various temporal spheres and registers.

Segregated from their children, the ageing salaryman fathers exclusively take on the role of reflecting on the passage of time. For this purpose, Ozu tends to use the settings of bars or restaurants and the activity of drinking, which repeatedly appear in the series of new salaryman films. Here, the fathers, who suffer dwindling masculinity at home, typically worry about marrying off their daughters, reminisce about the old days and lament the loss of their youth. Such places are the realm of old men, a special retreat not permitted to the preceding salaryman group of the *shōshimin* film in the 1930s. Women are excluded from this space, and their interruption – as seen in the restaurant scene in *Early Summer* – is precluded. In this place of safety, the fathers enjoy suggestive sexual jokes as if they are struggling to rekindle their dying masculine power. Nor can the younger generation become a genuine part of the drinking space. In *An Autumn Afternoon*, when the father Hirayama (Ryū Chishū) and his eldest son Kōichi (Sada Keiji) visit a bar, Torys, to talk about the *omiai* of their daughter/sister Michiko, Kōichi somehow looks unbecoming in this 'father's space'. In fact, he never drinks whisky as Hirayama does, but instead eats fried rice and drinks tea, deploying the same contrast between rice and *sake* as was seen with Shige and her father Shūkichi in *Tokyo Story*. Moreover, Kōichi does not agree with Hirayama's opinion that the bar's madam resembles his dead mother, which evinces his lack of sympathy for the father's desire to reincarnate the past out of the bar space.

The fathers' drinking in the new salaryman films is not generally connected to the historical recognition of war as in the drinking at the *pachinko* parlour in *The Flavour of Green Tea over Rice*, or the reunion sequence in *Tokyo Story*. In the late 1950s, war now seemed too distant a memory to be directly referred to through a dead son or friend. Instead, the past that the fathers struggle with is a more personal and ordinary one, often to do with the realisation that they get old while their children grow up and get married. But there are a few exceptions to this tendency. First, in a reunion party scene in *Equinox Flower*, the former classmates of the father Hirayama (Saburi Shin) sing a song together called *Sakurai no ketsubetsu/Parting at Sakurai*, which, dealing with a death of a loyalist samurai, was popular during wartime.[40] It is not that these singing fathers, whose eyes are closed with touching emotion, are missing war itself and lament the defeat: Hirayama in an earlier scene has clearly stated that he 'hates the war and the people who swaggered at that time'. But the song, in the context of the postwar, still signified 'particular evocations for people of an older generation, since it epitomises the sense of resignation, poignancy and *aware* (pathos) that surround the defeated Japanese hero', a sensitivity that distinguishes itself from a typical victim consciousness.[41] As mentioned in Chapter 1, the reunion party in *Tokyo Chorus* works as a collective antidote to the threat of Western capitalism. Twenty-seven years later, now grown old and betrayed by war, the salaryman fathers at the reunion in *Equinox Flower* look tired and lost in the face of the postwar society that they struggle to make sense of, just as the *pachinko* parlour owner Hirayama, who sings the song about a dead comrade in *The Flavour of Green Tea over Rice*.

A clearer historical consciousness returns in *An Autumn Afternoon*. The aforementioned Torys Bar becomes a memorial place for the war, just as were the room inside the *pachinko* parlour in *The Flavour of Green Tea over Rice* or Noriko's apartment in *Tokyo Story*. There, the father Hirayama (Ryū Chishū) shares drinks with Sakamoto, who is his former subordinate in the navy, and together they listen to the Gunkan March – the famous war tune also used in the reunion party scene in *Tokyo Story*. Cheered by the march, Sakamoto asks Hirayama, 'Why did Japan lose the war?' and 'What if we had won?', the first and the last time such fundamental questions are raised so directly in Ozu's films. Sakamoto then dreams of a Japanese-occupied New York and re-enacts a march with salute along with the Gunkan March. Again, the point of the scene is not to glorify wartime militarism; Sakamoto agrees that 'stupid blokes were swaggering' at that time. Rather, the wartime is perceived as the epitome of the past, in relation to which the changes to postwar society can be reflected upon. For the generation old enough to remember the war, time has now ripened and enabled these men to perceive this history as a detached object, which can be bantered about or played with over a simple drink. In other words, war is now truly a part of the everyday to consume. And the young Japanese, who Sakamoto grumbles 'imitate Americans by playing records and shaking their hips', are excluded from any enjoyment of this memory. No wonder that Hirayama, on another visit to the bar with Kōichi, does not let the madam play the Gunkan March again, preventing the son from listening to the music.

Thus in the new salaryman films, the generations are separated, even more so than before in Ozu's postwar cinema. And the separation is naturalised or taken for granted. Without an intermediary character such as Noriko in *Tokyo Story*, each generation does not seem to interact with the other in order to resolve differences. Rather, the conflict is transformed into a paternal character's inner turmoil after his realisation that there is no role left for him in his relationship with his child. It is a postwar version of the masculine lethargy that plagued the dwindling salaryman fathers in the *shōshimin* film. The Hirayamas of both *Equinox Flower* and *An Autumn Afternoon* reveal this symptom in the final scene of each film, where they murmur the melody of the past (namely, *Sakurai no ketsubetsu* and the Gunkan March) alone. The Hirayama of the former sings it on a train to Hiroshima to meet and reconcile with Setsuko, who is now married. A journey of an opposite direction to the train ride in *Tokyo Story*, where Noriko carries Tomi's past into her future, Hirayama's singing, as it was in the reunion sequence, is only a lament for the disappeared past and an expression of his alienation from the present. This is reconfirmed in the case of the latter, where the singing of the drunken father (Ryū Chishū) is interrupted by his younger son, who finds it annoying while he tries to sleep. In the end, what the two fathers show in common on their faces is absolute tiredness, which not only describes their loneliness, but also evidences how helpless their existence is in the changing postwar society. In that sense, Ozu succeeded in making the new salaryman films a tale for the old generation rather than the young one as he had originally intended.

A New Everyday Life

If their parents suffered from the burden of an unresolved past, the younger generation confronted the new reality of everyday life that they had to manage in the present. As mentioned in the previous chapter, one of the multiple aspects of the Japanese postwar that Gluck suggested is 'middle class postwar' or 'the postwar of private life', which was founded upon the motto of 'sameness, middleness, [and] homogeneity'.[42] As the Japanese economy gradually recovered from the destruction of the early postwar years, it presented more opportunities to Japanese consumers in the form of commodity culture. As Marilyn Ivy notes, mass products became the 'objects of desire, the signs of middle-class inclusion, the unparalleled commodity fetishes for the Japanese'.[43] Once out of the impoverishment of the immediate postwar years, Japanese consumers, faithfully responding to advertisements targeted at the masses, started to expand their collections of household goods at rapid speed after the mid-1950s. The 'Three Sacred Regalia' – television, washing machine and refrigerator – appeared, which was soon replaced by the 'Three Cs: car, cooler (air conditioner), and colour television' in the 1960s.

The universal satisfaction of these desires resulted in democratic 'equalisation' of every household, but negatively put, it could also mean the 'homogenisation' and 'privatisation' of middle-class society.[44] Three quarters of the population claimed to be 'middle class' at the beginning of the 1950s, and this number rose to 90 per cent in the late 1970s.[45] Under this system, the word 'class' in 'middle class' ironically meant 'classless'. This 'classless' consciousness implied not only that quality of life was perceived to be roughly equal throughout the population but also that the substance of their everyday life was standardised. Hence most Japanese would usually integrate themselves into the 'salaryman [and] full-time housewife system', working in the same company throughout their lives (*shūshinkoyōsei* or lifetime employment) and rearing a small number of children (usually two) in a *mochiie* (an owned house paid for by a lifelong loan).[46] Now more things were available to more consumers, but in exchange, they became more strongly integrated into a capitalistic wage labour system. The general social tendency accordingly moved towards political conservatism ('reprivatisation' in Lefebvre's term) and the protection of the status quo, while social differences are covered up under the myth of so-called 'middle-class-ness'.[47]

The advent of private life was partly due to the postwar experiences of the Japanese, who, 'liberated from the imperial state to *seikatsu*', faced the 'disjunction between what was called public sacrifice and private life'.[48] Ueno Chizuko called this type of postwar Japanese society '*shiminshakai* (私民社会/ private society), not *shiminshakai* (市民社会/ civil society)', which operates through the 'naturalism of desire' where 'the pursuit of private desire is shamelessly affirmed without being restricted by any other kind of values'.[49] Kano Masanao, quoting Hidaka Rokurō and Fujida Shōjō, similarly differentiated between the 'restoration of the everyday' in the immediate postwar period and the 'indulgence in the everyday' after the 1960s.[50] Ueno argued that the tendency toward privatisation was underlined by postwar conservative politics. The 'income-doubling plan', promoted by the Ikeda regime that took control of the nation in the midst of the Anpo crisis in 1960, was a 'policy with the intention of inducing the Japanese people to turn from political problems to the ideology of private life'.[51] In fact, during the very time of the 1960 crisis, Maruyama Masao specifically criticised the tendency of the postwar Japanese people to 'enjoy private life in the sphere of consumption', and worried that 'the political indifference of the privatised group . . . [was] very convenient for the governing elites who wish[ed] to "contain" activist groups'.[52]

However, the relationship between the everyday and politics was not simply reactive, but also proactive and creative. In this regard, Maruyama's point of view was directly opposed by the Japanese poet and critic Yoshimoto Takaaki, who characterised it as the 'typical logic of progressive enlightenment thought or false democracy', which neglected a 'consciousness . . . that . . . value[d] private self-interest over the interests of social sectors'.[53] According to Yoshimoto, true postwar democracy should be bourgeois democracy with a 'privatised consciousness' that 'neither idolises the organisation nor exalts state authority'.[54] In this sense, the privatisation of the masses did not necessarily mean political conservatism. Yoshimoto wanted, rather, to present his concerns about the bureaucratic tendency growing in all sectors of postwar Japanese society, whether it was conservatives or communists, officials or activists, which he thought was threatening every individual's fundamental rights to the everyday. Takabatake Michitoshi similarly understood the essential agenda of the postwar Japanese intellectual, as defined by the question of how to make sense of the 'common people', who were ambiguously positioned between 'blind devotion' to the 'occupational group' and 'anti-authority sentiment' that pushed them to 'defend everyday life'.[55] Even intellectuals themselves, Takabatake argued, were targets of the argument against authoritarianism. In this way, the tension between collectivism and individualism could not be resolved through the analysis and criticism of the intellectuals, but only through each individual's 'persistent commitment to the everyday' itself.[56]

Ozu's late postwar films exhibit the same kind of dilemma of urban Japanese people caught between the enjoyment of commodity consumption and resulting social privatisation and political indifference, through *hōmudorama*-style depiction of the banal everyday such as office life, commuting, eating and drinking, and family relationships. These subject matters had been similarly dealt with in the *shōshimin* film, though the prewar counterpart articulated more the salaryman father's struggle to survive in the economic depression. In the postwar new salaryman films, living per se is not of great concern; it is indeed possible to earn and spend, but not without accompanying fatigue and boredom, which are exchanged for the pleasure of purchase and possession. Ozu's everyday is thus finally 'modernised' in the sense that it starts to foreground the connections between waged labour and mass production and consumption. In a sense, this transformation in domestic everyday life signals an ironical achievement of the dream of the prewar urban middle classes, who aspired to Americanism and the consumerist's heaven.

On one side of this everyday life exists office space, the stronghold of the salaryman. Ozu's office scenes in the new salaryman films visualise one of the most tasteless and expressionless spaces he ever created. And he repeats almost the same *mise en scène* for this again and again throughout the period as if to confirm the banal nature of the space. The rigid colour palette is dominated by monotonous blues and greys, and seamlessly blended profile shots of a working salaryman father are repeatedly shown, whilst the sounds of noisy machinery or traffic are heard from outside. Typically, an acquaintance will walk down a long corridor to visit the salaryman in the office. And throughout such a scene the camera never moves an inch. Ozu, however, hardly permits the salaryman characters a reflection upon the meaning of this monotonous repetitiveness; for most of the time, they and their visitors talk about marriage and the opportunity of an *omiai*.

The exception to this tendency is *Early Spring*, where the main salaryman characters are much younger than the salaryman fathers at management level that we frequently see in the later films. These young salarymen are first presented in an early morning commuting scene, where one by one they gather at Kamata station, ending up in a huge cluster of commuters lined up on a platform. With the familiar elements of the suburb and the commuting train in the morning, this scene offers a variation on the final scene of *I Was Born But . . .*, where the salaryman Yoshii's two sons, still in doubt about their future, head to school with the other pupils. The whole film can actually be read as Ozu's delayed answer to the ambiguous conclusion of *I Was Born But . . .* regarding the fate of the salaryman. Nothing has fundamentally changed here; what is waiting for the children's generation after nearly a quarter century is the same everyday all over again, which the father Yoshii had hoped his children would avoid.

Early Spring faces this reality directly, with a self-reflexive attitude, which brings it closer to the 1930s *shōshimin* film than the later new salaryman films. In the following scene after the train commuting, two salaryman characters inside an office building look out of a window in order to watch other commuting salarymen hurrying along a street. One of them offers his impression, 'It's a flood of salarymen', and the other adds, 'There are 340,000 salarymen who commute to Tokyo station everyday'.[57] Their high-angled point-of-view shot over the street – a rare case in Ozu – permits them an 'objective' perspective. This allows them to realise the fact that they are merely part of this massive group of people. For these salarymen, the view thus becomes a sorrowful self-portrait, comparable to the father Yoshii's clown image, as seen through his boss's home movie in *I Was Born But . . . .*

What lies on the other side of this everyday life is domesticity. Ozu always excelled at depicting the domestic environment, but those of the new salaryman films are distinct for their more stable and affluent atmosphere. An important space that contributes to this change is the living room (*chanoma*) as a place for family gathering. It is not that Ozu had not deployed the space before, and I have discussed this in relation to female movement in the previous chapter. However, the *chanoma* in Ozu's previous films was used more as a specific 'meeting' place to have a meal, welcome a guest or talk about a serious familial issue such as marriage. Individual space accordingly received more attention, such as Noriko's upstairs room in *Late Spring*. This characteristic changes in the new salaryman films; the *chanoma* finally obtains its full function as an everyday space where family members encounter each other 'without a specific purpose' except relaxation – to talk, read or snack – creating a conventional middle-class domestic landscape (see Figure 5.1). The one who controls this space and time is not the patriarch but the housewife/mother, who, even while appearing subservient to her husband, adroitly mediates communication between the blunt father and the resistant child in order to maintain familial harmony. Ozu also strengthens this domestic stability with his static camera, which concentrates extensively on layered spatial structures and various domestic objects. Again, this is far from a novel experiment for the director, but in the new salaryman films, his virtuosity reaches the point of utmost visual pleasure. It would not be necessary to reconfirm the fact here that critics have already made on this formal refinement, except for the point that the use of colour, which Ozu began to employ from *Equinox Flower* in 1958 on, greatly contributed to the emphasis on domestic space and objects, which is effectively contrasted with the dullness of the office spaces mentioned earlier.[58]

Figure 5.1 A family spending evening time together in *Good Morning* – a typical scene of the domestic everyday, which ironically did not appear in Ozu's prewar *shōshimin* films

These new tendencies of the new salaryman films have attracted criticism. Wood, referring to Burch, argues that Ozu's work of the latter years fell into formalism ('academicism' in Wood's term) in order to defend his stylistic position:

> I agree – tentatively . . . – with Noel Burch, though for utterly different reasons, that Ozu finally declined into academicism. Only I set the date much later: the last colour films strike me as tired, the creative impetus weakened, a retreat into a formal play with colour that, at its worst, becomes almost a kind of painting-by-numbers.[59]

Sakamoto, as mentioned, understands Ozu's films of this period as fitting into the genre of *hōmudorama*, which is characterised by its restricted scope, focusing mostly on family life separate from any social context. Tanaka Masasumi defines the characteristics of the late Ozu as 'elaboration and jokes' in terms of style, and 'self-emulation' in terms of content, and suggests that the tendency had begun after the critical and commercial failure of *Tokyo Twilight* (1957).[60] Whatever the cause, I concur with the assertion that Ozu's late films evidence a gradual decline in the director's creativity, as he becomes too involved with formal consideration and repetitive subject matter. However, I also think that the emphasis on domesticity is not merely degeneration into formalism and the space 'inside' the home. Rather, Ozu maintained an aspect of social commentary by letting the symptoms of postwar everyday life – most importantly, consumerism – permeate into this static domestic space. The shiny consumer electronics that pervade the new salaryman films – such as rice cooker, vacuum cleaner, refrigerator and television – are not just there to evoke visual pleasure, but act as a strong signifier of the changing postwar society that is fundamentally influencing the lives of Ozu's characters, especially the younger ones. The obsessive interest they show towards these domestic objects can be none other than commodity fetishism.

The best example of this appears in *An Autumn Afternoon* in relation to the everyday life of Kōichi and his wife Akiko (Okada Mariko). Both being young salarymen, Kōichi is urged by Akiko to buy a refrigerator. Unable to afford it with their salary, Kōichi borrows money from his father. But he receives more money than he needs, which allows him to buy a set of used golf clubs from his colleague, without telling his wife. Akiko, learning of this fact and upset that she has been ignored, declares that she will also buy herself an expensive handbag, in return for allowing Kōichi to buy the clubs. The society that surrounds this young couple of the *shōwa hitoketa* generation is structured around a commodity culture that stimulates the 'homogenisation' of households, which is different from the community consciousness of the Shitamachi neighbourhood. Akiko's decision to buy a refrigerator is actually influenced by her neighbour in a *danchi* (a block of collective apartment buildings), who already owns one along with a TV and a vacuum cleaner. When she visits the neighbour to borrow a couple of 'chilled' tomatoes, her envious and admiring gaze does not miss the vacuum cleaner on the floor, which she tries turning on only to hear its motor sound. Kōichi is no exception to such fetishism when he swings and *caresses* the clubs several times saying, 'This is a good product' (see Figure 5.2). If the oppressed desire of the *taiyōzoku* is vented through sex and violence, Ozu's young characters pacify it through possession obsession. Although one is denied and the other accepted by social mores, both desires indicate fundamentally the same phenomenon: the reconfiguration of Japanese society according to its new postwar economic and political imperatives.

Crucially, Ozu develops the penetrating insight that what exists deep inside this phenomenon is the boredom of the everyday. As Akiko complains, Kōichi, a salaryman, almost always comes home late at night, only to immediately go to

Late Ozu   205

Figure 5.2   Kōichi's commodity fetishism

bed saying he is tired. But tiredness is the other name of commodity obsession, in which Akiko herself is participating. This is demonstrated in a night scene where Akiko talks about buying a refrigerator with Kōichi, who has just returned home and is 'sleepy'. A profile shot of Kōichi, who yawns while hearing her enthusiastic plan for the purchase, is followed by a reverse shot of Akiko, who, upset by the husband's indifferent response, devours a grape. In return, when Akiko objects to Kōichi's buying of the golf clubs, his languor transforms into resentment, which he expresses by being unresponsive to Akiko's conversation. This sequence is set on a peaceful Sunday morning, with sunshine brightening the apartment and the sound of a woman singing *Caro mio ben* with a piano audible outside. However, the morning as such also becomes the most lethargic time of the week. Staying at home on such a day foregrounds the banality of the everyday; Akiko is busy doing household chores, and Kōichi, lying on the floor and smoking without a word, is asked by his wife to wind up a wall clock, a visual metaphor of the repetitious everyday. For this couple, commodity fetishism is the only way to escape from this dead-end everydayness. Kōichi's boredom instantly dissipates when he finally obtains the clubs with Akiko's approval (and her declaration that she will buy the handbag as well) at the end of this sequence.

Seen from this perspective, commodity culture can be understood as a means of deviation from the terms of the everyday that I have discussed in this book. The salaryman in *An Autumn Afternoon* cannot skip his work as the children in *I Was Born But...* did to enjoy a day-off in an empty field. Instead they can indulge in the pleasure of planning and practising consumption in order to break the monotonous rhythm of the everyday. Granted, the salaryman's deviation is subordinate to the postwar capitalistic order, lacking the anti-establishment potential of the children's behaviour in *I Was Born But...*, but Ozu accepts it as a reality of contemporary society without making any value judgement. Such a position is more clearly stated in *Good Morning*. The film is usually regarded as a light comedy, but Ozu in fact asks a more fundamental question regarding the necessity of commodity culture and its effect on postwar society. Set in a small suburban town outside Tokyo, the film depicts how the impetus towards homogenisation – buying consumer electronics that a neighbour already has – influences the life of the middle-class residents. The child protagonists, whose normal everyday time and space is completely disrupted by watching a television owned by a young couple in their neighbourhood, demand that their salaryman father buy a TV set for the family. The father sternly rejects this, designating television (and the desire to possess in general) as a 'useless' thing. But as the main message of the film goes, even the world of adults is made up of such trivial desires anyway. What eventually persuades him to purchase one is less the children's demand than his consideration of his relationship with a neighbour, who has recently retired from a company and managed to get a new job as an electronics salesman, whose mild (yet earnest) request to buy any item the father can hardly ignore. After all, consumerism is already an indispensable part of Japanese daily life to an extent that it permeates and reconfigures community relationships.

Commodity fetishism in late Ozu then works to reiterate the director's typical thematic issue, the generational divide. For the young children, the act of television watching would have much more meaning than eye-catching entertainment; it is a form of cultural practice to connect their suburban everyday life to the contemporary world outside as it is happening now. In this sense, it is a revealing fact that the programme they watch is a live broadcast of a sports game (*sumō*) (see Figure 5.3). The 'nowness' of the absorbing image is in stark contrast to the wartime past lingering in the image of a dead son that the parents in *Tokyo Story* watch in Noriko's apartment (see Figure 4.8). As discussed through Iwasaki Akira, Ozu's depicting the indulgence of the younger generation in consumerist culture can be placed in the opposite position to the more resistant form of representation, whether the sex and violence of *taiyōzoku* films or politically charged Ōshima. But in the context of 'post-Occupation Japanese cinema', it may as well regard them together as the two sides of a coin, mirroring

Figure 5.3 Children engrossed in watching television (compare with Figure 5.2 and also with the retrospective gaze of the old parents in Figure 4.8)

reactions to the same economic and political topography of Cold-War-era Japan under American influence. In this regard, both indulgence and resistance are a modern phenomenon, borne out of the boredom of the everyday, and the desire to deviate from it.

Ozu's older characters continue on a separate path from this current. Their typical temporal sensitivity no longer reaches the younger generation, whose everyday life is encroached upon by commodity fetishism. As a result, the old salaryman fathers are alienated from their children, and confined within the memorial spaces of the bar and restaurant. There, they are permitted to lament the wartime as a distanced, abstracted concept of the past, an entity quite different to the one that directly troubled the elderly parents in Ozu's previous postwar films. In this sense, the new salaryman films faithfully succeeded the *shōshimin* film, sharing the central issue of weakened masculinity, although the cause of the threat and the extent of the middle-class consciousness are not exactly the same. It is undeniable that Ozu ultimately perceived postwar society from this older generation's point of view, concluding most of the new salaryman films with the images of tired and lonely parents. However, it should not be overlooked that the younger generation are also vulnerable to a similar fatigue, as evinced by the image of Kōichi's yawning in *An Autumn Afternoon*. The profile image of an enervated father has long been used in Ozu's cinema to imply the impending death of the past, but in the new salaryman films, such a shot gains another metaphoric dimension, in connection with the boredom and tiredness inevitable in the course of everyday life, where such things as ending or death do not exist.

Conclusion

I have so far explored Ozu's cinema from the perspective of the everyday. Despite the inherent complexity of the concept of the everyday, its relation to the work of Ozu has largely been taken for granted, and has not been given the examination that it deserves. That relation, I think, is not merely confined to the direct impression that viewers get from Ozu's films. Ozu's everyday may seem to be a void; one may choose to point to the silently flowing cloud shots that are frequently seen in his films in order to assert the 'emptiness' of the present, which essentially constructs the everyday. However, arguments such as this often miss out on the more significant point that such shots hardly stand alone in the narrative; the cloud implies the 'gaze' of a subject of the everyday (even if absent or elided), and, moreover, a 'drama' that has been building to necessitate the gaze. Ultimately, we do not merely respond to the beauty of the scenery Ozu presents us with; we also respond to the feeling it evokes, or a meaning that saturates Ozu's everyday.

In order to conceptualise that abstract affect, I have actively drawn upon the history of Japan and the Japanese film industry in my argument. Within that framework of enquiry, Ozu's everyday becomes a more concrete phenomenon, placed within the context of modern Japanese history. I have articulated the multiplicity of modern life, discussing the differentiated aspects of Japanese modernity, and how a cultural text – a woman's magazine, for example – can reveal the varied perspectives of the modern subject on the everyday. One of the major purposes of this book is to extend this principle of multiplicity to the subjects related to Ozu's cinema, including not only Shochiku and Ozu himself, but also the characters on screen.[1] The result reveals a much more multifaceted topography of Ozu's work, wherein the positions of each subject can be related and compared. I have distinguished the prewar suburban middle classes (*shōshimin*) from the inner-city lower-middle classes in the Shitamachi district (*shomin*), whose everyday lives were founded upon different aspects of modernisation – that is, expanding capitalism and pre-modern communalism – although both indicate the same critique of modernity. The contrast between male and female point of views has also been discussed with regard to the woman's film genre, in which female subjectivities are also divided – into categories such as *moga* and *ryōsai kenbo* – by their relationship with dominant patriarchal ideology conveyed through the 'failed *moga*' narrative. I have also shown how Ozu's use of domestic objects and space – such as mirrors and movement within a room – displays (and violates) this gender-based order of subjectivity.

The characterisation of modern subjects in Ozu's films experiences a gradual transition as Japan becomes involved in war and ends up in defeat. Even though his only attempt at a war film was not fulfilled, his postwar films – at least before the 'new salaryman films' – demonstrate that the war and its aftermath became the primary thematic issue for the director. I have suggested that Ozu's historical consciousness during this period can be seen to share a basic problematic with the wartime intellectuals of the Overcoming Modernity symposium, where the specificities of Japanese modernity were actively re-examined in the context of the current war with the US. Records of Ozu's utterances, as well as the frequent images of old capitals in his films, exhibit the extent to which he was engaging with the matter of 'Japaneseness' at this time. However, I would caution against equating 'Japaneseness' with traditionalism (both aesthetically and politically), or hastily concluding that Ozu was in agreement with militarism or nationalism, which, with all the records of Ozu's participation in war, still leaves ambiguous points. Rather, I interpret this 'Japaneseness' as Ozu's active contemplation and questioning of the concept of postwar Japan, specifically 'how Japan was led into this history' and 'what Japan can do from now on'. From this critical viewpoint wartime totalitarianism cannot be exempted.

Female subjectivity (in contrast with male subjectivity) was a conspicuous example of how Ozu successfully addressed Japan's historical dilemma of continuing the present while retaining the burden of the past. Women's predominance in the domestic everyday contrasts with the alienation of male characters from domesticity, which not only reveals a symptom of patriarchy in crisis, as found in the wartime films as well as *shōshimin* films, but also connotes the temporal conflict that existed in postwar society. The narrative of marriage, which has long been one of the main issues in Ozu studies, should thus be reconsidered within this historical context, not in the sense of a reflection of the democratic reformation of the US Occupation period, but as a narrative element facilitating a complex interaction between the temporal sensitivity towards the past and the present.

The contrast between classes also obtained a temporal dimension in the postwar. Kihachi's Shitamachi world and its communality rapidly loses its ground in postwar society, as depicted in *Tokyo Story*, while an urban daily life based around consumerism, which was mostly ignored in the prewar *shōshimin* films, finally finds agency in the new salaryman films. This stabilised everyday life owes its prototype to wartime bourgeois drama, where female characters began to emerge out of the world of *shinpa* tragedy as the subject of the present temporality as well as consumption activities. In contrast, the realm of the past is pushed into the dark recesses of memory, especially the memory of the loss of war, as visualised in the old fathers' bar and restaurant spaces in the new salaryman films. I have concluded that the success of Ozu's films largely depends upon this memory of the past permeating into the everyday of the present. This important role is mainly given over to Ozu's young female characters, as seen in the Occupation-era films, and in the character of Noriko in *Tokyo Story*. However, as they begin to lose their connection to the wartime past more and more in the new salaryman films, the tension inherent in Ozu's cinema seems to lose its greatest source of momentum. This can be regarded as the reason for the common underestimation of this late period as simple *hōmudorama*, but I have argued that this should not lead to the conclusion that Ozu turned his back on society and indulged in stories of private life. Rather, the new salaryman films exhibit a franker examination of the contemporary consumerist culture that dominated postwar everyday life, for which Lefebvre's analysis of French society can offer a theoretical background. The bored younger generation inherits the anxiety of the prewar *shōshimin* class in the form of commodity fetishism, while their parents are confined to a space of nostalgia.

I have deployed the concept of deviation to explain the characteristics of Ozu's everyday as discussed so far. It is a way of interpreting recurrent narrative and visual elements that set a different spatial and temporal tonality or rhythm against the usual, rationalised system of daily life. In the *shōshimin* films, intermediary spaces such as the empty field or public park, which are neither home, school nor workplace, function as alternative spaces, where the characters can not only deviate from, but also reflect upon, the capitalistic order that dominates their everyday life. During the wartime, the everyday in deviation appeared in the form of the trivial chatting of female characters in such a non-domestic space as a café, or as male characters' drinking, both of which leave a direct trace in Ozu's postwar films. The best example, however, can be the living room inside the *pachinko* parlour in *The Flavour of Green Tea over Rice*, which, just a step away from the bustling reality of postwar mass culture, affords the male characters a chance to look back on the wartime past. I have also pointed out that such a small-scale spatial 'displacement' and temporal 'retrogression' can be extended to larger-scale movements as found in Kihachi's vagrant movement to/from a Shitamachi town, or the escape from and return to Tokyo accompanied in the narrative of marriage in the Occupation-era films. The distancing from usual everyday space and time works as a critique of Japanese modernity in the above-mentioned cases. However, female characters, though the main subjects who perform the return to Tokyo through marriage, generally tend not to be involved in such spatial displacement. Women instead disrupt and restructure domestic space and time where their existence is firmly rooted, which is clearly contrasted with their male counterparts' choice to retreat to a secluded place. Their movements at home, or their ability to bring an unexpected object into the domestic space (such as the shortcake in *Early Summer*), generate a similar deviating effect, which breaks the normal everyday logic that governs the otherwise static domesticity.

How was Shochiku's style of *Kamata-chō/Ōfuna-chō* related to the everyday of Ozu's films? Although Ozu's work has been regarded as the epitome of Shochiku style, and the name of Shochiku also has been equated with the female-oriented family drama that Ozu excelled at, this study suggests a more complex relationship – both personal and artistic. It is undeniable that Kido's realism, that is, an aesthetic striving to represent the world as it is, became the basic principle for Ozu's style in depicting the everyday. However, both Kido and Ozu deviate from that commonality. Kidoism was more of a commercial sensitivity than an artistic belief in realism, and the Kamata/Ofuna studio reflected this tendency in its *shinpa*-flavoured melodramas and happy-ending family dramas, the tradition of which continued until the postwar period. On the other hand, Ozu wanted to further pursue his artistic ambitions for more serious subject matter and style, as revealed in the form of the deep pathos of his *shōshimin* films. Thus, in order for Ozu's cinema to exist within the realm of Shochiku, a compromise had to be made. It should not be underestimated that Ozu thought of himself as 'an employee of Shochiku', and as he himself acknowledged, some of the typical elements now understood to be the essence of Ozu – the themes of paternal or maternal love, for instance – were adopted for commercial reasons. But in spite of this compromise, it is also true that Ozu's way of dealing with the everyday was distinct from that of other Shochiku films (such as *What Is Your Name?* or *Our Neighbour Miss Yae*). The principal reasons for this differentiation are, as discussed, the wide variety of subjectivities and the issue of historicity that Ozu emphasises throughout his films, which I believe transcend the stereotypical *Kamata-chō/Ōfuna-chō* film that is largely devoid of social concerns. In this sense, Ozu's cinema may not represent the whole of Shochiku's *Kamata-chō/Ōfuna-chō*, although his works did share common aspects with the genre's stylistic legacy.

The discussion above also suggests an important point in relation to the complex interactions between a filmmaker, the text s/he produces, and the contextual influences on the production of the text (from the film company the filmmaker works for to the larger socio-political environment at the time of the production). Ozu's case demonstrates that the relationships surrounding his filmmaking practice were not as linear, discrete and hierarchical as Bordwell's 'concentric circle' model suggests.[2] As mentioned, Ozu's relationship with Shochiku was not simple at all, as it became entangled in continuing negotiations between commerciality and artistry. In comparison, Ozu's work was more directly responsive to the ever-changing issues of Japanese society, from the early *shōshimin* films of the Depression era to the later new salaryman films of the privatised postwar society. As in the example of the *pachinko* parlour in *The Flavour of Green Tea over Rice*, Ozu was quick to comment on cultural tendencies in contemporary society in his films. This can be partly attributed to the unique production system that Ozu was involved in (at least in the postwar period), in which he could supervise the whole process from the initial planning and writing stage with Noda Kōgo. Again, this does not mean that he was free of any kind of restriction during the production, as it appears that Ozu's wish to confront darker subject matter was checked by Noda's contributions. However, it is clear that both Ozu and Noda were concerned with maintaining close contact with contemporary society in order to provide the main subject matter of everyday life in Ozu's films. I would suggest that the reason that a film is detached from social context in Bordwell's model is because he devised it from the viewpoint of *cinematic form*; it would be unreasonable to assert a 'direct' connection between the change in Ozu's visual style and, for instance, the social reformation of the Occupation era. But seen from the content's point of view, such a connection becomes acutely necessary for studying the workings of the everyday. This of course does not mean that in rescuing Ozu from formal excessiveness, everything in Ozu's films can be reduced to a reflection of Japanese society. Rather, I have discussed some contradictory examples against 'reflectionism', especially with regard to the influence of social ideology on the formation of subjectivity in film (for instance, patriarchy versus female subjectivity, or nationalism versus the consumerist subject). The point I am making is not to ignore the importance of the text, but rather to prompt an examination of its complex contextual linkage in order to fully enrich its meaning.

The relation between Ozu and society finally leads us to the big question of, 'Is Ozu conservative?', which can be also related to another question, 'Is Ozu traditional?' This question needs clarification because there are both formal and thematic dimensions to the term 'conservative'. For example, Rosenbaum's similar question, 'Is Ozu slow?', approaches this matter from a point of view that focuses on the formal, even though he confirms that it is 'impossible to speak about one without speaking about the other'.[3] While I agree with his conclusion, I would like to think about this issue from the other point of view, that is, Ozu's thematic conservatism. Ozu was perennially exposed to the criticism of Japanese critics throughout his career under different terms: his petit-bourgeois ideology in the *shōshimin* films; anachronistic individualism in the wartime bourgeois dramas, escapism (or traditionalism) in the Occupation-era films; and apolitical conservatism in the new salaryman films. Although the concrete object of the criticisms changed over the years, these critical attacks were unanimous in their antagonism toward Ozu's lukewarm moderatism, which defied radical change and offered instead a compromise with ambiguous humanism, holding him back from consummating the potential social realism inherent in his films of the everyday. Although there were occasional efforts to overcome this limit with a more straightforward type of realism, such as in *A Hen in the Wind* and *Tokyo Twilight*, Ozu in the end hardly transcended the boundaries of everyday realism he himself set. Such a tendency seems to have worked most restrictively for his filmmaking during wartime and the early postwar years, when reality existed in an extremely harsh form for most of the Japanese. His war experience in China as a soldier being considered, it may be a regrettable deficiency that Ozu never transferred that reality onto screen in a more unequivocal way. Also his historical consciousness, though sensitive to Japanese modernity and its relationship with the West, failed to expand to a more general idea to include Japanese imperialism and its influence on Asia within its scope.

Seen from this perspective, the director Ozu may present an interesting case in film history that raises fundamental questions about the relationship between cinema and reality, and whether or to what degree the former is able to faithfully represent the latter on its screen. As discussed in the early part of this book, the history of Shochiku itself is established on the effort to bring these two entities closer, albeit in a technical sense, through adopting Western methodology. Speaking in defence of Ozu, he might have thought there is little possibility for the two realms to become completely homogeneous. His confession after returning from war, 'I have lost my confidence in cinema', must be a proof that reveals this scepticism.[4] The increasingly refined formal style can be his personal tactic to respond to the uncertainty of cinematic realism by suggesting an alternative way to reconstruct reality. In terms of theme and subject matter, Ozu rather chose a method of irony to depict reality with unreality, in the face of criticism that he abandoned true reality.

I would therefore like to reconfirm that Ozu's everyday does not suffice to present the reality; it only shows a slice of it, applicable to a particular group of people in a particular space and time through a peculiar method, leaving out other possibilities. However, his cinema as a whole has an advantage of having the breadth of realities that he had explored throughout his long career, resulting in a dynamic quality. Ozu himself thus noted, 'It may look all the same to you, but I begin each work with a new interest, trying to express new things'.[5] This statement makes a paradoxical yet complementary contrast with his famous quote, 'I'm a tofu seller so I only make tofu'. His conservatism thus should be understood as a form of versatility created in response to varying social realities in Japanese history, while, on the other hand, maintaining its basic principles within a necessary boundary. Concluding in his own rhetoric, Ozu actually made various kinds of tofu, each with different ingredients and tastes, but tofu is still tofu, always retaining intact its distinctively plain flavour of the everyday.

Notes

Introduction

1. Richie, 'The Later Films', p. 18.
2. Thompson, *Breaking the Glass Armor*, pp. 329–30.
3. Miner, 'Japanese Film Art', pp. 355, 363. The event was entitled 'Japanese Film Series' and jointly presented by University of California Los Angeles and the Motion Picture Association of Japan on five consecutive Sunday evenings in March and April. The screening included such films as *Ōsaka no yado/An Inn at Osaka* (dir. Gosho Heinosuke, 1954), *Yama no oto/Sound of the Mountain* (dir. Naruse Mikio, 1954), *Mugibue/Wheat Whistle* (dir. Toyoda Shirō, 1955), *Ikiru/Ikiru* (dir. Kurosawa Akira, 1952), and Ozu's *Tokyo Story*, which was introduced under the title, *Their First Trip to Tokyo*.
4. Richie, *Ozu*, p. xii.
5. Ibid., pp. xii-xiii, 52.
6. Thompson, pp. 19–20, 327–31; Bordwell, *Ozu and the Poetics of Cinema*, pp. 73–4.
7. Ibid., pp. 32, 33, 50.
8. Ibid., p. 172.
9. Bordwell, *Poetics of Cinema*, pp. 30–1.
10. Lefebvre, *Critique of Everyday Life, Vol. 1*, p. 18.
11. Blanchot, 'Everyday Speech', p. 13.
12. Highmore (ed.), *The Everyday Life Reader*, p. 1.
13. Lefebvre, *Critique of Everyday Life, Vol. 2*, p. 41.
14. Ibid., p. 18.
15. In Lefebvre's 'critique', 'structure' means 'a system of coherent relations', which, 'located on a certain level above phenomena', is constructed with a view to studying and understanding them. Inversely, 'structure' itself also becomes 'discrete, distinct and discontinuous units' of 'totality' (which means a universal entity such as whole society or mankind). Thus 'structure' is 'an intermediary and a mediation' between phenomena (or 'reality', where the everyday is located) and totality (or 'abstraction'). Ibid., pp. 157–9, 180.
16. Anderson and Richie, *The Japanese Film*, p. 67.
17. Tanaka (ed.), *Sengo goroku*, p. 118.
18. Schrader, *Transcendental Style*, p. 39.

19. Roberts, *Philosophising the Everyday*, p. 67.
20. 'Do the needs of the working class differ absolutely from the needs of the bourgeoisie? This study demonstrates that they do not ... While there is a quantitative and qualitative disparity (of "standards of living") between the extent to which these needs and desires are satisfied, needs tend to equalise ... Proletariat as such contains the total human phenomenon – need, work, pleasure'. Lefebvre, *Vol. 2*, pp. 32–3.
21. Ibid., p. 10.
22. Ibid.
23. Ibid., p. 11.
24. Sekino, 'Shinkyōbutsu no hasan', p. 22.
25. De Certeau, *The Practice of Everyday Life*, p. xiii. De Certeau uses an example of the relationship between the Spanish colonisers and the indigenous Indians. Although the former imposed their culture and law on the latter's everyday life, the latter made use of them to produce 'something quite different from what their conquerors had in mind'. Ibid.
26. Ibid., p. 36.
27. Ibid., pp. 37, 117. 'Space' has 'none of the univocity or stability of a "proper"' as inherent in 'place'. Ibid., p. 117.
28. Ibid., p.37.
29. Ibid., pp. xiii, 20.
30. Ibid., pp. 92, 97. Such movements include a pedestrian's sudden turns, detours, crossings, wanderings and avoidings, making the consequential paths 'opaque' and 'invisible' to the panoptic viewer's effort to map. In Merleau-Ponty's terminology, these pedestrian movements constitute an 'anthropological space', which is contrasted with a 'geometrical space ("a homogeneous and isotropic spatiality," analogous to [de Certeau's] "place")'. Ibid., p. 117.
31. Baudelaire, *The Painter of Modern Life*, p. 12.
32. Wada-Marciano, *Nippon Modern*, pp. 37–8.
33. Lefebvre, *Rhythmanalysis*, pp. 73–4.
34. De Certeau, p. 38. De Certeau explains with an example of walking and mapping; after the 'practice' of the former has *passed* through a space, the latter attempts to gather the 'trace left behind', becoming a 'relic set in the *nowhen*'. Ibid., p. 97.
35. Ibid., p. 108
36. Ibid., p. 107.
37. Highmore, *Everyday Life and Cultural Theory*, p. 66.
38. Benjamin, *Vol. 4*, p. 317.
39. Ibid., p. 315.
40. Ibid., pp. 337–8, pp. 253–4. In contrast, the 'technology of reproduction' prevailing in modern art 'detaches the reproduced object from the sphere of tradition. By replicating the work many times over, it substitutes a mass existence for a unique existence'. Ibid., p. 254.
41. Ibid., p. 314.

42. Ibid., p. 390. 'It's not that what is past casts its light on what is present, or what is present its light on what is past; rather an image is that in which the Then [or 'what-has-been'] and the Now come into a constellation like a flash of lightning. In other words: image is dialectics at a standstill'. Didi-Huberman, 'The Supposition of the Aura', p. 8.
43. Ibid.
44. Benjamin, *Vol. 4*, p. 391.
45. Hamacher, 'Now', p. 57.
46. Charney, *Empty Moments*, p. 48.
47. Ibid., pp. 6, 35.
48. Benjamin, *Vol. 4*, p. 255.
49. Didi-Huberman, p. 8.
50. Ross, 'French Quotidian', p. 21; Gardner, *Advertising Tower*, p. 8.
51. Lefebvre, *Vol. 2*, p. 19.
52. Harootunian, *History's Disquiet*, pp. 62–3.
53. Ibid., p. 106.
54. Ibid., p. 63.
55. Gardner, p. 14.
56. Takeuchi, *What Is Modernity?*, p. 54.
57. Ibid., p. 57.
58. Lefebvre, *Vol. 2*, p. 88.
59. Ross, *Fast Cars*, pp. 78–9, 106.
60. Takabatake, 'Nichijō no shisō', p. 24.
61. Ibid., p. 27–8.
62. Ibid., p. 27.
63. Harootunian, *History's Disquiet*, p. 286.
64. Smith, *The Everyday World as Problematic*, p. 3.
65. By tradition, Yoshimoto means 'manifestations, representations or reflections of the traditional Japanese world view, sensibility or aesthetic principles'. The critics who are against seeing Ozu from this viewpoint are 'modern'. Being reactionary or radical indicates the political implication of such a traditional or modern style. Yoshimoto, *Logic of Sentiment*, p. 114.
66. Ibid., p. 117.
67. Ibid, p. 113.
68. '[N]eoformalists . . . never try to use their film analyses for any ideological agendas'. Daisuke Miyao, 'Translator's Introduction', in Yoshida, *Ozu's Anti-Cinema*, p. xvi.
69. Nornes, 'The Riddle of the Vase', pp. 81–5.
70. Yoshimoto, *Logic of Sentiment*, p. 124, 128. For Mitsuyo Wada-Marciano, such a dichotomy is a result of an 'enlightenment historiography' or 'colonial model of history', which 'situates a Western subject as the viewer and reader' and frames the Japanese cinema as a 'belated national cinema following the trajectory of Hollywood'. Wada-Marciano, *The Production of Modernity*, p. 16.
71. Bordwell, *Ozu and the Poetics of Cinema*, p. 1

72. Standish, *A New History*, p. 25.
73. Hasumi, *Kantoku Ozu Yasujirō*, pp. 98–104.
74. Ibid., pp. 37–8.
75. Yoshida, p. 62.
76. Ibid., p. 2.
77. Wada-Marciano, *Nippon Modern*, p. 32, 84.
78. Phillips, 'The Salaryman's Panic Time', pp. 29–30.
79. Phillips, 'Pictures of the Past in the Present', p. 163.
80. Ibid., p. 160.
81. Russell, 'Naruse Mikio's Silent Films', p. 81.
82. Russell, *Cinema of Naruse Mikio*, pp. 32–3. Russell thus disagrees with Joan Mellen's view that Naruse 'almost obscenely idealise[d] the Japanese woman as housewife', evading 'the kind of upheaval that would make possible true equality for women in Japan'. Such a description, Russell argues, 'betrays a serious misunderstanding of the Japanese context'. Ibid., p. 25.
83. Ibid., p. 27.

Chapter 1

1. Seidensticker, *Low City, High City*, p. 15.
2. By the term, 'the modern', I mean a very general situation and process towards new social conditions including various kinds of phenomena that had been happening in Japan at least from the Meiji Restoration. In this sense, I expect it to be the closest translation of a Japanese word, *kindai*. Also, the modern in my context has a different meaning from its transliterated Japanese word *modan*, which Miriam Silverberg uses for her study of 1920s Japanese mass culture.
3. Minami (ed.), *Taishō bunka*, p. 6.
4. Tyler, *Modanizumu*, p. 21.
5. Standish, *A New History*, p. 34; Gerow, 'The *Benshi*'s New Face', p. 70.
6. Fujiki, '*Benshi* as Stars', p. 80.
7. *Tokyo nichinichi shinbun*, morning edition, 26 February 1920, p. 5.
8. At that time, Japanese theatre business was in a feudal state. People involved were bound to each other in a 'father and son' relationship, and staging a play was dependent on the boss's decision. Performers were regarded as saleable goods or 'toys' for the leisured classes. Ticketing was monopolised by the tea house of each theatre, whose owner thus exerted strong power over promotion and box-office management. Yokomizo, *Shōchiku no uchimaku*, p. 15.
9. Ibid., p. 16.
10. Nagayama (ed.), *Shōchiku hyakunenshi*, p. 163.
11. Anderson and Richie, *The Japanese Film*, p. 31; Powell, *Japan's Modern Theatre*, p. 13. The first *shinpa* production in 1887 was performed by political activists (*sōshi*), and the company was led by Sudō Sadanori, 'an ex-policeman and a journalist on one of the first anti-government newspapers'. Ibid., pp. 12–13.

12. Tanaka Jun'Ichirō, *Hattatsushi*, Vol. 1, p. 247.
13. Onoe himself was a former stage actor, from the age of six years old, who, after gaining popularity in theatrical plays, moved on to film performance. It was Makino Shōzō, the 'first man to deserve the name of director in the Western sense of the word', who gave him his first starring role in film. Anderson and Richie, pp. 31–2.
14. Drawn from various Japanese theatrical traditions such as *jōruri* in *bunraku* (puppet theatre), and *nagauta* in *kabuki*, the *benshi* had a unique existence that, along with live sound, represented an alternative mode of exhibition in contrast with the Western narrative system that was based around visual text. In *bunraku*, *jōruri* is narration recited on stage accompanied by both *shamisen* music and the manipulation of puppets. *Nagauta* is a school of *jōruri* adopted in *kabuki*, which developed in the early eighteenth century. Harris, *The Traditional Theatre of Japan*, pp. 143–7; Yoshinobu and Toshio, *The Traditional Theatre of Japan*, pp. 156–7, 172–6; McDonald, *Japanese Classical Theatre*, pp. 27–8.
15. Tanaka, *Hattatsushi*, Vol. 1, p. 346. In an ironic twist to its meaning of 'new wave', *shinpa* gradually became an 'old school' as its styles became as rigid and conservative as *kabuki*, and experienced a drop in popularity after the first half of the 1910s. Powell suggests the ongoing transmigration to the 'new medium of film' could have been 'distracting *shinpa* actors from what had been their main task, the creation of an alternative theatrical art'. Powell, p. 45.
16. Tanaka, *Hattatsushi*, Vol. 1, pp. 346, 349.
17. Ibid., p. 345.
18. It could be the matter of familiarity with (e.g. chance of exposure to) the American style in films that deterred Japanese audiences from accepting it without feeling uncomfortable. For instance, they had been so familiar with long still shots that, when facial close-up shots appeared in Shochiku's first film, *Shima no onna/A Woman of Island* (Henri Kotani, 1920), the spectators burst into laughter, to the bewilderment of the performers present in the cinema. Ibid., p. 317.
19. He was one of the central figures of the *shingeki* movement as a director of Jiyū Gekijō (Freedom Theatre, 1909–19) before joining Shochiku.
20. Poulton, 'The Rhetoric of the Real', p. 23. Poulton notes that this interest in the 'imitation of reality' was of a 'specifically ideological form that originated in the West and was deeply implicated in the project of Japan's modernisation'; 'realism in the theatre signifies "the mark of the modern" and, . . . the West provided the model of modernity'. Ibid., p. 19.
21. Tanaka, *Hattatsushi*, Vol. 1, p. 340.
22. Nomura became the head of Shochiku's Shimogamo studio in Kyoto, which specialised in producing *jidaigeki* (period drama) films. Kobayashi, *Nihon eiga o tsukutta otoko*, pp. 20–1.
23. Ibid., p. 21.
24. Kido, Takizawa and Ema, *Kido shirō kikigaki*, p. 3.
25. Sakamoto, *Kazoku imēji no tanjō*, p. 119.

26. Yamada, 'Shōchiku Kamata Satsueisho', p. 76.
27. Ibid.
28. Harootunian, *History's Disquiet*, p. 141.
29. Tosaka, *Nihon ideorogi-ron*, pp. 21–2.
30. Ibid., pp. 88–9.
31. Tosaka, *Tosaka Jun zenshū*, Vol. 4, p. 137.
32. Ibid., p. 284.
33. Ibid., p. 286.
34. Ibid., p. 287.
35. Kido, *Nihon eiga den*, pp. 39–40.
36. Sawamura, 'Nichijōsei sonchō eiga', pp. 201–2.
37. Jeong, 'Sosimin yeonghwa yeongu', pp. 59, 64.
38. Satō, *Nihon eigashi*, Vol. 1, p. 217.
39. Shimizu, 'Eiga to puchiburu', p. 53.
40. Powell, p. 19.
41. Quoted in Matsumoto, *Meiji engekiron shi*, pp. 511–12. Osanai found the reason for *shinpa*'s exaggerated performance style in the *shinpa* actors' ignorance of the basic principle of modern theatre, that is, to assume a stage surrounded by four walls and thus completely isolated from the audience's gaze. Being always conscious of the audience's existence, *shinpa* actors tended to show off, making their performance 'ostentatious and hypocritical'. Ibid., p. 512.
42. Tanaka, *Hattatsushi*, Vol. 1, p. 57.
43. Ibid., p. 58.
44. In fact, *chanbara* came before *jidaigeki*. In the course of experimenting with more cinematic technique of movement, realistic swordfighting scenes were introduced to 'replace the more abstract, formal, *kabuki*-style choreography seen in *kyūgeki* films', and then 'since swashbuckling needs a vehicle', the genre of *jidaigeki* followed. McDonald, *Japanese Classical Theatre*, p. 28. Mitsuhiro Yoshimoto also agrees that *jidaigeki*'s emergence had 'little to do with a return to tradition and more to do with a rebellion against the old forms and conventions of *kabuki* and *kyūgeki*'. Yoshimoto, *Kurosawa*, p. 217. Kido, however, contradictorily argues later that at the time he was beginning his career in Kamata, '*jidaigeki* was steadfastly theatrical. It thus progressed by words'. '*Gendaigeki*', on the other hand, depended on 'cuts'. Kido, Takizawa and Ema, p. 3.
45. Satō, *Nihon eigashi*, Vol. 1, p. 217. Yoshimura Kōzaburō also defines *Kamata-chō* with similar three principles: 'simple story', 'mixture of humour', and 'consideration of tempo'. Yoshimura, Ōba and Yamada, '*Ōfunachō towa nanika*', p. 85.
46. Kido, *Nihon eiga den*, p. 40.
47. Satō, *Nihon eiga no kyoshō*, p. 102.
48. Kinema Junpōsha, *Nihon eiga kantoku zenshū*, p. 205.
49. Yamada, 'Shōchiku Kamata Satsueisho', p. 70.
50. Kido, *Nihon eiga den*, p. 34.
51. Yamada, 'Shōchiku Kamata Satsueisho', p. 70.

52. Furukawa, 'Nichiyōbi', p. 25; Tanaka Saburō, 'Otōsan', p. 20.
53. Ibid., p. 25.
54. Yoshimura, 'Hyōden Shimazu Yasujirō', p. 220. The situation resembles an early history of Japanese television, where the simple and economic *hōmudorama* (home drama) format was favoured for various technological reasons.
55. *Tea Making Family* is a story about a family in the countryside, which, because of the greed of the second son, is faced with a crisis. The father in this film, in contrast with the one in *Father*, cannot fulfil the son's request for money, and sets fire to his tea roasting house in order to collect insurance. But he is identified as the arsonist, and in the end his daughter becomes a *geisha* in order to help her father and family. Kinema Junpōsha Henshūbu, '*Cha o tsukuru ie*', p. 22.
56. Oda says, 'as for us [i.e. the writers of theatrical origin], the form of *shinpa* drama clung to our body, and just getting out of it required an extraordinary effort'. *Tea Making Family* was his first such struggle, but 'it would be hard to say that there was no vestige of *shinpa* in the film'. Oda argues that traces of *shinpa* style composition can still be identified in more recent Japanese cinema and even in foreign films; 'I think it's the fate of cinema that, when a film is made with an easy attitude [to appeal to large audiences], it soon falls prey to the form of *shinpa* drama'. Quoted in Satō, *Nihon eigashi*, Vol. 1, pp. 214–15.
57. Ibid., p. 243.
58. Sakamoto, *Kazoku imēji*, pp. 102, 245–6; Satō, *Nihon eigashi*, Vol. 1, p. 242.
59. Sakamoto, pp. 173, 246–7.
60. Sasaki, 'Tonari no yae chan', pp. 164–5.
61. Leaving her husband, Kyōko finds herself helpless to make her own living. She even thinks about working as a café waitress, which is instantly disapproved of by her mother. Divorce also makes her feel disgraceful in comparison with 'pure' Yaeko. Her effort to seek a new love from Keitarō is denied, and she leaves home again, leaving a suicidal note behind.
62. Ibid., pp. 167, 172. Yaeko, however, never directly clashes with Kyōko, which would instantly have made this film another '*shinpa* drama'. Ibid., p. 172.
63. Ibid.
64. Kishi Matsuo evidences the contemporary audiences' dislike of Kyōko's character saying, 'what the spectators who watched this film commonly said was Okada Yoshiko [who played Kyōko] was ugly'. She is thus a 'witch-like' character, a typical female prototype in *shinpa* drama. Quoted in ibid., p. 165.
65. Ibid., p. 173.
66. Wada-Marciano, *Nippon Modern*, p. 117.
67. In 1931, *Tokyo Chorus* was ranked at number three in *Kinema Junpo*'s annual top ten list, and *I Was Born But*... would become Ozu's first number one film in the list in the following year.
68. Ōtsuka, '*Tōkyō no kōrasu*', p. 92.
69. Kido, *Nihon eiga den*, pp. 74–6.
70. Ikeda, 'Shōshimin eiga ron', p. 119; Wada-Marciano, *Nippon Modern*, p. 22.
71. Gordon, *A Modern History of Japan*, p. 149.

72. In Tokyo, the number of the salaryman workers rose from 6 per cent of the whole workforce in 1908 to 21 per cent in 1920. Ibid., p. 150.
73. Ikeda, 'Shōshimin eiga ron', p. 118.
74. Ibid.
75. Shimizu, 'Eiga to puchiburu', p. 53.
76. Ibid., pp. 53–4.
77. Ibid., p. 54.
78. Ōtsuka, 'Tōkyō no kōrasu', p. 92. Yoshimura Kōzaburō, himself later a renowned Shochiku director, was also very sceptical about the commercial appeal of shōshimin film to general audiences, who 'loathed realistic depiction of hardships in life in film' and did not 'understand the comparably intellectual techniques of the genre'; Yoshimura, 'Shinkyō eiga', p. 55.
79. Sekino, 'Shinkyōbutsu no hasan', p. 22. Since shōshimin film concentrated more on the various sentimental responses of the salaryman and his family than active analysis of and resistance to their socio-economic situation, Japanese critics tended to call the genre – in a negative nuance – shinkyō eiga (state of mind film). Jeong, 'Sosimin yeonghwa yeongu', p. 55.
80. Ikeda, 'Shōshimin film ron', pp. 121–3.
81. Sekino, 'Shinkyōbutsu no hasan', p. 22; Ōtsuka, 'Ozu Yasujirō ron', p. 45.
82. Passin, *Society and Education*, p. 137.
83. In 1923, 82 per cent of male university and professional school graduates could find jobs, but in 1928, the number plummeted to 54 per cent. Nagy, 'Middle-Class Working Women', p. 204.
84. Cutts, *An Empire of Schools*, p. 10.
85. Gluck, *Japan's Modern Myths*, pp. 206, 210.
86. Harootunian, *Overcome by Modernity*, pp. 204–5.
87. In this broader sense, the Japanese term modanizumu used here can be distinguished from the English term modernism that, in a narrow sense, designates the modern as shisō (ideology) and geijutsu (art), such as specific artistic and literary movements as well as discourses about the 'modern' offered by Japanese intellectuals and writers through media.
88. Tipton, *Modern Japan*, p. 107.
89. Catherine Russell evaluates this sequence as constituting 'a remarkable study of life in Ginza'. Russell, *Cinema of Naruse Mikio*, p. 74.
90. Jeong, 'Sosimin yeonghwa yeongu', pp. 92–5.
91. In a city centre scene in *Tokyo Chorus*, the housewife is seen riding a tram, but the purpose of her going out is not for shopping but to look for a job for her husband's sake.
92. Phillips, 'The Salaryman's Panic Time', p. 30. The Japanese government's effort to reorganise and control the contour of private everyday life took the form of sponsoring top-down public campaigns such as the Everyday Life Reform Movement, which 'emphasize[d] efficiency and economies yet encourage[d] people to avoid excess and immersing themselves too deeply in the new commodity culture'. Harootunian, *Overcome by Modernity*, p. 15.

93. Wada-Marciano, *Nippon Modern*, p. 50.
94. Jeong, 'Sosimin yeonghwa yeongu', p. 61.
95. Wada-Marciano, *Nippon Modern*, p. 50.
96. Jeong, 'Chichi, kokka, soshite kazoku', p. 248; Wada-Marciano, *Nippon Modern*, p. 51.
97. Inoue, *Ozu Yasujirō zenshū*, Vol. 1, pp. 39–51.
98. Ueno, *Kindai kazoku*, p. 69. As the history surrounding the enactment of the Code shows, patriarchy was not originally an absolute condition but an alternative. During a preliminary national survey for the Civil Code, the Meiji government discovered that there existed an inheritance system among wealthy farmer and merchant families that descended through the lineage of mother or youngest child, which contrasted with the samurai class's convention of a paternal lineage system. The controversy over the Civil Code continued for nearly twenty years, but the 'maternal system' was eventually dismissed as a '*shomin*'s barbaric custom'. Ibid., pp. 69–70.
99. Uno, 'Women and Changes', pp. 35–8; Ueno, 'Position of Japanese Women', pp. S78–S79.
100. Wada-Marciano, *Nippon Modern*, p. 58.
101. Joo, 'There Were Fathers', p. 33.
102. Ōmura in *Tokyo Chorus* is performed by Saitō Tatsuo, who also played the unemployed husband Takai in *Body Beautiful* and the stern father Yoshii in *I Was Born But . . .* His tall but slim body well visualises the authoritative but not so genuinely powerful male *shōshimin* characters in these films.
103. Satō, *Kanpon Ozu Yasujirō*, p. 256.
104. De Certeau, *Practice of Everyday Life*, p. viii.
105. Phillips, 'The Salaryman's Panic Time', p. 29; Standish, *A New History*, p. 47; Rosenbaum, *Essential Cinema*, pp. 148–9.
106. Hasumi, *Kantoku Ozu Yasujirō*, p. 40.
107. Wada-Marciano, *Nippon Modern*, p. 58.
108. De Certeau, pp. 97, 92–3.
109. Okamoto, 'Ozu Yasujirō sakuhin saikentō', p. 42.
110. Inoue, *Ozu Yasujirō zenshū*, Vol. 1, pp. 575, 583.
111. Scene 39- 54. Ibid., pp. 567–8.
112. Ibid., p. 562. *Hijōji* (a time of crisis or emergency) that the instructor mentions was a buzzword to describe every aspect of Japanese society. Since 1932, not only government and the military but also the press, school and even advertisers publicised the word to emphasise the increasing tension and unrest in and outside the country after the Manchurian Incident. Wilson, *The Manchurian Crisis*, pp. 62–7.
113. Inoue, *Ozu Yasujirō zenshū*, Vol. 1, p. 583. It is worth noting here that Fushimi Akira's original script of *I Was Born But . . .* also has an ending with a reference to the military. Instead of the children's hunger strike, it rather follows the elder son's

day out in a field where he happens to meet a group of marching soldiers and does an errand for one of them. His parents at home worry about the lost boy, but as the day closes, he comes home and everything goes back to normal. Satō, *Kanpon Ozu Yasujirō*, pp. 279–80.
114. Gerow, *Visions of Japanese Modernity*, p. 21.

Chapter 2

1. Quoted in Richie, *Ozu*, p. 5.
2. Kido, *Nihon eiga den*, pp. 69–70.
3. Ibid., pp. 71–2; Hikone, 'Madamu to nyōbō', pp. 18–19.
4. Anderson and Richie, *The Japanese Film*, pp. 76–7.
5. Satō, *Nihon eigashi Vol. 1*, p. 332. As High points out, this industry restructuring process eventually led to 'a period of unprecedented expansion' in the second half of the 1930s. 'In 1935, there were 1,586 movie theatres nationwide, with a total of 185 million admissions annually. By 1940, 2,363 theatres were selling over 400 million tickets'. High, *The Imperial Screen*, p. 149.
6. 'In 1935, talkies were, just barely, outnumbering silents. By 1937, only a handful of silents continued to be produced, almost all of them by marginals'. Ibid.
7. Shimazu, 'Sairento yori tōkī e', p. 66.
8. Ikeda, 'Tōkī no seisakuyoku', p. 69.
9. Masumoto, *Jinbutu Shōchiku*, p. 221, 229–32.
10. The last silent film from Kamata studio was *Bōya manzai/Hurray for the Kid* (dir. Munemoto Hideo) released on 9 February 1935, and the last *saundoban* film was *Watashi no haru/My Spring* (dir. Fukuda Shūzō) released on 8 April 1936. Nagayama (ed.), *Shōchiku hyakunenshi, eizō shiryō*, pp. 66–84.
11. Anderson and Richie, p. 72. Richie even asserts that Ozu, 'who had mastered the silent film, did not know how a talkie should be made'. Richie, *Ozu*, p. 224.
12. Burch, *To the Distant Observer*, pp. 154–85.
13. Ozu, *Zennikki*, p. 125.
14. Tanaka, *Ozu Yasujirō shūyū*, p. 135; Ozu, *Zennikki*, p. 125.
15. 'Kamata eiga no jōsei senden', p. 21.
16. 'Bangumi oyobi keikyō chōsa', p. 20.
17. Ōguro, 'Ozu Yasujirō wa naze', pp. 50–1.
18. Ōtsuka, 'Ukigusa monogatari', p. 222.
19. Tanaka, *Zenhatsugen*, p. 64.
20. Ibid., pp. 64–5.
21. Sasaki, 'Ozu Yasujirō shi e kōkaijō', p. 68.
22. Tanaka, *Zenhatsugen*, p. 68.
23. Ibid., p. 83.
24. Ibid., pp. 29, 63.
25. Ibid., p. 28.

26. Ibid., p. 17.
27. Ibid., pp. 27–33.
28. Ibid., p. 31.
29. Ibid., p. 32.
30. Dore, *City Life*, p. 11.
31. Ibid. If Yamanote was expanded in a half-circle shape to the higher district in the west of *shōgun*'s Edo castle, Shitamachi was an eastern part of it, surrounded by the Sumida River and Edo Bay, and including such areas as Nihonbashi, Kyōbashi, Kanda and Shitaya. Seidensticker, *Low City*, pp. 8–9.
32. Ibid., p. 8.
33. Ibid., p. 13.
34. Ibid., p. 14.
35. Pons, *Edo kara Tōkyō e*, p. 115.
36. Ibid., p. 124. For example, the sounds of morning include the newspaper and milk delivery man and various peddlers (such as a *nattō* seller) who arrive at different but regular times. In the evening a tofu seller visits, accompanied by a peculiarly sorrowful horn sound. At night the bell from a nearby temple is followed by a watchman beating wooden clappers to remind people to put out the fire before sleeping. Ibid.
37. Dore, p. 12.
38. Too ambiguous to be explained in words, *iki* could, however, be summarised as a refined manner and a highly sophisticated taste and regard for beauty. In *chōnin*'s real life, the quality of *iki* was mainly demanded in the relationship with courtesans and *geishas* in the pleasure quarters such as Yoshiwara. For more about *iki*, see Nishiyama, *Edo Culture*, p. 54.
39. Satō, *Eiga no naka no Tōkyō*, p. 78.
40. Pons, p. 132.
41. Ozu, 'Jisaku o kataru', p. 95.
42. Tanaka, *Zenhatsugen*, p. 47.
43. Ōtsuka, 'Ukigusa monogatari', p. 222.
44. Bordwell, *Ozu and the Poetics of Cinema*, pp. 257, 258.
45. Hazumi et al., 'Zadankai', p. 111.
46. Tanaka, *Zenhatsugen*, p. 48.
47. Tanaka, *Zenhatsugen*, p. 31.
48. Ibid.
49. Tanaka, *Ozu Yasujirō shūyū*, p. 121.
50. Tanaka, *Zenhatsugen*, p. 48.
51. Ibid.
52. Ibid., p. 31.
53. Seidensticker, p. 11.
54. Keene, *Dawn to the West*, pp. 421–3, 433–4.
55. Yoshimi, *Toshi no doramatourugi*, pp. 337–40.
56. Wada-Marciano, *Nippon Modern*, p. 27.

57. Ibid., p. 29.
58. Ibid., p. 31.
59. Ibid., p. 32.
60. Tanaka, *Ozu Yasujirō shūyū*, p. 129.
61. Osakabe, 'Tōkyō ondo', pp. 124–5.
62. Tanaka, *Ozu Yasujirō shūyū*, p. 130. In that sense, it would not be surprising if there had been a political intention regarding the promotion of the song and dance. Tanaka Masasumi, quoting Takada Tamotsu's writing in *Kaizō* in November 1933, reveals that the Ministry of Education and Ministry of Home Affairs as well as the military were actively involved in promoting the song with an 'intentional plan'. Tanaka also introduces nationalistic parts of the lyrics that are no longer sung today, which included such lines as, 'King and subjects, an eternal promise'. Ibid., p. 130–1.
63. Ibid., pp. 129, 131.
64. Satō, *Kanpon Ozu Yasujirō*, pp. 299, 308–12.
65. Ibid., p. 303; Tanaka, *Zenhatsugen*, p. 31.
66. Kinema Junpōsha, *Nihon eiga daihyō shinario*, p. 137.
67. Ibid.
68. Kitagawa, 'Deki kokoro', p. 97.
69. Hazumi et al., 'Zadankai', p. 111.
70. Iwasaki, 'Ozu Yasujirō to Nihon eiga', p. 62. Richie, who introduces Iwasaki's 'disappointment', misses this latter part of the quote.
71. This repeating formula of visiting and leaving resembles the basic narrative structure of the *Otoko wa tsurai yo/It's Tough Being a Man* series, wherein the protagonist *Tora-san* returns to his hometown, Shibamata, and leaves to travel again at the end. The appeal of the series is generally attributed to nostalgia for lost hometowns, but Richard Torrance argues that it is rather more complex, and includes a form of commentary on contemporary society using various parodies of popular culture and representations of class identity in the postwar period. Torrance, 'Otoko wa tsurai yo', pp. 226–49.
72. Sato, *New Japanese Woman*, p. 48.
73. The typical look of the *modan gāru* was a 'vapid young woman clad in a brightly coloured one-piece dress reaching only to the knees or a little below, favouring high-heeled shoes and sheer stockings that showed off her legs. A wide-brimmed floppy hat or cloche made of a soft material partially concealed her short hair, or *danpatsu*, which had been bobbed in the style of Hollywood idols Clara Bow, Pola Negri, Mary Pickford, and Gloria Swanson. In the Swanson tradition, she often pencilled in a thin line over her shaved eyebrows. Over her shoulder she casually slung a pouch bag'. Ibid., p. 51.
74. The term was first used in 1923 by the essayist Kitazawa Chōgo (also known as Kitazawa Shūichi), who, having lived in London for a few years, intended to introduce the English 'modern girl' to Japan. Kitazawa's first article mentioning the name '*modan gāru*' was 'Modan gāru no hyōgen – Nihon no imōto ni okuru

tegami/'The Emergence of the Modern Girl – A Letter to My Sister in Japan' published in *Josei Kaizō/Woman's Reform* in April 1923. The next year, he wrote another article 'Modan gāru' in the August 1924 issue of *Josei/Woman*, and from then on, the number of writings on *modan gāru* exploded on the pages of women's magazines. Ibid., pp. 57–8.
75. The Modern Girl Around the World Research Group, 'The Modern Girl as Heuristic Device', p. 4.
76. Fujiki, *Zōshokusuru perusona*, p. 295.
77. Ibid., p. 303.
78. For example, the Ministry of Railways and the Ministry of Interior deployed media to 'sensationally report the campaign of eradicating *moga* and *mobo* (acronyms of modern girl and modern boy)'. Tokyo's Metropolitan Police Department also campaigned for a '*mobo* and *moga* cleanup action'. Ibid., pp. 302–4.
79. Ibid., p. 304.
80. Sato, *New Japanese Woman*, p. 61.
81. Harootunian, *Overcome by Modernity*, p. 23.
82. Silverberg, *Erotic Grotesque Nonsense*, p. 55.
83. Ibid., p. 57.
84. Sato, *New Japanese Woman*, p. 56.
85. Ōya, *Modan sō*, p. 16. *Atarashii onna* indicates a group of young female intellectuals/writers/activists in the early twentieth century, such as Hiratsuka Raichō (1886–1971), Itō Noe (1895–1923), and Yosano Akiko (1878–1942), who were active in the magazine called *Seitō/Bluestockings* and became advocates of liberated femininity, preceding the *modan gāru* of the Showa era. Sato, *New Japanese Woman*, pp. 14, 19–20; Suzuki, *Becoming Modern Woman*, pp. 10–12.
86. Fujiki, *Zōshokusuru perusona*, pp. 296, 298–9.
87. Silverberg, *Erotic Grotesque Nonsense*, pp. 57–8, 66–7. According to the 'Survey regarding Working Women' released by the Tokyo Social Affairs Bureau in 1924, the category of the 'working woman' included not only office-based white-collar employees (teachers, typists, clerks, shopkeepers, nurses and telephone operators) but also workers of a more working-class nature (bus conductors, café waitresses and other employees in the service industry). Ibid., p. 66.
88. Ibid., p. 69.
89. According to a famous street fashion survey done by Kon Wajirō in 1925, even on the street of Ginza – the most likely place in the nation to encounter a modern girl – only 1 per cent of women were clad in the typical modern girl style. More than ten years later, a survey done by a women's magazine *Shufu no tomo* in 1937 showed 13 per cent of those surveyed in Tokyo wore Western-style dress. Sato, *New Japanese Woman*, p. 182.
90. Yoshimi, 'Teito to modan gāru', pp. 246–7; Yoshimi, 'Teikoku shuto Tōkyō', p. 51. Barbara Sato points out the same point that 'most young women entering the workforce never considered the possibility of sacrificing marriage for career'. Sato, *New Japanese Woman*, p. 137.

91. Yoshimi, 'Teikoku shuto Tōkyō', p. 44.
92. Ibid., pp. 44–5.
93. On women's magazines, see chapter 3 of Barbara Sato's *The New Japanese Woman*. Fujiki also notes that there existed various 'voices of women themselves' (such as café waitresses, schoolgirls and housewives) displayed on the pages of women's magazines, showing their subjective agency. Fujiki, *Zōshokusuru perusona*, p. 295.
94. Silverberg, *Erotic Grotesque Nonsense*, p. 58.
95. What mostly filled the pages of the magazines was '*katei kiji* (family articles)' that aimed to 'acquaint housewives with tips about home and family', such as 'bringing up children, information related to illnesses, cooking, sewing, knitting, flower arranging and other artistic pursuits, and proper etiquette'. Sato, *New Japanese Woman*, p. 97.
96. Sato, *New Japanese Woman*, p. 89; Silverberg, *Erotic Grotesque Nonsense*, pp. 148–9.
97. Wada-Marciano, *Nippon Modern*, p. 77.
98. Ibid.
99. Ibid., pp 82–3.
100. Ibid., p. 84.
101. Ibid., p. 107.
102. Ibid., p. 88.
103. Ibid., p. 108.
104. Ibid., p. 87.
105. Ibid., pp. 88–9.
106. Wada-Marciano, *Nippon Modern*, p. 88.
107. Sasaki, 'Tonari no yae chan', p. 168.
108. Sakamoto, *Kazoku imēji*, p. 105.
109. *The Lady and the Beard* was one of the most commercially popular Ozu films in the prewar era, especially compared to his *shōshimin* films. Ozu himself admitted that *The Lady and the Beard* and *Ojōsan/Young Miss* (1930) were the ones among his films that could be most easily received by audiences. Tanaka, *Zenhatsugen*, p. 49.
110. Before she appeared in *Woman of Tokyo* in 1933, Okada had been already involved in several extramarital love affairs, had an illegitimate son, and had also been barred from the film industry for five years because she walked out during the filming of *Tsubaki Hime/Camille* (Murata Minoru, Nikkatsu, 1927) with the leading actor, Takeuchi Ryōichi. Her star image as a modern girl is fixed by these offscreen scandals in addition to her physical appearance, which was exotically Western as well as sexual. Wada-Marciano, *Nippon Modern*, p. 95.
111. Ibid., pp. 97, 98.
112. Ibid., p. 99.
113. McDonald, *From Book to Screen*, p. 14.
114. Burch, *To the Distant Observer*, p. 161. Burch interpreted the pillow shot as a 'culturally and complexly determined sign of dissent from the world-view implicit in the Western mode' that is 'profoundly anthropocentric'. Thus in the pillow

shot, there is a 'prolonged or "unmotivated" absence of human beings from the screen . . ., [which] functions as a departure from the [Western] code'. Ibid.
115. Ibid., p. 160.
116. Inoue, *Ozu Yasujirō zenshū*, Vol. 1, p. 401.
117. Russell, *Cinema of Naruse Mikio*, pp. 73, 76.
118. Inoue, *Ozu Yasujirō zenshū*, Vol. 1, p. 387.
119. Miyao, *Aesthetics of Shadow*, p. 152.

Chapter 3

1. Bordwell, *Ozu and the Poetics of Cinema*, p. 275.
2. Nagayama (ed.), *Shochiku hyakunenshi, honshi*, p. 599.
3. The new motto of 'Kamata in the World (*sekaiteki kamata*)' had been announced in 1934 along with ten production policies, which included such pro-sound plans as the 'introduction of popular songs and singers', 'introduction of folk song artists', and 'film adaptation of all-female revue materials'. Ibid., p. 593.
4. Tanaka, *Hattatsushi*, Vol. 2, p. 300.
5. High, *The Imperial Screen*, p. 153.
6. Reischauer, pp. 101–2.
7. Irokawa, *Culture of the Meiji Period*, pp. 247–9; Beasley, *Rise of Modern Japan*, pp. 79–80; and Gluck, *Japan's Modern Myths*, p. 143.
8. Lee et al. (eds and trans.), *Taepyeongyang jeonjaeng*, p. 11. The English translation of the symposium can be found in Calichman (ed. and trans.), *Overcoming Modernity*. Also see Harootunian, *Overcome by Modernity*, pp. 34–94. Another similar symposium named 'The Standpoint of World History and Japan' was held three times in 1941 and 1942 by leading philosophers of the Kyoto School. This is serialised in the magazine *Chūō kōron* in 1942 and 1943, and then published as a book in 1943. Lee et al., p. 23. For an English translation of this, see Williams (ed.), *Philosophy of Japanese Wartime Resistance*.
9. Sun, 'In Search of the Modern', pp. 56–9.
10. Calichman, p. 149.
11. Ibid., p. 47.
12. Najita and Harootunian, 'Japan's Revolt', p. 264.
13. Calichman, p. 43.
14. Ibid., p. 49.
15. Sun, p. 63.
16. Lee et al., p. 12.
17. Tanaka, *Hattatsushi*, Vol. 3, pp. 14–15. High notes that film industry representatives did not see the law as a serious impediment to their business at the time. Since there had already been 'the arbitrary or capricious decisions of officials scattered throughout the government structure', they figured that the new legislation would institute 'clearly defined guidelines' that might afford them 'security and freedom'. In the end,

'the details of the Film Law, even after its enactment, did not add up to a system of total vertical control'. High, *Imperial Screen*, pp. 73–4, 151.
18. Tanaka, *Hattatsushi*, Vol. 3, p. 21; Standish, *A New History*, pp. 142–4.
19. Davis, *Picturing Japaneseness*, pp. 1–7.
20. High, *Imperial Screen*, pp. 251, 253.
21. Ibid., p. 224.
22. Ibid., pp. 224–5.
23. Tanaka, *Hattatsushi*, Vol. 3, p. 13.
24. Ibid., p. 41.
25. Ibid., p. 40; High, *Imperial Screen*, p. 164.
26. Kido, *Nihon eiga den*, p. 171.
27. Tanaka, *Hattatsushi*, Vol. 3, p. 40.
28. High, *Imperial Screen*, p. 165.
29. Standish, p. 53.
30. Tanaka, *Hattatsushi*, Vol. 3, p. 45. It took three years for Toho to complete *Flaming Sky*, a spectacular movie about air combat, which included the direct involvement and help of the army, using 947 aircrafts and fifteen cameras to record 328 hours of air combat scenes. Masumoto, *Shōchiku eiga no eikō*, p. 130.
31. Ibid., p. 122, and Tanaka, *Hattatsushi*, Vol. 3, p. 40.
32. Hase, 'Nihon eiga to zentai shugi', pp. 278–9; Calichman, pp. 118–27.
33. Hase, 'Nihon eiga to zentai shugi', pp. 278–9.
34. Tsumura, *Eiga to kanshō*, pp. 21–3.
35. Tanaka, *Hattatsushi*, Vol. 3, p. 41.
36. Masumoto, *Shōchiku eiga no eikō*, p. 126.
37. High, *Imperial Screen*, p. 211.
38. Ibid., p. 217.
39. Ibid., pp. 218–20.
40. Tanaka, *Hattatsushi*, Vol. 3, p. 42; Masumoto, *Shōchiku eiga no eikō*, p. 134.
41. Tanaka, *Hattatsushi*, Vol. 3, p. 132; High, *Imperial Screen*, p. 385.
42. Masumoto, *Shōchiku eiga no eikō*, p. 138.
43. Tanaka, *Ozu Yasujirō to sensō*, pp. 62–4.
44. Ibid., p. 65; Tanaka, *Zenhatsugen*, pp. 96,
45. Ibid., p. 110; Ozu, *Zennikki*, pp. 247–58.
46. Tanaka, *Ozu Yasujirō to sensō*, pp. 65–6.
47. Tanaka, *Zenhatsugen*, p. 103.
48. Ibid., p. 113.
49. Ibid., p. 110.
50. Ibid., p. 119.
51. Ibid., p. 101.
52. Ibid., pp. 110–11.
53. Ozu's field memo, reprinted in Tanaka, *Ozu Yasujirō to sensō*, p. 147.
54. Ibid.

55. Ibid.
56. Ibid., pp. 148–50.
57. High, *Imperial Screen*, p. 211.
58. Reprinted in Tanaka, *Ozu Yasujirō to sensō*, pp. 153–79.
59. Ozu, *Zennikki*, pp. 252, 254.
60. Tanaka, *Zenhatsugen*, 111–12.
61. Ibid., pp. 112–13.
62. High, 'Drama of Superimposed Maps', p.3.
63. Ozu, *Zennikki*, pp. 227–8, 252, 259, 262–3.
64. Tanaka, *Zenhatsugen*, p. 109.
65. Ozu, *Zennikki*, pp. 231–2
66. Ibid., p. 236.
67. See Mellen, *The Waves*, p. 155; Standish, p. 127.
68. Yonaha, *Teikoku no zan'ei*, pp. 36, 47, 59. Yonaha makes comparison with Shiga Naoya's novel *An'ya kōro/A Dark Night's Passing*, where the three colonial cities all appear as non-Japanese settings around which a female character Oei wanders after a break-up with the male protagonist Kensaku. Ozu was an avid reader of this novel. Ibid., pp. 34–6, 58.
69. Ozu actually mentioned, 'It's not that I haven't thought about making a war film, but I could not but give up that idea given the current state of facilities in Japanese studios'. Tanaka, *Zenhatsugen*, p. 163.
70. Ibid., p. 142.
71. Bordwell, *Ozu and the Poetics of Cinema*, p. 281.
72. Satō, *Kanpon Ozu Yasujirō no geijutsu*, p. 387.
73. Tanaka, '*Ochazuke no aji* kaidai, p. 48.
74. Bordwell, *Ozu and the Poetics of Cinema*, pp. 280, 281.
75. Ibid., p. 280.
76. In Ayako's own words: 'I could see his eyes were also full of tears. So I said, "No, please don't cry. You're a man. Going to war is . . .", but then he said, "Fool! Can't you understand my feeling?" and suddenly gave me a slap.' Ikeda and Ozu, *Ochazuke no aji*, p. 63.
77. Tanaka Masasumi thus groups these films together as Ozu's 'Yamanote *teitaku mono* (uptown mansion films)'. Tanaka, '*Ochazuke no aji* kaidai', p. 48.
78. Richie, *Ozu*, p. 226. Ozu said, 'The characteristic of this film is that the setting was moved from Shitamachi used until then to Yamanote . . . Since they said there had been comparably few films dealing with Yamanote, I wanted to take up that subject'. Ozu, 'Jisaku wo kataru', p. 96.
79. Bordwell, *Ozu and the Poetics of Cinema*, pp. 275–6.
80. Sawamura argued that Kihachi film's aesthetics of Shitamachi humanity (*ninjō*) are the basis and essence of Ozu's cinema. If the element of 'melancholy' and 'wisdom' is added to this, it becomes student/salaryman dramas. And what includes 'romanticism' instead becomes such films as *Beauty's Sorrows* (1930), *Until the Day We Meet Again* (1932), and *A Mother Should Be Loved* (1934). (However, exactly what the term 'romanticism' means is not clarified in his explanation.) Sawamura, *Gendai eiga ron*, p. 212.

81. As Tanaka Masasumi points out, it is also a noteworthy connection among the three films/television drama, *Equinox Flower, Late Autumn and Youth after School*, that they were all written in collaboration with a Japanese writer Satomi Ton (1888–1983), whose expert style in characters' conversation exerted an influence on Ozu's talkie films. Tanaka, 'TV shinario *Seishun hōkago* kaidai', p. 115.
82. Narita, *Kokyō*, pp. 64, 68.
83. Yoshimi, *Toshi no doramatourugi*, p. 340.
84. Narita, p. 145.
85. Sawamura, 'Kōhuku no toiki', pp. 135–6.
86. Bordwell, *Ozu and the Poetics of Cinema*, p. 279.
87. Ikeda and Ozu, p. 63.
88. Ibid., p. 50.
89. Ibid., p. 58.
90. Ibid.
91. Tanaka, *Zenhatsugen*, p. 162.
92. Ibid., p. 273.
93. Ibid., p. 227.
94. Ibid., p. 230.
95. Ibid., p. 231.
96. Davis, 'Back to Japan', p. 17.
97. Ibid., p. 23–4.
98. Standish, p. 38.
99. The other film with a family name in its title is *The Autumn of Kohayagawa Family* (*Kohayagawake no aki*), also known as *End of Summer* in English.
100. Bordwell, *Ozu and the Poetics of Cinema*, p. 283.
101. Due to postwar censorship, the existing print of the film does not include Ryōhei's answer, 'I've got A', to Horikawa's question, 'How did the physical examination go?', and some of the following Horikawa's congratulatory and encouraging remarks, such as a line from Man'yōshū, 'Since today I will not look back and set out to defend His Majesty', all of which can be found in the script. Inoue, *Ozu Yasujirō zenshū*, Vol. 1, p. 686.
102. Standish, p. 112.
103. Ueno, 'Modern Patriarchy', pp. 214–15.
104. Bruzzi, *Bringing Up Daddy*, p. 7.
105. Tsumura, *Eiga to kanshō*, pp. 156–7.
106. Ibid., p. 153.
107. Standish, p. 110.
108. High, 'Drama of Superimposed Maps', p. 5.
109. Ibid., pp. 5, 20–1.
110. Ibid., p. 18.
111. Reprinted in Tanaka, *Ozu Yasujirō to sensō*, pp. 180–202.
112. While stationed in Gushi county, Ozu slept at a school classroom, and its ceiling was papered with English newspapers, among which there was a colour picture of shortcake. Whenever Ozu lay down to sleep, it was seen right above his eyes; 'I

kept thinking everyday only the same thing, "wish I could eat whole of that"'. Ozu, 'Tegami', p. 64. Ozu's diary also confirms his struggle with hunger: 'It's better to eat much when it's possible. Otherwise, I would end up in a situation when I have to eat whatever available, clean or dirty. Also, the more I got tired, the more serious my appetite became, and I could not help it.' He even made a wishlist of the dishes he wanted to eat on returning home, one of which is none other than *ochazuke*. These real-life backgrounds provide a significant clue for properly analysing the allegorical references to food in Ozu's postwar films such as the *ochazuke* in *The Flavour of Green Tea over Rice* and the shortcake in *Early Summer*, as discussed in Chapter 4. Ozu, *Zennikki*, pp. 256, 240.
113. High, 'Drama of Superimposed Maps', pp. 15, 16–17.
114. Tanaka, *Zenhatsugen*, pp. 99–100, 107, 120–1.
115. Ibid., p. 107.
116. High, 'Drama of Superimposed Maps', p. 17.
117. Inoue (ed.), *Ozu Yasujirō zenshū*, Vol. 2, p. 534.
118. Ibid., p. 549.
119. Tanaka, *Zenhatsugen*, p. 108.
120. Tsumura, *Eiga to kanshō*, pp. 154–5.

Chapter 4

1. Gluck, 'The Past in the Present', p. 93; Kang, 'The Discovery of the "Orient"', p. 84.
2. Gluck, 'The "End" of the Postwar', pp. 4–9.
3. In the 'mythistoric postwar', 'history began anew, quite precisely on August 15, 1945'. This version of the postwar foregrounds an intentional effort to quickly convert Japan from war and militarism to peace and democracy, spurred on by the reign of the Occupation. In contrast, the 'inverted postwar' recognises the wartime past, but only as a negative experience, for which militarists are to blame. Japanese people purge themselves as victims and eventually erase all memory of the past. Ibid., p. 4.
4. Odagawa, 'Renzokusei ni tsuite', pp. 16–18.
5. Ibid., pp. 18–35.
6. Ibid., p. 19.
7. Ibid., pp. 26–7.
8. Ibid., pp. 30–5.
9. Gao, 'The Postwar Japanese Economy', p. 302.
10. Klopfenstein, 'Jobun', pp. 3–4.
11. Yoshimoto, *Kurosawa*, p. 87.
12. Ibid., p. 88.
13. Hirano, *Mr Smith Goes to Tokyo*, p. 4.
14. Ibid., p. 38; Satō, *Nihon eigashi*, Vol. 2, p. 163.
15. Ibid., p. 166.
16. Tanaka, *Hattatsushi*, Vol. 3, p. 215; Satō, *Nihon eigashi*, Vol. 2, p. 167.

17. For example, Conde, a non-professional in filmmaking, not only suggested the basic idea of a film *Minshū no teki/The Enemy of People* (Imai Tadashi, Toho, 1946), which dealt with the vices of militarists and capitalists during war, but also demanded revisions on over twenty points in the script. Imai, completing the film without the due revisions, had a hard time persuading Conde to approve it for release. Satō, *Nihon eigashi*, Vol. 2, pp. 176–7.
18. Ibid., p. 167.
19. Tanaka, *Ozu Yasujirō to sensō*, pp. 105–8. Also see Seki and Tanaka, 'Juron yokuryūsho', pp. 90–9 for Tanaka Masasumi's interview with Seki Tadashi, who spent the Jurong internment camp days with Ozu.
20. Tanaka, *Sengo goroku*, p. 22. Tanaka, *Ozu Yasujirō shūyū*, pp. 303–4.
21. Sun, 'In Search of the Modern', p. 62.
22. Ibid., p. 63.
23. Harootunian, *Overcome by Modernity*, pp. 43–4.
24. Calichman, *Overcoming Modernity*, p. 30.
25. Richie argued that 'so far as influences on his style went, the foreign films had no more impact than his army experience, the war itself, and the war's democratic aftermath'. Richie, *Ozu*, p. 232.
26. He mentioned three tendencies; first, realism based upon original novels such as John Ford's *Grapes of Wrath* (1940) and *Tobacco Road* (1941); secondly, films based upon the star system, which Hollywood had long excelled at; and thirdly, Technicolor films. Ozu understood that the second and third tendencies represented popular genre films, which 'back[ed] up' the more adventurous attempts of the realist films in terms of business. He thought such a balance exemplified the 'healthiness' of Hollywood studios. Ozu, 'Kongo no Nihon eiga', pp. 104–5; Tanaka, *Sengo goroku*, p. 24.
27. Tanaka, *Sengo goroku*, pp. 27–8.
28. Ibid., pp. 24, 27.
29. Fowler, 'Piss and Run', pp. 285–6.
30. Ibid., p. 286.
31. Calichman, p. 183.
32. Ibid.
33. Harootunian, 'Japan's Long Postwar', p. 99.
34. Ibid., p. 110.
35. Ibid., p. 107.
36. Ibid., p. 116.
37. Igarashi, *Bodies of Memory*, p. 5.
38. Ibid., p. 20.
39. 'Culture, or tradition, was a convenient medium through which to project continuity with Japan's past in order to mask the historical disjuncture of Japan's movement from a former enemy to ally of the United States'. Ibid., p. 73.
40. Tanaka, *Ozu Yasujirō shūyū*, p. 340.
41. Iwamoto and Makino, *Eiga nenkan, sengo hen*, pp. 418–24.

42. Ozu, 'Jisaku o kataru', p. 97.
43. Noda, 'Ozu Yasujirō to iu otoko', p. 42.
44. Satō, *Kanpon Ozu Yasujirō*, p. 434, 436.
45. Filming *The Moon Has Risen* was postponed several times during the years that Ozu was making *A Hen in the Wind*, *Late Spring*, and *The Munekata Sisters*. The first postponement was due to the seasonal setting of the script – autumn in Nara, for which the script was finished too late in November to begin filming – but the successive postponements were caused by the trouble with casting Takamine Hideko, who seemed essential for the main character Setsuko. The project was finally handed to Tanaka Kinuyo and released in 1954 under her direction. Tanaka, *Ozu Yasujirō shūyū*, pp. 331, 342–3.
46. In the original manuscript submitted to CIE for review, Ozu used the word '*yakeato* (ruins of fire)' to describe the state of Tokyo, which the censors marked for deletion. Nevertheless, the line survived into the final film, but the word was substituted with '*hokorippoi* (full of dust)'. Sorensen, *Censorship of Japanese Films*, pp. 138–9, 152.
47. Ibid., pp. 138–41. The completed script was submitted to CIE in November 1947, and just as in the case of *Late Spring*, 'from the outset, the censors were wary of the uses of the traditional and religious features of the ancient capitals of Japan'. Ibid., p. 138.
48. Regarding the contemporary critical response to *Late Spring*, refer to Sorensen, pp. 146–8.
49. Tanaka clarifies that the first time Ozu started to use the tofu maker metaphor was around the time he was making *Early Summer* in the autumn of 1951. Tanaka, *Sengo goroku*, p. 437.
50. Ibid., p. 67.
51. Thompson, *Breaking the Glass Armor*, pp. 317–18.
52. Wood, *Sexual Politics*, p. 120.
53. Tanaka, *Ozu Yasujirō shūyū*, p. 337. Originally a member of Shinkankakuha (New Sensationist School) – a group of young modernist writers influenced by the European avant-garde movement – in the 1920s, Yokomitsu later turned to a more nationalistic ideology, searching for the possibility of 'a rejection of the West and the rediscovery of a native cultural tradition', which became the central theme of his work *Ryoshū/Melancholy Journey* (1946). Lippit, *Topographies of Japanese Modernism*, p. 78, 200–2.
54. Tanaka, *Ozu Yasujirō shūyū*, pp. 335, 337.
55. Sorensen, p. 155.
56. Ibid., pp. 161–2.
57. That this social is 'monthly' is designated in the film's script. Inoue, *Ozu Yasujirō zenshū*, Vol. 2, p. 51.
58. Thompson, *Breaking the Glass Armor*, pp. 325–6.
59. Cazdyn, *Flash of Capital*, p. 230.
60. Ross, *Fast Cars*, p. 102.

61. Kano, *Nihon no kindai shisō*, pp. 184, 187.
62. Ibid., p. 184.
63. Kelly, 'Finding a Place', p. 208.
64. Kaneko, 'The Struggle for Legal Rights', pp. 10–12; Oda, *Basic Japanese Laws*, p. 8.
65. Eccleston, *State and Society*, pp. 187–8; Ueno, 'Onna no sengo bunkashi', p. 251.
66. Phillips, 'Pictures of the Past', p. 161; Wood, p. 126.
67. The cooked rice as a symbol of femininity also takes a central role in Naruse Mikio's *Meshi/Repast* (Toho, 1951), which is another film that stars Hara Setsuko. In the film, the meaning of *meshi* (another word for cooked rice) is duplicated. On the one hand, it is an everyday duty of the protagonist housewife Michiyo, and thus signifies 'a useless life, or the unglamorous necessities of life'. But as such, it also constitutes her feminine subjectivity and communality, as later confirmed when she visits her welcoming mother and shares a meal of warm *meshi*. Russell, *Cinema of Naruse Mikio*, p. 214.
68. Tanaka, *Ozu Yasujirō shūyū*, p. 362.
69. Ozu and Saitō, '*Tsuki wa noborinu*', p. 81.
70. Phillips, 'Pictures of the Past', p. 160.
71. Joo, 'Rethinking Noriko', p. 349.
72. For more detailed discussion on the marriage narrative of these films, see Joo, 'Rethinking Noriko'.
73. Tanaka, *Sengo goroku*, p. 232.
74. Tanaka, *Sengo goroku*, pp. 113, 116–17. This anecdote suggests that Ozu might have been thinking of something close to *Tokyo Story* as his next film for the year.
75. Ibid., p. 232.
76. Shimizu, 'Ochazuke no aji', p. 36.
77. Ibid.
78. Ibid.
79. Tanaka, *Ozu Yasujirō shūyū*, p. 373.
80. Tanaka, *sengo goroku*, p. 117.
81. Tanaka, *Sengo goroku*, p. 107.
82. For the taxi ride scene, according to Ozu's cinematographer Atsuta Yūharu, a special type of automobile was built because Ozu did not want to use rear projection. That car-body was installed on the loading platform of a truck, which not only the camera but also Ozu himself could get on. Atsuta and Hasumi, *Ozu Yasujirō monogatari*, pp. 189–90.
83. Inoue (ed.), *Ozu Yasujirō zenshū*, Vol. 2, p. 151.
84. Hasumi, *Kantoku Ozu Yasujirō*, pp. 101–3.
85. Having suffered an official ban during wartime, the *pachinko* industry was revitalised in the early years of the postwar. During the period from 1949 to 1953, when *The Flavour of Green Tea over Rice* was also made, the number of parlours increased to almost nine times the wartime figure. The general perspective on this new social phenomenon was, however, unfavourable, largely due to its gambling nature. Manzenreiter, 'Time, Space, and Money', pp. 359–65.
86. Ozu Yasujirō, 'Jisaku o kataru', p. 98.

87. In Ozu's own words: 'The idea of *Tokyo Story* did not suddenly occur, but had been discussed with Noda for a while. In fact, we tried to include it in *Early Summer*, but soon gave up'. Tanaka, *Sengo goroku*, p. 192.
88. Tanaka, *Ozu Yasujirō shūyū*, p. 359.
89. Tanaka, *Sengo goroku*, p. 186. Ozu was also fond of an aphorism of Akutagawa Ryūnosuke, 'The unhappiness of the human being begins with the parent-child relationship', which he used in the opening credits of *The Only Son*. Ibid., p. 449.
90. Ibid., p. 186.
91. Bordwell, *Ozu and the Poetics of Cinema*, p. 329.
92. From his comments after receiving the Japanese Geijutsusai [Art Festival] prize with *Tokyo Story*. 'Tatoeba tōfu no gotoku [Like Tofu, For Example]' in Tanaka, *Sengo goroku*, p. 202.
93. In 1950, Shochiku was second in domestic film revenue after Daiei, but regained the top spot in 1951, which it held until the fiscal year of 1955–6, when it started to lose ground to Toei.
94. Tanaka, *Hattatsushi, Vol. 3*, p. 304.
95. According to Richie, this film was 'one of the very few Japanese films to raise the question of responsibility for the war', and thus 'not the sort of film one expected from Shochiku'. Richie, *A Hundred Years*, p. 163.
96. Tanaka, *Hattatsushi, Vol. 3*, p. 308.
97. Ōba, 'Ōfunachō no senchū sengo', p. 196.
98. Ibid.
99. Togawa, '*Tōkyō monogatari*', p. 67.
100. Imamura, 'Saikin no Nihon eiga', p. 30.
101. Ibid., p. 31.
102. In the script, Shige's neighbourhood is specified as 'the outskirts of Tokyo: a town that is reconstructed after receiving war damage'. Inoue, *Ozu Yasujirō zenshū, Vol. 2*, p. 191.
103. The feeling of loss in the postwar urban space, however, was not necessarily bound to Tokyo but was rather a nationwide phenomenon. In a roundtable discussion about the customs and manners of contemporary Japanese society, Japanese director Yoshimura Kōzaburō pointed out that 'after the war, there disappeared the locality that had distinguished each city from others', leaving only 'Kyōto, Kanazawa, and Nara'. He thus declared, 'That's why it is Kyoto films these days. Kyoto is now exoticism'. Yoshimura et al., 'Dai issen yondai kantoku', p. 36.
104. Togawa, '*Tōkyō monogatari*', p. 67.

Chapter 5

1. Noguchi and Satō, 'Nemureru shishi', p. 60.
2. Ibid., p. 61.
3. Ōshima, *Cinema, Censorship and the State*, p. 36.

4. Ōshima, *Ōshima Nagisa chōsakushū*, p. 138. Even though Ōshima, graduating from Kyoto University, was trying hard to find a job, he was persuaded by a friend of his to apply together for Shochiku's entrance exam.
5. Ibid., pp. 130–1.
6. Ōshima, *Cinema, Censorship and the State*, pp. 37, 38, 40.
7. Toei, taking the initiative to implement the double feature exhibition system, had instantly risen to become the top-grossing company in the country. Toei's strategy can be summarised as 'mass productionism'. The films made for double feature were medium-length '*gorakuhan* (entertainment edition) movies', targeted at teenagers. Tanaka, *Hattatsushi*, Vol. 4, pp. 138–9.
8. Noguchi and Satō, 'Nemureru shishi', p. 69.
9. Some of them had to directly participate in the latter stages of the war as *shōnenhei* (child soldiers) and others stayed on the home front, but *shōwa hitoketa* can be commonly characterised as 'the generation that was old enough to have suffered but young enough not to have inflicted suffering'. Kelly, 'Finding a Place', p. 197.
10. From Article 1 of the Bilateral Security Treaty Between the United States of America and Japan. Mayo, 'The Occupation Years', p. 1071.
11. Hillenbrand, *Literature, Modernity*, p. 113.
12. Iwasaki, *Eigashi*, pp. 282–3.
13. Ibid., p. 283.
14. Ibid., p. 285. Named after the title of Ishihara Shintarō's original novel and Nikkatsu's filmic adaptation, the *taiyōzoku* films were characterised by a hedonistic and dissolute lifestyle, including sex and violence. Nikkatsu, which had had to sell off its production section during the wartime, was a newcomer in the postwar, and hence did not have as wide and strong an array of star actors/actresses as other studios. It thus concentrated on developing new subjects characterised by realism and 'fresh social sensibility'. Tanaka, *Hattatsushi*, Vol. 4, pp. 191–2. For more on the *taiyōzoku* phenomenon and *taiyōzoku* films, refer to Standish, *A New History*, pp. 222–37; Raine, 'Ishihara Yujiro', pp. 202–15.
15. Iwasaki, *Eigashi*, p. 285.
16. Noguchi and Satō, 'Nemureru shishi', p. 66.
17. Ibid.
18. Ibid., p. 67.
19. Ibid.
20. Ōshima, *Cinema, Censorship and the State*, p. 38.
21. Tanaka, *Hattatsushi*, Vol. 4, p. 325.
22. Ibid., p. 324.
23. Sakamoto, *Kazoku imēji*, pp. 173, 179, 247.
24. Ibid., p. 247.
25. Ibid., p. 251.
26. Sakamoto herself acknowledges that the change in Ozu is seen 'from the late 1930s to the 1940s', predating the real formation of the *hōmudorama* genre in the 1950s. Ibid., p. 258.

27. In Japan, television broadcasting began in February 1953. The first station was NHK, followed by Nihon Television in August of the same year. The diffusion of television sets, however, started to rise in 1955, rising to over 10 per cent in 1958, and 50 per cent in 1961, reaching a summit in 1964. This exactly matches the period of Shochiku's declining popularity. Hiramoto, *Nihon no terebi sangyō*, pp. 20, 30–1.
28. Muramatsu, *Terebi dorama*, pp. 57–8.
29. Tanaka, *Sengo goroku*, p. 411.
30. *Class Dismissed* was also later remade into a film, *Danshun/Warm Spring* (Nakamura Noboru, Shochiku, 1965). Tanaka, 'TV shinario *Seishun hōkago*', p. 114.
31. Ibid.
32. Tanaka, *Ozu Yasujirō shūyū*, pp. 390–2.
33. Tanaka, *Sengo goroku*, p. 297.
34. Ibid., p. 300.
35. Ibid. In the film, the father Hirayama (Saburi Shin) does not approve of the love marriage of his first daughter Setsuko (Arima Ineko), mainly out of disappointment that he was ignored during the process of her decision to marry. His objection continues even after the bridegroom-to-be turns out to be a very nice young man.
36. Among the major actresses of this generation, the only one who did not have a chance to play a prominent role in an Ozu film would be Kitahara Mie (b. 1933). Nikkatsu's heroine often formed a pair with Ishihara Yūjirō, whom she would later marry. However, she was not without connections to Ozu. Her film debut was a very small role in *The Flavour of Green Tea over Rice*, and after she moved to Nikkatsu, she would star in *Tsuki wa noborinu/The Moon Has Risen* (Tanaka Kinuyo, 1954), the film based on Ozu's original script in 1947, discussed in the previous chapter.
37. Atsuta and Hasumi, *Ozu Yasujirō monogatari*, p. 165.
38. Tanaka, *Sengo goroku*, p. 287.
39. Ibid. *Ubaguruma* is about the conflict between a father who maintains an extramarital family and the two women related to this affair (his wife and mistress). Ishihara, the brother of the mistress, together with the daughter of the father (Ashikawa Izumi), becomes 'instrumental in guiding the parent generation, acting as mediators between the two families'. Ishihara's image accordingly was 'softened' from that of a rebellious youth to a representative of social mores appropriate for the genre of family drama. Standish, pp. 230–2.
40. *Sakurai no ketsubetsu* tells the story of the last farewell between a samurai named Kusunoki Masahige and his son before the father goes to war and dies for his emperor. Due to their extreme loyalty, the Kusunokis became the icons of nationalist heroism during the Pacific War period, the elder Kusunoki being the 'most revered' figure among *kamikaze* pilots. After the war, the name of Kusunoki was officially removed from school textbooks, and the song *Sakurai no ketsubetsu* was also prohibited. Turnbull, *The Samurai*, pp. 97–8; Morris, *The Nobility of Failure*, pp. 131–7, 281, 314; Irokawa, *Culture of the Meiji*, pp. 300, 303.
41. Morris, *The Nobility of Failure*, p. 131.

42. Gluck, 'The "End" of the Postwar', p. 8.
43. Ivy, 'Formations of Mass Culture', p. 249.
44. 'If every household contained the same electric appliances in similarly constricted domestic spaces, then households were democratically equalised'. However, this can also mean 'homogenisation, an elimination of differences as nuclear familial units constructed themselves as "micro-utopias" sealed off from external conflict; or as privatisation, a dangerous shrinking of social networks and forms of association into the modular confines of "my home"'. Ibid., p. 250.
45. Gordon, 'Democracy and High Growth', p. 1084. In another newspaper survey, even 'presidents of major companies . . . identified themselves as middle class'. Eccleston, *State and Society*, p. 175.
46. Ueno, 'Onna no sengo bunkashi', pp. 249–52.
47. Gluck, 'The "End" of the Postwar', p. 9.
48. Ibid.
49. Ueno, 'Onna no sengo bunkashi', p. 247. She argues that it was the first time in Japanese history after the Meiji Reformation that 'private goals took priority over public goals'. Ibid.
50. According to Hidaka, in the concept of 'ko (個, individual)', which was advocated in the early postwar, both 'shi (私, private)' and 'kō (公, public)' coexisted in unification. He argues that this concept should be distinguished from the 'private life prioritism that was linked to political indifference' and prevalent in the post-high economic growth era after the 1960s. Fujida calls this privatisation tendency 'totalitarianism towards comfort' or 'private comfort-ism'. Quoted in Kano, *Nihon no kindai shisō*, pp. 187–9.
51. Ueno, 'Onna no sengo bunkashi', pp. 247–8. Gordon agrees, '[T]he ruling elites . . . moved to capture a growing political centre by co-opting programs of citizen's movements or left wing parties with initiatives such as the "income-doubling plan"'. Gordon, 'Democracy and High Growth', p. 1083.
52. Gordon, 'Democracy and High Growth', p. 1096.
53. Ibid., p. 1098.
54. Ibid.
55. Takabatake, 'Nichijō no shisō', p. 30.
56. Ibid., p. 27.
57. In the postwar, the salaryman became an even more prevalent demographic group than before, as the number of college graduates had constantly increased during the war and postwar period. Thus in 1955, when *Early Spring* was filmed, 'half of all households were headed by salaryman'. This expansion was 'linked to the processes and discourses of the re-emergence and successes of the state-capitalism system', which was also possible through Japan's integration into the Cold War politics. Roberson and Suzuki, *Men and Masculinities*, p. 7.
58. Ozu is known to have been sensitive to all the subtle differences of a colour, saying, 'There are about ten different shades of red'. He thus preferred Agfa film, instead of Fuji, Konishiroku or Eastman colour stock, and used it for all of his six colour films.

Agfa's was known to be more 'supple, more responsive to natural light, [and] paler', and also separated colours more softly to generate 'muted edges'. Okajima, 'Colour Film Restoration', pp. 32–3; Andrew, 'The Postwar Struggle for Colour', pp. 46–7; Bordwell, *Ozu and the Poetics of Cinema*, p. 83.
59. Wood, *Sexual Politics*, p. 137.
60. Tanaka, *Ozu Yasujirō shūyū*, pp. 389–91.

Conclusion

1. However, I have not included the audience in my discussion, whose subjectivity is too ambiguous an issue to examine without greatly expanding the scope of my study. For example, to show how Japanese female audiences constructed their subjectivity while watching Shochiku's woman's films, a more detailed investigation of the actual discourses produced by female audiences – for instance, through the pages of women's magazines – would be necessary.
2. In Bordwell's poetics, the concentric circle model is explained as that each different norm of analysis is situated in different hierarchical layers. For instance, Ozu's films are located at the centre, then towards the outside are his working environment (colleagues and their craft practices) and the circumstances of film industry and its trends (successively) placed, and at the outermost circle are the broader cultural forces of Japanese society and history. As such, Ozu's films at the centre lose a direct connection with marginal social forces. In fact, for Bordwell, such a relation between them is something to be cautioned, a mistake often found in what he calls 'reflectionism'. Bordwell, *Ozu and the Poetics of Cinema*, p. 17; Bordwell, *Poetics of Cinema*, pp. 30–2.
3. Rosenbaum, *Essential Cinema*, p. 146.
4. Tanaka, *Zenhatsugen*, p. 108.
5. Tanaka, *Sengo goroku*, p. 397.

Glossary of Japanese Terms

Bakufu (幕府)	A Japanese political system where a *shōgun* (将軍, general) rules the government. Also known as Shogunate
Benshi (弁士)	A performer in cinema who provided narration, commentary and translation of silent films for audiences
Bunka (文化)	Culture
Bushido (武士道)	'Way of the warriors'. The ethical code governing the behaviour of the warrior (*bushi*)
Chanbara (チャンバラ)	Films, television dramas or plays that highlight sword-fighting scenes
Chanoma (茶の間)	Living room (sometimes functioning as a dining room as well) in a Japanese-style house
Chichimono (父もの)	Japanese film genre that centres on a story of a father
Chōnin (町人)	The petit-bourgeois class (merchants or craftsmen) in Edo-period Japan.
Daimyō (大名)	Japanese feudal lords who served *shōgun* and hired samurai to manage their domains.
Edo (江戸)	The old name of Tokyo during the Tokugawa regime
Edokko (江戸っ子)	An Edo native
Engawa (縁側)	A wooden-floored corridor outside a room in a Japanese-style house
Futon (布団)	Japanese-style bedding that is usually laid on the floor to be used
Geisha (芸者)	Japanese female entertainers who entertain customers with various skills in traditional dances and musical performances
Gendaigeki (現代劇)	Japanese contemporary dramas with contemporary settings (after the Meiji Restoration)
Giri (義理)	Duty, obligation
Gunkan (軍艦)	Warship
Hahamono (母もの)	Japanese film genre that centres on a story of mother(s)

Hinomaru (日の丸)	Japanese national flag
Hōmudorama (ホームドラマ)	Japanese film genre that deals with family life, which became popular in the postwar period
Ie (家)	Japanese patriarchal family system
Jidaigeki (時代劇)	Japanese period dramas
Kabuki (歌舞伎)	Japan's traditional theatre since Edo period
Kamata-chō (鎌田調)	The characteristic style of the films made in Shochiku's Kamata studio
Kazoku kokka (家族国家)	Japan as family State, with the emperor as the head of the family
Kimigayo (君が代)	Japanese national anthem
Kimono (着物)	Japanese traditional garment
Kō (孝)	Filial piety
Kokusaku (国策)	National policy
Kokutai (国体)	The national polity or essence of the State of Japan, appearing in the form of the lineage of Japanese emperors that has descended eternally without a breakage
Koseki (戸籍)	A family registration system as stipulated in the Meiji Civil Code, where the position of each family member is identified in relation to the family head
Manzai (漫才)	Japanese-style stand-up comedy, usually with two performers
Modan gāru (モダンガール)	The Japanese translation for the English words 'modern girl'; these were popular during the 1920s and 1930s, and characterised by their interest in fashion and commodity culture as well as liberal pursuit of eroticism.
Moga (モガ)	An acronym of *modan gāru* (modern girl) with a nuance to emphasise her consumerist and morally liberated aspects.
Mono no aware (物の哀れ)	A traditional Japanese aesthetic consciousness about the sorrowful feeling towards the transience of the things in the world
Nagaya (長屋)	Japanese row houses
Nattō (納豆)	Fermented soybean
Ninjō (人情)	Human feelings, especially compassionate, warm-hearted
Ochazuke (お茶漬け)	Japanese dish that has steamed rice and savoury toppings over which green tea is poured
Ōfuna-chō (大船調)	The characteristic style of the films made in Shochiku's Ofuna studio
Okura (お蔵)	Literally, a storehouse; an act of suspending release, publication etc.

Glossary of Japanese Terms

Omiai (御見合い)	A meeting for an arranged marriage
Onnagata/Oyama (女形)	An actor who impersonates a female's role in *kabuki* theatre and in early Japanese cinema
Pachinko (パチンコ)	A Japanese game machine that resembles pinball. By passing a large number of small metal balls through pins, gamers aim to put them inside a certain location, releasing more balls.
Rakugo (落語)	Japanese verbal performance of a comic story
Ramen (らめん)	Japanese-style noodle soup
Risshin shusse shugi (立身出世主義)	Careerism, or literally, ideology of standing and advancing in the world
Ryōsai kenbo (良妻賢母)	Good wife and wise mother. One of the essential familial ideologies directed towards Japanese women by the Meiji government
Sake (酒)	Japanese alcoholic beverage
Samurai (侍)	Literally meaning 'those who serve', the word historically indicated supporters of the powerful landowners in the master-servant relationship. The *samurai*s from warrior families were named *bushi*.
Sashimi (刺身)	Raw fish
Saundoban (サウンド版)	Sound films with only background music and sound effects
Seikatsu (生活)	Life or living
Sengo (戦後)	Postwar (after World War II)
Shamisen (三味線)	Japan's three-stringed musical instrument
Shinpa (新派)	Literally, a new wave; A theatrical style that rose to popularity during the early twentieth century against the old *kabuki* style
Shintō (神道)	Japanese traditional religion
Shitamachi (下町)	Literally the town in the low. A region in Edo and Tokyo including such places as Nihonbahi, Kyōbashi, and Kanda, where the merchant and artisan classes resided
Shomin (庶民)	General term for middle classes or common people; a broader concept than *shōshimin* which indicates white-collar new middle classes.
Shōgun (将軍)	A hereditary military dictator in Japanese history who, though appointed by the Emperor, was the figure of authority with absolute power
Shōshimin (小市民)	Literally, petit-bourgeois, more exactly, Japanese urban, white-collar middle classes
Shōshimin eiga (小市民映画)	Japanese film genre that deals with white-collar middle-class life
Shōwa hitoketa (昭和一桁)	The generation in Japan born between 1925 and 1934

Sukiyaki (すき焼き)	Japanese hotpot with sliced beef
Sumō (相撲)	Japanese wrestling
Taiyōzoku (太陽族)	The sun tribe
Tatami (畳)	Japanese-style floor mat made of straw
Tōfu (豆腐)	Bean curd made from soy milk
Tokugawa (徳川) period	A period in Japanese history when Tokugawa *bakufu* (幕府) reigned the country from Edo (1603–1868)
Ukiyo-e (浮世絵)	Japan's woodblock printing that became popular from the Edo period
Yamanote (山手)	A region in Edo and Tokyo mainly in the western part of Edo castle, populated by noble samurai classes, and thus contrasting with Shitamachi region
Yose (寄席)	Vaudeville theatre that was popular among the commoners in Edo period
Yukata (浴衣)	Casual-style kimono often worn in summer or for loungewear or sleepwear

Select Filmography

Ozu Yasujiro's Films

(All films are made in Japan and the production company is Shochiku, except where specified.)

Akibiyori/Late Autumn (1960).
Bakushū/Early Summer (1951).
Banshun/Late Spring (1949).
Chichi ariki/There Was a Father (1942).
Daigaku yoitoko/College Is a Nice Place (1936).
Deki gokoro/Passing Fancy (1933).
Haha wo kowazuya/A Mother Should Be Loved (1934).
Hakoiri musume/An Innocent Maid (1935).
Higanbana/Equinox Flower (1958).
Hijōsen no onna/Dragnet Girl (1933).
Hitori musuko/The Only Son (1936).
Hogaraka ni ayume/Walk Cheerfully (1930).
Kaze no naka no mendori/A Hen in the Wind (1948).
Kohayagawa ke no aki/The End of Summer (Takarazuka Eiga, 1961).
Mata au hi made/Until the Day We Meet Again (1932).
Munekata kyōdai/The Munekata Sisters (Shintoho, 1950).
Nagaya shinshiroku/Record of a Tenement Gentleman (1947).
Nikutaibi/Body Beautiful (1928).
Ochazuke no aji/The Flavour of Green Tea over Rice (1952).
Ohayo/Good Morning (1959).
Ojōsan/Young Miss (1930).
Otona no miru ehon: Umarete wa mita keredo/I Was Born But . . . (1932).
Rakudai wa shitakeredo/I Flunked But . . . (1930).
Sanma no aji/An Autumn Afternoon (1962).
Shukujo to hige/The Lady and the Beard (1931).
Shukujo wa nani wo wasuretaka/What Did the Lady Forget? (1937).
Sōshun/Early Spring (1956).
Toda ke no kyōdai/The Brothers and Sisters of the Toda Family (1941).

Tōkyō boshoku/Tokyo Twilight (1957).
Tōkyō kōrasu/Tokyo Chorus (1931).
Tōkyō mongatari/Tokyo Story (1953).
Tōkyō no onna/Woman of Tokyo (1933).
Tōkyō no yado/An Inn in Tokyo (1935).
Ukigusa /Floating Weeds (Daiei, 1959).
Ukigusa monogatari/A Story of Floating Weeds (1934).
Gakusei romansu, Wakaki hi/Days of Youth (1929).
Wasei kenka tomodachi/Fighting Friends (1929).

Other Directors' Films

(All films are made in Japan except where specified.)

Aizen katsura/The Love-Troth Tree (Nomura Hiromasa, Shochiku, 1938).
Anjōke no butōkai/The Ball at the Anjo House (Yoshimura Kōzaburō, Shochiku, 1947).
Aoi sanmyaku/Blue Mountains (Imai Tadashi, Toho, 1949).
Aru onna/A Certain Woman (Shibuya Minoru, Shochiku, 1942).
Bakuon/Airplane Drone (Tosaka Tomotaka, Nikkatsu, 1939).
Cha wo tsukuru ie/Tea Making Family (Shimazu Yasujiro, Shochiku, 1924).
Champ (King Vidor, MGM, USA, 1931).
Danryū/Warm Current (Yoshimura Kōzaburō, Shochiku, 1939).
Danshun/Warm Spring (Nakamura Noboru, Shochiku, 1965).
Dokkoi ikiteru/And Yet We Live (Imai Tadashi, Shinsei Eiga, 1951).
Chikyōdai/Foster Sisters (Nomura Hōtei, Shochiku, 1932).
Fue no shiratama/Undying Pearl (Shimizu Hiroshi, Shochiku, 1929).
Fukōsha/A Bad Son (Shimazu Yasujiro, Shochiku, 1924).
Genroku Chūshingura/The 47 Ronin (Mizoguchi Kenji, Shochiku, 1941–2).
Gojira/Godzilla (Honda Ishirō, Toho, 1954).
Gonin no sekkōhei/Five Scouts (Tasaka Tomotaka, Nikkatsu, 1938).
Haha/Mother (Nomura Hōtei, Shochiku, 1923).
Haha/Mother (Nomura Hōtei, Shochiku, 1929).
Hō no namida/Tears of Law (Nomura Hōtei, Shochiku, 1921).
Honjitsu Kyūshin/The Doctor's Day Off (Shibuya Minoru, Shochiku, 1952).
Hutari no yūkanbai/A Couple Selling Evening Papers (Nomura Hōtei, Shochiku, 1921).
Ikite wa mita keredo/I Lived But . . . (Inoue Kazuo, Shochiku, 1983).
Itsuwareru seisō/Clothes of Deception (Yoshimura Kōzaburō, Daiei, 1951).
Izu no odoriko/Izu Dancer (Gosho Heinosuke, Shochiku, 1933).
Jigokumon/Gate of Hell (Kinugasa Teinosuke, Daiei, 1953).
Jinsei no onimotsu/Burden of Life (Gosho Heinosuke, Shochiku, 1935).
Junjō nijūso/Naïve Duet (Sasaki Yasushi, Shochiku, 1939).
Kabe atsuki heya/The Thick Walled Room (Kobayashi Masaki, Shochiku, 1956).
Kagiri naki hodō/Street without End (Naruse Mikio, Shochiku, 1934).

Kago no tori/A Bird in a Cage (Matsumoto Eiichi, Teikoku Kinema, 1924).
Kid (Charles Chaplin, Charles Chaplin Productions, USA, 1921).
Kimi no na wa/What Is Your Name? (Ōba Hideo, Shochiku, 1953–4).
Kojima no haru/Spring in Leper's Island (Toyoda Shiro, Tōkyō Hassei Eiga, 1940).
Kon'yaku sanba garasu/The Trio's Engagement (Shimazu Yasujirō, Shochiku, 1937).
La Kermesse héroïque/Carnival in Flanders (Jacques Feyder, Films Sonores Tobis, France and Germany, 1935).
Ladri di biciclette/Bicycle Thieves (Vittorio De Sica, Produzioni De Sica, Italy, 1948).
Madamu to nyōbō/The Neighbour's Wife and Mine (Gosho Heinosuke, Shochiku, 1931).
Mata au hi made/Until We Meet Again (Imai Tadashi, Toho, 1950).
Meshi/Repast (Naruse Mikio, Toho, 1951).
Mikaeri no tō/The Inspection Tower (Shimizu Hiroshi, Shochiku, 1941).
Minshū no teki/The Enemy of People (Imai Tadashi, Toho, 1946).
Moyuru ōzora/Flaming Sky (Abe Yutaka, Toho, 1940).
Nani ga kanojo wo sō saseta ka/What Made Her Do It? (Suzuki Shigeyoshi, Teikoku Kinema, 1930).
Nasanu naka/Not Blood Relations (Naruse Mikio, Shochiku, 1932).
Nichiyōbi/Sunday (Shimazu Yasujirō, Shochiku, 1924).
Nihon no higeki/A Japanese Tragedy (Kinoshita Keisuke, Shochiku, 1953).
Nihon no yoru to kiri/Night and Fog in Japan (Ōshima Nagisa, Shochiku, 1960).
Nijyūshi no hitomi/Twenty-four Eyes (Kinoshita Keisuke, Shochiku, 1954).
Nipponsengoshi: Madamu onboro no seikatsu/History of Postwar Japan as Told by a Barmaid (Imamura Shōhei, Nihon eiga shinsha, 1971).
Nishizumi senshachōden/Legend of Tank Commander Nishizumi (Yoshimura Kōzaburo, Shochiku, 1940).
Nora inu/Stray Dog (Kurosawa Akira, Eiga geijutsu kyōkai, 1949).
Norowaretaru misao/Damned Chastity (Shimazu Yasujirō, Shochiku, 1924).
Otoko wa tsurai yo/It's Tough Being a Man series (Yamada Yōji, Shochiku, 1969–96).
Otōsan no kisetsu/Father's Season (NHK, October 1958-March 1961).
Otōsan/Father (Shimazu Yasujirō, Shochiku, 1923).
Rashōmon/Rashomon (Kurosawa Akira, Daiei, 1950).
Rikugun/Army (Kinoshita Keisuke, Shochiku, 1944).
Rojō no reikon/Souls on the Road (Murata Minoru, Shochiku, 1921).
Seidon/Sunny Cloud (Nomura Hotei, Shochiku, 1933).
Seishun hōkago/Class Dismissed (NHK, 21 March 1963).
Shanhai rikusentai/The Naval Brigade at Shanghai (Kumagai Hisatora, Toho, 1939).
Shima no onna/A Woman of Island (Henri Kotani, Shochiku, 1920).
Shin josei mondō/New Woman's Dialogue (Sasaki Yasushi, Shochiku, 1939).
Shūbun/Scandal (Kurosawa Akira, Shochiku, 1950).
Stranger's Return (King Vidor, MGM, USA, 1933).
Taiyō no kisetsu/The Season of the Sun (Furukawa Takumi, Nikkatsu, 1956).
The Barker (George Fitzmaurice, First National Pictures, USA, 1928).
Tonari no Yae chan/Our Neighbour Miss Yae (Shimazu Yasujirō, Shochiku, 1934).

Tsubaki Hime/Camille (Murata Minoru, Nikkatsu, 1927).
Tsuchi/Earth (Uchida Tomu, Nikkatsu, 1939).
Tsuchi to heitai/Mud and Soldiers (Tasaka Tomotaka, Nikkatsu, 1939).
Tsuki wa noborinu/The Moon Has Risen (Tanaka Kinuyo, Nikkatsu, 1954).
Ubaguruma/The Baby Carriage (Tasaka Tomotaka, Nikkatsu, 1956).
Ugetsu monogatari/Ugetsu (Mizoguchi Kenji, Daiei, 1953).
Yogoto no yume/Every Night Dreams (Naruse Mikio, Shochiku, 1933).

Select Bibliography

Ai, Maeda, *Text and the City: Essays on Japanese Modernity* (Durham: Duke University Press, 2004).
Anderson, Joseph L. and Donald Richie, *The Japanese Film: Art and Industry* (Princeton: Princeton University Press, 1982).
Andrew, Dudley, 'The Postwar Struggle for Colour', *Cinema Journal*, 18: 2, Spring 1979, pp. 41–52.
Ashkenazi, Michael, *The Essence of Japanese Cuisine: An Essay on Food and Culture* (Richmond: Curzon, 2000).
Atsuta, Yūharu and Shigehiko Hasumi, *Ozu Yasujirō monogatari/Ozu Yasujiro Story* (Tokyo: Chikuma Shobō, 1989).
'Bangumi oyobi keikyō chōsa'/'Program and Business Investigation', *Kinema junpō*, 467, 11 April 1933, p. 20.
Baudelaire, Charles, *The Painter of Modern Life and Other Essays*, trans. Jonathan Mayne (New York: Da Capo, 1986).
Beasley, W. G., *The Rise of Modern Japan* (London: Weidenfeld and Nicolson, 1995).
Benjamin, Walter, *Selected Writings, Vol. 3, 1935–1938*, ed. Howard Eiland and Michael W. Jennings (Cambridge, MA: Belknap Press, 2006).
Benjamin, Walter, *Selected Writings, Vol. 4, 1938–1940*, ed. Howard Eiland and Michael W. Jennings (Cambridge, MA: Belknap Press, 2006).
Bernardi, Joanne, *Writing in Light: The Silent Scenario and the Japanese Pure Film Movement* (Detroit: Wayne State University Press, 2001).
Blanchot, Maurice, 'Everyday Speech', *Yale French Studies*, 73, *Everyday Life* (1987), pp. 12–20.
Bordwell, David, *On the History of Film Style* (Cambridge, MA: Harvard University Press, 1997).
Bordwell, David, *Ozu and the Poetics of Cinema* (Princeton: Princeton University Press, 1988).
Bordwell, David, *Poetics of Cinema* (New York: Routledge, 2008).
Bruzzi, Stella, *Bringing Up Daddy: Fatherhood and Masculinity in Postwar Hollywood Film* (London: British Film Institute, 2006).
Buckley, Sandra (ed.), *Encyclopedia of Contemporary Japanese Culture* (London: Routledge, 2002).

Burch, Noël, *To the Distant Observer: Form and Meaning in Japanese Cinema* (London: Scolar Press, 1979).
Calichman, Richard F. (ed. and trans.), *Overcoming Modernity: Cultural Identity in Wartime Japan* (New York: Columbia University Press, 2008).
Cazdyn, Eric, *The Flash of Capital: Film and Geopolitics of Japan* (Durham: Duke University Press, 2002).
Charney, Leo, *Empty Moments: Cinema, Modernity and Drift* (Durham: Duke University Press, 1998).
Charney, Leo and Vanessa R. Schwartz (eds), *Cinema and the Invention of Modern Life* (Berkeley: University of California Press, 1995).
Chiba, Machiko (ed.), *Ara, sentanteki ne: Taisho matsu Shōwa shoki no toshi bunka to shōgyō bijutsu/How Ultramodern!: The Urban Culture and Commercial Art in the Late Taisho and Early Showa* (Okazaki: Okazakishi Bijutsukan, 2009).
Chiba, Nobuo, *Ozu Yasujiro to nijisseiki/Ozu Yasujiro and the Twentieth Century* (Tokyo: Kokusyo Kankokai, 2003).
Cutts, Robert, L., *An Empire of Schools: Japan's Universities and the Molding of a National Power Elite* (Armonk: M. E. Sharpe, 1997).
Davis, D. William, 'Back to Japan: Militarism and Monumentalism in Prewar Japanese Cinema', in *Wide Angle*, 11: 3, July 1989, pp. 16–25.
Davis, Darrell William, 'Ozu's Mother' in David Desser (ed.), *Ozu's Tokyo Story* (Cambridge: Cambridge University Press, 1997), pp. 76–100.
Davis, Darrell William, *Picturing Japaneseness: Monumental Style, National Identity, Japanese Film* (New York: Columbia University Press, 1996).
De Certeau, Michel, *The Practice of Everyday Life*, trans. Steven Rendall (Berkeley: University of California Press, 1984).
Didi-Huberman, Georges, 'The Supposition of the Aura: The Now, The Then, and Modernity', in Andrew Benjamin (ed.), *Walter Benjamin and History* (London: Continuum, 2005), pp. 3–18.
Dore, Ron P., *City Life in Japan* (London: RoutledgeCurzon, 1999).
Eccleston, Bernard, *State and Society in Post-War Japan* (Cambridge: Polity Press, 1989).
Firumu Ātosha (ed.), *Ozu Yasujirō o yomu: Furuki mono no utsukushii fukken/Reading Ozu Yasujiro: Beautiful Restoration of the Old* (Tokyo: Firumu Ātosha, 1994).
Fowler, Edward, 'Piss and Run: Or How Ozu Does a Number on SCAP', in Dennis Washburn and Carole Cavanaugh (eds), *Word and Image in Japanese Cinema* (Cambridge: Cambridge University Press, 2001), pp. 273–92.
Frisby, David, *Fragments of Modernity: Theories of Modernity in the Work of Simmel, Kracauer and Benjamin* (Cambridge: Polity, 1985).
Fujiki, Hideaki, '*Benshi* as Stars: The Irony of Popularity and Respectability of Voice Performance in Japanese Cinema', *Cinema Journal*, 45: 2, 2006, pp. 68–84.
Fujiki, Hideaki, *Zōshokusuru perusona: Eiga sutadamu no seiritsu to Nihon kindai/Proliferating Persona: The Formation of Film Stardom and Japan's Modernity*, (Nagoya: The University of Nagoya Press, 2007).

Furukawa, Roppa, '*Nichiyōbi*'/'*Sunday*', *Kinema junpō* 161, 1 June 1924, p. 25.
Gao, Bai, 'The Postwar Japanese Economy', in William M. Tsutsui (ed.), *A Companion to Japanese History* (Malden: Blackwell Publishing, 2007), pp. 299–314.
Gardiner, Michael E., *Critiques of Everyday Life* (London: Routledge, 2000).
Gardner, William O., *Advertising Tower: Japanese Modernism and Modernity in the 1920s* (Cambridge, MA: Harvard University Asia Centre, 2006).
Gerow, A. A., 'The *Benshi*'s New Face: Defining Cinema in *Taishō* Japan', *Iconics*, 3, 1994, pp. 69–86.
Gerow, Aaron, *Visions of Japanese Modernity: Articulations of Cinema, Nation, and Spectatorship, 1895–1925* (Berkeley: University of California Press, 2010).
Gluck, Carol, 'The "End" of the Postwar: Japan at the Turn of the Millenium', *Public Culture*, 10: 1, 1997, pp. 1–23.
Gluck, Carol, 'The Past in the Present', in Andrew Gordon (ed.), *Postwar Japan as History* (Berkeley: University of California Press, 1993), pp. 64–98.
Gluck, Carol, *Japan's Modern Myths: Ideology in the Late Meiji Period* (Princeton: Princeton University Press, 1985).
Gordon, Andrew, 'Democracy and High Growth', in William Theodore de Bary, Carol Gluck, and Arthur E. Tiedemann (compilers), *Sources of Japanese Tradition, second edition, Vol. 2* (New York: Columbia University Press, 2005), pp. 1082–112.
Gordon, Andrew, *A Modern History of Japan: From Tokugawa Times to the Present* (Oxford: Oxford University Press, 2003).
Hamacher, Werner, '"Now": Walter Benjamin on Historical Time', in Andrew Benjamin (ed.), *Walter Benjamin and History* (London: Continuum, 2005), pp. 38–68.
Harootunian, Harry, 'Japan's Long Postwar: The Trick of Memory and the Ruse of History', in Tomiko Yoda and Harry Harootunian (eds), *Japan after Japan: Social and Cultural Life From the Recessionary 1990s to the Present* (Durham: Duke University Press, 2006), pp. 98–121.
Harootunian, Harry, 'The Execution of Tosaka Jun and Other Tales: Historical Amnesia, Memory and the Question of Japan's "Postwar"', in Sheila Miyoshi Jager and Rana Mitter (eds), *Ruptured Histories: War, Memory, and the Post-Cold War in Asia* (Cambridge, MA: Harvard University Press, 2007), pp. 150–71.
Harootunian, Harry, *History's Disquiet: Modernity, Cultural Practice, and the Question of Everyday Life* (New York: Columbia University Press, 2000).
Harootunian, Harry, *Overcome by Modernity: History, Culture, and Community in Interwar Japan* (Princeton: Princeton University Press, 2000).
Harris, John Wesley, *The Traditional Theatre of Japan: Kyogen, Noh, Kabuki, and Puppetry* (Lewiston, NY: The Edwin Mellen Press, 2006).
Hase, Masato, 'Nihon eiga to zentai shugi: Tsumura Hideo no eiga hihyō o megutte'/'Japanese Cinema and Totalitarianism: In Relation to Tsumura Hideo's Film Criticism', in Iwamoto Kenji (ed.), *Nihon eiga to Nashonarizumu/Japanese Cinema and Nationalism* (Tokyo: Shinwasha, 2004), pp. 273–94.
Hasumi, Shigehiko, *Eigaron kōgi/Lecture on Film Theory* (Tokyo: Tōkyō Daigaku Shuppankai, 2008).

Hasumi, Shigehiko, *Kantoku Ozu Yasujirō/Director Ozu Yasujiro*, trans. Yongsun Yun (Seoul: Hannarae, 2001).

Hazumi, Tsuneo, Tomoda Jun'ichirō, Tachibana Kōichirō, Sugimoto Shun'ichi, Suzuki Jyūzaburō, Ogawa Hiroshi and Kikuchi Sannosuke, 'Zadankai: 1933 nen no Shōchiku eiga o okuru'/'Roundtable Talk: Reviewing Shochiku's Films in 1933', *Kamata*, 12: 12, December 1933, pp. 107–13.

Hendry, Joy, *Understanding Japanese Society* (London: Routledge, 2003).

High, Peter B., 'A Drama of Superimposed Maps: Ozu's *So Far from The Land of Our Parents*', in *Gengobunkaronshū/Journal of Language Culture*, 29: 2, March 2008, pp. 3–21.

High, Peter B., *The Imperial Screen: Japanese Film Culture in the Fifteen Years' War, 1931–1945* (Madison: The University of Wisconsin Press, 2003).

Highmore, Ben, *Everyday Life and Cultural Theory* (London: Routledge, 2002).

Highmore, Ben (ed.), *The Everyday Life Reader* (Oxon: Routledge, 2002).

Hikone, Tōkichirō, 'Madamu to nyōbō kara Ren annai made'/'From *The Neighbour's Wife and Mine* to *A Studio Romance*', *Kinema shūhō/Weekly Kinema*, 117, 8 July 1932, pp. 18–19.

Hillenbrand, Margaret, *Literature, Modernity and the Practice of Resistance: Japanese and Taiwanese Fiction, 1960–1990* (Leiden: Brill, 2007).

Hiramoto, Atsushi, *Nihon no terebi sangyō/Television Industry in Japan* (Kyoto: Mineruba Shobo, 1994).

Hirano, Kyoko, *Mr Smith Goes to Tokyo: Japanese Cinema under the American Occupation, 1945–1952* (Washington: Smithsonian Institution Press, 1992).

Igarashi, Yoshikuni, *Bodies of Memory: Narratives of War in Postwar Japanese Culture, 1945–1970* (Princeton: Princeton University Press, 2000).

Ikeda, Hisao, 'Shōshimin eiga ron: Akarusa, yūmoa, pēsosu no kaikyūsei'/'A Comment on *Shōshimin* Film: The Class Consciousness of Cheerfulness, Humour, and Pathos', *Eiga hyōron/Film Criticism*, 13: 4, April 1932, pp. 118–23.

Ikeda, Tadao and Ozu Yasujirō, *Ochazuke no aji/The Flavour of Green Tea over Rice*, reprinted in *Kinema junpō rinji zōkan: Ozu to kataru/Kinema Junpo Special Issue: Talking with Ozu*, 1136, 7 July 1994, pp. 50–64.

Ikeda, Yoshinobu, 'Tōkī no seisakuyoku' / 'My Desire for Talkie', *Kamata*, 12: 1, January 1933, p. 69.

Imamura, Taihei, 'Saikin no Nihon eiga'/'Recent Japanese Cinema', *Eiga hyōron/Film Criticism*, 11: 6, June 1954, pp. 24–33.

Inoue, Kazuo (ed.), *Ozu Yasujirō zenshū/Complete Screenplays of Ozu Yasujiro*. Vols 1 and 2 (Tokyo: Shiinshokan, 2003).

Irokawa, Daikichi, *The Culture of the Meiji Period*, trans. Marius B. Jansen (Princeton: Princeton University Press, 1985).

Ivy, Marilyn, 'Formations of Mass Culture', in Andrew Gordon (ed.), *Postwar Japan as History* (Berkeley: University of California Press, 1993), pp. 239–58.

Iwamoto, Kenji and Mamoru Makino (compilers), *Eiga nenkan, sengo hen/The Film Almanac: Postwar Years*, Vol. 11–20 (Tokyo: Jiji Tsushinsha, 1950–1960; reprinted by Tokyo: Nihon Tosho Sentā, 1998–9).

Iwasaki, Akira, 'Ozu Yasujirō to Nihon eiga'/'Ozu Yasujiro and Japanese Cinema', in Kinema Junpōsha (ed.), *Kinema junpō zōkan: Ozu Yasujirō, hito to geijutsu/ Kinema Junpo Special Issue: Ozu Yasujiro, A Man and His Art*, 358, Feb 1964, pp. 56–70.

Iwasaki, Akira, *Eigashi/History of Film* (Tokyo: Tōyō Keizai Shinpōsha, 1961).

Jacoby, Alexander, *A Critical Handbook of Japanese Film Directors: From the Silent Era to the Present Day* (Berkeley: Stone Bridge Press, 2008).

Jansen, Marius B., *The Making of Modern Japan* (Cambridge, MA: Harvard University Press, 2000).

Jeong, Suwan, 'Chichi, kokka, soshite kazoku'/'Father, Nation, and Family', in Iwamoto Kenji, *Kazoku no shōzō: hōmudorama to merodorama/A Portrait of a Family: Home Drama and Melodrama* (Tokyo: Shinwasha, 2007).

Jeong, Suwan, 'Sosimin yeonghwa yeongu: ilbon ui ijungjeok geundaihwa rul jungsim euro'/'A Study of *Shōshimin* Films: On the Double Modernisation of Japan' (PhD dissertation, Dongguk University, 2000).

Jinnai, Hidenobu, *Tokyo: A Spatial Anthropology* (Berkeley: University of California Press, 1995).

Joo, Woojeong, 'Rethinking Noriko: Marriage Narrative as Historical Allegory in Ozu Yasujiro's *The Moon Has Risen* and other occupation-era films', *Screen*, 56: 3, 2015, pp. 335–56.

Joo, Woojeong, 'There Were Fathers: Representation of Father Figures in Ozu Yasujiro's Films', MA dissertation, University of Warwick, 2007.

'Kamata eiga no jōsei senden o: Zenkoku jōeikan ni kiku'/'Marketing the Now of the Kamata Films: Nationwide Cinema Survey', *Kinema Junpō*, 462, 21 February 1933, p. 21.

Kaneko, Sachiko, 'The Struggle for Legal Rights and Reforms: A Historical View', in Kumiko Fujimura-Fanselow and Atsuko Kameda (eds), *Japanese Women: New Feminist Perspectives on the Past, Present, and Future* (New York: The Feminist Press, 1995).

Kang, Sangjung, 'The Discovery of the "Orient" and "Orientalism"', in Richard F. Calichman, *Contemporary Japanese Thought* (New York: Columbia University Press, 2005), pp. 84–100.

Kano, Masanao, *Nihon no kindai shisō/Modern Japanese Thought*, trans. Hyeju Choi (Seoul: Hanwul Academy, 2003).

Katō, Shuichi, *A History of Japanese Literature, Vol. 3: The Modern Years*, trans. Don Sanderson (Tokyo: Kodansha International, 1983).

Keene, Donald, *Dawn to the West: Japanese Literature of the Modern Era* (New York: Columbia University Press, 1998).

Kelly, William W., 'Finding a Place in Metropolitan Japan: Ideologies, Institutions, and Everyday Life', in Andrew Gordon (ed.), *Postwar Japan as History* (Berkeley: University of California Press, 1993), pp. 189–238.

Kido, Shirō, *Nihon eiga den: Eiga seisakusha no kiroku/The Life of Japanese Cinema: A Record of a Film Producer* (Tokyo: Bungei Shunzyū Shinsha, 1956).

Kido, Shirō, *Waga eiga ron*/*My Film Theory* (Tokyo: Shōchiku, 1978).
Kido, Shirō, Osamu Takizawa and Michio Ema, *Kido Shirō kikigaki*/*A Record of Kido's Dictation*, interviewed in March 1973 (Kyoto: Kyoto Bunka Hakubutsukan, 1997).
Kinema Junpōsha, *Kinema junpō bessatsu: Nihon eiga daihyō shinario zenshū*/*Kinema Junpo Separate Issue: The Complete Scenarios of the Major Japanese Films, Vol. 2* (Tokyo: Kinema Junpōsha, 1958).
Kinema Junpōsha, *Kinema junpō zōkan: Nihon eiga kantoku zenshū*/*Kinema Junpo Special Issue: Complete Collection of Japanese Film Directors*, 698, 24 December 1976.
Kinema Junpōsha, *Kinema junpō zōkan: Nihon eiga sakuhin zenshū*/*Kinema Junpo Special Issue: Complete Works of Japanese Cinema*, 619, 20 November 1973.
Kinema Junpōsha (ed.), *Nihon eiga jinmei jiten, Dan'yū, Jōyū, Kantoku*/*Illustrated Who's Who of Japanese Cinema, Actors, Actresses, Directors* (Tokyo: Kinema Junpō sha, 1996).
Kinema Junpōsha (ed.), *Ozu Yasujirō shūsei*/*A Compilation of Ozu Yasujiro* (Tokyo: Kinema Junpōsha, 1993).
Kinema Junpōsha henshūbu, 'Cha o tsukuru ie'/'Tea Making Family', *Kinema junpō*, 161, 1 June 1924, p. 22.
Kirihara, Donald, *Patterns of Time: Mizoguchi and the 1930s* (Madison: University of Wisconsin Press, 1992).
Kitagawa, Fuyuhiko, 'Deki kokoro'/'Passing Fancy', *Kinema junpō*, 184, 1 October 1933, p. 97.
Kitagawa, Fuyuhiko, 'Ozu dokutoku no tenpo'/'Ozu's Unique Tempo', *Kinema junpō*, 68, 15 October 1949, pp. 24–5.
Kitagawa, Fuyuhiko, 'Ukigusa monogatari'/'A Story of Floating Weeds', *Kinema junpō*, 526, 11 December 1934, p. 84.
Klevan, Andrew, *Disclosure of the Everyday: Undramatic Achievement in Narrative Film* (Wiltshire: Flicks Books, 2000).
Klopfenstein, Eduard, 'Jobun', in Eduard Klopfenstein and Suzuki Sadami (eds), *Nihon bunka no rennzokusei to hirennzokusei*/*Continuity and Discontinuity in Japanese Culture, 1920–1970* (Tokyo: Bensei Shuppan, 2005), pp. 1–12.
Kobayashi, Kyūzō, *Nihon eiga o tsukutta otoko: Kido shirō den*/*The Man Who Created Japanese Cinema: Kido Shirō Biography* (Tokyo: Shinjinbutsu ōraisha, 1999).
Le Fanu, Mark, *Mizoguchi and Japan* (London: BFI Publishing, 2005).
Lee, Kyunghun, Song, Taeuk, Kim, Yeongsim, and Kim, Gyeongwon (eds and trans), *Taepyeongyang jeonjaeng ui sasang*/*The Thought behind the Pacific War* (Seoul: Imaejin, 2007).
Lefebvre, Henri, *Critique of Everyday Life, Vol. 1: Introduction*, trans. John Moore (London: Verso, 2002).
Lefebvre, Henri, *Critique of Everyday Life, Vol 2: Foundations for a Sociology of the Everyday*, trans. John Moore (London: Verso, 2002).
Lefebvre, Henri, *Everyday Life in the Modern World*, trans. Sacha Rabinovitch (London: Allen Lane, The Penguin Press, 1971).

Lefebvre, Henri, *Rhythmanalysis: Space, Time and Everyday Life* (London: Continuum, 2004).
Liddle, Joanna and Sachiko Nakajima, *Rising Suns, Rising Daughters* (London: Zed, 2000).
Lippit, Seiji M., *Topographies of Japanese Modernism* (New York: Columbia University Press, 2002).
Manzenreiter, Wolfram, 'Time, Space, and Money: Cultural Dimensions of the "Pachinko" Game', in Sepp Linhart and Savine Fruhstuck (eds), *The Culture of Japan as Seen through Its Leisure* (Albany: SUNY Press, 1998), pp. 359–82.
Masumoto, Kinen, *Jinbutu Shōchiku eigashi: Kamata no jidai/A Person-Centred History of Shochiku Cinema: The Age of Kamata* (Tokyo: Heibonsha, 1987).
Masumoto, Kinen, *Shōchiku eiga no eikō to hōkai – Ōfuna no jidai/The Glory and Collapse of Shochiku Cinema: Ofuna's Age* (Tokyo: Heibonsha, 1988).
Matsumoto, Shinko, *Meiji engekiron shi/The History of Meiji Theatre Study* (Tokyo: Engeki Shuppansha, 1980).
Mayo, Marlene, 'The Occupation Years, 1945–1952', in Wm. Theodore de Bary, Carol Gluck and Donald Keene (compilers), *Sources of Japanese Tradition, Second edition, Volume Two: 1600 to 2000* (New York: Columbia University Press, 2005), pp. 1021–81.
McDonald, Keiko I., *From Book to Screen: Modern Japanese Literature in Film* (New York: M. E. Sharpe, 2000).
McDonald, Keiko I., *Japanese Classical Theatre in Films* (Cranbury: Associated University Presses, 1994).
Mellen, Joan, *The Waves at Genji's Door: Japan through Its Cinema* (New York: Pantheon Books, 1976).
Minami Hiroshi (ed.), *Nihon modanizumu no kenkyū: Shisō, seikatsu, bunka/A Study of Japanese Modernism: Ideology, Living, Culture* (Tokyo: Burēn Shuppan, 1982).
Minami, Hiroshi (ed.), *Taishō bunka/Taisho Culture 1905–1927* (Tokyo: Keisō Shobō, 1987).
Miner, Earl Roy, 'Japanese Film Art in Modern Dress', *The Quarterly of Film Radio and Television*, 10: 4, Summer, 1956, pp. 354–63.
Miyao, Daisuke, *The Aesthetics of Shadow: Lighting and Japanese Cinema* (Durham: Duke University Press, 2013).
Morikawa, Shigeo, 'Tōkyō no onna ni tsuite'/'On Woman of Tokyo', *Kinema junpō*, 463, 1 March 1933, p. 65.
Morris, Ivan, *The Nobility of Failure: Tragic Heroes in the History of Japan* (New York: Holt, Rinehart and Winston, 1975).
Muramatsu, Yasuko, *Terebi dorama no joseigaku/Women's Studies of Television Drama* (Tokyo: Sōtakusha, 1979).
Nagayama, Takeomi (ed.), *Shōchiku hyakunenshi, honshi, eizō shiryō/100 Years History of Shochiku: Main History, Film Materials* (Tokyo: Shochiku Kabushiki Kaisha, 1996).
Nagy, Margit, 'Middle-Class Working Women During the Interwar Years', in Gail Lee Bernstein (ed.), *Recreating Japanese Women, 1600–1945* (Berkeley: University of California Press, 1991), pp. 199–216.

Najita, Tetsuo and H. D. Harootunian, 'Japan's Revolt Against the West', in Bob Tadashi Wakabayashi (ed.), *Modern Japanese Thought* (Cambridge: Cambridge University Press, 1998), pp. 207–72.

Narita, Ryūichi, *Kokyō to iu monogatari/A Story Called Hometown* (Tokyo: Yoshikawa Kōbunkan, 1998).

Nihon Eigashi Kenkyū Kai (ed.), *Nihon eiga sakuhin jiten, Senzen hen/Complete Dictionary of Japanese Movies from 1896 to 1945 August* (Tokyo: Kagaku Shoin, 1996).

Nihon Eigashi Kenkyū Kai (ed.), *Nihon eiga sakuhin jiten, Sengo hen/Complete Dictionary of Japanese Movies from 1945 August to 1988 December* (Tokyo: Kagaku Shoin, 1996).

Nishiyama, Matsunosuke, *Edo Culture: Daily Life and Diversions in Urban Japan, 1600–1868* (Honolulu: University of Hawai'i Press, 1997).

Noda, Kōgo, 'Ozu Yasujirō to iu otoko'/'The Man Who Was Called Ozu Yasujirō', in Kinema Junpōsha (ed.), *Kinema junpō zōkan, Ozu Yasujirō: hito to geijutsu/ Kinema Junpo Special Issue, Ozu Yasujiro: A Man and His Art*, 358, Feb 1964, pp. 38–43.

Noguchi, Yūichirō and Tadao Satō, 'Nemureru shishi – Shōchiku Ōfuna'/'Sleeping Lion: Shochiku's Ofuna Studio', *Eiga Hyōron/Film Criticism*, 16: 6, June 1959, pp. 60–74.

Nolletti, Arthur, *The Cinema of Gosho Heinosuke: Laughter Through Tears* (Bloomington: Indiana University Press, 2005).

Nornes, Abé Mark, 'The Riddle of the Vase: Ozu Yasujirō's *Late Spring* (1949)', in Alastair Phillips and Julian Stringer (eds), *Japanese Cinema: Texts and Contexts* (London: Routledge, 2007), pp. 78–89.

Nornes, Abé Mark and Aaron Gerow, *Research Guide to Japanese Film Studies* (Ann Arbor: Center for Japanese Studies, The University of Michigan, 2009).

Ōba, Hideo, 'Ōfunachō no senchū sengo'/'The Wartime and the Postwar of Ōfunachō', in Imamura Shōhei, Satō Tadao, Shindō Kaneto, Tsurumi Shunsuke and Yamada Yōji (eds), *Kōza Nihon eiga 4 – Sensō to Nihon eiga/Lectures in Japanese Cinema, Vol. 4: War and Japanese Cinema* (Tokyo: Iwanami Shoten, 1986), pp. 184–97.

Oda, Hiroshi, *Basic Japanese Laws* (Oxford: Clarendon Press, 1997).

Odagawa, Daisuke, 'Renzokusei ni tsuite no mitsu no monogatari: seiji kenkyū no tachiba kara'/'Three Stories about Continuity: From the Position of Political Science', in Eduard Klopfenstein and Suzuki Sadami (eds), *Nihon bunka no rennzokusei to hirennzokusei/Continuity and Discontinuity in Japanese Culture, 1920–1970* (Tokyo: Bensei Shuppan, 2005), pp. 15–52.

Oguma, Eiji, *Minshu to aikoku: Sengo Nihon no nashonarizumu to kōkyōsei/Democracy and Patriotism: Nationalism and the Sense of Public in Postwar Japan* (Tokyo: Shinyōsha, 2002).

Ōguro, Toyoshi, 'Ozu Yasujirō wa naze chinmoku surunoka'/'Why Ozu Keeps Silent?', *Kamata*, 14:5, May 1935, pp. 50–1.

Okajima, Hisashi, 'Colour Film Restoration in Japan: Some Examples', in *Journal of Film Preservation*, 66, October 2003, pp. 32–6.

Okamoto, Susumu, 'Ozu Yasujirō sakuhin saikentō'/'A Review of Ozu Yasujiro's Works', *Kinema junpō*, 443, 1 August 1932, pp. 41–2.

Osakabe, Yoshinori, 'Tōkyō ondo no sōshutsu to eikyō: ondo no media kōka'/'The Birth and Influence of *Tokyo Ondo*: The Media Effect of Ondo', *Shōgaku kenkyū/The Studies of Business and Industry*, 31, March 2015, pp. 106–28.

Ōshima, Nagisa, *Cinema, Censorship and the State: The Writings of Nagisa Oshima, 1956–1978*, ed. Annette Michelson, trans. Dawn Lawson (Cambridge, MA: MIT Press, 1992).

Ōshima, Nagisa, *Ōshima Nagisa chōsakushū daiichikan – Wagaokori, wagakanashimi / The Writings of Ōshima Nagisa, Vol. 1: My Anger, My Sorrow* (Tokyo: Gendai Shichō Shinsha, 2008).

Ōtsuka, Kyōichi, 'Ozu Yasujirō ron'/'A Comment on Ozu Yasujiro', in *Eiga hyōron/Film Criticism*, 8: 4, April 1930, pp. 40–5.

Ōtsuka, Kyōichi, 'Tōkyō no kōrasu'/'*Tokyo Chorus*', *Eiga hyōron/Film Criticism*, 11: 3, September 1931, pp. 91–2.

Ōtsuka, Kyōichi, '*Ukigusa monogatari*'/'A Story of Floating Weeds', *Eiga hyōron/Film Criticism*, 18: 1, January 1935, pp. 222–3.

Ōya, Sōichi, *Modan sō to modan sō/The Modern Class and the Modern Look* (Tokyo: Daihōkaku Shobō, 1930).

Ozu, Yasujirō, 'Jisaku o kataru'/'Talking about His Works', in Kinema Junpōsha (ed.), *Ozu Yasujirō: hito to geijutsu, Kinema junpō zōkan/Ozu Yasujiro: A Man and His Art*, Kinema Junpo Special Issue, 358, Feb 1964, pp. 92–9.

Ozu, Yasujirō, 'Kongo no Nihon eiga'/'Japanese Cinema, From Now On', in Nishiguchi Tōru (ed.), *Ozu Yasujirō: Eien no eiga/Ozu Yasujiro: The Cinema of Eternity* (Tokyo: Kawade Shobō Shinsha, 2003), pp. 102–5.

Ozu, Yasujirō, 'Tegami'/'A Letter', in *Kinema junpō*, 667, 1 January 1939, pp. 64–5.

Ozu, Yasujirō, *Zennikki Ozu Yasujirō/The Complete Diary of Ozu Yasujiro* (Tokyo: Firumu Ātosha, 1993).

Ozu, Yasujirō and Ryōsuke Saitō, 'Tsuki wa noborinu'/'The Moon Has Risen', in *Kinema junpō rinji zōkan: Ozu to kataru/Kinema Junpo Special Issue: Talking with Ozu*, 1136, 7 July 1994, pp. 80–92.

Ozu, Yasujirō Hito to Shigoto Kankōkai (ed.), *Ozu Yasujirō: Hito to shigoto/Ozu Yasujiro: A Man and His Work* (Tokyo: Banyūsha, 1972).

Passin, Herbert, *Society and Education in Japan* (New York: Bureau of Publications, Teachers College, Columbia University, 1965).

Phillips, Alastair, 'Pictures of the Past in the Present: Modernity, Femininity and Stardom in the Postwar Films of Ozu Yasujiro', *Screen*, 44: 2, July 2003, pp. 154–66.

Phillips, Alastair, 'The Salaryman's Panic Time: Ozu Yasujiro's *I Was Born, But* . . . (1932)', in Alastair Phillips and Julian Stringer (eds), *Japanese Cinema: Texts and Contexts* (London: Routledge, 2007), pp. 25–36.

Pincus, Leslie, *Authenticating Culture in Imperial Japan* (Berkeley: University of California Press, 1996).

Pons, Philipe, *Edo kara Tōkyō e: Chōnin bunka to shomin bunka/From Edo to Tokyo: The Culture of Chōnin and Shomin*, trans. Mikio Kamiya (Tokyo: Chikuma Shobo, 1992).

Poulton, M. Cody, 'The Rhetoric of the Real', in David Jortner, Keiko McDonald and Kevin J. Wetmore Jr (eds), *Modern Japanese Theatre and Performance* (Lanham, MD: Lexington Books, 2006), pp. 17-32.

Powell, Brian, *Japan's Modern Theatre: A Century of Change and Continuity* (London: Japan Library, 2002).

Raine, Michael, 'Ishihara Yujiro: Youth, Celebrity, and the Male Body in Late-1950s Japan', in Dennis Washburn and Carole Cavannaugh (eds), *Word and Image in Japanese Cinema* (Cambridge: Cambridge University Press, 2001), pp. 202-25.

Reischauer, Edwin O. and Marius B. Jansen, *The Japanese Today: Change and Continuity* (Cambridge, MA: Belknap Press of Harvard University Press, 1995).

Reynolds, Jonathan M., 'The Bunriha and the Problem of "Tradition" for Modernist Architecture in Japan, 1920-1928', in Sharon A. Minichiello (ed.), *Japan's Competing Modernities: Issues in Culture and Democracy, 1900-1930* (Honolulu: University of Hawai'i Press, 1998), pp. 228-46.

Richie, Donald, 'The Later Films of Yasujiro Ozu', *Film Quarterly*, 13: 1, Autumn 1959, pp. 18-25.

Richie, Donald, *A Hundred Years of Japanese Film* (Tokyo: Kodansha International, 2005).

Richie, Donald, *Ozu* (Berkeley: University of California Press, 1974).

Roberson, James E. and Nobue Suzuki, *Men and Masculinities in Contemporary Japan: Dislocating the Salaryman Doxa* (London: Routledge, 2003).

Roberts, John, *Philosophising the Everyday: Revolutionary Praxis and the Fate of Cultural Theory* (London: Pluto Press, 2006).

Rosenbaum, Jonathan, *Essential Cinema: On the Necessity of Film Canons* (Baltimore: Johns Hopkins University Press, 2004).

Rosenfeld, David M., *Unhappy Soldier: Hino Ashihei and Japanese World War II Literature* (Oxford: Lexington Books, 2002).

Ross, Kristin, 'French Quotidian', in Lynn Gumpert (ed.), *The Art of the Everyday: The Quotidian in Postwar French Culture* (New York: Grey Art Gallery, 1997), pp. 19-30.

Ross, Kristin, *Fast Cars, Clean Bodies: Decolonisation and the Reordering of French Culture* (Cambridge, MA: The MIT Press, 1996).

Russell, Catherine, 'Naruse Mikio's Silent Films: Gender and the Discourse of Everyday Life in Interwar Japan', *Camera Obscura* 20: 60, 2005, pp. 57-89.

Russell, Catherine, 'Tokyo, the Movie', *Japan Forum*, 14: 2, 2002, pp. 211-24.

Russell, Catherine, *The Cinema of Naruse Mikio: Women and Japanese Modernity* (Durham: Duke University Press, 2008).

Sakamoto, Kazue, *Kazoku imēji no tanjō: Nihon eiga ni miru hōmudorama no keisei/The Birth of the Family Image: The Formation of Home Drama Found in Japanese Films* (Tokyo: Shinyōsha, 1997).

Sand, Jordan, 'At Home in the Meiji Period: Inventing Japanese Domesticity', in Stephen Vlastos (ed.), *Mirror of Modernity* (Berkeley: University of California Press, 1998), pp. 191-207.

Sand, Jordan, 'The Cultured Life as Contested Space: Dwelling and Discourse in the 1920s', in Elise K. Tipton and John Clark (eds), *Being Modern in Japan* (New York: Taylor and Francis, 2000), pp. 99–118.

Sand, Jordan, *House and Home in Modern Japan: Architecture, Domsetic Space, and Bourgeois Culture, 1880–1930* (Cambridge, MA: Harvard University Asia Centre, 2003).

Sasaki, Suekichi, 'Ozu Yasujirō shi e kōkaijō'/'An Open Letter to Mr Ozu' in *Kinema junpō*, 543, 11 June 1935, p. 68.

Sasaki, Yoriaki, 'Tonari no yae chan o meguru gekisekai no hensen'/'The Change of Dramatic World Surrounding *My Neighbour, Miss Yae*', in Iwamoto Kenji (ed.), *Nihon eiga to modanizumu/Japanese Cinema and Modernism: 1920–1930* (Tokyo: Libropōto, 1991), pp. 164–77.

Sato, Barbara, *The New Japanese Woman: Modernity, Media, and Women in Interwar Japan* (Durham: Duke University Press, 2003).

Satō, Barbara, (ed.), *Nichijō seikatsu no tanjō: Senkanki Nihon no bunka henyō/The Birth of Everyday Life: Acculturation of Japan in the Interwar Period* (Tokyo: Kashiwa Shobō, 2007).

Sato, Tadao, *Currents in Japanese Cinema: Essays*, trans. Gregory Barrett (Tokyo: Kodansha International, 1982).

Satō, Tadao, *Eiga no naka no Tōkyō/Tokyo in Film* (Tokyo: Heibonsha, 2002).

Satō, Tadao, *Kanpon ozu Yasujirō no geijutsu/The Art of Ozu Yasujiro, the Complete Edition* (Tokyo: Asahi Shinbunsha, 2004).

Sato, Tadao, *Kenji Mizoguchi and the Art of Japanese Cinema*, trans. Brij Tankha (Oxford: Berg, 2008).

Satō, Tadao, *Nihon eiga no kyoshō tachi/The Masters of Japanese Cinema* (Tokyo: Gakuyō Shobō, 1996).

Satō, Tadao, *Nihon eigashi/History of Japanese Cinema Vol. 1–3* (Tokyo: Iwanami Shoten, 1995).

Satō, Takumi, *Kingu no zidai/The age of King* (Tokyo: Iwanami Shoten, 2002).

Sawamura, Tsutomu, 'Kōhuku no toiki wa kanashii'/'A Sigh of Happiness Is Sad', *Eiga Hyōron/Film Criticism*, 19: 4, April 1937, pp. 133–6.

Sawamura, Tsutomu, 'Nichijōsei sonchō eiga no kansei'/'A Completion of the Film of Respect for the Everyday', *Eiga hyōron/Film Criticism*, 18: 1, January 1936, pp. 199–202.

Sawamura Tsutomu, *Gendai eiga ron/A Theory of Contemporary Film* (Tokyo: Yumani Shobō, 2003; reprint of Tokyo: Tōkei Shobō, 1941).

Schrader, Paul, *Transcendental Style in Film: Ozu, Bresson, Dryer* (New York: Da Capo, 1988).

Seidensticker, Edward, *Low City, High City: Tokyo from Edo to the Earthquake* (Cambridge, MA: Harvard University Press, 1991).

Seki, Tadashi and Tanaka Masasumi, 'Juron yokuryūsho no omoide'/'Memory of Jurong Detention Camp', in *Ozu Yasujirō, eien no eiga/Ozu Yasujiro, the Cinema of Eternity* (Tokyo: Kawade Shobō, 2003), pp. 90–9.

Sekino, Yoshio, 'Shinkyōbutsu no hasan to Ozu Yasujirō no zento'/'The Bankruptcy of the State of Mind Film and the Future of Ozu Yasujiro', *Eiga hyōron* 9: 1, July 1930, pp. 20–4.

Shimazu, Yasujirō, 'Sairento yori tōkī e'/'From Silent to Talkie', *Kamata*, 12: 1, January 1933, p. 66.

Shimizu, Chiyota, '*Ochazuke no aji*: Ozu Yasujirō no gobyū'/'A Mistake of Ozu Yasujiro', *Kinema junpō*, 49, 1 October 1952, p. 36–7.

Shimizu, Shunji, 'Eiga to puchiburu no seikatsu'/'Film and the Life of the Petit-Bourgeois', *Eiga hyōron/Film Criticism*, 11:3, September 1931, pp. 53–4.

Shindō, Kaneto, 'Shinarioraitā ga umareta'/'Scenario Writer Was Born', in Imamura Shōhei et al. (eds), *Tōkī no jidai: Kōza Nihon eiga/The Age of Talkie: A Lecture in Japanese Cinema, Vol. 3* (Tokyo: Iwanami Shoten, 1986), pp. 110–55.

Shirai, Akira, 'Aru kyoshō no teimei'/'A Slump of a Master', *Kinema junpō*, 142, 1 April 1956, pp. 124–5.

Shōchiku Kabushiki Kaisha Eizō Hankenshitsu (ed.), *Ozu Yasujirō eiga tokuhon: Tōkyō soshite kazoku/A Reader for Ozu Yasujiro's Films: Tokyo and Family* (Tokyo: Firumu Ātosha, 2003).

Shōji, Tōru, 'Ozu Yasujirō e no ichi ketsuron'/'A Conclusion about Ozu Yasujiro', *Kinema junpō*, 463, 1 March 1933, pp. 64–5.

Silverberg, Miriam, 'Constructing the Japanese Ethnography of Modernity', in *The Journal of Asian Studies*, 51: 1, February 1992, pp. 30–54.

Silverberg, Miriam, *Erotic Grotesque Nonsense: The Mass Culture of Japanese Modern Times* (Berkeley: University of California Press, 2006).

Simmel, Georg, *Simmel on Culture* (London: Sage, 1997).

Smith, Dorothy E. *The Everyday World as Problematic: A Feminist Sociology* (Milton Keynes: Open University Press, 1987).

Sorensen, Lars-Martin, *Censorship of Japanese Films during the US Occupation of Japan: The Cases of Yasujiro Ozu and Akira Kurosawa* (Lewiston: The Edwin Mellen Press, 2009).

Standish, Isolde, *A New History of Japanese Cinema: A Century of Narrative Film* (New York: Continuum, 2005).

Sun, Ge, 'In Search of the Modern: Tracing Japanese Thought on "Overcoming Modernity"', trans. Peter Button, in Thomas Lamarre and Nae-hui Kang (eds), *Impacts of Modernities* (Hong Kong: Hong Kong University Press, 2004), pp. 53–76.

Suzuki, Michiko, *Becoming Modern Woman: Love and Female Identity in Prewar Japanese Literature and Culture* (Stanford: Stanford University Press, 2010).

Suzuki, Sadami, *The Concept of 'Literature' in Japan*, trans. Royall Tyler (Kyoto: International Research Centre for Japanese Studies, 2006).

Suzuki, Sadami (ed.), *Modan gāru no yūwaku/The Temptation of Modern Girl* (Tokyo: Heibonsha, 1989).

Takabatake, Michitoshi, 'Nichijō no shisō to wa nanika'/'What Is the Thought of the Everyday?', in Takabatake Michitoshi (ed.), *Nichijō no shisō/The Thought of the Everyday* (Tokyo: Chikuma Shobō, 1970), pp. 3–34.

Takeuchi, Yoshimi, *What Is Modernity?: Writings of Takeuchi Yoshimi*, trans. Richard F. Calichman (New York: Columbia University Press, 2005).

Tanaka, Jun'Ichirō, *Nihon eiga hattatsushi/The History of Development of Japanese Cinema*, Vol. 1-4 (Tokyo: Chūō Kōronsha, 1976).

Tanaka, Masasumi, '*Ochazuke no aji* kaidai'/'Introduction to *The Flavour of Green Tea over Rice*', in *Kinema junpō rinji zōkan: Ozu to kataru/Kinema Junpo Special Issue: Talking with Ozu*, 1136, 7 July 1994, pp. 48-9.

Tanaka, Masasumi, '*Tsuki wa noborinu* kaidai'/'Introduction to *The Moon Has Risen*', in *Kinema junpō rinji zōkan: Ozu to kataru/Kinema Junpo Special Issue: Talking with Ozu*, 1136, 7 July 1994, pp. 78-9.

Tanaka, Masasumi, 'TV shinario *Seishun hōkago* kaidai'/'Notes on TV script *Youth after School*', in *Kinema junpō rinji zōkan: Ozu to kataru/Kinema Junpo Special Issue: Talking with Ozu*, 1136, 7 July 1994, pp. 114-15.

Tanaka, Masasumi, *Ozu Yasujirō shūyū/An Excursion to Ozu Yasujiro* (Tokyo: Bungei Shunjū, 2003).

Tanaka, Masasumi, *Ozu Yasujirō to sensō/Ozu Yasujiro and War* (Tokyo: Misuzu Shobō, 2005).

Tanaka, Masasumi (ed.), *Ozu Yasujirō sengo goroku shūsei/Ozu Yasujiro, Compilation of His Utterances: 1946-1963* (Tokyo: Firumu Ātosha, 1993).

Tanaka, Masasumi (ed.), *Ozu Yasujirō zenhatsugen/Complete Utterances of Ozu: 1933-1945* (Tokyo: Tairyūsha, 1987).

Tanaka, Saburō, 'Otōsan'/'*Father*', *Kinema junpō*, 147, 1 January 1924, p. 20.

The Modern Girl around the World Research Group, 'The Modern Girl as Heuristic Device: Collaboration, Connective Comparison, Multidirectional Citation', in The Modern Girl around the World Research Group (ed.), *The Modern Girl around the World: Consumption, Modernity, and Globalization* (Durham: Duke University Press, 2008), pp. 1-24.

Thompson, Kristin, *Breaking the Glass Armor: Neoformalist Film Analysis* (Princeton: Princeton University Press, 1988).

Tipton, Elise K., *Modern Japan: A Social and Political History*, 2nd edn (London: Routledge, 2008).

Tipton, Elise K. and John Clark (eds), *Being Modern in Japan* (New York: Taylor and Francis, 2000).

Togawa, Naoki, 'Tōkyō monogatari'/'*Tokyo Story*', *Kinema junpō*, 78, November 1953, pp. 67-8.

Tokyo Metropolitan Culture Foundation and Tokyo Metropolitan Museum of Photography (eds), *Rhapsody of Modern Tokyo* (Tokyo: Tokyo Metropolitan Museum of Photography, 1993).

Tokyo Metropolitan Museum of Photography (ed.), *Tokyo: A City Perspective* (Tokyo: Tokyo Metropolitan Museum of Photography, 1990).

Tokyo Shiyakusho, *Tokyo, Capital of Japan: Reconstruction Work, 1930* (Tokyo: Municipal Office, 1930).

Torrance, Richard, 'Otoko wa tsurai yo: Nostalgia or Parodic Realism?', in Dennis Washburn and Carole Cavanaugh (eds), *Word and Image in Japanese Cinema* (Cambridge: Cambridge University Press, 2001), pp. 226–49.

Tosaka, Jun, *Nihon ideorogi-ron/A Study of Japanese Ideology* (Tokyo: Iwanami Shoten, 1977).

Tosaka, Jun, *Tosaka Jun zenshū/The Complete Collection of Tosaka Jun, Vol. 4* (Tokyo: Keisō Shobō, 1966).

Tsumura, Hideo, *Eiga to kanshō/Appreciating Film* (Tokyo: Sōgensha, 1941).

Turnbull, Stephen, *The Samurai: A Military History* (London: RoutledgeCurzon, 2002).

Tyler, William Jefferson, *Modanizumu: Modernist Fiction from Japan, 1913–1938* (Honolulu: University of Hawai'i Press, 2008).

Ueno, Chizuko, 'Modern Patriarchy and the Formation of the Japanese Nation State', in Donald Dennon, Mark Hudson, Gavan McCormack and Tessa Morris-Suzuki (eds), *Multicultural Japan: Palaeolithic to Postmodern* (Cambridge, Cambridge University Press, 2001), pp. 213–23.

Ueno, Chizuko, 'Onna no sengo bunkashi: Shōgai to shōhi no bunri o koete'/'A Postwar Cultural History of Women: Beyond the Separation between Life and Consumption', in Yōichi Komori et al. (eds), *Towareru rekishi to shutai/History and Subject Inquired* (Tokyo: Iwanami Shoten, 2003), pp. 235–77.

Ueno, Chizuko, 'Position of Japanese Women Reconsidered', *Current Anthropology*, 28: 4, August–October 1987, pp. S75–S84.

Ueno, Chizuko, *Kindai kazoku no seiritsu to shūen/The Rise and Fall of Modern Family* (Tokyo: Iwanami Shoten, 1994).

Uno, Kathleen S., 'The Death of "Good Wife, Wise Mother"?', in Andrew Gordon (ed.), *Postwar Japan as History* (Berkeley: University of California Press, 1993), pp. 293–324.

Uno, Kathleen S., 'Women and Changes in the Household Division of Labor', in Gail Lee Bernstein (ed.), *Recreating Japanese Women, 1600–1945* (Berkeley: University of California Press, 1991), pp. 17–41.

Vlastos, Stephen, *Mirror of Modernity: Invented Traditions of Modern Japan* (Berkeley: University of California Press, 1998).

Wada-Marciano, Mitsuyo, 'Construction of Modern Space: Tokyo and Shochiku Kamata Film Texts', in Aaron Gerow and Abe Mark Nornes (eds), *In Praise of Film Studies: Essays in Honor of Makino Mamoru* (Victoria: Trafford, 2001), pp. 158–75.

Wada-Marciano, Mitsuyo, 'Imaging Modern Girls in the Japanese Woman's Film', *Camera Obscura*, 20: 60, 2005, pp. 15–55.

Wada-Marciano, Mitsuyo, *Nippon Modern: Japanese Cinema of the 1920s and 1930s* (Honolulu: University of Hawai'i Press, 2008).

Wada-Marciano, Mitsuyo, *The Production of Modernity in Japanese Cinema: Shochiku Kamata Style in the 1920s and 1930s*, PhD thesis, University of Iowa, 2000.

Williams, David (ed.), *The Philosophy of Japanese Wartime Resistance* (London: Routledge, 2008).

Wilson, Sandra, *The Manchurian Crisis and Japanese Society, 1931–33* (London: Routledge, 2002).
Wood, Robin, *Sexual Politics and Narrative Film* (New York: Columbia University Press, 1998).
Yamada, Yōji, 'Shōchiku Kamata Satsueisho'/'Shochiku Kamata Studio', in Imamura Shōhei, Satō Tadao, Shindō Kaneto, Tsurumi Shunsuke and Yamada Yōji (eds), *Musei eiga no kansei: Kōza Nihon eiga/Completion of Silent Cinema: A Lecture in Japanese Cinema, Vol. 2* (Tokyo: Iwanami Shoten, 1986), pp. 62–81.
Yano, Christine R., *Tears of Longing: Nostalgia and the Nation in Japanese Popular Song* (Cambridge, MA: Harvard University Asia Center, 2002).
Yokomizo, Tatsuhiko, *Shōchiku no uchimaku/The Inside Story of Shochiku* (Tokyo: Kengensha, 1957).
Yomota, Inuhiko, *Nihon eiga to sengo no shinwa/Japanese Cinema and the Myth of the Postwar* (Tokyo: Iwanami Shoten, 2007).
Yonaha, Jun, *Teikoku no Zan'ei: Heishi Ozu Yasujirō no Shōwashi/The Afterimage of Empire: A History of Showa through the Soldier, Ozu Yasujiro* (Tokyo: NTT Shuppan, 2013).
Yoshida, Kiju, *Ozu's Anti-Cinema*, trans. Daisuke Miyao and Kyoko Hirano (Ann Arbor: Center for Japanese Studies, 2003).
Yoshimi, Shun'ya, 'Teikoku shuto Tōkyō to modanitei no bunka seiji'/'The Imperial Capital, Tokyo, and the Cultural Politics of Modernity', in Komori Yōichi, Sakai Naoki, Shimazono Susumu, Narita Ryōichi, Chino Kaori and Yoshimi Shun'ya (eds), *Kakudai suru modaniti/Expanding Modernity*, trans. Yeongugonggan Suyu+Nomo (Seoul, Somyungchulpan, 2007), pp. 17–78.
Yoshimi, Shun'ya, 'Teito to modan gāru'/'Imperial Capital and Modern Girl', in Satō Barbara (ed.), *Nichijō seikatsu no tanjō: Senkanki Nihon no bunka henyō/The Birth of Everyday Life: Acculturation of Japan in the Interwar Period* (Tokyo: Kashiwa Shobō, 2007), pp. 228–50.
Yoshimi, Shun'ya, *Toshi no doramatourugi/Dramaturgy of City* (Tokyo: Kawade Shobō Shinsha, 2008).
Yoshimoto, Mitsuhiro, *Kurosawa: Film Studies and Japanese Cinema* (Durham: Duke University Press, 2000).
Yoshimoto, Mitsuhiro, *Logic of Sentiment: The Postwar Japanese Cinema and Questions of Modernity*, PhD thesis, University of California, San Diego, 1993.
Yoshimura, Kōzaburō, 'Hyōden Shimazu Yasujirō'/'A Critical Biography of Shimazu Yasujirō', in Imamura Shōhei et al. (eds), *Tōkī no jidai: Kōza Nihon eiga/The Age of Talkie: A Lecture in Japanese Cinema, Vol. 3* (Tokyo: Iwanami Shoten, 1986), pp. 214–33.
Yoshimura, Kōzaburō, 'Shinkyō eiga ni tsuite'/'About State of Mind Film', in *Eiga hyōron/Film Criticism*, 18: 1, January 1936, pp. 50–5.
Yoshimura, Kōzaburō, Hideo Ōba and Yōji Yamada, 'Ōfunachō towa nanika'/'What Is Ōfunachō?', in Imamura Shōhei, Satō Tadao, Shindō Kaneto, Tsurumi Shunsuke

and Yamada Yōji (eds), *Musei eiga no kansei: Kōza Nihon eiga/Completion of Silent Cinema: A Lecture in Japanese Cinema*, Vol. 2 (Tokyo: Iwanami Shoten, 1986), pp. 82–93.

Yoshimura, Kōzaburō et al., 'Dai issen yondai kantoku gendai Nihon fūzoku o kataru'/'Four Major Japanese Directors Talk about Contemporary Japanese Customs and Manners', *Kinema Junpō*, 29, 1 January 1952, pp. 32–8.

Yoshinobu, Inoura and Kawatake Toshio, *The Traditional Theatre of Japan* (Warren, CT: Floating World Editions, 2006).

Index

Note: italics signify illustration, 'n' signifies note, 't' signifies table

acting schools, 24–6
actresses, 86, 195
Adachi (character in film), 137
Aihara (character in film), 137
Aizen katsura/The Love-Troth Tree (1938), 153, 174
Akibiyori/Late Autumn (1960), 72, 186, 192–5
Akiko (character in film), 204–5
Akutagawa, Ryūnosuke, 238n
Amano (character in film), 55–6
Americanisation, 26, 58, 82–3, 110, 150, 201
And Yet We Live/Dokkoi ikiteru (1951), 4
Anderson, Joseph L., 64
Anpo crisis (1960), 200
An'ya kōro/A Dark Night's Passing (novel), 232n
Arashi no naka no shojo/Maiden in the Storm (1932), 61
Arima, Ineko, 195
atarashii onna, 228n
Atsuta, Yūharu, 195, 237n
An Autumn Afternoon/Sanma no aji (1962), 165, 186, 194–8, 204–6, 208
'aura', 9–10
Ayako (character in film), 118–20, 126–7, 164, 232n

The Baby Carriage/Ubaguruma (1956), 195, 240n
A Bad Son/Fukōsha (1924), 33
Bai, Gao, 144
Bakushū/Early Summer (1951)
    family dining scenes, 4, 171, 180, 183
    family life, 173
    female bonding, 125, 160–2
    Kamakura, 158
    marriage, 164–6, 196
    postwar Japan, 149
Banshun/Late Spring (1949)
    family life, 173
    family relationships, 152–4, 156–60

    female bonding, 125
    Ginza, 168
    marriage, 165, 196
    Occupation-era, 15, 162
    postwar Japan, 146, 149, 176–7
    postwar Tokyo, 179
    spatiality, 202
    suburbs, 42–3
Baudelaire, Charles, 7, 8
Benjamin, Walter, 8–10, 19
benshi (explainer), 22, 25, 26, 61, 105, 220n
A Bird in a Cage/Kago no tori (1924), 31
Biruma sakusen: Harukanari fubo no kuni/Burma Campaign: Far away from the Motherland (1942), 117, 134–9
Blanchot, Maurice, 3
Body Beautiful/Nikutaibi (1928), 36, 37, 45–6
Bokuto kitan/A Strange Tale from East of the River (1937), 74
Bon Odori, 75
Bordwell, David
    bourgeois, 120, 130
    class, 104–5
    'concentric circle' model, 213, 242n
    didactic, 174
    formalism, 73–5, 156
    Hollywood influence, 2–3
    moga, 124
    'neo-formalists', 14–16
    Ofuna, 118–19
bourgeois ladies, 118–28, *123*
box office, 36–7, 65, 72–4, 152, 166, 174, 176
The Bride Talks in Her Sleep/Hanayome no negato (1933), 65
The Brothers and Sisters of the Toda Family/Todake no kyōdai (1941), 116–17, 120, 125, 129–30, 132–4, 136, 158, 182
Bruzzi, Stella, 132
Buddhist images, 2, 138, 153–4

Bungakukai (Literary Society), 106, 107
bunka (culture), 21–2
bunka seikatsu (cultured life), 41
bunmei (civilisation), 21–2
Burch, Nöel, 14–15, 64, 203, 229–30n
Burden of Life/Jinsei no onimotsu (1935), 43, 86–7
Burma Campaign: Far away from the Motherland/ Biruma sakusen: Harukanari fubo no kuni (1942), 117, 134–9

Calichman, Richard F., 148
Cazdyn, Eric, 159
censorship, 108, 118–19, 233n
Cha o tsukuru ie/Tea Making Family (1924), 33, 222n
chanbara (sword fighting), 30–1
Chaplin, Charlie, 66
Charney, Leo, 9
Chichi ariki/There Was a Father (1942), 117, 128–32, 134–7
chichimono (father films), 34, 134
Chieko (character in film), 89
Chijin no ai/A Fool's Love (1924), 83
Chikako (character in film), 93–9, 95, 97, 98
China, 111, 214
  anti-Japanese propaganda, 115
chōnin (Shitamachi people), 69–70, 72, 80, 226n
Cinema of Naruse Mikio, 219n
Civil Code (1947), 160, 224n
Civil Information and Education Section (CIE), 145–6
Class Dismissed/Seishun hōkago (1963), 193
Clothes of Deception/Itsuwareru seisō (1951), 157, 175
Cold War, 189, 207
College is a Nice Place/Daigaku yoi toko (1936), 55–6, 73–4, 113
commercialism, 26, 69, 73, 175
commodity fetishism, 205, 206–7
Conde, David, 145–6, 235n
consumerism, 13, 41, 43–4, 204–7, 211
A Couple on the Move/Hikkoshi fufu (1928), 36

Daiei, 174, 175, 188
Daigaku wa detakeredo/ I Graduated But . . . (1929), 36, 81, 90
Daigaku yoi toko/College is a Nice Place (1936), 55–6, 73–4, 113
Damned Chastity/Norowaretaru misao (1924), 33
A Dark Night's Passing/An'ya koro (novel), 232n
Date, Satoko, 89, 91, 124
Davis, Darrel William, 108, 129
De Certeau, Michel, 6–7, 8, 19, 50, 52, 217n
Desser, David, 14
'deviation', 8, 19, 49–58, 78–9, 157

Didi-Huberman, Georges, 218n
Dokkoi ikiteru/And Yet We Live (1951), 4
Dragnet Girl/Hijōsen no onna (1933), 73, 93–4, 99–100, 101
drinking sequences, 180–1, 197, 211

Early Spring/Shōshun (1956), 186, 195, 201–2, 241n
Early Summer/Bakushū (1951)
  family dining scenes, 4, 171, 180, 183
  family life, 173
  female bonding, 125, 160–2
  Kamakura, 158
  marriage, 164–6, 196
  postwar Japan, 149
Edo (Tokyo's old name), 21, 68, 69, 74, 76
edokko (child of Edo), 70
Eiga hyoron/Film Criticism (film magazine), 36, 39, 66, 72
eigaho (Film Law) (1939), 107
The End of Summer/Kohayagawa ke no aki (1961), 195
Engekai kairyo kai (Association of Theatre Improvement), 24
Equinox Flower/Higanbana (1958), 72, 186, 192–8, 202, 233n
'Erfahrung', 8–10
'Erlebnis', 8–9
Everyday Life Reform Movement, 223n
everyday realism
  definition, 27–9
  Kamata-chō, 49, 118, 212
  Kido, Shirō, 29–34, 212
  shōshimin film, 21–58, 60, 77
Excitement of a Young Day/Wakaki hi no kangeki (1931), 62

'failed moga', 87, 89, 90, 93–5, 119, 122, 210
family melodrama, 59–102
Father/Otōsan (1923), 27, 32–3
fathers, 128–40, 133, 162–3, 196–7
female audience, 4, 86, 92–3, 109, 242n
female employment, 83–5
female movement, 159, 212
female rights, 159–61
female solidarity, 160–2
female subjectivity, 18, 210
Film Law (eigahō) (1939), 107
Five Scouts/Gonin no sekkōhei (1938), 110, 136–7
Flaming Sky/Moyuru ōzora (1940), 231n
The Flavour of Green Tea Over Rice/Ochazuke no aji (1940)
  bourgeois ladies, 117–28
  class, 176–8
  Kitahara Mie, 240n

Index

marriage, 163
modernity, 165-73
　Occupation-era, 142
　pachinko parlour, 181, 197, 211, 213, 237n
　urban modernity, 184
　younger generation, 186
'flower in mud', 155-6, 157, 162
A Fool's Love/Chijin no ai (1924), 83
Fowler, Edward, 149
Fue no shiratama/Undying Pearl (1929), 87
Fujida, Shojo, 200
Fujiki, Hideaki, 82, 83
Fukōsha/A Bad Son (1924), 33
Fumiko (character in film), 178, 183
Fushimi, Akira, 224-5n

geinin (performing entertainer), 80
gendaigeki (contemporary drama), 1, 2, 14, 65, 146
Gerow, Aaron, 22, 58
Ginza, 21, 43, 74-5, 159, 167-8, 178-9, 228n
giri (sense of duty), 69, 77
Gluck, Carol, 40, 143, 199
Godzilla/Gojira (1954), 151
Gojira/Godzilla (1954), 151
Gonin no sekkōhei/Five Scouts (1938), 110, 136-7
Good Morning/Ohayo (1959), 186, 192, 195, 203, 206
gorika (rationalization), 85
Gosho, Heinosuke, 1, 43, 62, 75, 86-7
Great Depression era, 75, 78, 186
Great Kanto Earthquake, 21-2, 26, 27, 40, 74, 82

hahamono (mother films), 34, 134, 175
Haha/Mother (1923), 34
Haha/Mother (1929), 34, 62
Hakoiri musume/An Innocent Maid (1935), 59, 80, 127, 152
Hanayome no negato/The Bride Talks in Her Sleep (1933), 65
Hara, Setsuko, 173, 195
Harootunian, Harry, 10, 148, 150-2
Hasegawa, Shigure, 74
Hasumi, Shigehiko, 17, 19, 50, 169
Hawai marei-oki kaisen/The War at Sea from Hawaii to Malaya (1942), 111, 131
Hayashi, Fusao, 106
Hazumi, Tsuneo, 66, 67-8, 73
A Hen in the Wind/Kaze no naka no mendori (1948), 152, 153, 156, 177
Hidaka, Rokura, 200
Higanbana/Equinox Flower (1958), 72, 186, 192-8, 202, 233n
High, Peter, 16-17, 110, 113, 115, 116, 135, 136-7, 225n, 230-1n

hijoji (time of crisis or emergency), 224n
Hijōsen no onna/Dragnet Girl (1933), 73, 93-4, 99-100, 101
Hikkoshi fufu/A Couple on the Move (1928), 36
Hillenbrand, Margaret, 189
Hino, Ashihei, 114
Hirayama (character in film), 171-3, 172, 197-8, 240n
Hitori musuko/The Only Son (1936), 64, 66, 103-4, 121-2, 166, 173, 175-7
Hogaraka ni ayume/Walk Cheerfully (1930), 89, 90, 124
Hollywood, 2, 14, 76, 148-9
Home Ministry, 135
homogenisation, 192, 199, 204, 206, 241n
homudorama, 34, 191-4, 201, 203, 211, 222n
Honma, Shigeo, 30
Horikawa (character in film), 130-2, 137
housewives, 80-1, 85, 101, 159, 199
humanism, 29, 31, 138, 190
humanist war films, 110, 134, 136

I Graduated But.../Daigaku wa detakeredo (1929), 36, 81, 90
I Was Born But.../Otona no miru ehon: Umareta wa mita keredo (1932)
　deviated temporality, 78-80, 157
　family life, 192
　intergenerational conflict, 186
　middle-class life, 36-9
　military, 224-5n
　patriarchy, 47-50
　salaryman, 201-2, 206
　sound, 66
　spatiality, 41-4, 52-5
　Tokyo suburb, 8, 18, 42, 72-3
ianfu (comfort women), 116
Igarashi, Yoshikuni, 151
Iida, Chōko, 71
Ikeda, Tadao, 37, 76-7, 118
Ikeda, Yoshinobu, 62
Ikeda regime, 200
Ikeda, Hisao, 38-9
iki (aesthetic ideal), 70, 226n
Imamura, Taihei, 176-7
Imperial Screen, 16-17
Inagaki, Hiroshi, 190
Indian National Army, 111
Information Bureau (Jōhōkyoku), 107-8, 128
An Inn in Tokyo/Tokyo no yado (1935), 59, 66, 78-9, 177
An Innocent Maid/Hakoiri musume (1935), 59, 80, 127, 152
inter-gender gaze, 89-90, 95-6
intra-gender gaze, 89, 96-9, 100-1

Ishihara, Shintarō, 239n
Ishihara, Yūjirō, 190, 195–6
Itō, Daisuke, 190
It's Tough Being a Man/Otoko wa tsurai yo series (1969–96), 227n
Itsuwareru seisō/Clothes of Deception (1951), 157, 175
Ivy, Marilyn, 199
Iwasaki, Akira, 59, 77, 189, 206
Izu Dancer/Izu no odoriko (1933), 75
Izu no odoriko/Izu Dancer (1933), 75

Japan
　attack on US, 107
　historical relationship with the West, 11
　US Occupation, 11, 15, 20, 145, 167
　war with China (1937–45), 68, 105, 107
Japanese Film Series, 216n
Japanese iconography, 73
Japaneseness, 1–2, 14, 107–8, 129, 132, 148, 210
Jeong, Su-wan, 29–30, 43
jidaigeki (period drama), 1, 30–1, 110, 146, 220n, 221n
Jinsei no onimotsu/Burden of Life (1935), 43, 86–7
jissaisei (act-uality), 28
Jiyutsushin/The Liberty Report (newspaper), 147
josei eiga (woman's film), 59–60, 81–102
jun'eiga undō (Pure Film Movement), 22, 30–1, 58

Kabe atsuki heya/The Thick Walled Room (1956), 174–5
kabuki, 24–6, 30, 67
Kagiri naki hodō/Street without End (1934), 43, 54
Kago no tori/A Bird in a Cage (1924), 31
Kaishain sekatsu/The Life of an Office Worker (1929), 36
kakyo kukan (hometown space), 74–5
Kamakura, 8, 154, 157–8, 159, 167
Kamata (Shochiku's fan magazine), 61–2
'Kamata in the World' (*sekaiteki kamata*), 230n
Kamata studio, 13, 19, 21, 24, 25, 26, 60, 62t, 87; see also Shochiku
　transferred to Ofuna, 105
Kamata-chō
　everyday realism, 49, 118, 212
　modernity, 18, 22–3, 57, 190
　and *shinpa*, 60, 121
　Westernisation, 26–38, 108
　see also Shochiku
Kamei, Katsuichiro, 106–7
Kanda district, Tokyo, 32
Kang, Sangjung, 143
Kanki no ichiya/A Night of Joy, 61
Kano, Masanao, 159, 200

Kantoku Ozu Yasujirō/The Director Ozu Yasujiro, 17
kateigeki (home drama), 33, 34, 36
kateishinbun (home newspapers), 87
kateishōsetsu (home novel), 34, 87–8
　adapted to *shinpa* melodrama, 88t
katsudo shashin (moving pictures), 22
Kawabata, Yasunari, 145, 156
Kawakami, Tetsutarō, 107
Kawasaki, Hiroko, 89
Kaze no naka no mendori/A Hen in the Wind (1948), 152, 153, 156, 177
kazoku kokka (family state), 44, 105–6, 133
Kazuko (character in film), 99–100
keiko eiga (politically progressively tendency film), 37
Kido, Shirō
　bourgeois, 120
　everyday realism, 29–34, 212
　head of Kamata studio, 13, 22–3
　humanism, 190
　Kamata-chō, 26–7
　'Shochiku boom', 109
　and *shoshimin* films, 36–8, 57
　talkies, 60–2, 65, 68, 105
Kido-ism, 174–6, 193, 212
kigeki (comedy), 30–1, 118, 166
Kihachi (character in films), 71–2, 77–80, 79, 121, 211
Kihachi series, 59–60
　family relationships, 175
　marriage, 127
　modernity and tradition, 149
　and nostalgia, 68–80, 150, 157
　private life, 177
　shinpa-esque elements, 101–2
　Shitamachi district, Tokyo, 210–11
　Shitamachi humanity, 232n
Kikuchi, Kan, 83
Kikugoro no kagamijishi/Lion Dance of Onoe Kikugoro (1935), 65
Kimi no na wa/What is Your Name? trilogy (1953–4), 151, 174–5, 184, 187–8, 195
kindai (modernity), 11, 18, 60, 106–7, 150, 156, 190, 209, 219n
　and tradition, 149
　urban, 28, 169, 184
Kindai Eiga Kyōkai, 175
Kindai no chōkoku (Overcoming Modernity) symposium, 106, 107, 110, 147–8, 150, 156, 163, 210, 230n
Kinema Junpo, 66, 72–3, 152, 166
Kinoshita Keisuke, 176, 187, 191, 194
Kinugasa, Teinosuke, 64, 190
Kishi, Keiko, 195

Kishi, Matsuo, 34–5
Kitahara, Mie, 240n
Kitakamakura, 43, 153
Kitakawa, Fuyuhiko, 73, 77
Klopfenstein, Eduard, 144–5
Kōaeiga, 110
Kobayashi, Masaki, 139, 174–5
kofu (old-fashioned), 72
Kohayagawa ke no aki/The End of Summer (1961), 195
Kōichi (character in film), 160–1, *161*, 177–80, 182–3, 197, 204–5, *205*, 208
'*kokumin eiga* (national film)' competition, 128
kokusaku (national policy), 129, 131, 134
war film, 135
kokutai (national body), 105–6, 144
'Kongo no nihon eiga/Japanese Cinema, From Now On', 148–9
Korean War, 189
Kotani, Henry, 25
Kubota, Mantarō, 74
Kuga, Yoshiko, 195
Kumagai, Hisatora, 108
Kurishima, Sumiko, 24
Kurosawa, Akira, 145
Kyōko (character in film), 34–5, 81, 222n
Kyoto, 21, 24, 34, 110, 157, 167

The Lady and the Beard/Shukujo to hige (1931), 89, 124, 127, 229n
A Lady Crying in Spring/Naki nureta haru no onna ya (1933), 67
Late Autumn/Akibiyori (1960), 72, 186, 192–5
Late Spring/Banshun (1949)
family life, 173
family relationships, 152–4, 156–60
female bonding, 125
Ginza, 168
marriage, 165, 196
Occupation-era, 15, 162
postwar Japan, 146, 149, 176–7
postwar Tokyo, 179
spatiality, 202
suburbs, 42–3
Lefebvre, Henri, 3, 5–6, 8, 10, 11–12, 211, 216n, 217n
Legend of Tank Commander Nishizumi/Nishizumi senshachōden (1940), 110
The Life of an Office Worker/Kaishain sekatsu (1929), 36
Lion Dance of Onoe Kikugoro/Kikugoro no kagamijishi (1935), 65
'lotus in mud', 155–6, 157, 162
The Love-Troth Tree/Aijen katsura (1938), 153, 174

Madamu to nyōbō/The Neighbour's Wife and Mine (1931), 43, 61, 62, 86–7
Maiden in the Storm/Arashi no naka no shojo (1932), 61
Makino, Shōzō, 220n
Malay, 111
Marching On/Shingun (1929), 60
marriage, 156, 163–4, 173, 184–5, 194, 196, 212; *see also omiai*
Maruyama, Masao, 143–4, 200
Masumoto, Kinen, 62, 111
Mata au hi made/Until the Day We Meet Again (1932), 93, 96, 101, 113, 187
Meiji Civil Code (1898), 46, 83
Meiji Constitution (1889), 105
Meiji era (1868–1912), 21, 40, 74, 106
Mellen, Joan, 219n
memory, 9, 142, 150–2, 184–5
Merleau-Ponty, Maurice, 217n
Meshi/Repast (1951), 237n
militarism, 143, 145, 161, 198, 210
Minami, Hiroshi, 21–2
Minamikaze/Stranger's Return (1933), 67
Ministry of Home Affairs, 108, 110, 119, 226n
mirai kūkan (future space), 74–5
mise en scène, 96, 168, 177, 201
Mitsuhiro, Yoshimoto, 14–15, 145
Miyao, Daisuke, 14–15, 101
Miyazawa, Toshiyoshi, 144
modan gāru (modern girl), 13, 18, 43, 81, *91*, 122–4, 227–8n
modan raifu (modern life), 41
modanizumu (modernism), 22, 41, 223n
'modern, the', 21–2, 219n
modernisation, 13, 19, 38, 49, 56–7, 74, 82, 147–8
modernity (*kindai*), 11, 18, 60, 106–7, 150, 156, 190, 209, 219n
and tradition, 149
urban, 28, 169, 184
moga, 83, 84, 100, *100*, 210
moga failed, 87, 89, *90*, 93–5, 119, 122, 210
Mokichi (character in film), 118–20, 169–73
The Moon Has Risen/Tsuki wa noborinu, 152–4, 156–7, 163–5, 196, 236n, 240n
Mother/Haha (1923), 34
Mother/Haha (1929), 34, 62
Moyuru ōzora/Flaming Sky (1940), 231n
Mud and Soldiers/Tsuchi to heitai (1939), 110, 114
Munekata kyōdai/The Munekata Sisters (1950), 117, 149, 159, 163, 165
The Munekata Sisters/Munekata kyōdai (1950), 117, 149, 159, 163, 165

Nagai, Kafū, 74
nagaya (shabby row houses), 69, 71, 78
Nagaya shinshiroku/Record of a Tenement Gentleman (1947), 146–7, 152
Naki nureta haru no onna ya/A Lady Crying in Spring (1933), 67
Nani ga kanojo o sō saseta ka/What Made Her Do It? (1930), 4
naniwa-bushi (story recitation and singing), 71
Nara, 154, 157, 164–5, 167
Narita, Ryūichi, 122
Naruse, Mikio, 1, 18, 43, 54, 64, 73, 100, 219n, 237n
Nasanu naka/Not Blood Relations (1932), 87–9
national policy (*kokusaku*), 129, 131, 134
The Naval Brigade at Shanghai/Shanhai rikusentai (1939), 108
The Neighbour's Wife and Mine/Madamu to nyōbō (1931), 43, 61, 62, 86–7
New Deal idealism, 143, 145
A New History of Japanese Cinema, 16
'new salaryman films', 8, 167, 186–208, 210–11, 214; *see also* salaryman films
NHK, 193, 240n
nichijōsei (the everyday), 32
Nichiyōbi/Sunday (1924), 27, 32–3
Night and Fog in Japan/Nihon no yoru to kiri (1960), 190
A Night of Joy/Kanki no ichiya, 61
Nihon no yoru to kiri/Night and Fog in Japan (1960), 190
Nijyūshi no hitomi/Twenty-four Eyes, 187
Nikkatsu, 105, 109, 189, 239n, 240n
Nikutaibi/Body Beautiful (1928), 36, 37, 45–6
ninjō (humane) realism, 69, 77
Nippon Modern: Japanese Cinema of the 1920s and 30s, 18
Nishitani, Keiji, 149–50
Nishizumi senshachōden/Legend of Tank Commander Nishizumi (1940), 110
Noda, Kōgo, 152–3, 155, 166, 167, 173–4, 194, 213, 238n
Noguchi, Yuichiro, 187–8, 190
Noguchi, Yukio, 144
Nomura, Hiromasa, 109
Nomura, Hōtei, 25–6, 27, 32, 33–4, 62, 220n
Nomura-ism, 25–6, 32
Noriko (character in film)
  female movement, 158–62
  intergenerational conflict, 187, 195–6
  marriage, 18, 142, 156, 164, 173
  memory, 211
  spatiality, 177–83
Nornes, Abé Mark, 15
Norowaretaru misao/Damned Chastity (1924), 33

nostalgia, 68–80, 150–2, 157
Not Blood Relations/Nasanu naka (1932), 87–9

Ōba, Hideo, 175
Occupation-era, 143–6, 213
  films, 196, 211, 214
  Tokyo, 152
Ochazuke no aji/The Flavour of Green Tea over Rice (1940)
  bourgeois ladies, 117–28
  class, 176–8
  Kitahara, Mie, 240n
  marriage, 163
  modernity, 165–73
  Occupation-era, 142
  pachinko parlour, 181, 197, 211, 213, 237n
  urban modernity, 184
  younger generation, 186
Oda, Takashi, 33, 222n
Ōe, Kenzaburō, 189
Ōendanchō no koi/Romance of a Cheerleader (1933), 65
Ōfuna eiga (Ofuna film), 64
Ofuna studio, 104–17, 105, 152, 187–9
Ōfuna-chō, 108, 109–10, 174–5, 188, 190–1, 193–4, 212; *see also* Shochiku and Kamata-chō
Ōguro, Toyoshi, 66
Ohayō/Good Morning (1959), 186, 192, 195, 203, 206
Okada, Mariko, 195
Okada, Yoshiko, 89, 90–2, 93, 229n
Okajima (character in film), 44–7, 47, 49–50, 53–4, 78, 89–90, 91
Okamoto, Kihachi, 139
omiai (meeting between marriage partners), 127, 160–1, 163–4, 168, 196, 197, 201; *see also* marriage
The Only Son/Hitori musuko (1936), 64, 66, 103–4, 121–2, 166, 173, 175–7
onnagata (or *oyama*, male in female role), 24–5, 86
Onoda, Isamu, 193
Onoe, Matsunosuke, 25, 220n
'An Open Letter to Mr Ozu', 66
Osanai, Kaoru, 25, 30, 32, 221n
Ōshima, Nagisa, 187–8, 189, 190–1, 239n
Ōtani, Hiroshi, 190
Ōtani, Takejirō, 24
Otoko wa tsurai yo/It's Tough Being a Man series (1969–96), 227n
Otona no miru ehon: Umareta wa mita keredo/I Was Born But . . . (1932)
  deviated temporality, 78–80, 157
  family life, 192
  intergenerational conflict, 186

middle-class life, 36–9
military, 224–5n
patriarchy, 47–50
salaryman, 201–2, 206
sound, 66
spatiality, 41–4, 52–5
Tokyo suburb, 8, 18, 42, 72–3
Otōsan/Father (1923), 27, 32–3
Ōtsuka, Kyōichi, 66, 72
Otsune (character in films), 71–2, 78, 79, 81
Our Neighbour Miss Yae/Tonari no Yae chan (1934), 34–6, 57, 81, 87, 89
Overcoming Modernity (Kindai no chōkoku) symposium, 106, 107, 110, 147–8, 150, 156, 163, 210, 230n
Ōya, Sōichi, 83
Ozu and the Poetics of Cinema, 15–16
Ozu's Anti-Cinema/Ozu Yasujirō no haneiga, 14–15, 17
Ozu, Yasujirō
  as auteur, 14, 36, 57, 175
  and China, 115–17, 162
  and colour, 241–2n
  as *edokko*, 70
  in Gushi county, 233–4n
  humanistic war drama, 128–40
  Occupation-era film, 141–85
  shōshimin (petit-bourgeois) film, 36–49
  as soldier, 111–14, *112*, 214
  studies of, 1–2, 14–20
  and the talkie, 60–8
  in transition, 59–102
  woman's films, 80–102
Ozu Yasujirō no haneiga/Ozu's Anti-Cinema, 17
Ozu-gumi (Ozu's production staff), 64–5

pachinko, 168–73, 172, 197, 211, 213, 237n
Passing Fancy/Deki gokoro (1933), 59, 71–4, 76–8, 80
pātō tōkī (part-talkie), 61
patriarchy, 34, 40–1, 44–9, 72, 81, 83, 89, 129–31
PCL (Photo Chemical Laboratory) Studio, 64
Pearl Harbor attack, 105
'permeation', 10, 76–7, 150–1, 158, 164–5, 171–3, 181, 184, 196, 211
Phillips, Alastair, 18, 19, 44, 160, 223n
'A Plan for Schochiku's Talkie Production in 1933', 61–2
Pons, Philipe, 69
'post-Occupation generation', 189, 194–5
postwar (*sengo*), 141, 142–3, 147
  continuity/discontinuity between war and, 143–6
Poulton, M. Cody, 220n

The Practice of Everyday Life, 217n
privatisation, 187, 199–201, 241n
Proust, Marcel, 8
puchi buru mono (petit-bourgeois genre), 39
Pure Film Movement (*jun'eiga undō*), 22, 30–1, 58

'la quotidienneté (everydayness)', 5
'le quotidian (the everyday)', 5

Record of a Tenement Gentleman/Nagaya shinshiroku (1947), 146–7, 152
'relations of ruling', 13
Repast/Meshi (1951), 237n
'reprivatisation', 11–12, 13, 199
'reverse course (*gyaku kōsu*)', 144, 190
Richie, Donald, 1–2, 14, 64, 148, 235n
risshin shusse shugi (careerism), 40, 72, 177
Ritsuko (character in film), 45–6
The River Sumida/Sumidagawa (1909), 74
Rojō no reikon/Souls on the Road (1921), 32
Romance of a Cheerleader/Ōendanchō no koi (1933), 65
Rosenbaum, Jonathan, 213
Ross, Kristin, 10, 12, 159
Russell, Catherine, 18, 19, 100, 219n
Ryōhei (character in film), 132–4, *133*, 137
ryōsai kenbo
  and failed *moga*, 90
  female subjectivity, 80
  housewives, 97
  kiss with *moga*, *100*
  and *modan gāru*, 86–7, 90, 93–4, 122
  women's education, 46
Ryū, Chishu, 132, 137, 161, 163, 172

Sada, Keiji, 195
Saitō, Ryōsuke, 153
Sakamoto, Kazue, 34, 191–2, 203, 239n
Sakura ondo (1933) (4 films), 75
Sakurai no ketsubetsu (song), 197–8, 240n
Salaryman (*sararīman*), 120–1, 241n; *see also* 'new salaryman films'
  classlessness, 199
  consumerism, 204–6
  economic depression, 201–2
  family life, 186
  fear of unemployment, 57
  public and private realms, 46, 52
  shōshimin film (petit-bourgeois), 40–1, 43–4
San Francisco Peace Treaty (1951), 189
Sanma no aji/An Autumn Afternoon (1962), 165, 186, 194–8, 204–6, 208
Sano, Shūji, 137

sarariman (salaryman), 120–1, 241n;
  see also 'new salaryman films'
  classlessness, 199
  consumerism, 204–6
  economic depression, 201–2
  family life, 186
  fear of unemployment, 57
  public and private realms, 46, 52
  shōshimin film (petit-bourgeois), 40–1, 43–4
Sasaki, Yoriaki, 34–5, 87
Satō, Barbara, 82, 84–5
Satō, Tadao, 30, 31, 50, 76, 119, 153, 187–8, 190
Satomi, Ton, 193, 233n
Satsueijo romansu: renai annai/A Studio Romance (1932), 62
saundoban (sound films), 61, 62–4, 66
Sawamura, Tsutomu, 29, 108, 120, 123, 129, 232n
SCAP (Supreme Commander for Allied Powers), 143, 149, 159–60
Schrader, Paul, 5, 14, 17
The Season of the Sun/Taiyō no kisetsu (1956), 189–90
Second Company for Field Gas Operation, 111–13
Seidensticker, Edward, 69
Seidon/Sunny Cloud (1933), 87
seikatsu (everyday life), 177, 182, 184, 199–200
Seishun hōkago/Class Dismissed (1963), 193
Seishun no yume ima izuko/Where are the Dreams of Youth (1932), 127
sengo (postwar), 141, 142–3, 147
  continuity/discontinuity between war and, 143–6
sensō (war), 141
Setsuko (character in film), 124–5, 127, 132–4, 163–5, 167–8, 196, 198, 236n, 240n
setsumesha (explainer), 22
shajitsusei (actual reality), 28–9
Shanghai Expeditionary Army, 111–13
Shanhai rikusentai/The Naval Brigade at Shanghai (1939), 108
Shidō monogatari/A Story of Leadership (1941), 108
Shiga, Naoya, 232n
Shige (character in film), 177–83, *183*, 197
Shigehara, Hideo, 64–5, 66–8
Shima no onna/A Woman of Island (1920), 220n
Shimazu, Chiyota, 166
Shimazu, Yasujirō, 22–3, 27, 32–5, 61–4, 81
shiminshakai (private society), 200
Shimizu, Hiroshi, 39, 67
Shindō, Kaneto, 175
shingeki ('New Drama') movement, 26

Shingun/Marching On (1929), 60
Shinkankakuha (New Sensationist School), 236n
Shinoda, Masahiro, 191
shinpa ('new school')
  conservative, 30–1
  emotionalism, 49
  josei eiga (woman's film), 81, 87–8, 93, 100
  kateishōsetsu adapted to, 88t
  modern woman, 109
  new wave, 219n, 220n
  Ozu and, 56–7, 60, 121
  Shochiku, 24–6
  theatre, 221n, 222n
  tragedies, 27, 33–6, 175, 211
shinpa-esque elements, 59–60, 101, 122, 134, 212
Shintoho, 188
Shirai, Matsujirō, 24
Shiroi, Shintarō, 24
Shitamachi district, Tokyo
  deviation in everyday, 157
  family relationships, 173
  Great Kanto Earthquake, 21
  homogenisation, 204
  humanity, 232n
  Kihachi series, 68–80
  lower middle-class, 38, 176–80, 184, 209–11
  nostalgia, 19
  postwar Japan, 167
  spatiality, 8, 10, 121–2, 171
Shitamachi-mono (story of Shitamachi), 32
Shochiku
  birth of, 23–5
  censorship, 108–9, 135
  gendaigeki studio, 22
  Kamata studio, 13, 18, 19, 21, 27, 87
  Kamata studio transferred to Ofuna, 105
  key directors' transition to talkie films, 63t
  Kido, Shirō, 27
  Osanai and Nomura, 23–6
  popularity, 73, 166, 174
  production policy, 4
  Shimogamo studio, Kyoto, 220n
  sound system, 61
  and television, 192–3
  top grossing films in the early 1950s, 176t
Shochiku Cinema Institute (Shochiku Kinema Kenkyūsho), 26, 32
'Shochiku daiichi shugi (Shochiku Number One-is)', 65
Shochiku Nouvelle Vague, 189, 190–1
Shōjirō (character in film), 133–4
shokugyō fujin (working woman), 83–5, 100, 228n

shomin (lower middle class), 30, 32, 38, 121, 193, 209
shomin ninjōgeki (humane drama of the common people), 60
shomingeki, 38
shōshimin (petit-bourgeois), 39–41, 209
shōshimin film (petit-bourgeois)
   abandoned, 118
   distinguished from Kihachi series, 68–9
   economic depression, 19
   as escapist, 108
   everyday realism, 21–58, 60, 77
   intergenerational conflict, 186, 189–92
   military, 113
   modernity, 150
   modernity and tradition, 11
   neighbourhood, 72
   'new salaryman films', 207
   Ozu, 23
   patriarchy, 210–14
   reality, 139
   salaryman, 6, 196, 201–2, 223n
   urban bourgeoisie, 121–3
   women, 80, 101
Showa era, 21–2, 31, 192
shōwa futaketa (double-digit) generation, 189
shōwa hitoketa (single-digit) generation, 189, 195, 239n
Shūkichi (character in film), 183
Shukujo to hige/The Lady and the Beard (1931), 89, 124, 127, 229n
Shukujo wa nani wo wasuretaka/What Did the Lady Forget? (1937), 103–4, 120–5, 127, 158, 166, 176
Silverbeg, Miriam, 83–5
Simmel, Georg, 8
Singapore, 111, 147, 148, 172
Sino-Japanese War (1895), 24
Smith, Dorothy E., 13
Sono yo no tsuma/That Night's Wife (1930), 101
Sorensen, Lars-Martin, 154–5, 157
Sōshun/Early Spring (1956), 186, 195, 201–2, 241n
Souls on the Road/Rojō no reikon (1921), 32
sound, 59–102, 105
spatiality, 7–8, 41–2, 50–4, 71, 74, 95–9, 159
'spiritist film', 108, 110, 111, 113, 115, 128, 134
Standish, Isolde, 16, 22, 109, 129–30
A Story of Floating Weeds/Ukigusa monogartari (1934), 59, 71, 73–4, 77–8, 80, 135, 195
A Story of Leadership/Shidō monogatari (1941), 108
A Strange Tale from East of the River/Bokuto kitan (1937), 74
Stranger's Return/ Minamikaze (1933), 67

'strategy', 7–8
Street without End/Kagiri naki hodō (1934), 43, 54
A Studio Romance/Satsueijo romansu: renai annai (1932), 62
Sumidagawa/The River Sumida (1909), 74
Sun, Ge, 106, 148
Sun Tribe (*taiyōzoku*) films, 189–90, 195–6, 206, 239n
Sunday/Nichiyōbi (1924), 27, 32–3
Sunny Cloud/Seidon (1933), 87
Super Mohara Sound System, 64–5
Supreme Commander for the Allied Powers (SCAP), 143, 149, 159–60

tabemono (something to eat), 160–2
'tactic', 7–8
Taishō era (1912–26), 21–2, 31
Taiyō no kisetsu/The Season of the Sun (1956), 189–90
taiyōzoku (Sun Tribe) films, 189–90, 195–6, 206, 239n
Takabatake, Michitoshi, 12, 200
Takai (character in film), 45–6
Takamine, Hideko, 152, 236n
Takamura, Kiyoshi, 152
Takanawa, 104–5
Takasugi, Ichirō, 107
Takeuchi, Yoshimi, 11, 147–8, 150
talkies, 27, 60–4, 105, 225n
Tanaka, Jun'ichiro, 174
Tanaka, Kinuyo, 43, 87, 109
Tanaka, Masasumi, 17, 65, 119, 152, 155–7, 167, 203–4, 226n, 233n
Tanizaki, Jun'ichirō, 21, 77, 83, 145
Tasaka, Tomotaka, 109, 139
Tea Making Family/Cha o tsukuru ie (1924), 33, 222n
television, 192–3, 207, 222n, 240n
tennosei (emperor system), 144
That Night's Wife/Sono yo no tsuma (1930), 101
theatre, 24, 219n
'Theory of the August Revolution', 144
There Was a Father/Chichi ariki (1942), 117, 128–32, 134–7
The Thick Walled Room/Kabe atsuki heya (1956), 174–5
Thompson, Kristin, 2, 14–15, 155, 156, 158
Todake no kyōdai/The Brothers and Sisters of the Toda Family (1941), 116, 117, 120, 125, 128, 129–30, 132, 133–4, 136, 158, 182
Toei, 188, 239n
tofu, 5, 155, 196, 215, 236n
Togawa, Naoki, 176
Toho, 105, 109, 111, 174, 231n
Tokugawa era (1603–1868), 68

Tokyo, 21, 74, 157, 159, 164–5, 166–85, *179*, 211–12, 236n
  geopolitical transformation (1932), 75–6
  post-earthquake, 36
  war-torn, 149
Tōkyō boshoku/Tokyo Twilight (1957), 117, 194–5, 204
Tokyo Chorus/Tōkyō kōrasu (1931), 36–50, *48*, 53–4, 56, 72, 78, 80, 197, 223n
Tōkyō kōrasu/Tokyo Chorus (1931), 36–50, *48*, 53–4, 56, 72, 78, 80, 197, 223n
Tōkyō mongatari/Tokyo Story (1953), 142, 146, 166, 173–84, 187, 194, 197–8, 206, 210–11, 238n
Tōkyō nichinichi shinbun (Tokyo Daily News), 23
Tōkyō no onna/Woman of Tokyo (1933), 90, 93–9, 101, 122, 125
Tōkyō no yado/An Inn in Tokyo (1935), 59, 66, 78–9, 177
Tōkyō ondo (adapted traditional-style song), 75–6
Tokyo Story/Tōkyō mongatari (1953), 142, 146, 166, 173–84, 187, 194, 197–8, 206, 210–11, 238n
Tokyo Twilight/Tōkyō boshoku (1957), 117, 194–5, 204
Tonari no Yae chan/Our Neighbour Miss Yae (1934), 34–6, 57, 81, 87, 89
Tosaka, Jun, 12, 19, 28–9, 110
Toyoda, Shirō, 1
traditionalism, 1–2, 14, 153–5, 158, 184
Tsuchi to heitai/Mud and Soldiers (1939), 110, 114
Tsuchihashi Shiki Shochiku Fōn, 61
Tsuji, Kiyoaki, 144
Tsukasa, Yōko, 195
Tsuki wa noborinu/The Moon Has Risen, 152–4, 156–7, 163–5, 196, 236n, 240n
Tsumura, Hideo, 109–10, 133, 139
Twenty-four Eyes/Nijyūshi no hitomi, 187

Ubaguruma/The Baby Carriage (1956), 195, 240n
Ukigusa monogartari/A Story of Floating Weeds (1934), 59, 71, 73–4, 77–8, 80, 135, 195
Undying Pearl/Fue no shiratama (1929), 87
Uneno, Chizuko, 200
Until the Day We Meet Again/Mata au hi made (1932), 93, 96, 101, 113, 187

'victim consciousness', 138, 151–2, 164, 197, 234n
Vidor, King, 67

Wada-Marciano, Mitsuyo, 7–8, 18, 37, 46, 52, 75, 86–7, 90, 218n
Wakaki hi no kangeki/Excitement of a Young Day (1931), 62
Wakao, Ayako, 195
Walk Cheerfully/Hogaraka ni ayume (1930), 89, 90, 124
The War at Sea from Hawaii to Malaya/Hawai marei-oki kaisen (1942), 111, 131
Westernisation, 11, 23–7, 82–3
What Did the Lady Forget?/Shukujo wa nani wo wasuretaka (1937), 103–4, 120–5, 127, 158, 166, 176
What is Your Name?/Kimi no na wa trilogy (1953–4), 151, 174–5, 184, 187–8, 195
What Made Her Do It?/Nani ga kanojo o sō saseta ka (1930), 4
Where are the Dreams of Youth/Seishun no yume ima izuko (1932), 127
'Why Ozu Keeps Silent?', 65–6
A Woman of Island/Shima no onna (1920), 220n
Woman of Tokyo/Tōkyō no onna (1933), 90, 93–9, 101, 122, 125
women's magazines, 85, 209, 229n
Wood, Robin, 155, 156, 160, 203

Xiu River Crossing Operation (March 1939), 112

Yaeko (character in film), 35
yakeato (burnt-out ruins) generation, 189
Yamada, Yōji, 28
Yamamoto, Fujiko, 195
Yamanaka, Sadao, 112–13
Yamanote district, Tokyo, 69, 120, 153, 226n, 232n
Yamanouchi, Yasushi, 144
Yamauchi, Daisuke, 193
Yasue (character in film), 89
Yokohama Bay, 7
Yokomitsu, Riichi, 156, 236n
Yonaha, Jun, 116–17, 139, 232n
yose (variety hall), 70, 71
Yoshida, Kiju, 14, 17, 19
Yoshida, Yoshishige, 191
Yoshii (character in film), 44, 47–50, *49*, 53–5, 72, 201–2
Yoshimi, Shun'ya, 74, 84
Yoshimoto, Takaaki, 200, 218n
Yoshimura, Kōzaburō, 27, 110, 157, 175, 223n, 238n
Youth after School/Seishun hokago (1963), 233n

EU representative:
Easy Access System Europe
Mustamäe tee 50, 10621 Tallinn, Estonia
Gpsr.requests@easproject.com